COMMERCIAL LAW

COMMERCIAL LAW

General Editor
Sylvia McNeece

 BLACKSTONE
PRESS LIMITED

Published by
Blackstone Press Limited
Aldine Place
London
W12 8AA
United Kingdom

Sales enquiries and orders
Telephone +44-(0)-20-8740-2277
Facsimile +44-(0)-20-8743-2292
e-mail: sales@blackstone.demon.co.uk
website: www.blackstonepress.com

ISBN 1-84174-176-0
© Law Society of Ireland 2001
First published 2001

British Library Cataloguing in Publication Data
A catalogue record for this book is available from the British Library

Typeset in 10/12pt Meridien by Hewer Text Ltd, Edinburgh
Printed and bound in Great Britain by M & A Thomson Litho Ltd, East Kilbride

AUTHORS

Michael Carrigan is a partner in Eugene F. Collins, Solicitors. He specialises in commercial property and is also a practising arbitrator. He is a Fellow of the Chartered Institute of Arbitrators and has recently been appointed member for Ireland of the ICC International Court of Arbitration. Michael lectures on commercial law on the Professional Practice Course and is the author of *Handbook on Arbitration Law in Ireland.*

John Darby is a solicitor in McCann Fitzgerald, Solicitors. He practises in the corporate and commercial department where he specialises in EU law and merger control. John lectures on commercial law on the Professional Practice Course.

Brendan Heneghan is a partner in William Fry, Solicitors. He practises in the area of mergers and acquisitions with particular focus on transactions involving listed companies, including public takeovers and venture capital investments. Brendan lectures on commercial law on the Professional Practice Course and is the author of a number of publications, including the Irish chapter in *A Practitioner's Guide to the Acquisition of Private Companies in the European Union.*

Kevin Hoy is a partner in Mason Hayes & Curran, Solicitors, where he leads the financial services unit. His work includes acquisition financing, development financing and project financing. Kevin lectures on commercial law on the Professional Practice Course and he is also the internal examiner for the Law Society final examination—Part I Contract Law.

Howard Linnane is the information manager with William Fry, Solicitors. Before taking up that position Howard was the co-ordinating solicitor with responsibility for commercial law on the Law Society student courses. Howard lectures on commercial law on the Professional Practice Course.

Sylvia McNeece is a solicitor with the Law Society. She is responsible for designing and managing the Law Society's diploma and certificate courses including the Society's commercial law and e-commerce diplomas. Prior to joining the Law Society Sylvia worked as a solicitor with IONA Technologies plc.

Michael Moran is a practising in-house solicitor and a Community Trade Mark Attorney with Deloitte & Touche, Chartered Accountants. He specialises in company law and company secretarial practice and procedure. Michael lectures on commercial law on the Professional Practice Course.

Joseph O'Sullivan is a barrister specialising in commercial and chancery. He was formerly a solicitor in the corporate department of William Fry, Solicitors. In that capacity he worked in a wide range of matters such as mergers and acquisitions, commercial contracts, competition law, insurance law and general public company work. Joseph lectures on commercial law on the Professional Practice Course.

AUTHORS

Carol Plunkett is partner in Evans & Company, Solicitors. She specialises in intellectual property law and has acted in many of the patent, copyright, trade mark and passing-off cases which have come before the courts in recent years. Carol lectures on commercial law on the Professional Practice Course.

Imelda Reynolds is the managing partner in Beauchamps, Solicitors. She specialises in commercial property and franchising law and practice. Imelda lectures on commercial law on the Professional Practice Course and has written extensively on franchising.

Michael Twomey specialises exclusively in partnership law. He is the author of *Partnership Law* (2000, Butterworths) and lectures in partnership law in Trinity College Dublin and also on the Professional Practice Course. He acts as a consultant in partnership law, providing advice to law firms and their clients in this area.

PREFACE

This textbook is designed to support the teaching of the Commercial Law module on the Law Society's Professional Practice Course. It follows the prescribed syllabus for apprentice training as determined by the Law Society's Curriculum Development Unit. The book aims to equip apprentices with a knowledge of theory and practice in commercial law areas likely to be encountered at the outset of their legal careers. The text is not designed to be a comprehensive exposition of commercial law. It is hoped, however, that the work will be of interest to all who find that commercial law touches upon their practice, whether in the public or private sector.

While every effort has been made to ensure that this text is accurate, neither the authors, the editor, nor the Law Society of Ireland accept legal liability for any errors, omissions or mis-statements of law. Any comments or queries on the contents of this manual should be sent to the general editor at the Law Society.

Special thanks to Anne-Marie Cotter, Howard Linnane, Jane Moffatt and Brid Moriarty for their assistance in proofreading various chapters of this book. Thanks also to Margaret Cherry and Blackstone Press.

Sylvia McNeece
The Law School
May 2001

CONTENTS

CONTENTS

CONTENTS

CONTENTS

TABLES OF LEGISLATION

TABLE OF STATUTES

TABLE OF STATUTES

TABLE OF STATUTES

TABLE OF ORDERS, RULES AND REGULATIONS

TABLES OF INTERNATIONAL MATERIALS

Table of Treaties and Conventions

Table of European Secondary Legislation

LIST OF CASES

LIST OF CASES

CHAPTER 1

SECRETARIAL MANAGEMENT

1.1 Introduction

1.1.1 TYPES OF COMPANY

One of the principal ways of carrying on business is by way of a company. In Ireland, the usual form of entity that is used to conduct business is a private company limited by shares. The membership may simply consist of one person, as in the case of a single member company, but usually it consists of at least two persons, which is the prescribed minimum for all other types of private companies. There is a maximum limit of fifty members in private companies (not including employee members). Public limited companies (which may or may not be quoted on a Stock Exchange) may be used where there is a need to have a larger membership (i.e. more than fifty) and to raise money from the public to finance the business. A recent example was the case of the flotation of Eircom (formerly Telecom Eireann). Another type of company, namely a company limited by guarantee and not having a share capital, is very commonly used where the purpose is a charitable one or involves the promotion of sport. The principal difference is that in this type of company the members do not have to subscribe for shares but instead agree to contribute a specified amount if there are insufficient funds to meet the company's liabilities on a winding-up.

1.1.2 ADVANTAGES OF INCORPORATION

The advantages of incorporation are:

(a) a company has a separate and distinct legal personality from that of its members;

(b) a company has perpetual succession until it is either wound up or struck off the Register of Companies; and

(c) a company is liable for its own debts and may be sued by creditors and may itself sue debtors. Financial institutions usually prefer to lend money to a company rather than to individuals and a company, unlike an individual, may give a floating charge as security.

As against these favourable criteria, there is a requirement that every company (except an unlimited one, where members have unlimited liability for its debts) file its financial statements with the Registrar of Companies on an annual basis. These are available for public inspection on payment of the prescribed fee. Sole traders and partnerships are only obliged to file their financial records with the Revenue Commissioners and they are not available for public inspection.

1.1.3 COMPANY LAW

1.1.3.1 Statutory regulation

Companies are principally governed by the Companies Acts 1963–1999. Semi-state companies, e.g. An Post and Aer Lingus, are also governed by their own legislation, e.g. Postal and Telecommunications Services Act 1983, which should be read in conjunction with the Companies Acts. In addition to primary legislation in the form of Acts of the Oireachtas, secondary legislation in the form of statutory instruments also regulates companies, e.g. European Communities (Single-Member Private Limited Companies) Regulations 1994 (SI 275/1994). Most of the statutory instruments relating to company law have been drafted to implement EU directives. The EU is involved in an ongoing process of updating and harmonising company law in the Member States. The impact of judicial decisions is very important in the interpretation of the Companies Acts; there are hundreds of reported cases which provide authoritative interpretations of the legislation. In addition, judicial decisions of other common law jurisdictions, especially in the United Kingdom, are of persuasive authority in Ireland.

The Companies (Amendment) (No. 2) Act 1999 ('C(A)(No.2)A 1999') introduced new provisions regarding Irish companies:

- A company will not be registered unless the Registrar of Companies is satisfied that when registered it will carry on an activity in Ireland being an activity referred to in its memorandum of association: C(A)(No.2)A 1999, s. 42. A declaration is required to this effect, and it forms part of the revised Companies Registration Office Form A1.

- A company is obliged to have at least one director resident in Ireland, unless a bond in the prescribed form to the value of £20,000 has been entered into by the company: C(A)(No.2)A 1999, s. 43. The purpose of the bond is to meet any fine imposed under the Companies Acts 1963–1999, or the Taxes Consolidation Act 1997 or a penalty under the latter Act in respect of any offences committed by the company. For existing companies there are transitional provisions until 18 April 2001 but thereafter C(A)(No.2)A 1999 will apply to all Irish registered companies.

- The requirement that a company must have an Irish resident director or, alternatively, give a bond may be dispensed with if the Registrar of Companies grants to a company, on application in the prescribed form, a certificate stating that the company has a real and continuous link with one or more economic activities that are being carried on in Ireland.

- C(A)(No.2)A 1999, s. 45 imposes an upper limit of twenty-five on the number of directorships a person may hold. There are a number of exceptions to this rule, e.g. directorships of public limited companies and of groups of companies are excluded in the calculation of this number.

1.1.3.2 The single currency

Another feature which is currently topical is the EMU and the single currency. The Economic and Monetary Union Act 1998 provides for a mechanism for the conversion into Euros of existing capital denominated in currencies which are part of the EMU.

There are transitional provisions available to companies incorporated prior to 1 January 1999 which allow for the redenomination and renominalisation pending the introduction of the Euro as a single currency which is to take place on 1 January 2002. On this date all relevant currencies will be automatically converted into Euros. It is therefore important when adopting a capital in a newly-formed company to adopt a Euro denomination. The procedures for redenomination and renominalisation are set out in C(A)(No.2)A 1999.

1.1.3.3   Taxation of companies

The Taxes Consolidation Act 1997, and subsequent Finance Acts, in particular the Finance Act 1999, are relevant in the context of the taxation of Irish companies. Under the Taxes Consolidation Act 1997, every company incorporated in Ireland is obliged to furnish certain information to the Revenue Commissioners within thirty days from the date of incorporation on a Form 11 F CRO. The Finance Act 1999 contains provisions to deal with the taxation of Irish registered companies. The Irish government deemed it necessary to introduce these provisions to curb abuses which had arisen regarding the use of Irish non-resident companies. A dividend withholding tax was introduced with effect from 6 April 1999 in respect of dividends paid by companies resident in the State. All companies deemed to be Irish resident under the Act will be subject to the new dividend withholding tax rules. The Finance Act 1999 provides that a company incorporated in Ireland will be tax-resident in Ireland. The general rule is, however, subject to a number of exceptions, e.g. if the company is quoted on a stock exchange or is resident in another country under a tax treaty between Ireland and that other country.

Companies must also comply with the general law of the State.

1.1.4   PRE-INCORPORATION CONTRACTS

Individuals incorporating their business as a company are often called promoters.

A promoter may enter into a contract on behalf of a company which is about to be incorporated. The Companies Act 1963 ('CA 1963') recognises such contracts in s. 37. Once the company has been incorporated it may then ratify and take over the contract from the promoter and assume all rights and obligations under it but, until such time, the promoter or promoters will remain personally liable under the contract and the company is not bound by it.

1.1.5   ULTRA VIRES

At common law, unless the activity or contract entered into by a company was within its principal objects clause as specified in the memorandum of association, such activity or contract would be void. This doctrine was somewhat modified by the CA 1963, s. 8 and further modified by the European Communities (Companies) Regulations 1973 (SI 163/1973), reg. 6 which implemented the EC First Company Law Directive.

Essentially, as a result of these changes an outsider who enters into a transaction unaware of the contents of the memorandum and articles of association is now able to enforce the transaction against the company even though it was ultra vires.

1.2   A Company's Constitutional Documents

A company has two main constitutional documents: the memorandum of association and the articles of association.

1.2.1   MEMORANDUM OF ASSOCIATION

The memorandum of association sets out the purposes for which the company is being established. The memorandum of a limited company is divided into the following parts:

    (a)   the name of the company;

(b)   the objects and powers of the company;

(c)   a statement that the liability of the members of the company is limited;

(d)   the authorised share capital of the company, which is the number of shares the company may issue; and

(e)   the 'association' clause, whereby the initial subscribers agree to come together to form the company.

In the case of a public limited company, the words 'public limited company' or its Irish language equivalent 'cuideachta phoiblí teoranta' or their respective abbreviations 'plc' or 'cpt' must be included as the last word of the name. A private limited company must usually have the word 'Limited' in its name, or the Irish word 'Teoranta', or their abbreviations 'Ltd' or 'Teo'.

Slightly different provisions apply to an unlimited company in that heads (c) and (d) above are not inserted. In the case of a company limited by guarantee and not having a share capital, a statement that liability is limited is inserted as at head (c) above but instead of a statement as to capital, a clause is inserted to the effect that the members of the company will guarantee the liabilities of the company up to a specified sum which may be as low as £1 or as high as the members so decide.

The principal objects are set out in the memorandum of association. Usually the principal objects are set out in the first three paragraphs or so and the remaining paragraphs contain the powers which will enable the company to carry out the principal objects such as the power to acquire real and personal property, to apply for intellectual property rights, to lend and borrow and give guarantees, to mention but a few. It is important when drafting the main objects and powers of the company to ensure that they are comprehensive and cover the activities which the company proposes to do.

Where a company is seeking charitable status or exemption as a sporting entity, additional special clauses should be included in the memorandum of association to comply with Revenue Commissioner requirements.

1.2.2   THE ARTICLES OF ASSOCIATION

The articles of association establish how the business of the company will be carried on. CA 1963 contains model articles of association in the form of Tables A, C, D and E, which are suitable for the different types of company. For example, Table A, Part I is suitable for a public limited company, whilst Table A, Part II is suitable for a private limited company. The difference between Table A, Part I and Table A, Part II is that Part II contains alterations to the provisions of Part I, to make it suitable for a private limited company. In reality the articles set out in Table A, Part I and Table A, Part II are almost always modified to make them more suited to the conduct of business by modern companies.

Some of the main provisions of Table A, Part I are as follows:

article 5	directors' powers to allot shares (subject to Companies (Amendment) Act 1983, s. 20 authority)
articles 22–28	provisions dealing with the transfer of shares
articles 47–74	provisions relating to the holding of general meetings
articles 75–78	appointment and remuneration of directors
articles 80—89	provisions relating to powers and duties of directors
articles 101–109	proceedings of directors
articles 116—124	dividends and reserves
articles 133—136	notices

The provisions of Table A, Part II which modify Table A, Part I are as follows:

article 2   a statement that the company is private and stating the principal consequences (required by CA 1963, s. 33). The most important consequences are that the right to transfer shares freely is restricted, the number of members is limited to fifty and any invitation to the public to subscribe for shares is restricted.

article 3   gives the directors an absolute right to refuse to register a transfer (as contrasted with the more limited right under Table A, Part I, article 24 which is excluded).

article 4   different notice periods for the calling of meetings are stipulated. (Table A, Part I, article 51 is excluded.)

article 5   the quorum for members meetings is fixed at two. (Table A, Part I, article 54, which is excluded, specifies three.)

article 6   gives power to allow members' resolutions to be made in writing rather than at an actual meeting.

article 7   gives the directors the right to vote on matters in which they are interested (in contrast with the more limited rights under Table A, Part I, articles 84 and 86). Section 194 of CA 1963 as amended by Companies Act 1990, s. 47 requires directors to declare their interests.

article 8   gives the directors authority to vote as they think fit in respect of shares in any other company held or owned by the company.

article 9   allows alternate directors to be appointed.

The articles of association of a company form a contract between a company and its members and deal with the internal regulation of a company. They may be very straightforward and adopt the relevant Table A in the appropriate form or amended to deal with a particular company's rights, especially where there are different classes of shareholders.

In practice, when preparing a set of articles of association for a private limited company many modifications to the standard format set out in Table A are made, depending on the company's requirements. It may be necessary to insert details of offer round provisions to override the power of the directors to refuse to register a transfer as provided in Table A, Part II, article 3. It may also be necessary to provide in detail for how the directors of the company are to be appointed and to be removed instead of adopting the Table A provisions for retirement by rotation. In addition, the share capital of the company may be divided into different classes with different rights attaching to the various classes of shares which rights are usually set out in detail in the articles of association.

It is quite common to provide that the provisions of Table A, Part I and/or Part II as appropriate, will apply subject to certain stated exceptions. The articles which have been removed will be replaced with paragraphs setting out the new variables.

It is a useful practice to attach a copy of Table A, Parts I and II to a set of articles of association, where they have not been reproduced in full, so that shareholders who are unfamiliar with the content of Table A may refer to them in conjunction with the specified articles of association which apply in a particular case.

.2.3   EFFECT OF MEMORANDUM AND ARTICLES OF ASSOCIATION

Section 25 of CA 1963 provides that the memorandum and articles of association bind the company and its members as if they had been signed and sealed by each member and contain covenants on the part of each member to observe the provisions. When a member sues to enforce a personal right given to him by the articles, he may do so by way of personal action. (The rule in *Foss v Harbottle* has no application in the case of an infringement of a member's personal rights.)

1.2.4 PREPARING MEMORANDUM AND ARTICLES OF ASSOCIATION

The Solicitors Act 1954, s. 58 and CA 1963, s. 397 provide that with certain exceptions it is illegal for any person other than a solicitor of the Court of Justice in Ireland to perform the act of drawing or preparing a memorandum or articles of association for the purposes of the Companies Acts 1963–1999.

1.3 Incorporation

1.3.1 TYPES OF COMPANIES WHICH MAY BE INCORPORATED

1.3.1.1 Companies limited by shares

The overwhelming majority of all companies are private companies limited by shares. The members of such a company are those who have agreed to become members and whose names have been entered on the register of members. Their liability to creditors is limited to paying the full amount payable on their shares.

1.3.1.2 Single member companies

Prior to October 1994, it was not possible to have a limited liability company with a single member. Section 36 of CA 1963 provides that where a company carries on business with less than the required minimum number of members (two in a private company and seven in a public company) for more than six months, each member is personally liable for the payment of the debts of the company at that time. With the introduction of the European Communities (Single Member Private Limited Companies) Regulations 1994 on 1 October 1994, it is now permitted to form, or convert existing companies into, single member private limited companies with only one shareholder.

It is important to note, however, that all companies must have a minimum of two directors and the 1994 Regulations do not dispense with the requirement to file an annual return or accounts in the case of single member companies.

All the powers exercisable by a company in general meeting may be exercised by the sole member without the need to hold any meeting for that purpose except the powers contained in CA 1963, s. 160(2)(b), (5) and (6), being the power to remove an auditor from office. In that situation, it is necessary to hold the requisite meeting.

1.3.1.3 Public limited company

A public limited company may be listed or 'quoted' on a Stock Exchange or remain unquoted. It must have at least seven members, and a nominal and issued share capital of at least £30,000 of which at least 25 per cent must be paid up together with the entire premium.

1.3.1.4 Unlimited companies

Members of an unlimited company have unlimited liability to contribute to the company's assets in the event of the company being unable to pay its debts. However, such members do not have personal liability to creditors.

1.3.1.5   Companies limited by guarantee and not having a share capital

Companies limited by guarantee and not having a share capital are often used for clubs and charities which are not trading and do not need capital and where members may pay an annual subscription and undertake to pay a further amount (the guarantee) specified in the memorandum of association in the event of insolvency. All companies of this type are public (as private companies must always have a share capital: CA 1963, s. 33).

1.3.1.6   Private company limited by guarantee and having a share capital

The liability of a private company limited by guarantee and having a share capital is limited to the amount the members have undertaken to contribute to the assets of the company in the event of its being wound up, in addition to the amount, if any, unpaid on shares held by them. In practice, such companies are rarely used.

1.3.1.7   External companies

Until the introduction of the European Communities (Branch Disclosures) Regulations 1993 (SI 395/1993), any foreign company which established a place of business within Ireland was required to register with the Registrar of Companies, as an external company under CA 1963, Part XI.

Under the 1993 Regulations, there are different requirements as to registration imposed on a company incorporated in a Member State and companies incorporated in other countries. The regulations apply where a foreign company has established a 'branch' in the State. If the foreign company has established a 'place of business', it must continue to register under CA 1963, Part XI. The Regulations contain no definition of 'branch', but it may be taken that a branch is regarded as a place of business, which is permanent and carries on business with a management team, and not merely a postal address.

1.3.2   COMPANY NAMES

Generally speaking a new company name or a change of name for an existing company will not be registered if:

(a)   it is identical to a name already on the register of companies;

(b)   in the opinion of the Minister for Enterprise, Trade and Employment it is offensive; or

(c)   it would suggest State sponsorship.

Every company name should be unique. Consequently CA 1963, s. 23(2) provides that if through inadvertence or otherwise a company is registered by a name which is too similar to that of an existing company then the second company may be ordered by the Minister to change its name. An objection to a name pursuant to s. 23(2) must be received within six months of the registration of the name.

Section 21 of CA 1963 provides that no company may be registered by a name which, in the opinion of the Minister, is undesirable. In general, the following types of name are regarded as undesirable:

(i)   names which are identical, or confusingly similar to names already on the register;

(ii)   names that could be regarded as deceptive or misleading, i.e. could imply State sponsorship;

(iii)   names which include a year date are not acceptable.

For a private limited company, 'Limited' or 'Teoranta' (or their respective abbreviations 'Ltd' or 'Teo') must be the last word in the name. If the company is non-profit making or formed for charitable purposes, a licence to omit the word 'limited' may be obtained from the Minister for Enterprise, Trade and Employment under CA 1963, s. 24. If the word 'bank' is to be used in a company name, a licence must be obtained from the Central Bank. This would apply even in the case of a name such as 'Hollybank Construction Limited'.

The word 'insurance' may only be included if the company is to engage in the business of insurance and has been licensed by the Minister for Enterprise, Trade and Employment to do so. If the company carries on the business of insurance broking then the words 'insurance' or 'insurance broking' may be used. The word 'co-operative' may not be used in a company name. This is to avoid confusion between entities registered in the Registry of Friendly Societies and limited companies. The word 'Society' may be used if permission has been obtained from the Registrar of Societies.

A dissolved company may be restored to the register under CA 1963, s. 310 within a two-year period of its dissolution. A company struck off the register under CA 1963, s. 311 may be restored within a period of twenty years. Consequently, these names may not be re-used until these time limits have expired.

A company trading under a name other than its own is obliged to register under the Registration of Business Names Act 1963. This Act is in the course of being replaced by new legislation on business names due to be published in 2001.

Registration of a business name confers no protection of the name and there is no crosscheck between the Business Names Register and the Company Register.

In certain cases it may also be necessary to carry out a search of the Register and Pending Register of Trade Marks maintained pursuant to the Trade Marks Act 1996 to ensure that no intended trade mark or service mark is already registered or pending registration and thus avoid any action for possible infringement. In exceptional cases a search of the Trade Marks Register and Pending Register maintained by the Office for the Harmonisation of the Internal Market in Alicante, Spain, may be necessary. Care should also be taken not to infringe domain names and the necessary searches of the relevant domain registry may also have to be made.

1.3.3 DOCUMENTS LEADING TO INCORPORATION OF PRIVATE LIMITED COMPANY

The main documents required to incorporate a private limited company are as follows:

1.3.3.1 Memorandum and articles of association

It is necessary that the memorandum and articles of association be signed by at least two subscribers (one in the case of a single member company) and in the case of the memorandum that each of the subscribers sets opposite their names the number of shares which they are going to take up with a minimum of one share each. This must be expressed in words. The signature of a subscriber must then be witnessed by an independent person and dated.

1.3.3.2 Company registration form A1

A Form A1 has to be completed by the directors and the secretary with a consent by each of these persons to act as directors or secretary. (At least one director should be resident in Ireland; alternatively, a bond for £20,000 in the prescribed form may be lodged instead.) Directors must be natural persons but a secretary may be a body corporate or a firm. The form must also be signed on behalf of the subscribers and have the company's capital duty section completed by a director or secretary. In addition, it must state the address of the registered office of the company.

C(A)(No.2)A 1999, in addition to the statutory declaration made to the effect that all the requirements of CA 1963 have been met, introduced new provisions which require the declarant to state the classification of the activity of the company in accordance with the NACE Rev 1 (which is the common basis for statistical classifications of economic activities within the EU) and to describe the general nature of the activity of the company or, where it is not possible to classify the activity, to describe the activity. The declarant goes on to further declare the place or places in Ireland where it is proposed to carry on the activity and where the central administration of the company will normally be carried on.

The declaration must be completed by a director, secretary or by a practising solicitor before a commissioner for oaths, a practising solicitor, a notary public or a peace commissioner.

1.3.3.3   Registration fees

The Registrar's fees currently for the incorporation of a private company limited by shares are £51, and £50 for a company limited by guarantee without a share capital.

1.3.4   PROCEDURE FOR INCORPORATION OF A COMPANY

In relation to the incorporation of new companies, there are two systems at present in operation in the Companies Registration Office.

1.3.4.1   Fé Phráinn

The Fé Phráinn system is restricted to private limited companies, unlimited companies and companies limited by guarantee and not having a share capital and is available to all applicants who use a standard form of memorandum and articles of association which has been approved by the Companies Registration Office. All copies of the memorandum and articles of association submitted under this system must be printed and certain information only needs to be inserted such as the company's name, principal objects clause and nominal share capital. If the documentation furnished is correct and complete a company will be incorporated within ten days from the date of lodgement at the Companies Registration Office.

A modification of the Fé Phráinn scheme is Crodisc. The information on the Form A1 is recorded on a computer disk and submitted with the hard copies of Form A1 (signed and declared) together with the standard memorandum and articles. If the documentation is in order, incorporation will take place within five days from the date of lodgement in the Companies Registration Office.

1.3.4.2   Ordinary List

The Ordinary List comprises companies which do not belong to the Fé Phráinn scheme and public limited companies. A time scale for the incorporation of companies on the Ordinary List is between three and four weeks.

The principal difference from the Fé Phráinn Scheme is that hard copies of the documentation, which may include memoranda and articles of association which have not received the approval of the Companies Registration Office, are lodged with the Companies Registration Office. Such documentation is then manually checked to ensure that it complies with the Companies Acts 1963–1999.

1.3.5 CERTIFICATE OF INCORPORATION

When all the documents and fees have been lodged in the Companies Registration Office and the Registrar is satisfied that all formalities have been completed, a certificate of incorporation is issued for the company which is conclusive evidence that the company has been properly incorporated.

1.3.5.1 Post formation

The company must keep certain statutory books and have a common seal. The company may trade under a different name which must be registered under the Registration of Business Names Act 1963.

The subscribers become members on incorporation. Even if they are nominees, their names should be entered on the register of members and then they should transfer their shares. Alternatively, they may renounce their rights to take shares (without ever becoming shareholders) in favour of the persons to whom it is intended to allot the shares.

The directors should order notepaper as soon as possible so as to be sure that they comply with the provisions of the Companies Acts 1963–1999 as regards letterheads etc.

1.3.5.2 Nameplate

A nameplate must be affixed outside every office or place in which the company carries on business. The plate(s) must be affixed in a conspicuous position and the name must be shown in letters which are easily legible.

1.3.5.3 Company letterheads etc.

Every company is required to have the following particulars on its letters and order forms:

(a) the place of and number of registration of the company;

(b) the address of its registered office;

(c) in relation to a company exempted from the requirement to add 'Limited' or 'Teoranta' to its name, the fact that it is a limited company;

(d) the full name of the company (note that the only permissible abbreviation is Ltd for Limited or plc for Public Limited Company or their Irish language equivalents, Teo or cpt respectively);

(e) the names and any former names of the directors and nationality, if not Irish: CA 1963, s. 196; and

(f) Companies (Amendment) Act 1983 ('C(A)A 1983'), s. 47(9) requires public investment companies as defined by s. 47(3) of that Act to include the expression 'investment company' on their letters and order forms.

1.3.5.4 Company seal

An embossed seal must be obtained and, when required, affixed to documents.

When a company carries on business abroad, and if the articles of association of the company so permit, it may have a seal for use abroad. The only difference is that the name of every territory, district or place where it is to be used must be added to the name of the company on the common seal.

A public limited company may also have a special seal for sealing share certificates.

1.4 Meetings and Resolutions

1.4.1 CALLING AND CONDUCT OF MEETINGS AND PASSING OF RESOLUTIONS

The day-to-day business of a company is conducted by the board of directors of that company.

It is occasionally necessary for the members to be consulted regarding the business of a company. This may occur where it is proposed, e.g. to amend the memorandum and articles of association, or increase the authorised share capital or for a number of other purposes. At least once in each year, apart from the company's first year of existence, the members must meet for an Annual General Meeting.

A minimum of three (in the case of a public limited company) or two (in the case of a private company) shareholders of a company may pass resolutions.

For a resolution to be valid, it must be passed by the requisite majority of those persons who are entitled to attend and vote and do vote in person or by proxy (where permitted by the articles of association) at a meeting where a quorum is present and of which notice has been duly given.

1.4.2 ANNUAL GENERAL MEETING

Every company is obliged to hold an Annual General Meeting (AGM) of its shareholders:

(a) It must be held once in each calendar year, and not more than fifteen months after the previous one: CA 1963, s. 131.

(b) Provided the first AGM is held within eighteen months of incorporation, one need not be held in the year of incorporation or the following year.

(c) If an AGM is not held, the Minister for Enterprise, Trade and Employment may order it to be held on application by the company or any member.

(d) Twenty-one clear days' notice of the AGM must be given unless all entitled to attend and vote agree to accept shorter notice.

(e) The only business which must be dealt with at the AGM is the laying before the meeting of the balance sheet, profit and loss account, auditors' report and directors' report on the state of the company's affairs for consideration by the shareholders. However, the articles of association may provide that the following matters are dealt with also at the meeting as ordinary business:

    (i) the declaration of a dividend;

    (ii) the election of directors in place of those retiring;

    (iii) the re-appointment of the retiring auditor; and

    (iv) the fixing of the remuneration of the auditors.

Under the standard form of articles in Table A any business save that deemed as 'ordinary business', which is usually the above four items along with the presentation of the accounts and reports, transacted at the AGM or at an Extraordinary General Meeting (EGM) is treated as 'special business' (article 53, Table A). The auditors' report must be read at the meeting and must be open to inspection by any of the members (CA 1990, s. 193(2)). (For provisions on AGMs see CA 1963, s. 131 as amended by C(A)A 1982, Sch. 1.)

1.4.3   TIMETABLE FOR THE AGM

The timetable leading up to the AGM is as follows:

(a)   Determine the financial year end of the company.

(b)   As soon as practicable after the financial year end, the auditors will commence the audit.

(c)   Auditors submit draft accounts to the directors, who review them and agree any adjustments with the auditors.

(d)   A directors' meeting is called to sign the accounts, and prepare the directors' report and instruct the secretary to convene the AGM. The chairman considers preparing his speech. The directors may recommend the declaration of a dividend.

(e)   The secretary sends out notice convening the meeting to members, accompanied by the accounts, the chairman's address and the auditors' report.

(f)   The secretary must make sure to give twenty-one days' clear notice, and thus this will usually mean sending out the notice at least twenty-four days in advance of the meeting. He will have booked the room in advance, and may have notified the press if necessary. Some public limited companies use their annual accounts as a form of advertisement to attract new investments and they will therefore contain extra information about the company.

(g)   Hold the AGM—prepare minutes of the meeting as soon as practicable after its conclusion.

(h)   File the annual return within sixty days of the AGM together with the appropriate financial statements.

1.4.4   EXTRAORDINARY GENERAL MEETING

Any meeting of the shareholders of a company, other than the AGM, is an Extraordinary General Meeting.

Unless all entitled to attend and vote agree to accept shorter notice, fourteen clear days' notice is required for an EGM in the case of a public limited company, seven clear days' notice in the case of a private company to pass an ordinary resolution and twenty-one clear days if a special resolution is to be passed. The articles may provide for longer periods of notice of meetings.

The EGM may be convened by the directors (see Table A, Part I, article 50). In addition, the members may require the directors to convene such meetings. The directors must convene an EGM on a requisition of a member or members holding at the date of the requisition not less than one-tenth of the paid-up capital which carry a right to vote at a general meeting. This provision may not be excluded by the articles: CA 1963, s. 132.

1.4.5   TYPES OF RESOLUTION

1.4.5.1   Special

A special resolution requires twenty-one clear days' notice regardless of the type of meeting and three-quarters majority; a special resolution is necessary in any case where the Companies Acts 1963–1999 or the articles so specify, e.g. change of name, objects, articles.

The Acts specify a special resolution is required as follows:

- to change the name;
- to permit the giving of financial assistance for the purchase of its shares;

- to reduce the share capital;
- to alter the memorandum and/or articles of association; or
- to wind up the company.

1.4.5.2   Ordinary resolution

The required notice depends on the type of meeting: a simple majority suffices. An example of an ordinary resolution is where there is an increase in the authorised share capital of the company.

Certain ordinary resolutions must be filed which relate to attaching, restricting or varying rights on shares.

Extended notice (twenty-eight days minimum) must be given for certain ordinary resolutions, i.e. resolutions removing a director or auditor.

1.4.6   CONTENTS OF NOTICE

A notice of a general meeting must contain:

(a)   The date, time and place of meeting (Table A, Part I, article 51).

(b)   A statement that every member entitled to attend and vote is entitled to appoint a proxy, who need not be a member. (This may be excluded by the articles of association of a company limited by guarantee and not having a share capital.)

(c)   The general nature of any special business, which should be sufficiently specified so that members may decide whether or not they wish to attend. All business at an EGM is special and all business at an AGM is special other than declaring a dividend, the consideration of accounts, balance sheets and the reports of directors and auditors, the election of directors in place of those retiring, the reappointment of the retiring auditors and the fixing of the remuneration of the auditors.

(d)   The exact wording of special resolutions.

1.4.7   VOTING

Resolutions are decided by a show of hands unless a poll is demanded. Except on the question of adjourning the meeting or electing a chairman, the articles of association may not exclude the right to demand a poll by the following: CA 1963, s. 137:

(a)   the chairman;

(b)   five or more voting members or their proxies;

(c)   a member or members holding one-tenth of the total voting rights; or

(d)   a member or members holding shares representing at least one-tenth of the total paid-up capital conferring a right to vote.

See Table A, Part I, articles 59 and 62.

Note that the chairman may have a casting vote: see Table A, Part I, article 61.

Voting is usually on a show of hands unless a poll is demanded (before or on the declaration of the result of the show of hands). If a poll is duly demanded it must be taken in such manner as the chairman directs. On a show of hands, one vote per member is counted; while on a poll each share is accorded the number of votes to which it is entitled under the articles or terms of issue. This allows for the use of weighted votes and a member with a large number of shares can influence the vote: see articles 59–67, Table A, Part I.

Any member of a company entitled to attend and vote at a meeting of the company is entitled to appoint another person (whether a member or not) as his proxy to attend, speak and vote instead of him. A proxy so appointed has the same right as the member to speak at the meeting and to vote on a show of hands and on a poll: CA 1963, s. 136(1).

The instrument appointing a proxy and the power of attorney or other authority, if any, under which it is signed must be deposited, not less than forty-eight hours before the meeting, at the appropriate venue specified for that purpose in the notice convening the meeting (Table A, Part I, article 70) unless the articles specify otherwise.

The chairman must conduct the meeting and must accord the members a reasonable opportunity to express their views. He must also proceed through the agenda efficiently.

1.4.8 AFTER THE MEETING

Printed copies of special and certain ordinary resolutions passed at a meeting or written resolutions which have effect as special or ordinary resolutions must be sent within fifteen days for filing to the Registrar of Companies: CA 1963, s. 143.

Minutes of the proceedings of general meetings and meetings of directors must be entered in books kept for that purpose: CA 1963, s. 145.

1.4.9 WRITTEN RESOLUTIONS

Where the articles of association provide, it is possible in most cases to pass the relevant resolution by all the members entitled to attend and vote at general meetings, consenting in writing to the passing of the resolutions. The written resolution is not effective until the last signatory has signed it. It is not possible to transact the business of an AGM by way of written resolution and such a meeting must actually take place. Similarly, where there is a serious loss of capital, an extraordinary general meeting must take place as provided in Companies (Amendment) Act 1983 ('C(A)A 1983'), s. 40.

1.4.10 SINGLE MEMBER COMPANIES

In the case of a single member company resolutions may be replaced by written decisions of the sole member.

1.5 Administrative Records of Private Limited Company

Every company is obliged to maintain statutory registers and minute books pursuant to the Companies Acts 1963–1999.

1.5.1 REGISTER OF APPLICATIONS AND ALLOTMENTS

A company is not required by law to maintain a register of applications and allotments, but a register has proved to be a useful link in the company's records, as it provides a continuous visual diary of the movement of the company's share capital.

The cross-referencing in the headings in this register also becomes a useful index to the several operations relating to share transactions.

The directors may not exercise any power to allot shares unless duly authorised under C(A)A 1983, s. 20. Pre-emption rights in favour of existing holders of shares must be observed unless excluded: C(A)A 1983, s. 23.

In the context of the allotment and issue of new shares, the 'pre-emption provisions' referred to in s. 23 mean that before any 'equity securities' as defined in the section are allotted and issued to any third party, they must first be offered to the existing shareholders on a 'pro rata' basis, i.e. in proportion to their existing shareholdings.

1.5.2 REGISTER OF TRANSFERS

Similarly, a company is not required by law to keep a register of transfer of shares, but such a register has proved to be a very useful and necessary adjunct to the records of a company and will assist in the preparation of annual returns. The register provides a continuous visual diary and indicator of share transfers. The cross-referencing in the headings on the register also becomes an index to the several related operations.

1.5.3 REGISTER OF MEMBERS

The register of members contains details of each member in the company.

If the register is kept at a place other than the registered office of the company the Registrar of Companies *must be notified* within fourteen days of the place, or any change in the place, where the register is kept. Form B3 is used for this purpose: CA 1963, s. 116(5)–(8).

Save for the subscribers to the memorandum of association, a person does not become a member in a company until he has agreed to become a member and his name has been entered in the register of members, or cease to be a member until a like entry has been made transferring out his shares. The secretary should therefore ensure that all duly authorised changes in membership are recorded promptly in the appropriate registers, subject to the prior stamping of the relevant instrument.

The register must be open to the inspection of any member of the company without charge for not less than two hours daily during business hours and likewise to any other person on payment of not more than 5p: CA 1963, s. 119.

A copy of the register or any part of it must be furnished within ten days of a request by a member or any other person on payment of the appropriate fee per 100 words or part of 100 words copied: CA 1963, s. 119(2).

1.5.4 REGISTER OF DIRECTORS AND SECRETARIES

The register of directors and secretaries contains details of directors to include their full names, residential addresses, nationality (if not Irish), date of birth, details of directorships held worldwide during the preceding ten years and particulars of appointment and retirement/removal. A director must be an individual—bodies corporate may not be directors.

The register must be open to the inspection of any member of the company without charge for not less than two hours daily during business hours, and likewise to any other person on payment of not more than £1: CA 1963, s. 195(10).

It is not necessary for particulars to be recorded in the register of 'other directorships' held by a director (CA 1963, s. 195(3)):

(a) in companies of which the company is the wholly-owned subsidiary, or

(b) in companies which are the wholly-owned subsidiaries, either of the company *or* of another company, of which the company is the wholly-owned subsidiary.

The expression 'company' for this purpose includes any body corporate incorporated in the Republic of Ireland and a body corporate shall be deemed to be the wholly-owned subsidiary of another if it has no members except that other and that others' wholly-owned subsidiaries and its or their nominees.

Section 174 of CA 1963 states that every company must have at least two directors.

Any changes of directors or in the particulars in this register must be notified to the Companies Registration Office on Form B10 within fourteen days of the occurrence: CA 1963, s. 195 as amended by C(A)A 1982, s. 8.

The register of directors and secretaries contains details of the secretary or joint secretaries and includes the full name of the secretary/joint secretaries and address. A secretary may be either an individual or a body corporate or a partnership.

Generally, where all the partners in a firm are joint secretaries, the name and the principal office of the firm may be stated in the register instead of the detailed particulars and the names etc. of those partners: CA 1963, s. 195(4)(b) and (5).

Anything required or authorised to be done by or to the secretary may, if the office is vacant or there is for any other reason no secretary capable of acting, be done by or to any assistant or deputy secretary or, if there is no assistant or deputy secretary capable of acting, by or to any officer of the company authorised generally or specially in that behalf by the directors: CA 1963, s. 175(2).

Any changes of secretary or joint secretaries or in the particulars in this register must be notified to the Companies Registration Office on a Form B10 within fourteen days of the occurrence: CA 1963, s. 195 as amended by C(A)A 1982, s. 8.

1.5.5 REGISTER OF INTERESTS

The register of directors' and secretaries' interests contains particulars of directors, secretaries and connected persons, e.g. spouses and minor children's interests in shares and debentures in the company. If the company's register of members is kept at its registered office, then the register of interests must also be kept there. Alternatively, if the register of members is not so kept, then the register of interests must be kept either at the company's registered office or at the place where the register of members is kept. The company must notify the Registrar of Companies of the place where the register is kept and of any change in that place.

The register must be available for inspection during business hours (subject to such reasonable restrictions as the company in general meeting may impose, so that not less than two hours in each day be allowed for inspection) by any members of the company without charge and by any other person on payment of 30p or such lesser sum as the company may prescribe for each inspection. The company must maintain an index of names entered on the register to enable the information kept therein to be readily accessible: Companies Act 1990 ('CA 1990'), s. 60.

CA 1990, s. 53 applies to directors, secretaries, shadow directors and their respective families. It provides that any such person who is interested in shares in, or debentures of, the company or any other body corporate, being the company's subsidiary or holding company or a subsidiary of the company's holding company, must notify such interest in writing to the company within five days of the event. Any subsequent change in that interest must also be notified and the company must maintain a register of such interests.

1.5.6 REGISTER OF CHARGES

Every company is obliged to keep a copy of every instrument creating a charge which is required to be registered with the Registrar of Companies under CA 1963, Part IV at the registered office.

Copies of such instruments may be inspected during normal business hours by any creditor of the company free of charge.

1.5.7 REGISTER OF SEALINGS

A company is not required by law to keep a register of sealings, but such a register is a useful adjunct to the records of a company.

Every company must have a common seal with its name engraved on it in legible characters. The seal should be kept in safe custody at all times and be used only with the authority of the directors.

It should be affixed only in the manner allowed by the articles of association of the company, which commonly provide that documents to which the seal is affixed shall be attested by two directors, or by a director and the secretary, or a director and one other authorised person. Every care should be taken to ensure that the description of the document sealed will be sufficient to identify that document beyond doubt. As an added precaution against substitution it is advisable to endorse the document with the consecutive number of the entry in the sealings register.

Entries should always be made and authenticated at the time of affixing the seal.

When a company transacts business abroad it may, if its articles allow, have an 'official' seal for use abroad but with the addition on its face of the name of every territory, district or place where it is to be used: CA 1963, s. 41(1).

A company may in writing under its common seal empower any person, either generally or otherwise, as its attorney, to execute deeds on its behalf in any place outside Ireland: CA 1963, s. 41(3).

1.5.8 MINUTES

Every company must keep minutes of proceedings at general meetings of the company *and* meetings of its directors: CA 1963, s. 145(1).

The minutes are the permanent record of business transacted at a meeting and must be absolutely impartial. They must record the decisions reached at a meeting and be expressed in clear and unambiguous terms. Special care should be taken to record relevant dates and figures.

Minutes when signed by the chairman of the meeting, or by the chairman of the next succeeding meeting, are prima facie evidence of the proceedings: CA 1963, s. 145(2).

Looseleaf minute books are permissible, but for security reasons precautions must be taken to guard against falsification and to facilitate discovery: CA 1963, s. 378(2).

As an added precaution each page of the minutes should be initialled at the foot of the page.

It is preferable to keep the minutes of general meetings separated from those of directors' meetings because members have a right to inspection only of the former.

The minutes of proceedings of all general meetings must be kept at the registered office of the company and be open to inspection by any member: CA 1963, s. 146(1).

Minutes of general meetings of the company must be open to the inspection of any member of the company without charge for not less than two hours daily during business hours: CA 1963, s. 146(1).

Copies of any minutes of general meetings must be supplied within seven days after a request by a member at a charge of not more than 5p for every 100 words: CA 1963, s. 146(2).

1.5.9 SHARE CERTIFICATE

Every member of a company is entitled to a certificate specifying the shares held by him and such certificate issued under the seal of the company shall be prima facie evidence of the title of the member to the shares. The company must have the certificate ready for delivery to the shareholder within two months of allotment of the shares or the lodgement of a properly completed transfer: CA 1963, ss. 86 and 87.

Share certificates should be completed with the full name(s) of the shareholder(s) and it should be ensured that the details on the certificate correspond exactly with the entry in the register of members. The certificate should be sealed and the sealing witnessed as provided by the articles of association of the company. On the issue of a certificate the counterfoil should be completed and kept by the company. Appropriate cross-references should be made to the register of allotments or transfers and to the register of sealings.

1.5.10 LOCATION OF STATUTORY BOOKS

The statutory books of the company must be kept at the registered office of the company or at such other address in Ireland that has been certified to the Registrar of Companies on Form B3: CA 1963, s. 146. The minute book of general meetings of the company must be kept at the registered office.

1.5.11 COMPUTERISATION OF RECORDS

Section 4 of the Companies (Amendment) Act 1977 introduced provisions to allow the statutory records of a company other than minute books of directors and general meetings to be kept on a computer. However, such records must be able to be reproduced in a legible, i.e. written, form.

1.6 Shares

1.6.1 GENERAL

A shareholder in a company has a statutory right to transfer his/her shares, in the 'manner provided by the articles of the company': CA 1963, s. 79. A private company is a company which inter alia restricts the right to transfer its shares: CA 1963, s. 33(1)(a).

The articles of association of a private company usually provide that the directors have a power to refuse to register a transfer either for certain reasons or a general power, without the necessity to state any reasons; for instance article 3, Part II, Table A provides that:

> *The directors may, in their absolute discretion and without assigning any reason therefor, decline to register any transfer of any share, whether or not it is a fully paid share.*

Three principles govern the construction of this type of clause:

18

(a) If the company refuses to register a transfer, it must send a notice of refusal to the transferee within the period of two months from the date the transfer is lodged with the company: CA 1963, s. 84(1). If the notice is not given in two months, then unless there are special circumstances, the right to veto will be deemed to have lapsed.

(b) The courts will, where a clause has more than one potential meaning, take the narrowest construction.

(c) Where the directors have discretion to refuse, they must exercise their power bona fide in what they consider the best interests of the company: *Clark v Workman* [1920] 1 IR 107. In practice, it is difficult to prove that directors were not acting bona fide and in the best interests of the company, especially if they do not have to state their reasons for refusing to register the transfer.

Alternatively, the articles of association of a private company may contain pre-emption (right of first refusal) provisions. Under these provisions, a prospective transferor would first have to offer his/her shares to the remaining members of the company.

There are also statutory pre-emption provisions contained in C(A)A 1983, s. 23. These relate to the allotment of shares and not their transfer. C(A)A 1983, s. 23(10) allows a private company to exclude the relevant s. 23 provisions by a provision contained in either the memorandum or the articles of association of the company.

Alternatively, where the directors have been authorised to allot shares, the provisions of C(A)A 1983, s. 23 may be disapplied by special resolution passed pursuant to C(A)A 1983, s. 24.

1.6.2 TRANSFER FORM

Registered securities may be transferred by means of an instrument under hand in the prescribed form. The prescribed form is that set out in the First Schedule to the Stock Transfer Act 1963 as amended by the Stock Transfer (Forms) Regulations 1996 (SI 263/1996). The form must set out:

(a) particulars of consideration;

(b) description of security;

(c) number, or amount of security;

(d) name and address of transferor; and

(e) name and address of transferee.

The transfer form must be signed by the transferor: Stock Transfer Act 1963, s. 4(1). However, the form need not be attested. Further, the form need not be signed by the transferee provided that the share is fully paid. However, in an unlimited company the transferee must sign.

If the share being transferred is only part paid, then the standard transfer form must be amended to provide for signature by the transferee. A form common or usual before the commencement of the Stock Transfer Act 1963 will be valid if it complies with the requirements as to execution and contents which apply to a stock transfer.

A *'transfer in blank'* is a transfer on which the name and address of the transferee have not been inserted. In practice, it is not uncommon for nominee shareholders to execute share transfers in blank, and these transfer forms are handed over to the client. While this is perfectly in order, it is an offence for the transferee or the person(s) acting on his/her behalf to part with possession of the transfer form until the name(s) of the transferee(s) have been inserted: Stock Transfer Act 1963, s. 4(1). This offence is punishable by a fine and the transferee or anyone acting on his/her behalf must also pay the unpaid stamp duty.

Section 81 of CA 1963 provides that it shall not be lawful for a company to register a transfer of shares in or debentures of the company unless a proper instrument of transfer has been delivered to the company. If a secretary or registrar of a company receives a transfer form on which any of the details referred to above have been omitted, he will be entitled to refuse to register the transfer. Section 81(1) of CA 1963 shall not prevent the company registering as shareholder or debenture holder a person to whom the right to any shares has been transmitted by operation of law: CA 1963, s. 81(2).

A person may become entitled to shares in a company by operation of law, e.g. the personal representative of a deceased shareholder is entitled to be registered as the holder of the shares without production of an executed share transfer form. That person would, however, have to produce to the registrar or secretary of the company evidence of their right to be registered as owner of the shares, e.g. a grant of probate.

1.6.3   STAMP DUTY ON TRANSFERS

Stamp duties are a form of tax levied on documents used to transfer property. The Revenue Commissioners are charged with the assessment and collection of this tax.

Stamp duty is imposed on the market value or the consideration, whichever is greater, and not the nominal value of the shares transferred.

Duty, generally, is levied at one of two rates:

(a)   under the head 'Conveyance or Transfer on Sale' transfers in which a beneficial interest passes attract ad valorem duty. This is calculated at the rate of l per cent of the market value or the consideration (whichever is greater) of the shares; or

(b)   under the head 'Any Case other than a Sale' transfers or securities in which no beneficial interest passes (e.g. transfer of subscriber shares, nominee shares); such transfers no longer attract a duty.

A registrar or secretary of a company has a duty to satisfy himself that the correct stamp duty has been paid on the transfer before registering the transferee as a member of the company. It is the responsibility of the transferee to lodge the instrument, but under the Stamp Duties Consolidation Act 1999, s. 129, the secretary is liable to a fine if she/he registers or records any instrument not duly stamped. However, it appears that the transfer is valid if registered, notwithstanding the fact that it is not properly stamped.

A person/company may hold shares in a company through a nominee. The nominee is registered as the owner of the shares, but in fact he holds these shares 'in trust for' some other person/company (the beneficial owner). On transfer to the nominee by the legal owner, no beneficial interest will pass and stamp duty is levied on the transfer form at the nominal rate. Where shares are held by a nominee that person/company executes a declaration of trust in favour of the beneficial owner. The declaration of trust is itself no longer stampable even at the nominal rate.

In passing, it should be noted that under CA 1963, s. 123, a registrar or secretary of a company is not permitted to receive notice of or register the existence of a trust and must register the trustee as the shareholder.

In certain transactions, before a transfer form may be stamped, it must first be adjudicated. An example of a transaction in which this arises is a company reconstruction or amalgamation qualifying for relief from stamp duty under the Stamp Duties Consolidation Act 1999, s. 80.

A transfer form which has not been stamped or which has been improperly stamped, is still a legal transfer of the security to which it refers. However, the transfer document itself is not producible as evidence in court, unless correctly stamped or not chargeable for duty except in criminal cases or in civil proceedings by the Revenue Commissioners: Stamp Duties Consolidation Act 1999, s. 127.

1.6.4 COLLECTION AND ENFORCEMENT OF STAMP DUTY

The Finance Act 1991 introduced new provisions regarding the collection and enforcement of stamp duty. These sections brought stamp duty into line with the collection and enforcement provisions of other taxes and have now been reproduced in Part 2 and Part 10 of the Stamp Duties Consolidation Act 1999.

The payment of stamp duty is now mandatory and must be made within thirty days of the date of execution of the stampable instrument, regardless of where execution took place, e.g. if the stampable instrument is executed in France, it must be stamped in Ireland within thirty days. Failure to have an instrument properly stamped within the prescribed period will result in penalties, interest, and surcharges being payable. Surcharges are also payable if the consideration on the instrument is understated. Where an instrument is lodged for adjudication and stamp duty is assessed, it must be paid within fourteen days of the issuance of an assessment.

The register of members will be prima facie evidence of any matters directed or authorised to be contained in it: CA 1963, s. 124. A person wishing to have a name removed from the register, or, alternatively, added to the register, may apply to the court (under CA 1963, s. 122(1)) to have the register rectified. The transferee of shares in a company has a right, subject to anything contained in the memorandum or articles of association of the company, to be entered on the register as a member of the company.

Where a contract to sell shares is in existence, then, in the absence of an express stipulation to the contrary, there is an implied undertaking on the part of the transferor that he will do nothing to prevent or delay registration of the transferee as a member. There is, however, no implied term that the transferee will be registered.

.6.5 SHARE CERTIFICATES

CA 1963 provides that:

(a) A share certificate under the common seal of a company specifying the shares held by a member shall be prima facie evidence of the title of the member to the shares: CA 1963, s. 87(1).

(b) The date that a share certificate has been issued and the number of the share certificate is recorded in the register of members.

(c) A purported transfer of shares in respect of which a share certificate has been issued will not be accepted for registration unless the relevant share certificate is presented with the transfer form.

(d) If a share certificate is lost, a duplicate may be obtained from the company on the terms provided in the company's articles of association. The company will usually require that an indemnity in respect of the lost certificate be given to the company.

.6.6 DIVIDENDS

The payment of dividends mechanism is usually set down in the memorandum and articles of association. A fundamental principle of company law is that dividends must be paid out of 'distributable profits' and may not be paid out of capital of the company since this would effectively be an unauthorised reduction of the company's capital.

The procedure in regard to the declaration of dividends is usually set down in the company's articles. The company in general meeting may declare dividends, but no dividend should exceed the amount recommended by the directors: Table A, Part I, article 116.

The directors are allowed to declare such interim dividends as appear to them to be justified by the profits of the company: Table A, Part I, article 117.

Additionally, the directors are entitled to set aside certain of the profits of the company to a reserve.

It is also possible for the general meeting declaring a dividend to make a distribution of paid-up shares in lieu of a dividend: Table A, Part I, article 122.

The EC Second Directive on Company Law, which was implemented by C(A)A 1983, made specific regulations regarding the distribution of profits. Previously the only definitions in company law of distributable profit (other than in a company's memorandum or articles) were to be found in case law. Distributions are now restricted to those permitted by C(A)A 1983, Part IV subject to any further restrictions which may be included in a company's articles of association or in case law.

The rules of distribution may be summarised as follows:

The definition of 'profits available for distribution' is by reference to the excess of realised profits over realised losses as shown in the accounts: C(A)A 1983, s. 45(2).

There is an additional restriction for public limited companies. A public limited company may not allow a distribution to reduce its net assets below the amount of its called-up share capital and undistributable reserves: C(A)A 1983, s. 46(1).

A public limited company which is an investment company as defined (principally a listed investment trust) may as an alternative to the foregoing distribute the excess of its realised revenue profits over its realised and unrealised revenue losses but may not let the distribution reduce the value of its assets below one and one half times its liabilities: C(A)A 1983, s. 47(1).

1.6.7 MERGERS CLEARANCE

A further matter to be considered under the heading 'share transfers', is that of mergers clearance. The Mergers, Take-overs and Monopolies (Control) Act 1978 ('the 1978 Act') as amended restricts certain mergers and take-overs if they come within the provisions of the Act.

A merger may occur, for example, where Company A purchases the assets and undertaking of Company B in return for shares in Company A. Company B is then dissolved leaving the business of the two companies effectively merged. A take-over may occur, for example, where one company purchases all the shares in another company.

1.7 Division of Powers

1.7.1 DIRECTORS

1.7.1.1 Generally

The articles usually delegate to the directors the exercise of all the powers of the company not required by the articles or by the Companies Acts 1963–1999 to be exercised by the company in general meeting: Table A, Part I, articles 80–90. The directors' powers may be usurped by a court-appointed examiner pursuant to C(A)A 1990, s. 9. The general rule is that powers given exclusively by the articles to the directors may not be altered by the members in general meeting except by changing the relevant article by special resolution under CA 1963, s. 15. However, the power to dismiss directors may not be taken away from the members by any provision in the articles: CA 1963, s. 182. A court-appointed examiner may amend a company's memorandum and articles in accordance with C(A)A 1990, s. 24(7). The powers granted to directors enable them to conduct and manage the day-to-day business of the company and would include such powers as borrowing money, using the company seal, recruiting employees and entering into contracts.

1.7.1.2   Appointment and removal of directors

The first directors of a company must be named in a statement delivered to the Registrar of Companies: C(A)A 1982, s. 3. Any subsequent directors of the company must be appointed in the manner set out in the articles of association. If no format of appointment is set down, directors must be elected by the members in general meeting. It is not allowed to propose the election of more than one director by a single resolution, unless by prior unanimous resolution of the members: CA 1963, s. 181. It is normal that the directors have power to fill casual vacancies in their number: Table A, Part I, article 98.

The manner of appointment of subsequent directors will depend upon the articles: see Table A, Part I, articles 98–100.

The company must keep a register of directors and secretaries and must notify the Registrar of Companies of all changes: Form B10.

The articles may prescribe a maximum number of directors. There is no statutory maximum.

The articles may require directors to hold qualification shares. Table A, Part I, article 77 provides that no shareholding qualification is required unless and until so fixed by the company in general meeting.

A person may be disqualified from acting as a director either under the general law or under the articles.

An undischarged bankrupt may not act as a director: CA 1963, s. 183 as substituted by CA 1990, s. 169.

The court may disqualify persons from acting or being appointed as, inter alia, directors, auditors or managers for a five-year period, or such other period as the court may order, if they are convicted of any indictable offence in relation to a company or an offence involving fraud or dishonesty: CA 1990, s. 160. The court may also make a disqualification order for as long as it sees fit on certain grounds.

1.7.1.3   Restriction of directors

For disqualification under the articles, see Table A, Part I, article 91.

The articles may provide that directors must retire by rotation: see Table A, Part I, articles 92–97.

The articles of association adopted by a company may include a special article facilitating the removal of a director. This would apply for instance in the case of a subsidiary company, where the holding company may be entitled to appoint or remove a director by notice in writing to the secretary or by leaving notice at the registered office.

1.7.1.4   Removal of directors

The directors of a company may be removed by an ordinary resolution of the company in general meeting: CA 1963, s. 182. Unless the directors are directors of a private company holding office for life, this provision may not be altered by the articles of association. At least twenty-eight days' notice must be given of a resolution proposing to remove a director and a director must have an opportunity to speak at the meeting and must receive a copy of the notice of the resolution. The director whose removal is being sought is allowed to make representations in writing to the company upon receipt of the notice of the resolution.

Removal by s. 182 does not deprive the director concerned of right to damages etc., irrespective of any claim under employment protection legislation.

The articles of association may be modified to confer loaded voting rights on a director where it is proposed to pass a resolution to dismiss him, thus enabling the director to remain in office: *Bushell v Faith* [1970] AC 1099.

The court may disqualify a director under CA 1990, s. 160(2).

1.7.1.5 Powers of directors

The directors' powers will be conferred on them by the articles or by resolution of the company: see Table A, Part I, articles 79 and 80.

Directors' powers are exercisable by them collectively by resolution at board meetings. The conduct of board meetings will be laid down by the articles: see Table A, Part I, articles 89 and 101–109.

1.7.1.6 Delegation of powers by directors

Directors may not delegate their powers unless the articles so permit: see Table A, Part I, article 105.

In particular, articles invariably enable directors to appoint a managing director: see Table A, Part I, article 110. The managing director is often given powers co-extensive with the powers of the board as a whole: see Table A, Part I, article 112.

The board of directors may delegate any of its powers to committees consisting of such member or members of the board as it thinks fit: see Table A, Part I, articles 105–108.

Special articles may be inserted to provide for the appointment of alternate directors who act as a substitute director for the appointing director when the latter is absent from the meetings of directors.

1.7.1.7 Statutory and fiduciary limitations on powers of directors

A director owes his duty to the company, not to the individual shareholders: *Percival v Wright* [1902] 2 Ch 421.

A director must not make a personal profit out of his position: *Cook v Deeks* [1916] AC 554.

A director must account to the company for any personal profit as a result of a transaction, which he would not have entered into but for his directorship: *Regal (Hastings) Ltd v Gulliver* [1942] 1 All ER 378. Directors must exercise their powers for the benefit of the company.

A director must exercise a duty of skill and care in accordance with the following criteria:

- Directors are only required to perform their duties with the degree of skill which may be reasonably expected from persons with their particular knowledge and experience.

- Directors need not give continuous attention to the affairs of the company.

- Directors may delegate their functions to other officials in the absence of suspicious circumstances (subject to there being power to do so in the articles).

- In exercising their duties to the company directors are now under a duty to have regard to the interests of the company's employees in general (CA 1990, s. 52), as well as the interests of its members.

24

1.7.1.8   Statutory provisions concerning directors

To prevent them from abusing their position, directors are subject to a considerable number of statutory controls. Thus:

Remuneration

Accounts laid before the company in general meeting must disclose aggregate amounts of directors' emoluments, aggregate amounts of directors' or past directors' pensions and aggregate amounts of compensation in respect of loss of office: CA 1963, s. 191.

Compensation for loss of office

A company may not pay compensation for loss of office gratuitously to a director unless disclosed to and approved by members: CA 1963, s. 186.

Register of directors' and secretaries' interests

There must be maintained a separate register of the interests of directors, their spouses and minor children and of 'connected persons', in the company's shares: CA 1990, s. 59.

Substantial property transactions involving directors and loans to directors

CA 1990, ss. 29 and 31–40 regulate certain 'substantial property transactions' and the giving of loans or other similar financial benefits by a company to its directors. A director includes 'shadow director' and 'connected person'.

Interest in contracts

A director who is interested directly or indirectly in a contract or proposed contract with his company must declare the nature of his interest at a board meeting: CA 1963, s. 194. This rule also applies to a shadow director, who must declare his interest by written notice to the directors: CA 1990, s. 27(3).

1.7.1.9   Meetings of directors

The management of a company is vested in its board of directors. It is at meetings of the board that many decisions which affect the company must be formally taken. The articles of association of the company set down the regulations pertaining to the holding of directors' meetings. Directors may meet together as and when they think fit. A director is entitled to and the secretary, if requested by a director must, at any time summon a meeting of directors: Table A, Part I, article 101.

The quorum for the transaction of the business of directors is fixed by them and unless so fixed is two: Table A, Part I, article 102.

Every director is entitled to reasonable notice of a meeting of directors save that it is normal to provide that a director who is abroad does not have to receive notice of the meeting if the directors so resolve: Table A, Part I, article 101.

Where due notice is not given of a meeting or a quorum is not present it is an irregular meeting and its decisions are not valid (although the 'indoor management' rule may apply in the case of an outsider without notice).

It is a matter of choice as to whether the chairman is given a casting vote at directors' meetings. Article 101 of Table A, Part I provides that the chairman has a casting vote and therefore care should be taken in the event of Table A articles being used in companies in which there is likely to be any contention in this matter. A casting vote of the chairman will arise where there is an equal number of votes in favour of and against a resolution. To break the deadlock the chairman (if authorised by the articles of association) is given a second or casting vote.

It is also normal for a provision to be set down in the articles of association that a resolution in writing signed by all the directors entitled to receive notice of a meeting is as valid as a resolution passed at a duly convened meeting of directors. Such a provision is particularly helpful for a company where many of the directors are overseas: Table A, Part I, article 109.

It should be noted that the use of the company seal is dependent upon the authority being given by the directors or a committee of the directors and it is normal for the articles to set down the signing requirements attaching to the sealing of a document, e.g. under article 115, Table A, Part I, two directors, a director and secretary or a director and a person duly authorised by the board of directors for that purpose.

As regards directors' meetings, most solicitors will be called upon to be present at the first directors' meeting of a company. This meeting will usually deal with the following matters:

(a) approval of the company's seal;

(b) formal approval of the registered office of the company;

(c) opening a bank account and signing of mandate;

(d) appointment of auditors pending the first AGM;

(e) appointment of solicitors;

(f) issue of shares;

(g) disclosure of directors' interests;

(h) formal ratification of the board of directors;

(i) formal ratification of the appointment of the secretary; and

(j) approval of transfer of subscriber shares.

1.7.1.10 Disclosure in the company's accounts

CA 1990, s. 41 increases both the details of disclosure necessary and the range of persons to whom disclosure should be made in regard to certain transactions by requiring same to be disclosed in the company's accounts, e.g. disclosure of directors' loans, quasi loans etc.

1.7.1.11 Inspection of directors' service contracts

CA 1990, s. 50 requires that a company must keep at either its registered office, the place where its register of members is kept if other than its registered office, or its principal place of business:

(a) in the case of each director whose contract of service is in writing, a copy of that contract;

(b) in the case of each director whose contract of service with the company is not in writing, a written memorandum setting out the terms of that contract;

(c) in the case of each director who is employed under a contract of service with a subsidiary of the company, a copy of that contract or, if it is not in writing, a written memorandum setting out the terms of that contract; and

(d) a copy or written memorandum, as the case may be, of any variation of any contract of service, referred to in sub-paragraphs (a), (b) and (c) above.

Members of the company may inspect such documents during normal business hours by virtue of s. 50(6). Section 50(7) provides for a range of penalties if these provisions are breached.

These requirements do not apply to the unexpired portion of the term of the service contract if that is less than three years, or where the company may, within the next three years, terminate the contract without payment of compensation.

1.7.2 SECRETARY

Every company must have a secretary. Any act required to be done by or to a director and a secretary may not be performed by the same person acting in both capacities.

The secretary is the principal administrative officer of the company, with apparent authority to enter into contracts connected with the administrative side of the company's business: *Panorama Developments (Guildford) Ltd v Fidelis Furnishing Fabrics Ltd* [1971]2 QB 711.

The secretary is an officer of the company and therefore shares, with the directors, the responsibility of ensuring compliance with all those provisions of the Companies Acts 1963–99 where a penalty for non-compliance is imposed on an officer.

1.7.3 AUDITORS

1.7.3.1 Generally

Every company must have a duly qualified independent auditor. CA 1990, s. 187 (as amended by the Companies Act 1990 (Auditors) Regulations 1992) lists those who are not qualified for appointment as auditor of a company or as a public auditor of a society. These include a present officer or servant of the company or society or a person who has been an officer or servant of the company within a period in respect of which accounts would fall to be audited by him; a parent, spouse, brother, sister or child of an officer of the company; a person who is a partner or in the employment of an officer of the company; or a person who is disqualified from appointment as auditor of any other body corporate that is a subsidiary or holding company of the company. If during his term of office as auditor of a company or public auditor a person becomes disqualified under the Companies Acts 1963–1999 for appointment to that office, he must immediately vacate his office, giving notice in writing to the company or society.

The auditors' primary duty is to make a report to the members on the accounts examined by them and to state whether they give a 'true and fair view' of the company's financial position and whether they have been prepared in accordance with usual accountancy standards and procedures.

1.7.3.2 Appointment of auditors

The first auditors of a company may be appointed by the directors at any time before the first AGM of the company. If the directors fail to do so the Minister for Enterprise, Trade and Employment may do so instead. Normally the auditors will be appointed at each AGM and hold office until the next AGM and the auditors' remuneration must also be fixed. There is now provision that an auditor may be removed and replaced by an ordinary resolution at an EGM of a company as well as at an AGM. Extended notice (which means at least twenty-eight days) of such a resolution is required and notice of the removal must be filed in the Companies Registration Office.

Under CA 1963, s. 160 a company may remove an auditor by ordinary resolution before the expiry of his term of office.

Pursuant to CA 1990, s. 184 shareholders of a company are now accorded the option of being able to appoint new auditors if a casual vacancy should arise. Previously only the board of directors could fill such a vacancy.

1.7.3.3 Removal of auditors

Extended notice being at least twenty-eight days' notice must be given of a resolution at the AGM or EGM proposing the appointment of someone other than the retiring auditors as auditor of the company. An auditor has a right to attend and to be heard at any general meeting at which it is proposed to remove him from office and also at the AGM at which his term would have expired. He is entitled to receive all notices and other communications relating to any such meeting which are sent to members of the company.

1.7.3.4 Resignation of auditors

CA 1990, s. 185 allows auditors of an Irish company to resign or decline to be reappointed, if they so wish. The auditors are entitled to require an EGM to be convened to consider the situation: CA 1990, s. 186. If they consider that their reasons should be brought to the notice of the shareholders and creditors, they must state these reasons in writing and forward a copy to the Registrar of Companies and the company must forward a copy to each shareholder. If the auditors require an EGM to be held, the directors on receiving such a notice from the auditor are bound within fourteen days to convene a general meeting of the company for a day not more than twenty-eight days after such notice. The auditors of course have the right of audience at such meetings and are entitled to receive all notices and communications relating to such a meeting.

1.7.3.5 Removal of statutory requirement for an audit for small companies

Part III of C(A)(No.2)A 1999 introduced new provisions which allow small private limited companies to claim exemption from the requirement to have their accounts audited. The company must satisfy certain criteria to avail of this exemption and must have:

(a)   turnover not exceeding £250,000 per annum;
(b)   balance sheet total not exceeding £1.5 million;
(c)   number of employees not exceeding fifty persons; and
(d)   the company is a company to which C(A)A 1986 applies.

The exemption is not available if the company is a parent company or subsidiary, or holds a bank licence, insurance licence or is one of the companies listed in the Second Schedule of that Act.

The annual return of the company must be furnished to the Companies Registration Office in compliance with the requirement of CA 1963, s. 127(1), that is that the return must be completed *within sixty days after the AGM for the year and forwarded to the Registrar of Companies within this period.*

Unless the financial year in respect of which the exemption is being claimed is the first financial year of the company, the company must also have satisfied all the conditions set out in s. 32(3) in respect of the preceding financial year: s. 32(1)(b). This means, for instance, that where a company has failed to file its annual return on time either during the preceding financial year or it fails to file its return on time during the financial year in respect of which it wishes to claim the exemption, that company is not entitled to the exemption from the requirement to have its accounts audited, notwithstanding that it may satisfy all of the remaining conditions.

If the exemption is available the appointment of an auditor may be terminated for so long as the exemption may be claimed.

A company which has claimed the exemption will still have to prepare annual accounts and submit them to the members at the AGM and file them in the Companies Registration Office with the annual return.

1.7.3.6 Qualifications

Basically, persons undertaking company audit work in Ireland must possess qualifications as accountants. Usually they will be a member of a body of accountants recognised by the Minister for Enterprise, Trade and Employment or have an accountancy qualification from a body of accountants which, in the opinion of the Minister, is of a similar standard to that required for membership of a recognised body of accountants.

The Minister is given wide powers in relation to the recognition or authorisation of bodies of accountants as to their qualifications as auditors. The Minister may attach such terms and conditions to his recognition or authorisation as she/he believes necessary and may at any time, by notice in writing, revoke or suspend such recognition and may further require the recognised body of accountants to prepare and submit for his approval a code of professional conduct and standards: CA 1990, s. 192.

1.7.3.7   Statutory report

The contents of the auditors' report are now set out in CA 1990, s. 193. CA 1990, s. 193(6) states that an auditor is under a general duty to carry out audits with professional integrity. The 1990 Act does not state what this consists of, but it will presumably entitle the company to take action against the auditor if he fails to observe the appropriate standard. The auditor is now entitled to require from the officers any information within the knowledge of the directors etc., which he thinks necessary for the performance of his duties. In the report itself, the auditors must state whether they are satisfied that proper books of accounts have been kept by the company and that proper returns adequate for their audit have been received from branches of the company not visited by them.

1.7.3.8   Subsidiary companies

The auditor of a holding company is empowered to request information and explanations from the subsidiary company. The subsidiary and its auditors must give information and explanations as may reasonably be required by the auditors of the holding company for the purposes of their duties as such. It is the duty of the holding company, if required by its auditors to do so, to take all such steps as are reasonably open to it to obtain from the subsidiary the information required: CA 1990, s. 196(1). If a company or auditor fails to comply within five days of the making of the requirement, the company and every officer in default or the auditor shall be guilty of an offence: CA 1990, s. 196(2).

1.7.3.9   Book of accounts

The company has a duty to provide accurate information to enable auditors to keep proper books of accounts.

An officer of a company who knowingly or recklessly makes a statement, which is misleading, false or deceptive is guilty of an offence. It is also provided that an officer must within two days provide the auditor with any information which the auditor requires as an auditor of the company and which is within the knowledge of, or may be procured by, the officer: CA 1990, s. 197. This puts an onus on the officers in question to provide accurate information at all times.

Every company must, on a continuous and consistent basis, keep proper books of accounts which correctly record and explain the transactions of the company and at any time will enable the financial position of the company to be determined with accuracy: CA 1990, s. 202. If a company is being wound up and is unable to pay all its debts and has not kept proper books of accounts and the court considers that such contravention has contributed to the company's inability to pay all its debts, or has resulted in a substantial uncertainty as to the assets and liabilities of the company or has impeded the ordinary winding-up of the company, every officer of the company who is in default is guilty of an offence: CA 1990, s. 203.

The court on the application of a liquidator or any creditor or contributory of the company may declare that any one or more of the officers or the former officers who is or are in default in relation to this matter shall be personally liable without any limitation of liability for all or such part as may be specified by the court of the debts and other liabilities of the company: CA 1990, s. 204.

1.7.4 POWERS OF MEMBERS

The members of a company are:

(a) the subscribers to the memorandum provided they have not transferred their shares;

(b) those others who have agreed to become members, having taken shares from the company (on allotment), from another member (by transfer) or on a transmission by operation of law (e.g. personal representatives) and whose names are entered on the register of members.

The members' powers comprise those powers of the company which have not been or cannot be delegated to the directors. Members can exercise their powers at general meetings, which have been duly convened (see below). In general terms, a member may vote in relation to his shares in whatever manner he wishes. However, there is authority to the effect that he must exercise his powers 'bona fide for the benefit of the company as a whole' and that any exercise of the powers is subject to equitable considerations which may make it unjust to exercise (them) in a particular way: *Ebrahimi v Westbourne Galleries Ltd* [1973] AC 360, quoted in *Clemens v Clemens Bros Ltd* [1976] 2 All ER 268.

1.7.5 ANNUAL RETURNS

It should also be noted that every company must make an annual return: CA 1963, s. 125(6). The return must be completed within sixty days after the AGM and a copy thereof signed by a director and the secretary of the company must be forwarded to the Companies Registration Office. The return is made up to a date which falls fourteen days after the AGM.

The requirements for the annual return of a company having a share capital are detailed in Part I, Fifth Schedule of CA 1963 and the form itself is set out in Part II (equivalent to the CRO Form B1). A shortened form annual return (Form B1S) is also available.

All companies must attach to the annual return a certified copy of the profit and loss account, balance sheet, auditors' report and directors' report as required by CA 1963, ss. 128 and 157 and C(A)A 1986, s. 16 unless an exemption is granted pursuant to C(A)A 1986, ss. 10–12 or the exemption in respect of subsidiaries provided by the 1986 Act, s. 17 (as amended) is availed of.

1.7.6 COMPANIES (AMENDMENT) ACT 1986

C(A)A 1986 as amended by the European Communities (Accounts) Regulations 1993 (SI 396/1993), reg. 4 introduced new accounting formats and disclosure requirements for all companies. It created the concept of small and medium-sized companies and imposed disclosure requirements accordingly.

The level of detail required to be included in a company's financial statements varies depending on the classification of a company as large, medium or small.

Section 8, as amended, sets out the definitions as follows:

1.7.6.1 Small companies

A small company is a private company which complies with at least two of the following three conditions:

- its balance sheet total for the year does not exceed £1.5 million;
- its turnover for the year does not exceed £3 million; or
- the average number of people employed by the company for the year did not exceed 50.

In the case of a small company, the abridged accounts will include a special auditors' report and the balance sheet together with notes to the balance sheet which are required so that the abridged financial statements show a true and fair view.

1.7.6.2 Medium companies

A medium company is a private company which complies with at least two of the following three conditions:

- its balance sheet total for the year does not exceed £6 million;
- its turnover does not exceed £12 million for the year; or
- its average number of employees for the year does not exceed 250.

In the case of a medium sized company, the abridged financial statements will be similar to the full accounts except that the profit and loss account will commence with gross profit but is not required to include turnover or costs of sales.

1.7.6.3 Subsidiaries

Where a private company is a subsidiary of a parent company established under the laws of a Member State of the EU, the company shall, as respects any particular financial year of the company, be exempted from the provisions of C(A)A 1986, s. 7 (other than subsection (1)(b); i.e. the need to annex a copy of its accounts to the annual return) if the following conditions are fulfilled:

(a) every person who is a shareholder of the company on the date of the holding of the next AGM of the company after the end of that financial year shall declare his consent to the exemption;

(b) there is in force in respect of the whole of that financial year an irrevocable guarantee by the parent company of the liabilities of the subsidiary company in respect of that financial year and the company has notified in writing every shareholder of the guarantee;

(c) the annual accounts of the company for that financial year are consolidated in the group accounts prepared by the parent company and the exemption of the parent company under this section is disclosed in a note to the group accounts;

(d) a notice stating that the company has availed of the exemption in respect of that financial year and a copy of the guarantee and notification referred to in paragraph (b) of this subsection, together with a declaration by the company in writing that paragraph (a) of this subsection has been complied with in relation to the exemption, is annexed to the annual return for the financial year made by the company to the Registrar of Companies;

(e) the group accounts of the parent must be drawn up in accordance with the requirements of the Seventh Council Directive; and

(f) the group accounts of the parent company are annexed to the annual return as aforesaid and are audited in accordance with article 37 of the Seventh Council Directive.

1.8 Compliance

There is now an emphasis on compliance by companies and their officers with the provisions of the Companies Acts 1963–1999 and the secondary legislation relating to companies in the form of statutory instruments. This was given impetus by the publication in June 2000 of the Company Law Enforcement Bill 2000, whose main provisions flow directly from recommendations in the Report of the Working Group on Company Law Compliance and Enforcement which was published in March 1999. The principal provisions of the Bill provide for the establishment of the post of Director of Corporate Enforcement and the transfer to the Director of the functions of the Minister for Enterprise, Trade and Employment relating to the investigation and enforcement of the Companies Acts 1963–1999. The Bill also recognises the need for ongoing review of company legislation to deal with changes in the commercial world and it envisages the establishment of a statutory Company Law Review Group to monitor, review and advise the Minister for Enterprise, Trade and Employment on matters relating to company law.

1.9 Future Developments

There are also further far-reaching developments such as the creation of a 'European company' and the consolidation of the Companies Acts 1963–1999 into a single Act in the same way as the consolidation of the tax legislation into the Taxes Consolidation Act 1997. The role of technology will also be very important in both compliance by way of electronic filing and the exchange of information such as the availability of forms and legislation on the internet.

CHAPTER 2

SHAREHOLDERS' AGREEMENTS

2.1   Introduction

A shareholders' agreement is an agreement between the shareholders of a company pursuant to which the shareholders agree certain matters in relation to the management and operation of the company. Parties enter into a shareholders' agreement to provide for how certain important matters relating to the company, such as the conduct of its business or the payment of dividends, will be dealt with and to afford certain protections to shareholders who are in a minority position or who do not have an active involvement in the day-to-day operation of the company. In many cases, a shareholders' agreement will be drawn up when a person makes an investment in a company.

2.2   Parties

A shareholders' agreement only binds those persons who are a party to it. Therefore, it is normal practice for all shareholders in the company to be a party to the agreement. It is possible to have an agreement between some and not all of the shareholders but such an agreement will only have effect as between the contracting parties. It is also standard practice to join the company itself as a party to the agreement though particular attention should be paid to the covenants which the company agrees to become bound by. In *Russell v Northern Bank Development Corporation* [1992] 1 WLR 588, it was confirmed that a company could not, by its articles or otherwise, deprive itself of its statutory power (as set out in the UK equivalent of the CA 1963, s. 68) to increase its share capital by special resolution. Accordingly, it was held that an undertaking by a company in a shareholders' agreement not to increase its share capital was unenforceable against the company. However, such a covenant was binding on the shareholders who were a party to the agreement.

To address this issue, shareholders' agreements now provide that the shareholders agree *as between themselves* that they will not exercise their votes as shareholders in the company in such a way so as to increase the share capital of the company. While the company may be a party to the shareholders' agreement, it is not a party to this particular undertaking but the practical effect is the same in that the company's share capital may only be increased in accordance with the terms of the shareholders' agreement.

As a result of the *Russell* case, it is not considered advisable to make a company a party to covenants in a shareholders' agreement which may limit its statutory power. As with the covenant relating to an increase in share capital, it is the shareholders only who are parties to such covenants. If the company is made a party to a covenant which may fetter its statutory powers then a severance provision should be included in the agreement.

2.3   Advantages of a Shareholders' Agreement

The key advantages of a shareholders' agreement are, first, that it provides certainty as to specific matters relating to the operation of the company and, secondly, it may provide minority shareholders with protection which they may not otherwise have.

2.3.1   CERTAINTY

As regards certainty, persons who become shareholders in a company may wish to have some certainty that specific matters will not change. For instance, they will not wish the company in which they become a shareholder to change the nature of its business or they might wish that profits over a certain level will be distributed by way of dividend. If these matters are agreed when a person becomes a shareholder, this can be recorded in the shareholders' agreement thereby ensuring clarity for the future operation of the company.

2.3.2   PROTECTION OF MINORITY INTERESTS AND ENFORCEABILITY

As regards the protection of minority interests, a company's articles of association will normally provide that all shares of the same class carry equal voting rights. Therefore, a shareholder with a small interest (e.g. 10 per cent) will, in practice, have very little influence on all matters that are put to a vote at a shareholders' meeting. A shareholders' agreement may provide such a shareholder with protection in that, pursuant to it, the other shareholders may agree and undertake to exercise (or not to exercise) their voting rights in a particular way. If the majority acts in breach of this undertaking, the minority shareholder has a direct right of action against them for breach of contract pursuant to the shareholders' agreement. This avoids some of the complicated issues that may arise in seeking to enforce a shareholder's rights pursuant to the articles of association alone as such rights are only enforceable by and against shareholders in their capacity as shareholders.

2.3.3   CONFIDENTIALITY

If the shareholders' agreement does not have to be registered with the Registrar of Companies pursuant to CA 1963, s. 143, its contents may be kept confidential to the parties to it as it will not be available for inspection by the public in the Companies Office. For further discussion on the consequences of CA 1963, s. 143 for shareholders' agreements, see **2.4.11.3**.

2.4   Drafting a Shareholders' Agreement

2.4.1   GENERALLY

The clauses to be inserted into a shareholders' agreement obviously depend on the purposes for which it is required. There are a number of relatively standard clauses which are found in nearly all shareholders' agreements. Where a shareholders' agreement is drafted to provide certain assurances for persons investing in a company, it generally contains a number of additional clauses which are not found in agreements drafted between existing shareholders. An outline of clauses which are typically found in shareholders' agreements is set out below. These clauses are additional to clauses containing recitals and a definition section which are found at the start of most commercial agreements.

2.4.2 CONDITIONS PRECEDENT

A conditions precedent clause is generally only found in an agreement where one or more persons are investing in the company. It sets out the conditions which must be satisfied before the investors subscribe for new shares in the company. The obligations of the investors pursuant to the agreement are contingent on the satisfaction of these conditions. This clause has exactly the same purpose as it has in a share purchase agreement and reference should be made to the more detailed discussion of this topic in Chapter 3 which deals with share purchase agreements. Similar issues, such as the requirement for an 'end date', arise in relation to shareholders' agreements as they do in relation to share purchase agreements.

2.4.3 SUBSCRIPTION/COMPLETION

Again, a subscription/completion clause is only found in situations where new investors are buying shares in the company. It provides for the procedure to be followed when new shareholders apply for their shares and the company issues and allots the shares to them. The meeting at which these events take place is often referred to as the 'completion'. At completion, the events described in the next paragraph occur.

Subject to the satisfaction or waiver of the pre-conditions (if any), the investors submit written applications to the company for the issue to them of a specified number of shares at a specified price and, at the same time, pay the amount due in respect of the new shares to be allotted to them (sometimes, the manner of payment is provided for in the clause). On receipt of these applications the existing shareholders undertake to convene a meeting of the board of directors of the company at which the applications are accepted, the new shares are allotted to the investors, share certificates are issued and other matters relevant to the arrangements between all the shareholders are attended to. These other matters may include the appointment of the nominees of the new shareholders to the board of directors of the company and the alteration of the company's bank mandates to include the signature of a nominee director of the new shareholders.

The section dealing with completion may also provide that, at completion, the existing shareholders (or a majority of them) will deliver to the new shareholders a deed of indemnity in respect of pre-existing tax liabilities of the company. Typically, such a deed is required in a situation where an investor such as a venture capitalist is investing in a company which has, up to that point, been held and operated by a small group of people. The investor will not want a situation to arise where, shortly after the making of its investment, the company incurs a significant tax liability in respect of liabilities arising prior to the date of the investment and a substantial amount of the money which it invested in the company goes towards discharging these liabilities. In a small tightly run company, the existing shareholders should be in a position to know whether or not there is a risk of such tax liabilities arising and so are generally the appropriate parties to give the indemnity. In summary, the deed of indemnity in this situation serves a similar purpose as the deed of indemnity in a share purchase transaction and readers are referred to the discussion of this topic in Chapter 3.

In a situation where new shareholders are coming into the company, the clause providing for subscription often also provides that the existing shareholders waive any right or claim which they may have against the company. From the new shareholders' point of view, the logic of such a clause is clear: a person will not wish to invest in a company only to find that an existing shareholder takes a successful legal action against the company and that the investment money is used to discharge the liability arising pursuant to this action. Whilst such a waiver is drafted in general terms, it often also contains a specific undertaking by the existing shareholders that they will not have any claim against the company in respect of any inaccurate information provided to them by the company to enable them to give the warranties to the new shareholders. There is a further discussion on the role of warranties in shareholders' agreements below.

2.4.4 WARRANTIES AND UNDERTAKINGS

A clause relating to warranties and undertakings is also generally only found where an investor is subscribing for new shares in the capital of the company. Pursuant to this clause, the existing shareholders give warranties to the investor about the state of affairs of the company. Where an investor suffers loss by reason of a matter which constitutes a breach of a warranty, it may seek to recoup the amount of this loss from the warrantor. The company does not give the warranties as it would defeat the underlying rationale for the warranties if the investor had to recover any loss arising from a breach of warranty from the company in which it had invested. The issues arising in relation to warranties in shareholders' agreements are identical to those arising in relation to warranties in share purchase agreements and the reader is referred to the discussion of that topic in Chapter 3. It should be noted that, as with share purchase agreements, the warranties will generally be made subject to a disclosure letter furnished by the warrantors to the investor which will disclose matters which constitute a breach of warranty. As with share purchase agreements, where there is a gap between signing and completion, a shareholders' agreement may provide a right of rescission on the part of the investor if a matter occurs between signing and completion which constitutes a breach of warranty.

2.4.5 NON-COMPETITION

Many shareholders' agreements contain covenants by some or all of the shareholders that they will not, for the duration of their shareholding in the company and for a certain period thereafter, compete with the business of the company. The purpose of such a clause is to protect the 'goodwill' of the company. 'Goodwill' is not a legal term but may be defined as the reputation of a business and its customer connection. A shareholder (particularly one with an active involvement in a company) may be very much associated in the minds of the customers of a company with the company and may have a lot of information in relation to its operations and methods of business. If such a shareholder were to set up a business competing with the company, this could seriously undermine the company's business. The purpose of the non-compete clause is to prevent this situation arising and to protect the goodwill of the company. However, a non-compete clause that is unnecessarily wide or otherwise contrary to law will not be enforceable. A brief outline of the general principles relating to the enforceability of non-compete clauses is set out below.

The legal position governing non-compete restrictions in shareholders' agreements is very similar to the principles governing such restrictions in share purchase agreements. Generally speaking, a non-compete restriction must be limited in terms of subject matter, geographical territory and duration to what is necessary to protect the goodwill of the company. This is the general common law position in relation to both shareholder agreements and share purchase agreements and has, to a large extent, been confirmed by developments under the Competition Acts 1991–1996.

Guidance on the extent of the restrictions which it is permissible to place shareholders under is set out in Competition Authority Decision No. 489 'Category Certificate in Respect of Agreements Involving a Merger and/or Sale of a Business' Competition vol. 6, 1996–1997 p. 260. The provisions of the category certificate are dealt with in detail in Chapter 3: Share Purchase Agreements.

2.4.6 TRANSFER OF TITLE TO COMPANY'S ASSETS

This is another clause which is generally only found in agreements where an investor is subscribing for new shares in a company. It is not uncommon in small companies involving a small number of people for an asset which is crucial to the operation of the business of the company (e.g. a patent) to be held in the name of a person other than the company and to be used on an informal basis by the company. Pursuant to this clause, the existing shareholders undertake to procure the transfer of the ownership of the said asset to the company so that the investor will be taking shares in an entity which has full title to the assets necessary for the conduct of the business.

2.4.7 COMPLIANCE BY THE COMPANY

Due to some doubts as to the enforceability of certain covenants given by a company (as raised by the decision in *Russell v Northern Bank*), shareholders' agreements contain covenants given by all parties that no party will exercise his or its voting or other rights in relation to the company in such a manner as would cause the company to be in breach of any of the provisions of the agreement. Accordingly, in the event that a company acts in breach of one of the provisions of the agreement (for example the requirement to give information to a party), the party who has suffered by virtue of this breach may take an action pursuant to this clause requiring the other shareholders to exercise their voting rights in the company in such a manner as will ensure that the company acts in compliance with its obligations. Accordingly, if a covenant is not enforceable against the company directly, it should, at least, be enforceable against the other shareholders.

2.4.8 COVENANTS CONCERNING THE COMPANY

While the clauses referred to above set out certain matters governing the relationship between the shareholders on certain issues (such as the warranties) the covenants which are outlined below set out the agreement between the parties as to how the company will be operated. The purpose of these covenants is to give a specific shareholder or a specified proportion of shareholders a right of veto (which they would not otherwise have) over certain matters. For example, under company law, the holder of 20 per cent of the voting rights in a company does not have the power to prevent the holders of the other 80 per cent of the voting rights from adopting new articles of association for that company. However, in a shareholders' agreement, the parties can agree that they will not adopt new articles of association without the consent of the 20 per cent holder. In this situation, if the majority purport to adopt new articles without the consent of the 20 per cent holder, that holder may prevent them from doing this by seeking to enforce the relevant provisions of the agreement.

In some shareholders' agreements, it is provided that a shareholder will only be able to rely on these covenants if his holding exceeds a certain specified percentage. Therefore, if he sells some of his shares so that his holding is brought below the specified percentage, he will no longer be able to rely on these covenants. It should be noted that this does not affect the continuation of the other clauses in the agreement which continue in force until such time as they otherwise cease.

Broadly speaking, these covenants may be divided into positive covenants and negative covenants, covenants that the company will do certain matters and covenants that the company will not do certain matters.

The 'positive' covenants normally provide for the following matters:

- there will be no material change in the nature and scope of the business of the company;
- the management of the company will be carried out by its board of directors and no other party;
- the board of directors will consist of a certain number of persons with each shareholder having the right to act as a director or to nominate a person to act as a director;
- the memorandum and articles of association of the company will not change;

- the quorum for both shareholder and board meetings will consist of a representative of each shareholder or a designated number of shareholders;

- all shareholders will have access to the books and records of the company and will be given full information about its activities;

- profits shall be distributed on a basis as set out in the agreement; and

- the auditors of the company will be a certain named firm of auditors.

The 'negative' obligations generally deal with a range of matters which the parties agree the company shall not do. In most agreements, the parties agree that the company shall not do any of the following without the consent of all or a specified percentage of the shareholders:

- create or issue any new share or loan capital;

- create or suffer to exist any charge, mortgage, lien or other encumbrance over any part of its undertaking;

- enter into any onerous or unusual contract or arrangement (i.e. a contract outside the ordinary course of its business or which is not terminable by it within twelve months without penalty);

- dispose of a substantial part of its assets;

- pay salaries over a certain specified level;

- allow its borrowings to exceed a certain level;

- incur any capital expenditure over a certain level; and

- acquire any interest in any other business.

It is these covenants which are essential to ensuring that the interests of a minority shareholder in a company are properly protected. Other matters which are of concern to the minority shareholders may be addressed by additional covenants. It should be noted that the existence of these obligations in the agreement does not mean that the company may never do or not do (as the case may be) any of the matters referred to. The parties may, of course, in any one particular circumstance, agree that a certain matter should be done thereby waiving their rights of enforcement under the agreement. For example, parties may agree that, notwithstanding an undertaking to the contrary, a new set of articles should be adopted. In this situation, all the shareholders simply pass the necessary resolutions and the articles are adopted in the usual way and, as each party has effectively agreed to waive its rights to enforce the relevant provisions of the shareholders' agreement, no action is taken to enforce the provisions preventing the adoption of a new set of articles.

2.4.9   TERMINATION

As it is intended that the parties will only benefit from the provisions of the agreement whilst they are shareholders, some shareholders' agreements contain provisions relating to the termination of the agreement. Typically, these clauses provide that the agreement will terminate in the following events:

(a)   the company going into liquidation, or

(b)   in relation to any particular shareholder, upon that shareholder ceasing to own any shares in the company.

Not all shareholders' agreements contain a termination clause, but if one is used it is important to make it clear that the provisions which are intended to survive after the termination of the agreement (such as a non-compete clause) remain enforceable notwithstanding the termination.

2.4.10 DEADLOCK

'Deadlock' is the word used to describe a situation where the shareholders do not agree on an important matter relating to the company, thereby making it impossible for the company to do anything. Typically, deadlock arises where there are two shareholders holding equal shares in the company and they do not agree on anything so that no resolutions (ordinary or special) may be passed by the company. Usually, deadlock has consequences for the day-to-day business of a company and not just for specific legal formalities. For instance, most companies which are held by two shareholders (who also serve as directors) will operate a practice whereby all cheques issued by the company must be signed by both directors. When deadlock arises, either or both of the directors may refuse to sign cheques thereby making it impossible for any funds to be transferred by the company. A deadlock clause seeks to deal with this impasse by setting out precisely what will occur when a deadlock arises. There are a number of ways in which this may be done but two of the most common types of deadlock resolution mechanisms are outlined below:

- either party may serve a notice in the event of a deadlock arising and, if the deadlock is not resolved within a specified number of days of the service of the notice, the parties agree to wind up the company, or

- where there are two shareholders and in the event of a deadlock not being resolved within a specified period of time after service of a notice of deadlock by either party, one or other of the parties (the 'offeror') may serve a notice offering to buy the other party's (the 'offeree's') shares at a certain price (the 'offer price'): the offeree then has a certain period of time either to accept the offer and sell the shares held by it to the offeror for the offer price or to buy the offeror's shares for the offer price: in this way the deadlock is resolved in that one shareholder is bought out of the company: the advantage of this mechanism is that it encourages the party who initiates the process to set a price for the shares which is fair as it is the price at which that party's own shares may be bought out.

It should be noted that not all shareholders' agreements contain deadlock provisions as the parties will sometimes prefer to deal with a deadlock situation if and when it arises in the context of the respective rights and obligations of the parties under the agreement itself, the articles of association and under general law.

2.4.11 GENERAL PROVISIONS

A shareholders' agreement will also contain provisions dealing with general matters such as the survival of obligations and the giving of notices. These are the 'General Provisions' found at the end of most commercial agreements. In the context of shareholders' agreements, the general clauses dealing with the following four issues warrant special reference:

(a) arbitration;

(b) costs;

(c) conflict with the articles; and

(d) partnership.

2.4.11.1 Arbitration

The parties may agree that any matters in dispute be referred to arbitration. The principal advantage of arbitration is that it is held in private, thereby ensuring that any disputes between the shareholders are not aired in public. However, arbitration may not be appropriate in all shareholder situations and reference should be made to Chapter 9 which deals with the relative advantages and disadvantages of arbitration.

2.4.11.2 Costs and expenses

In situations where a substantial amount of time has been spent in negotiating and completing a shareholders' agreement and related documentation, a clause will often be inserted setting out who will be responsible for the costs and expenses incurred in completing the agreement. Very often, the agreement will provide that the company itself will be responsible for the costs involved. It is important to note that the payment by a company of professional fees incurred during the acquisition by subscription of shares in the company may be in contravention of CA 1963, s. 60, which prohibits a company from giving financial assistance in connection with a purchase of or subscription for shares in the capital of the company.

It is arguable that where a company pays legal fees incurred by a person in the course of acquiring shares in the company, it is providing indirect financial assistance in connection with the subscription for shares in itself. For this reason, where a company is to pay fees in such circumstances, it is prudent to ensure that it complies with the procedure set out in CA 1963, s. 60(2) regarding matters such as the passing of a shareholders' special resolution and the swearing and filing of a statutory declaration by the directors. Further information on the provisions and procedures set out in s. 60 are contained in Chapter 4.

2.4.11.3 Conflict with articles of association

It has been common practice for shareholders' agreements to contain a provision that, in the event of a conflict between the shareholders' agreement and the articles of association, the shareholders' agreement shall prevail. This has raised issues under CA 1963, s. 143 which sets out some of the principal requirements regarding the registration of company documents with the Companies Office.

Under s. 143(4) the following types of document, amongst others, must be registered with the Companies Office:

> resolutions which have been agreed to by all the members of a company, but which, if not so agreed to, would not have been effective for their purpose unless they had been passed as special resolutions.

It is arguable that where a shareholders' agreement to which all shareholders are a party contains a clause providing that the agreement prevails over the articles of association, such a clause is, in effect, a resolution which, if not agreed to by all the members, would only have been effective for its purpose (i.e. prevailing over the articles of association) if it had been passed as a special resolution.

On this basis, the shareholders' agreement would appear to be a document which, under the provision of s. 143(1), should be filed in the Companies Office. This possible requirement raises serious concerns for shareholders as shareholders' agreements usually contain commercially sensitive information which the shareholders do not wish the public to have access to. In practice, the following approaches are commonly used to address this issue, thereby removing the requirement for registration of the shareholders' agreement:

(a) the clause providing for the priority of the shareholders' agreement may be omitted provided that there is no actual conflict between the agreement and the articles; or

(b) the clause may be redrafted to provide that as between the parties, if there is any conflict between the agreement and the articles of association, then the provisions of the agreement should prevail but not so as to amend the articles.

The current view is that a clause of the type set out at (b) above removes the necessity for registration in the Companies Office but it must be said that there is some uncertainty on the issue.

2.4.11.4 Partnership

Given the practical similarities that exist between a business partnership and a company in which a number of persons have a shareholding, a question may arise that the relationship between the shareholders constitutes a partnership or a quasi-partnership. This may have undesirable consequences for the respective rights and obligations of the parties. To deal with this, a clause is often inserted providing that the relationship between the parties does not constitute a partnership.

2.5 Articles of Association

2.5.1 GENERAL

It is normal practice for most private companies to adopt Part II of Table A of CA 1963 (which itself incorporates most of Part I of Table A) as their articles of association. Nearly all companies will have their own specific requirements which will mean that some of the articles in Part II will need to be excluded or modified. There is further discussion on this in Chapter 1 which deals with the drafting of articles of association. In the context of a company in respect of which a shareholders' agreement is in place, there are a number of specific issues that need to be provided for in the articles for such companies and further discussion on these issues is set out below.

2.5.2 ISSUE OF NEW SHARES

The shareholders' agreement will usually contain a provision that no new shares may be issued without the consent of all or a specified percentage of the shareholders. Where shares are issued, it is still necessary to provide for a right of pre-emption on the part of existing shareholders. To ensure that the level of each shareholder's equity interest in a company may not be diluted by the issue of new shares to other shareholders and third parties, the articles usually provide that any new shares which are issued should first be issued to existing shareholders on a basis that is pro rata to their existing shareholding in the company and that any shares which are not taken up on a first round will be offered to the other shareholders on a similar basis. For this reason, article 5 of Part I of Table A, which gives the directors general discretion in relation to the issue of shares, is generally excluded from the articles of any such company or a clause is inserted that article 5 is modified by reference to the article dealing with allotment.

2.5.3 TRANSFER OF SHARES

Most investors in a company will want to realise their investment at some stage by selling their shares whereas existing shareholders will generally not want shares in the company to be sold to parties whom the shareholders do not know. To deal with these competing requirements, the articles of private companies normally contain detailed provisions concerning the transfer of shares. The procedure set out in such articles is often referred to as the 'exit mechanism' meaning that the provisions provide a mechanism which allows shareholders to 'exit' the company.

Typically, most articles provide a right of pre-emption for existing shareholders in that a shareholder who wishes to sell his shares must first offer them to other shareholders on a basis that is pro rata to their existing shareholding in the company. The articles relating to the transfer are very detailed in that, as well as the procedure for transfer, the articles usually set out a mechanism for setting the price at which the shares will be sold: either the price is set by the auditors on a certain basis or the price is set by the selling shareholder. Articles usually provide that if none of the existing shareholders will buy the shares on offer, the selling shareholder may sell these shares to a non-shareholder subject to the important stipulation that the price at which the shares are sold to the non-shareholder must not be less than the price at which the shares were offered to the existing shareholders. It is important to note that, once the pre-emption provisions are complied with, the directors do not generally retain an unfettered discretion to refuse to register a transfer (otherwise the vendor might never be able to find a buyer for his shares which would be acceptable to the directors). For this reason, article 3 of Part II of Table A (which grants directors of a company an unfettered discretion to refuse to register a transfer) is generally excluded from the articles of companies with such detailed transfer provisions. The transfer provisions also generally provide for what will happen to a shareholder's shares on death.

2.5.4   MEETINGS OF SHAREHOLDERS

As important decisions of a company are taken at meetings of the shareholders, each shareholder will want to ensure that a meeting cannot take place without him or his representatives. For this reason, the shareholders' agreement or the articles usually provide that a quorum of a general meeting will be a certain minimum number of shareholders and that a meeting may not take place in the absence of such a quorum. Typically, this is done by dividing the capital of the company into different classes of shares (such as 'A' shares, 'B' shares etc.), all of which rank equally. Each shareholder holds a different class of shares. The provisions relating to quorum normally stipulate that for each meeting, a quorum will consist of the presence of at least one shareholder from each separate class. In companies in respect of which a shareholders' agreement is in place, it is inappropriate for a chairman to have a casting vote and for this reason, a clause is inserted into the relevant article that article 61 of Part I of Table A (which grants the chairman of general meetings a casting vote) is modified accordingly. Likewise, a clause is inserted into the article dealing with shareholders' meetings that article 54 of Part I of Table A (which contains provisions dealing with the quorum for shareholders' meetings) is modified accordingly.

2.5.5   MEETINGS OF DIRECTORS

The shareholders' agreement usually provides that the board of directors will contain a specified number of persons, each of whom is nominated by a different shareholder. To give further effect to this principle, the articles will contain a provision stipulating that a quorum for a board meeting will comprise a certain number of directors which must include the designated nominees of each shareholder. As with general meetings, it is generally inappropriate for a chairman to have a casting vote and therefore a clause is inserted into the relevant article that article 101 of Part I of Table A (which grants the chairman of the meeting of the board of directors a casting vote) is modified accordingly. Article 102 of Part II of Table A is also generally excluded as this contains provisions dealing with the quorum of directors' meetings.

2.5.6   BORROWING POWERS

Article 79 of Part I of Table A is also generally excluded as this puts restrictions on the borrowing powers of a company. In most companies in respect of which a shareholders' agreement is in place, this is not seen to be appropriate as provisions relating to borrowing powers are generally set out in the shareholders' agreement.

2.5.7 APPOINTMENT AND RETIREMENT OF DIRECTORS

Other articles in the standard Table A which are generally excluded are articles 75 and 92–100 which deal with the appointment and rotation of directors. In a private company in respect of which a shareholders' agreement is in place, it is generally not desirable for there to be an ongoing rotation of directors as the appointment and removal of directors will be dealt with by the provisions set out in the shareholders' agreement alone.

2.6 Joint Ventures

The term 'joint venture' is frequently used to describe business relationships between different entities and companies. It is not a legal term and the types of legal agreement or agreements which are used to give effect to a joint venture very much depend on the nature of the joint venture and the requirements of the parties involved. In general terms, a joint venture consists of two persons who are otherwise unconnected with each other coming together to combine their respective resources for a new business venture. This may be structured by way of investment in a new company in which both parties are shareholders. Alternatively, it may be structured in a different way such as a distribution agreement or an exclusive supply agreement between the joint venture partners. Where a joint venture is structured by way of a company, there will generally be a shareholders' agreement setting out the relationship between the parties as shareholders and there may also be ancillary agreements, such as a supply agreement pursuant to which one party supplies products to the joint venture company. In summary, there is no 'standard' joint venture agreement and the structure and composition of each joint venture depends on its purpose and the requirements of the parties involved.

2.7 Conclusion

The foregoing sets out the matters of principal concern that need to be taken into account in advising on and drafting a shareholders' agreement and related articles of association. However, in any particular situation, these may not be the only matters that need to be addressed. It is essential to take full instructions from the clients so as to assess their precise requirements so that any other issues of particular concern may be taken into account and provided for in drafting the relevant documentation.

CHAPTER 3

SHARE PURCHASE AGREEMENTS

3.1   Introduction

The purpose of this chapter is to explain the principal features of transactions under which shares are purchased and sold. The following pages assume that what is being purchased is 100 per cent of a company ('the target company') and that accordingly a normal share purchase agreement is being drawn up. The features discussed in this chapter are the standard features of a share purchase agreement for the entire issued share capital of the target company. It is of course possible to effect a share purchase on the basis of a much simpler form of agreement and indeed in many instances the formal agreement may be dispensed with in its entirety, particularly in the purchase of a small shareholding where a share transfer form is all that is completed.

The most basic form of a share purchase is by way of completion of a share transfer form. The format of the share transfer form is prescribed by the Stock Transfer Act 1963. It has been possible since 1996, however, to transfer shares pursuant to the Companies Act 1990 (Uncertificated Securities) Regulations 1996 (SI 68/1996) without requiring an instrument in writing at all. This facility allows for the operation of the CREST system in the context of publicly listed companies and allows for a paperless format for share transfers.

3.2   Structuring of Transactions

3.2.1   GENERAL CONSIDERATIONS

When a transaction is first proposed, careful consideration needs to be given as to whether the transaction is best structured as a purchase of the shares of a target company or the purchase of the assets and liabilities of that target company. In most, but not all cases, having considered the factors involved, the decision would be taken to proceed by way of share purchase. However, this is an issue which must be considered at the outset of every transaction. The salient concerns are:

Share purchase	Asset purchase
All assets and liabilities pass to purchaser	Purchaser has flexibility to choose assets and liabilities
Stamp duty is levied at a rate of 1%	Stamp duty is leviable at rates up to 6%
Tax losses pass, subject to the various anti-avoidance legislation	Difficult to secure tax losses
Employees pass automatically	May be some flexibility not to take employees but this is rendered difficult by European Communities (Safeguarding of Employees' Rights on Transfer of Undertakings) Regulations 1980 (SI 306/1980)
Consideration paid to vendor	Consideration paid to target company which then has to pay it to the vendor

3.2.2 CHOICE OF ASSETS AND LIABILITIES

Choice of assets and liabilities is likely to be the most significant issue, based on which a purchaser will decide to go on the asset purchase route. This choice in particular may be taken where the company has uncertain liabilities, such as a pending legal claim. The purchaser will require only the assets and will not want to take on liabilities which could turn out to be substantial. In such an instance the purchaser will always be conscious that if the liability is subsequently not met, the creditor may seek to challenge the transaction. Therefore it is important that the transaction be carried out at arm's length and that the price be demonstrably fair. Careful thought is also required as to how the sales proceeds will be disbursed as, if a purchaser is in any way party to an arrangement where a creditor is being ignored, they may have difficulty if a transaction is subsequently challenged. The mechanism might also be used if there are assets in the target company which the purchaser does not want and it is not possible to extract those assets from the target company in advance of completing the transaction without creating excessive tax liabilities. In these circumstances, it is usually a question of assessing whether the taxation liabilities are more onerous if the assets are extracted or if the assets and relevant liabilities are sold by the target company.

3.2.3 STAMP DUTY

It is provided by the Stamp Duties Consolidation Act 1999 that stamp duty at a rate of 1 per cent is payable on the transfer of shares. Consequently a share purchase attracts stamp duty at a rate of 1 per cent. On a transfer of assets, the rate of stamp duty depends very much on the assets which underlie the business. However, in a business which consists substantially of items such as property, goodwill, intellectual property or book debts, stamp duty is payable at the rate of 6 per cent on those assets. This usually results in the stamp duty being significantly greater for the purchaser on an asset purchase. On the other hand, assets such as stock and loose plant and machinery may, if the transaction is properly structured, pass by delivery and it is theoretically possible (but unlikely) that an asset purchase may be cheaper if the entire assets of the target company consist of this type of assets.

3.2.4　TAX LOSSES

If a target company which has ongoing tax losses is acquired, it may be possible for the purchaser to utilise those tax losses in the future trading of the target company. There are some restrictions on this imposed by the Taxes Consolidation Act 1997, s. 401 which prevent significant changes in the nature of the business. It is conversely regarded as extremely difficult to transfer tax losses when a business is acquired by way of an asset purchase. The issue of transfer of tax losses is becoming gradually less significant with the reduction in corporation tax rates to the 12 per cent intended for 2003. Nevertheless if a business has very significant tax losses, this might be a relevant consideration.

3.2.5　NAME

If the target company's shares are purchased, the name of the target company is automatically acquired. If, on the other hand, the transaction is conducted by way of asset purchase through a shelf company or other vehicle of the purchaser, it would be necessary for that vehicle to change its name and for the target company to change its name. This is not a very difficult procedure where the parties are in agreement but is an inconvenience and may give rise to practical difficulties with things such as bank accounts.

3.2.6　EMPLOYEES

If the shares in a target company are purchased, all of the employees of that target company will be unaffected by the purchase and will therefore automatically (albeit indirectly) pass to the purchaser. In an asset purchase scenario, it used to be possible to pick and choose as between employees when the assets of a business were being purchased as the employees could be regarded as assets/liabilities not required. However, since the European Communities (Safeguarding of Employees' Rights on Transfer of Undertakings) Regulations 1980, there is an automatic transfer of the rights and obligations of the vendor company to the purchaser company on a transfer of an undertaking or business. It is, however, possible notwithstanding these regulations to have situations where the regulations do not apply; for example, if the assets being purchased form part of a business, it may be permissible not to take any employees or to take only those employees who relate to that part of the business. This is a specialist area on which there is a considerable volume of case law.

3.2.7　CONSIDERATION

If a person carries out a transaction by way of a share purchase, the proceeds of sale are paid to the holders of the shares in the target company and they are subject to taxation if they have made a gain on those shares. On the other hand, if the assets are purchased from the target company, the target company gets the proceeds, is the chargeable entity and its tax liabilities will undoubtedly differ from those of its shareholders. If the target company then wishes to pass the sale proceeds to its shareholders, there will be tax payable by those shareholders on what they have obtained from the target company. There are therefore two possible tax events on an asset purchase, whereas the share sale will involve one taxable event. An added complication with an asset purchase is that the target company, depending on its trading position, may be prohibited for reason of prudence, from immediately handing over the sale proceeds to its shareholders. Thus, for example, if there are significant liabilities in the target company which are unquantified, it may be appropriate to await quantification of those liabilities before the target company distributes the proceeds out to its shareholders.

3.3 Due Diligence

3.3.1 GENERALLY

When instructed in relation to a share purchase, one of the first items which needs to be attended to in relation to the target company is the carrying out of a number of investigations, usually referred to as due diligence. This should include:

- accounting due diligence
- general legal due diligence
- Companies Office/statutory books review
- investigation of title
- actuarial due diligence
- insurance review
- environmental review
- areas specific to target company

The level of detail into which these investigations will go very much depends on the nature of the target company. As a general principle, the level of investigation will be greater where the purchase price is greater, but this principle would not always apply. For example, a company acquired for £1 may have very significant liabilities and a very extensive investigation to quantify these may be appropriate.

3.3.2 ACCOUNTING DUE DILIGENCE

It is important that every acquisition of a target company be the subject of some form of accounting review. This is usually carried out by a financial adviser to the purchaser. In a simple case, this may involve reviewing the last few sets of audited accounts and reviewing projections for a future period. In a more complex situation, a very detailed accountants' report would be prepared pointing out any deficiencies in an accounting sense of the target company and very detailed work would be done on the future position. The scope of this work is largely outside the territory of the legal adviser but it is critical that a legal adviser should advise the client to make sure that this matter is attended to as it is likely to be the most fundamental review that requires to be carried out. The accounting review should also cover the tax affairs of the target company, in particular where the target company is a member of a group, as leaving a group often crystallises tax problems.

3.3.3 GENERAL LEGAL DUE DILIGENCE

It is good practice at an early stage in an acquisition to look for a copy of all legal documentation which has been entered into by a company. Apart from areas specifically dealt with below, this would include a review of employment-related contracts, distribution/agency agreements, agreements relating to trademarks, patents and other intellectual property rights, hire purchase/leasing agreements and conditions of sale. Given the increasing importance of technology and the increasing frequency with which technology companies are acquired, particular attention needs to be paid to intellectual property rights. It is critical to establish that the target company either owns or has proper licences for all of its intellectual property as otherwise there may be litigation by third parties alleging breach. Furthermore, in a company that supplies technology, there must be a full understanding of the basis on which that technology is made available to others, with particular focus on arrangements where exclusive licences have been agreed or where the licence arrangements permit the customer to distribute onwardly the technology or a product incorporating same.

The legal due diligence is very much the province of the legal adviser and there will usually be a report made to the purchaser as to any material issues established following this review.

3.3.4 COMPANIES OFFICE/STATUTORY BOOKS REVIEW

If asked to acquire a target company, the legal adviser should at an early stage conduct a Companies Office search against that target company and its subsidiaries. Consideration should also be given in searching against any company with a similar name as this may disclose potential passing-off problems or issues being raised about the name of the target company. Obviously, this is only practical where a name is somewhat unusual. It may also be appropriate to check domain names and trade mark registrations. The Companies Office search gives the purchaser's solicitor useful information at an early stage such as a list of registered charges, a list of the directors filed in the Companies Registration Office and information as to when the last annual return is made up to. This may indicate deficiencies in paper work. It is useful at an early stage also to obtain a copy of the memorandum and articles of association of the target company and its subsidiaries. This will highlight issues which may need to be dealt with in the course of the acquisition such as the waiver of pre-emption rights. The due diligence in this regard should also cover a review of the statutory books of the target company and its subsidiaries. This is often left until the last moment but in practice should be conducted as early as possible in the transaction as clearly the entries in the statutory books should mirror details in the share purchase contract and in the Companies Registration Office.

3.3.5 INVESTIGATION OF TITLE

Many target companies include among their assets valuable lands and buildings. In these circumstances it is critical that some form of title investigation is carried out. The most usual format of investigation involves raising requisitions on title and enquiries in the same way as if the property itself is being bought and getting various documents on completion in the same way as the completion of a property transaction. A possible alternative is to have the vendor's solicitors certify the title. A certificate of title may be the only practical way to proceed if there are a significant number of properties and there is a commercial urgency in completing the transaction. A less satisfactory alternative to investigation or certificate of title is to rely on the warranties given by the vendor as part of the share purchase agreement. This is sometimes done when the properties are comparatively insignificant in value compared to the target company as a whole or where there are a lot of properties none of which individually is particularly material and where the purchaser has some degree of confidence that they have been acquired and managed in a competent fashion. As in a property transaction, it is of course always advisable that a purchaser should conduct a survey of the property. A purchaser should always be advised that this is an appropriate course of action. (It is a commercial decision for a purchaser to weigh up the cost of the survey as against the benefits.)

3.3.6 ACTUARIAL DUE DILIGENCE

If the target company has set up a pension scheme, it is important that some form of investigation (usually known as an actuarial investigation) be carried out into the pension scheme. This will specifically focus on whether the assets of the pension scheme are sufficient to meet its liabilities. If it is found that a pension scheme is inadequately funded, there is often an adjustment in the purchase consideration to reflect this. There are two different types of schemes encountered, being defined benefit schemes (where the members are promised a definitive amount when they retire, e.g. one-half of final salary) and defined contribution schemes (where the members receive what their aggregate contributions will buy at the time of retirement). Defined benefit schemes are usually more problematic and generally require more thorough investigation than defined contribution schemes but both would need to be reviewed by specialists in the area. The review should also encompass any promises that have been made to employees in relation to their pension.

3.3.7 INSURANCE REVIEW

The purchaser should review the insurances put in place by the target company as if they complete the purchase and the insurance turns out to be inadequate, it is the purchaser who will suffer the loss. This task is usually carried out by handing over a schedule of insurance policies to the purchaser's insurance brokers. The review needs to cover property and public liability insurance, employers' liability, product liability and directors' and officers' insurance.

3.3.8 ENVIRONMENTAL REVIEW

Given the increasing legislative importance that is being placed on care of the environment, it is important, particularly with a company which has a significant environmental impact, that an environmental assessment be carried out. This may involve a thorough review (similar to a survey) carried out by appropriately qualified personnel. The focus would be on whether the company causes air, water, noise or other pollution, how waste products are disposed of and compliance with any existing licences which the company has. Particular attention may need to be paid as to whether the land on which the company operates has been historically contaminated as this may give rise to problems in the future which would be expensive to remedy. While not specifically an environmental area, thought should also be given to issues concerning the safety of employees as the internal environment may give rise to as many problems as the external environment.

3.3.9 OTHER ISSUES

While the above headings enumerate the principal issues which need to be looked at as a part of due diligence, thought should always be given to the particular circumstances of the target company. Depending on the business the target company is engaged upon, there may be further aspects which need to be looked at. For example, if a company is heavily involved in the processing of data, compliance with the data protection legislation becomes enormously relevant; if a company is involved in mineral exploration, compliance with appropriate legislation and with licences is critical. The purchaser should be readily able to identify the areas that are likely to require focus given the specifics of the target company.

3.4 Pre-Conditions to Share Purchase Agreement

3.4.1 GENERALLY

In a number of cases where the commercial details of a share purchase agreement are agreed, it is not possible for the parties to proceed immediately to complete the matter because of the necessity to get a consent of a third party. The device which is used in these circumstances to enable the parties to commit to their agreement is the insertion in the share purchase agreement of a number of pre-conditions. This enables the parties to sign and therefore be bound by their agreement subject only to these pre-conditions being satisfied.

A technical distinction should be drawn between conditions precedent to an agreement and conditions precedent to completion. In the case of conditions precedent to an agreement, no contract exists and no contractual obligations on the parties arise if the conditions are not fulfilled. No contract is even deemed to have existed until the conditions are fulfilled. In the case of conditions precedent to completion a contract exists but the parties have the right to rescind on the terms of the contract if the pre-conditions are not fulfilled. The parties may therefore incur contractual obligations to each other even though the contract is never completed. The standard types of pre-conditions tend to be conditions precedent to completion.

3.4.2   STANDARD CONDITIONS PRECEDENT

The most common types of matters, which give rise to conditions precedent, are the need to obtain:

(a)   clearance under the Mergers, Take-overs and Monopolies (Control) Act 1978;

(b)   clearance under the Competition Act 1991;

(c)   consent of a grant authority such as Enterprise Ireland, Shannon Development, Udaras Na Gaeltachta;

(d)   consent of bankers to or other parties having a contract with the target company; or

(e)   consent of shareholders.

These are discussed in detail below.

3.4.3   'NEGATIVE' CONDITIONS PRECEDENT

If conditions precedent of the type listed in **3.4.2** are being inserted in a contract, however, consideration needs to be given to the insertion of other conditions precedent which broadly consist of things which should not happen during the period while the substantive condition is being fulfilled. Examples of the types of 'negative' conditions that would be included would be a condition that no substantial damage should occur to the assets of the company by reason of fire, explosion or other similar hazard and a condition to the effect that there should be no substantial breach of warranty between the date of signing and completion. Clearly a purchaser faced with the situation where a premises has burnt down or substantial litigation against a target company has been initiated at some stage between signing and completion will want to be able to decide not to proceed with the contract and therefore the insertion of such pre-conditions will normally be required by the purchaser. Purchasers may also seek to insert conditions concerning a due diligence process, such as a condition to the effect that they should be satisfied with the due diligence process in general or certain aspects thereof. This, however, is normally resisted by the vendor as it gives the purchaser too much room to decide not to proceed with the contract.

3.4.4   END DATE

If a contract contains pre-conditions, there is a possibility that third parties who have to give the relevant consents/approvals may take some considerable length of time to do so, or indeed may never do so. It is also possible that by the time they get around to issuing their approval or consent, circumstances will have radically changed. It is therefore practice to include a latest date by which all of the conditions are to be satisfied (which may normally be extended by agreement). This means that either of the parties is free not to proceed with the contract if the pre-conditions are not satisfied within a reasonable time period. While there is no set practice for the length of time involved, normally a reasonable estimate as to how long it is going to take to fulfil the conditions will be made and a period of approximately one month added to this to allow for slippage.

3.4.5 SUBSTANTIVE CONDITIONS

3.4.5.1 Mergers, Take-overs and Monopolies (Control) Act 1978

The Mergers, Take-overs and Monopolies (Control) Act 1978, as amended (the 'Mergers Act') is a very technical piece of legislation introduced in 1978 to control mergers. In technical terms, its focus is a situation where 'two or more enterprises, at least one of which carries on business in the State, come under common control'. A takeover by a purchaser of a target company will clearly come within this as common control is deemed to happen 'if the decision as to how or by whom each shall be managed can be made either by the same person, or by the same group of persons acting in concert'. Clearly after the acquisition the same people will 'call the shots' in both purchaser and target company.

By reason of various elaborations contained in the Mergers Act, the acquisition of shares in a target company which carry voting rights will trigger the Mergers Act, if after the acquisition the acquiror holds more than 25 per cent of total voting rights. The figure of 25 per cent was introduced by the Competition Act 1991, s. 15(2) with the previous threshold being 30 per cent. An exception arises where the purchaser has more than 50 per cent of voting rights before the acquisition, in which event they may acquire further shares without requiring Mergers Act sanction.

Thresholds

On the basis of the test as set out above, it is clear that nearly every acquisition involving the attainment of more than 25 per cent of voting rights in a target company would be subject to the Mergers Act. The Mergers Act is, however, only concerned with substantial transactions and there are therefore thresholds specified for transactions to fall within the legislation. The thresholds are set out in the Mergers Act 1978, s. 2(1). The thresholds provide that in the most recent financial year the value of the gross assets of each of two or more of the enterprises to be involved in the proposal is not less than £10 million or alternatively that the turnover of each of two or more enterprises involved in the proposal is not less than IR£20 million. These thresholds do not apply to newspapers by reason of the Mergers, Take-Overs and Monopolies (Newspapers) Order 1979 (SI 17/1979) so any takeover of a newspaper is notifiable. The current thresholds were fixed by the Mergers, Take-overs and Monopolies (Control) Act 1978 (Section 2) Order 1993 (SI 135/1993) and are overdue for revision. These figures are assessed by reference to the most recent financial year which is commonly taken in practice to refer to the most recent audited accounts. If, however, a company has substantially completed its accounts but they are not audited, an argument may be made that it is those unaudited accounts that should be considered.

Enterprises involved in proposal

It can be difficult to assess which enterprises are involved in a proposal. It is universally accepted that a target company and the purchaser are involved in the proposal. Where there are multiple vendors and one of these happens to be over the threshold, it is generally accepted that such a person is involved in the proposal and clearance would be sought, although based on past practice, the Minister may have a different view on this issue. Difficulties arise where persons become involved as lenders or guarantors but it is common in practice that such a relationship would be regarded as too distant to constitute involvement in the proposal.

The definition of enterprise is also quite technical, meaning 'a person or partnership engaged for profit in the supply or distribution of goods or the provision of services' and it is sometimes argued that this definition excludes an individual and it clearly excludes a non-profit making body. Issues may also arise as to what constitutes carrying on business in the State—e.g. is an address where letters are received enough? This criterion is often the basis on which non-Irish acquisitions by Irish companies are structured so as to avoid the application of the Mergers Act, by making the acquisition through a non-Irish subsidiary which does not carry on a business in Ireland.

Letter of notification

If it is determined that the Mergers Act applies to a transaction, the process involves notifying the Minister for Enterprise, Trade and Employment of the proposal. This is done by way of a letter setting out the details of the transaction including the parties involved. A fee, currently IR£4,000, is payable in connection with a notification. If one party to a transaction is delegated to make the notification it is critical that the notification is stated to be made on behalf of all of the parties. This is because the Mergers Act, s. 5 (as amended) requires each of the enterprises involved to notify the Minister and substantial fines are prescribed for enterprises who fail so to notify.

It was traditional in a mergers notification to address the criteria formerly contained in the Schedule to the 1978 Act which was repealed by the Competition Act 1991, s. 17. This is still practice. These criteria address the impact of the merger on issues such as continuity of supplies or services, level of employment, regional development, rationalisation of operations in the interest of greater efficiency, research and development, increased production, access to markets, shareholders and partners, employees and consumers.

Time limits

Apart from very substantial fines prescribed for non-notification of proposed mergers, the Mergers Act, s. 3 specifically provides the title to the shares or assets concerned shall not pass until either (a) the Minister has stated in writing that he has decided not to make an order in relation to the proposed merger or takeover; or (b) the Minister has stated in writing that he has made a conditional order in relation to the proposed merger; or (c) the relevant period prescribed by the Mergers Act has elapsed without an order having been made.

The relevant period is a period of three months in which the Minister must make a decision. This period of three months runs from the date of written notification, but the Minister has a right to request further information within one month of the date of receipt of a notification. If such a request is made the three months run from the date of receipt of the information. Consequently the time scale for obtaining clearance may be upwards of four months depending on the timing of a request for further information and the provision of that information. In practice, on account of the Mergers Act, s. 7, the Minister would appear to have to make a decision, within thirty days of notification/receipt of further information, to refer the matter to the Competition Authority, in default of which the Minister would appear to have no option but to indicate that he is not making an order.

Exemptions

It should be stressed in the interest of completeness that certain very large mergers are subject to control at the European Union level. In addition there are certain exemptions from the Mergers Act for transfers within a group (s. 1(3)(g)), for receivers or underwriters (s. 1(3)(f)) and for testamentary dispositions (s. 2(3)).

Checklist

The standard procedure for assessing whether mergers clearance is required is accordingly:

(a) Is more than 25 per cent of shares in a company being acquired?

(b) If yes, do two or more enterprises involved in the proposal exceed the relevant thresholds?

(c) If yes, does one of the enterprises which comes under common control carry on business in the State?

(d) If yes, a letter should be sent to the Minister outlining details of the transaction and purporting to be made on behalf of all parties involved in the proposal.

(e) Completion of the transaction must await receipt of confirmation of the Minister pursuant to the Mergers Act, s. 3 or the three-month period elapsing.

3.4.5.2 Competition Act 1991

The Competition Authority established under the Competition Act 1991 has asserted (somewhat controversially) jurisdiction to police mergers separate and distinct from that given to the Minister for Enterprise, Trade and Employment. This in particular becomes relevant where two companies in a similar business (sometimes referred to as 'a horizontal merger') merge in such a way as to reduce the number of competitors in that market. This authority was first asserted in the Competition Authority decision on *Woodchester Bank Ltd/ UDT Bank Ltd* 4 August 1992 and has been asserted in a number of subsequent decisions.

The Competition Authority issued a Certificate for Merger and/or Sale of Business Agreements on 2 December 1997 which outlined its position in this matter. In general whether a merger is problematic is determined by reference to two tests, namely the Herfindahl Hirschman Index (HHI) or by reference to the four largest firms concentration ratio. The HHI test involves squaring the market shares of all firms in the relevant markets. If the sum of all of these is less than 1,000, there generally would not be a problem but if it is above 1,800, there is liable to be an issue. The four largest firms test focuses on whether the market share of the four largest firms exceeds 40 per cent of the market.

If it is felt that the acquisition of a target company will infringe the Competition Act 1991, s. 4 (which prohibits agreements between undertakings which have as their object or effect the prevention, restriction or distortion of competition in trade in any goods or services in the State), Competition Authority clearance may be inserted as a pre-condition. This may give rise to practical difficulties as the Competition Authority has no clear cut time scale (unlike the Minister for Enterprise, Trade and Employment) to reach a decision.

.4.5.3 Consent of grant authority

It is common that Irish companies, particularly those in the manufacturing sector, will have received grant assistance from grant authorities. The most usual grant authorities encountered are Enterprise Ireland, Shannon Development (which administers grants in the mid-west region) and Udaras Na Gaeltachta (which administers grants in Irish-speaking areas). The grant agreements used by these bodies typically provide that the controlling interest in a grant-aided target company will be held directly or indirectly by certain persons unless otherwise agreed to, by the grant authority in writing. It is also frequently provided that payment of the grant may be stopped and the amount paid recalled if there is a breach of this condition. Therefore it is necessary on a share purchase to get a written consent from the authority involved. This is a fairly simple procedure which involves liaising with the authority concerned, usually by the target company or the vendor. However, it is prudent to make an application for this as early as possible in the acquisition process as the matter may require to be placed on the formal agenda for a board meeting of the grant-aiding authority and this may take a couple of weeks.

3.4.5.4   Banking consent

If the target company has banking facilities, it is quite possible that the bank may have provided in its banking facilities that its consent is required to a change of control and if it is not obtained that this amounts to an event of default. It is important in these circumstances that bank consent is obtained as even if the bank is aware of the situation, it is unsatisfactory to create technical defaults. The purchaser should make enquiries into this matter at an early stage in the transaction. Obviously if a search as part of the due diligence process indicates there is a charge registered by a bank against the target company, an enquiry should immediately be made as to whether bank consent is required.

In a way similar to banks, other persons who contracted with the target company may impose a condition which allows that party to take certain action if control of the company changes. For this reason it is prudent to establish that none of the important contracts to which the company is a party is subject to such a change of control clause. This is often done by way of warranties. Again if there is such a change of control clause, the necessary consent should be obtained and this may be included in a pre-condition to the contract.

3.4.5.5   Consent of shareholders

In some cases the consents of the shareholders of the vendor or of the purchaser will be required. This in particular arises:

(a)   in large transactions for publicly quoted companies where the Stock Exchange rules require it; and

(b)   where the purchaser or the vendor is a director or connected with a director, in which event it may be required by Companies Act 1990, s. 29 or by Stock Exchange rules.

3.5   Warranties

3.5.1   GENERALLY

By far the most substantive part of a typical share purchase agreement is the section, usually contained in the main body of the agreement, providing for the giving of warranties by the vendors which is inevitably accompanied by a schedule to the agreement setting out a very detailed list of warranties. For example, in the Dublin Solicitors Bar Association specimen share purchase agreement (1999 edition) the substantive agreement at clauses 6 and 7 includes provisions relating to warranties and this is accompanied by a schedule extending to twenty-four pages. The warranties tend to be the aspect of the agreement which gives rise to most discussion between the parties and accordingly they should be regarded as of great significance.

3.5.2   WHY SHOULD A PURCHASER SEEK WARRANTIES?

If a purchaser purchases a target company based on a share transfer alone (which is entirely permissible), the purchaser is in receipt of very little comfort in relation to the affairs of the target company. Thus, if it emerges after completion that the target company has a substantial undisclosed litigation claim which was asserted against it before the transaction was concluded, the principle of caveat emptor applies and the purchaser and the target company have to deal with the matter as best they can. It is accordingly commonplace in most share purchase transactions that the purchaser will seek fairly extensive statements in relation to the target company, the substantive effect of which is a series of promises to the effect that the target company is virtually perfect.

Exceptional situations do arise where, as a matter of contractual negotiations, no warranties are given. In particular this arises in:

(a) situations where one shareholder in a target company is buying the shares of other shareholders;

(b) management buyouts because management already has sufficient knowledge of the company's affairs;

(c) share purchases for very nominal consideration, although in these instances, the purchaser ought to be conscious of the possibility that there could be very substantial liabilities which could turn the acquisition into a 'nightmare'; and

(d) an acquisition of a listed or quoted company where, because of the large number of shareholders in the target, it is impractical to get warranties.

It is sometimes argued by vendors that, where a very extensive due diligence process has been carried out, warranties should not be given or should be significantly watered down. This is usually resisted by a purchaser, as no matter how extensive the due diligence process is, it is no substitute for warranties from those people who know the company best.

3.5.3 WHO SHOULD GIVE THE WARRANTIES?

In most situations, the vendor or, if there are more than one, all of the vendors will give the warranties. However, care should be taken to ensure that the warranties are not being given by a 'man of straw' as no matter how perfect the warranties are in a technical sense, they are of no benefit if they are not given by someone with substance to back them.

Particular care should be taken when acquiring from a vendor which is a member of a group of companies. Ideally in these circumstances, the most appropriate warrantor may be the holding company within the group, although it may be prudent to get warranties from the vendor company and perhaps other group companies with substantial assets.

If there is more than one vendor, the purchaser will normally seek to have warranties given on a joint and several basis. This means that the purchaser may make his warranty claim against every vendor and may choose to enforce against any of them. Conversely, vendors will sometimes seek to have liability established on a several basis only which means that each particular vendor is liable only for a proportion of a claim. This is unsatisfactory from a purchaser's viewpoint as it may mean that they may only recover part of their claim in the event that some of the warrantors turn out to be difficult to locate or of inadequate means.

While this chapter is primarily concerned with share purchase agreements, warranties may also arise in the context of a subscription for new shares. In such circumstances, the warranties are often given by the company. It would clearly be inappropriate to do this in a share purchase as the purchaser will end up owning the vehicle giving the warranties. In the case of a subscription, the person investing in the company may well accept this but they should, however, look for warranties from other shareholders as well. There is a question mark as to whether the giving of warranties by a company might constitute financial assistance within the meaning of the Companies Act 1963, s. 60—the prevailing view is that it is permissible to give warranties, however, as they are merely incidental to a transaction and do not constitute 'financial assistance'. This matter is not, however, entirely free of doubt.

3.5.4 MEASURE OF DAMAGES

The measure of damages which may be obtained should there be a breach of warranty is a matter which gives rise to much debate. The prevailing view is that a court is required to look at the market value of the shares held in the target company by the purchaser in the light of what has happened and compare this with what their market value would have been had the position been as it was warranted. This is quite a difficult exercise and, from the point of view of the purchaser, it will not necessarily result in the target company being put in the position that it would have been in had the breach of warranty not taken place. In some instances, to cover this point, the purchaser may seek a provision that the measure of damages should be sufficient to effect restitution—however, this would usually be resisted by vendors as effectively amounting to an indemnity.

3.5.5 SUBJECT MATTER OF WARRANTIES SOUGHT

The subject matter of warranties is discussed in greater detail below. The subject matter, however, will cover every conceivable aspect of the target company's affairs, ranging from its accounts and its taxation affairs to matters relating to its employees, its assets and debtors and any litigation against it. A considerable number of warranties have the function of gathering detailed information in relation to the target company rather than seeking to ascertain that there are no issues which may result in substantial liability.

3.5.6 PREPARATION FOR POTENTIAL WARRANTY CLAIM

If a purchaser has some concern that warranty claims may arise, there are a number of possible further steps that should be taken. One possibility is for the purchaser to seek to retain a portion of the purchase price which is only to be paid over in the future if no warranty claims have been asserted by a point in time. This is sometimes referred to as 'retention for warranties'. It may also be possible to get insurance cover against warranty claims. This is normally something which is obtained by a vendor and involves giving a copy of the agreement and the underlying disclosure letter to the insurer who is then in a position to assess the premium payable for taking the risk.

3.5.7 LIMITS ON WARRANTIES

If a vendor or vendors give warranties, he or they are potentially exposed to risk of being sued for breach of warranty for as long as the Statute of Limitations 1957 permits. In addition they could be exposed to a claim for an amount greater than they received for the target company or they could be subjected to trivial claims being asserted by a purchaser, usually for ulterior motives. For this reason it is usual for a vendor to seek to negotiate limits on warranties. Typical variations which a vendor will seek are the following:

- A provision that any warranty claim must be notified to them in writing by the purchaser within an agreed time scale. It is practice in this area to distinguish between claims relating to tax and other claims. In the case of tax claims, there is a view that the Revenue may in practice go back six periods of account if a tax liability comes to light and therefore to seek protection for a period of up to six years. In practice the time limit agreed for tax claims usually falls out somewhere in the spectrum three years to six years. In the case of non-tax claims, a vendor will usually seek a shorter period of liability and in this instance periods of the order of one year to three years are common. From a purchaser's point of view, it is often considered that two separate audits which are finished after completion should be sufficient to bring to light any warranty claims and in negotiating a limiting period, a purchaser may therefore seek sufficient time to complete two full audits post completion.

- A vendor will usually seek to cap the aggregate liability which may arise on foot of the warranties. Quite frequently the cap is the purchase consideration. The purchaser should, however, always be advised that in extreme circumstances their loss may be considerably greater than the purchase price and they will obviously lose the benefit of an alternative use to which they could have put the money. Care should also be taken by purchasers when the purchase price is relatively low. If there are provisions for increasing or varying the consideration, any limit agreed should bear this in mind.

- The purchaser will usually seek to negotiate a minimum threshold which claims have to exceed before they may be brought. This is often known as a 'de minimis' provision. The level of this will vary from transaction to transaction. A vendor will sometimes seek to have this amount constitute an excess so that if a claim arises this amount will be in any event a matter for the purchaser—this is not normally acceptable to a purchaser. The vendors will also sometimes seek to rule out any individual claim which falls below a certain amount. From a purchaser's point of view this practice is dubious as it is possible there could be a very large number of very small claims which in the aggregate would have a significant financial effect.

- Where there is more than one vendor, the vendors may seek to apportion liability on a several basis. This is discussed at **3.5.3** above.

- The vendor may seek to avoid responsibility for claims which arise because of change in law happening after completion. This is normally acceptable.

- The vendor may seek to be relieved of liability if the warranty claim arises as the result of any action by the purchaser after completion. The purchaser will often resist this and try and confine it, if agreed, to actions outside the normal course of business.

- The vendor will try and exclude matters which are covered by a provision or reserve in the company's accounts. To the extent that something is specifically provided for or reserved, this should be acceptable.

- The vendor will try and exempt liability for anything which is covered by a policy of insurance maintained by the company; again this is normally acceptable.

- A vendor will sometimes seek to reduce its level of exposure in a warranty by giving the warranty 'to the best of their knowledge, information and belief' or 'so far as the vendor is aware'. The qualification of warranties by these words is often the subject of considerable debate in the context of a purchase transaction but is generally resisted by a purchaser except for fairly trivial warranties.

- The limits frequently do not apply in case of fraud or wilful concealment by the vendor.

- By reason of the decision in *Eurocopy plc v Teesdale* [1992] BCLC 1067, a purchaser may not have a remedy for a breach of warranty, if it knew of the breach before it signed the share purchase agreement.

3.5.8   FINANCIAL MATTERS

Warranties which may be sought on financial matters include:

- A warranty that the latest set of audited accounts comply with all applicable laws and with generally accepted accounting principles (GAAP) and that they give a true and fair view of the assets and liabilities and financial position of the target company. This is commonly regarded as the most essential warranty obtained on any share purchase, and if this warranty is obtained, it may well give coverage against the bulk of claims which are likely to arise even in the absence of any other warranties. If a company has a trading record, it is important to focus on whether accounts are consistent with previous accounting periods and if not, why not.

- It is usual to seek some comfort that apart from transactions in the ordinary course of business, there have been no material changes since the date to which the last audited accounts have been made up. This is a particularly important matter to cover if the last audited accounts are relatively old. In addition, if the last audited accounts are quite old, the vendor may be asked to warrant management accounts.

- Extensive provision is usually made in warranties to deal with taxation. These warranties principally focus on whether the company has paid all of its tax which has become due prior to the date of completion. They also focus on whether the company is registered for all taxes for which it is liable and whether it has made returns on time. The warranties frequently focus on points of detail within the tax code, for example, whether the company has claimed roll-over relief under the capital gains legislation and whether it has ever incurred balancing charges. For companies which are trading companies and which have employees, these warranties should focus very clearly on VAT, PAYE and PRSI as non-payment of these taxes may quite quickly give rise to very substantial financial liability.

- Warranties are usually given as to the borrowing facilities available to the company, whether these are guaranteed or otherwise secured by the vendor, and the level of borrowing which have been incurred up to completion.

- It is not unusual to seek a warranty to the effect that the net assets of the company are not less than a stated figure. If such a warranty is given at completion of the transaction, it acts as an assurance that there have not been any major negative changes since the end of the last audited accounting period.

3.5.9   CONSTITUTION OF TARGET COMPANY

Warranties under constitution of the company include warranties:

(a)   that the memorandum and articles of the target company are as supplied;

(b)   as to who the directors and secretary are;

(c)   as to filing and returns to the Companies Registration Office;

(d)   as to who owns the share capital;

(e)   that proper records including statutory books are being kept by the company;

(f)   that no petition has been presented to wind up the company;

(g)   as to dividend payments; and

(h)   as to whether there have been any breaches of the Companies Acts, particularly investigations under Part II of CA 1990 and disclosure issues under Part IV of CA 1990.

3.5.10   ASSETS OF TARGET COMPANY

The various warranties will focus on matters relating to the assets of the company. In particular:

(a)   Warranties as to the ownership of intellectual property (e.g. trademarks, patents, and copyrights) used by the target company. In a target company which is substantially dependent upon intellectual property, material issues to consider include whether it has the right to use all the intellectual property which it is using. If the target company is selling a product which incorporates intellectual property, it is important to ensure that the right to use covers the right to incorporate that intellectual property in the product sold and generally to ascertain that such a company has not given any exclusive licence.

(b)   The warranties will focus on whether the target company is party to any unusual agreements such as long-term contracts or guarantees.

(c)   The warranties will focus on whether the target company owns all of its assets and whether they are subject to lease, hire purchase etc.

(d) Warranties will often focus on the state of the target company's assets and whether they are in good repair or are likely to require replacement. These warranties are often resisted by a vendor who might require purchasers to take their own view on assets.

(e) A warranty is usually sought that stock in trade is in good condition and, somewhat more controversially, that stocks are not excessive or slow moving or obsolete.

(f) A warranty is frequently sought that the book debts of the target company will be collected in the normal course and within a set time period after completion. This is frequently the subject of debate between vendor and purchaser, as the vendor will not want to guarantee their collectability.

(g) It is not unusual that extensive warranties would be given in relation to the properties occupied by the target company. This would normally focus on the target company having good and marketable title to the property and any encumbrances which may exist. The warranties would also cover the planning on the property and any notices which have been served affecting the property.

(h) There is usually a warranty as to whether the assets include amounts owed to the target company by the vendor or its associates. These will usually be collected at completion.

(i) A warranty is usually sought that the target company has all the licences it needs to carry on its business.

(j) A warranty will be sought as to distribution and agency agreements to which the target company is party.

(k) Warranties are usually sought as to the insurance held by the target company. This is frequently disclosed against by producing all of the insurance policies and requiring the purchaser to take its own view as to the appropriateness of same.

3.5.11 LIABILITIES OF TARGET COMPANY

A warranty will usually focus on any litigation to which the target company may be subject. Issues addressed include:

(a) whether there is any litigation in which the target company is involved or litigation which is contemplated;

(b) whether the target company has been in breach of any environmental law, in particular those relating to air pollution, water pollution, noise and waste; and

(c) whether it has sold defective products.

There is usually a warranty to the effect that the target company has complied with its statutory obligations generally without any specific statute being averted to.

There is usually a warranty seeking to establish whether the target company has any grants. If this is the case, there may be a liability to repay if there is default.

There is sometimes a warranty focusing on whether customers or suppliers have indicated that they are going to cease dealing with the target company or are winding down their level of dealing.

There is usually a warranty seeking to ascertain whether the target company owes any money to the vendors or persons associated with them. If there is a disclosure against this, the money is often discharged at completion.

3.5.12 EMPLOYEE-RELATED MATTERS

This section of the warranties usually focuses on the status of employees. This area would include a warranty:

(a) warranting a list of employees and details of their benefits, including salary;

(b) that no one is entitled to a significant period of notice;

(c) that there are no liabilities for unfair dismissal or redundancy;

(d) that there are no trade disputes;

(e) that all employee safety legislation has been complied with; and

(f) in relation to the pension schemes which are in place for employees and that they are properly funded.

3.5.13 OTHER ISSUES

There is usually concern on the part of the purchaser that notwithstanding the details of all of the specific warranties set out above, there are issues which they ought to be aware of as a purchaser. For this reason, it is not unusual to find a warranty to the effect that the vendor has disclosed to the purchaser any matter which would render any information otherwise given as untrue or misleading or any matter which ought to be disclosed to an intending purchaser of shares in the company. The inclusion of this type of warranty is sometimes resisted by the vendor. This type of warranty may be useful if there are personal circumstances connected with the vendor or senior officers of the vendor or the target company which cause difficulty at a subsequent stage.

3.5.14 CONCLUSION

The general categories of warranties which arise and were discussed above are as follows:

- Financial matters
- Constitution of target company
- Assets of target company
- Liabilities of target company
- Employee-related matters

However, the warranties which are typically given in a share purchase transaction vary to some extent from transaction to transaction. While most purchasers' advisers tend to have their own typical list of warranties, thought should always be given to whether specific warranties are needed in the context of the transaction. For example, if the target company's assets largely consist of intellectual property, it may be prudent to expand the intellectual property warranties over and above those which appear in a standard type of list of 'off the shelf' warranties. If the target company has substantial involvement with data, it may be appropriate to look carefully at legislation such as the Data Protection Act 1988 and draft specific warranties to ensure compliance. The above are merely examples to illustrate the principle that the particular circumstances of the target company should always be looked at.

3.6   Disclosure Letter

In every share purchase transaction where there are warranties, the net effect of those warranties is to state that the company is 'perfect'. Clearly no company will reach the state of perfection required by warranties and the vendor is therefore given an opportunity to set out clearly in a letter where the company deviates from 'perfection'. This is known as the disclosure letter. This is an extremely important document from the vendor's point of view and must be prepared with enormous care. The preparation of the letter involves the vendor being brought through each of the warranties and being asked as to whether there are any matters associated with the target company which would be a deviation from those warranties. In addition specialist areas such as tax warranties and pension warranties are usually referred to the target company's tax and pension advisers for their comment.

While this list can only be regarded as generally indicative, typical disclosures would include:

(a)   banking facilities available;

(b)   Companies Office filings not being up to date;

(c)   litigation by or against the company;

(d)   all of the company insurance policies;

(e)   disputes concerning employees;

(f)   assets which are leased by the company;

(g)   the company's pension affairs;

(h)   issues with title to property;

(i)   non-compliance with legal obligations;

(j)   arrears of taxation or past occasions when taxation was discharged late; and

(k)   areas where there might be a doubt as to the tax payable.

It is normal that the disclosure letter is prefaced by a number of general disclosures. These may be quite contentious as between vendor and purchaser as some standard general disclosure may be construed as putting the purchaser on notice of matters that he could ascertain by inspection. Therefore disclosures of Companies Registration Office records and statutory registers which are actually given to a purchaser would be regarded as acceptable. However, a disclosure of everything which might be ascertained by inspecting the premises and records of the target company is normally regarded as inappropriate as this, for example, would put a purchaser on notice of everything that might be in the company's filing cabinets or anything that might be found out about the property as a result of a survey.

The disclosure letter is usually written by the vendor to the purchaser. It is occasionally written on behalf of the respective clients by the firms of lawyers involved, in which event it should be clearly stated by the vendor's lawyers that it is based on instructions from their client and that they themselves disclaim the contents.

3.7   Consideration Payable Under Share Purchase Agreement

3.7.1   GENERALLY

There are a number of ways in which the consideration payable under a share purchase agreement may be discharged, principally:

(a) cash;

(b) allotment of shares in the purchaser;

(c) discharge of loan;

(d) payment of dividend by target company; and

(e) loan notes.

3.7.2 PAYMENT IN CASH

Payment in cash is the simplest and most common form of consideration and applies in most transactions.

3.7.3 ALLOTMENT OF SHARES IN PURCHASER

Allotment of shares in purchaser is somewhat unusual but arises in a few cases. It most often arises where the purchaser is a public limited company, particularly one which has a listing or quotation for its shares. It is settled law that a company must not issue its shares at a discount. However, historically this has not created any particular problem where a purchaser was issuing shares as, except in the most extreme of circumstances, it would be clear-cut that the shares in the target company represent sufficient to pay up the shares being allotted. However, the Companies (Amendment) Act 1983 has introduced an important qualification to this principle which is particularly important for the vendor to appreciate. Section 30 of that Act severely regulates the circumstances in which a public limited company may allot shares paid up otherwise than in cash. Subject to an exception, which is dealt with below, in general a public limited company may not allot shares without a valuation of the consideration for those shares being done by a person qualified to be the auditor of the company. A report in respect of value must be made to the company during the six months immediately preceding the allotment of the shares and a copy of that report must be sent to the proposed allottee. If the allottee does not receive a report or, to the knowledge of the allottee, there is some other contravention, the allottee is liable to pay the company the nominal value of the shares together with any premium and interest at 5 per cent per annum. This is quite a draconian sanction. If, for instance, a vendor was allotted shares in the purchaser deemed to be worth £1 million (including premium) at the time of an acquisition, the vendor could find itself liable to the purchaser in the sum of £1 million plus interest. Thus it is extremely important to comply with the section.

An important exception to the provision which applies to most share purchases is contained in s. 30(2). This provides that, where there is an arrangement providing for the allotment of shares in a company, on terms that the whole or part of the consideration for the shares allotted is to be provided by the transfer to that company of all or some of the shares of a particular class in another company, the procedure does not apply. However, the arrangement to take shares must be available to all the holders of the shares in the other company. Thus, if a purchaser is acquiring the shares in a target company from six vendors and the arrangement to take shares is available only to one of them, the exception would not apply. Given the draconian nature of the section, it is critical that the vendor satisfies itself that the exception applies. In case of any doubt, the valuation procedures are recommended to be followed although they are rather cumbersome.

The acquisition of a target company for shares in the purchaser may be attractive because it may qualify for stamp duty and capital duty relief under the Stamp Duties Consolidation Act 1999, ss. 80 and 119 respectively (formerly Finance Act 1965, s. 31 and Finance Act 1973, s. 72). It may also qualify for roll-over capital gains tax relief.

3.7.4   DISCHARGE OF LOAN

It is often the case that a target company owes money to the vendors or to persons associated with the vendors. It is usually a good idea to obtain a warranty to ascertain that there are no sums outstanding to such persons or a warranty which results in the disclosure as to the amounts outstanding and the arrangements whereby they are to be paid back. This is a matter which should always be looked at. Clearly if a target company owes money to the vendors post the transaction, there should be a clear-cut basis on which this is to be repaid.

3.7.5   DIVIDEND

If the target company has dividend payment capacity, there may be scope to discharge part of the consideration by paying dividends from the target company rather than the purchaser paying consideration. The attractiveness of this route has much reduced with various tax changes surrounding dividends, but it may be still appropriate in particular circumstances.

3.7.6   LOAN NOTES

A possible method of paying consideration otherwise payable in cash is by way of loan notes. These are still sometimes attractive, particularly in a transaction which has been concluded close to a tax year-end. If a vendor of shares receives loan notes, the capital gain on those shares is rolled over until the loan notes are cashed. With relatively low inflation rates and low capital gains tax rates, these are no longer as attractive as they used to be but they are still used from time to time. The vendors need to focus on whether the loan notes are secured or unsecured and whether they are guaranteed by a relatively financially stable third party such as a bank.

3.7.7   OTHER CONSIDERATIONS RELATING TO THE CONSIDERATION

3.7.7.1   Deferred consideration

A device which is commonly used in share purchase transactions is to defer the payment of part of the consideration. Frequently the amount which is deferred is uncertain and is computed by reference to future events, most notably the financial performance of the target company. If a vendor agrees to payment of deferred consideration which is dependent upon the financial performance of the target company, considerable thought needs to be given to controls placed on the purchaser as to how the target company will behave during the period by reference to which the deferred consideration is computed. The vendor would want to ensure that profits are calculated on a basis consistent with what they have been used to and is likely to insist on a right to have an independent review of the basis on which the calculation is made and appeal to a third party in the event that they are dissatisfied with the results as produced by the purchaser's auditors. Deferred consideration is also somewhat unsatisfactory from the point of view of the vendor, in that it may seem convenient to the purchaser to withhold payment of deferred consideration if there is any issue of warranty claims arising. For this reason, there are sometimes extensive negotiations if the vendor looks for a specific assurance in the agreement from the purchaser that payment will not be withheld on account of pending warranty claims.

3.7.7.2   Form CG50A

Section 980 of the Taxes Consolidation Act 1997 contains provisions the purpose of which is to stop the avoidance of capital gains tax on the disposal of land in Ireland and certain other assets. If land in Ireland is being disposed of, it is necessary for the purchaser to either get a clearance (known as a Form CG50A) of the vendor from capital gains tax or, alternatively, to withhold 15 per cent of the purchase price at source.

Clearly it would be easy to avoid this particular provision by putting land into a company and then selling the shares in the company. The Revenue has therefore extended this principle to shares in a company, the value or the greater part of whose value is derived from land situated in Ireland and also from certain other assets, most notably mineral and exploration rights. The Revenue Commissioners have a fairly liberal interpretation as to what constitutes deriving the greater part of the value of shares in a company from land. It is therefore necessary to look very closely at the target company's accounts to determine whether this requirement applies. If in doubt, the purchaser should insist on a certificate. In practice any target company which owns substantial lands is one to which the section may apply and it is usually prudent to seek a CG50A clearance. This is something which requires to be obtained by the vendor and is normally obtained by the vendor fairly quickly by means of an application in the appropriate form to the inspector of taxes who deals with its affairs.

If a transaction is completed in which a form CG50A ought to have been obtained and it was not, the purchaser may subsequently be called upon by the Revenue to pay over 15 per cent of the sale proceeds to the Revenue Commissioners so it is a serious problem for a purchaser not to obtain such a certificate when one is required. As a result of an anti-avoidance measure introduced in 1995, it is also necessary to get this clearance even where something other than cash is paid for land. This procedure does not apply to small transactions, with the current threshold being fixed at IR£300,000 (by Finance Act 2000, s. 87 replacing the previous threshold of IR£150,000).

3.7.7.3   Companies Act 1963, s. 60

Section 60 of CA 1963 prohibits a target company from giving financial assistance in connection with a purchase of or subscription for its own shares. This does not give rise to any particular problem where a purchaser is proposing to fund a purchase entirely from within its own resources. However, if the purchaser intends in some way to use the financial resources of the target company to fund the purchase, the provisions of s. 60 will require consideration. Section 60 renders it

> unlawful for a company to give, whether directly or indirectly, and whether by means of a loan, guarantee, the provision of security or otherwise, any financial assistance for the purpose of or in connection with a purchase or subscription made or to be made by any person of or for any shares in the company.

The section most commonly arises in practice where the purchaser is taking a bank loan to fund the purchase and the bank proposes to secure the facilities not only on the purchaser and its assets but also on the assets of the target company or companies. The security being given by the target company or companies would constitute financial assistance and is unlawful unless the procedure for derogating from s. 60 is carried out. This procedure is dealt with elsewhere in this book but involves the swearing of a statutory declaration as to solvency by the directors and the passing of a special resolution permitting the financial assistance by the members. If s. 60 is an issue, it should be flagged early in the transaction as the derogation procedure will require co-operation from the vendor.

It was noted above that consideration may include the payment of dividends or the discharge of indebtedness to the vendor. Neither of these is caught by s. 60 as s. 60(12) specifically allows for the payment of a dividend properly declared by a company or the discharge of a liability lawfully incurred by it.

It is critical for the vendor to satisfy itself that s. 60 is not breached as any transaction in breach of the section is voidable by the company as against a person who had notice of the facts which constitute the breach. It is extremely likely that the vendor would have notice of such facts and would be so caught.

Section 60 is dealt with in more detail in Chapter 4: Commercial Lending.

3.8 Non-Compete

A share purchase agreement usually includes a non-compete clause. Guidance on the extent of the restrictions which it is permissible to place vendors under is set out in Competition Authority Decision No. 489 'Category Certificate in Respect of Agreements Involving a Merger and/or Sale of a Business', Competition, vol. 6 1996–1997 p. 260 (the certificate). The certificate is stated to apply to mergers and/or sale of business agreements. Any restrictions on competition which come within the terms set out in the certificate benefit from its terms which, in effect, constitute the official view of the Competition Authority that the restrictions are not in breach of the Competition Acts and should therefore be enforceable. For the precise effect of a certificate under the Competition Acts, reference should be made to the Law Society manual on *Applied European Law* (Blackstone).

Save for exceptional circumstances (more details of which are given below) non-compete restrictions in share purchase and shareholder agreements are generally drafted to come within the terms of the certificate. This removes any necessity to make an individual application to the Competition Authority in respect of the agreement in question.

Article 4(a) of the certificate effectively provides that, to benefit from the terms of the certificate, a share purchase agreement and the non-compete restriction contained therein must comply with the following requirements. The agreement must involve the sale of the goodwill of the business and the restriction on the vendor competing, soliciting customers, soliciting employees and/or doing any other things in competition with the purchaser must not:

(a) exceed two years from the date of completion of the sale;

(b) apply to any location outside the territory where the products concerned were manufactured, purchased or sold by the vendor at the time of the agreement; or

(c) apply to goods or services other than those manufactured, purchased or sold by the vendor at the time of the agreement.

In most transactions involving the sale of a business, goodwill effectively passes by delivery and there is no clause in the relevant agreement specifically transferring goodwill. The goodwill is transferred to the purchasers in that they acquire the assets, business and reputation of the company and benefit from the non-compete restrictions.

In certain situations, the view may be taken by the purchasers of a business that a non-compete restriction of a period that is longer than two years is required to effectively protect the goodwill of the business which is being acquired. An example of this would be where the business in question has infrequent contact with its customers. A restriction which is longer than two years may be inserted into an agreement but this means that the agreement does not benefit from the certificate. However, an individual application to the Competition Authority in respect of the particular agreement may be made. In some cases, the Competition Authority has granted certificates in respect of agreements which contain restrictions which are longer than two years where it has been satisfied that such restrictions are necessary to protect the goodwill of the company being acquired. However, it should be noted that exceptional circumstances are required to justify a restriction which is longer than two years.

Another situation where a restriction of more than two years is acceptable is where the business involves the use of 'technical know-how'. This is defined in article 4(b) of the certificate as 'a body of technical information that is secret, substantial and identified in an appropriate form'. Under article 4(b), a restriction on the vendor competing with the purchaser or soliciting customers of the business for up to a maximum of five years from the date of sale of the business is acceptable provided that the restriction ceases to apply once the know-how comes into the public domain.

Generally speaking, a restriction which is unlimited in time preventing a vendor from disclosing confidential information regarding the company which is being sold benefits from the certificate under the terms of article 4(c) thereof. However, such a restriction may not be enforceable if its effect is to prevent a vendor from re-entering the relevant market after a valid non-compete restriction has expired.

The principles set out above apply to agreements for the sale of a business but similar principles apply in relation to agreements where the vendor remains as a shareholder. As regards restrictions on an existing shareholder, article 5(a) of the certificate effectively provides that a restriction which prevents a shareholder for as long as he remains engaged in the company as a shareholder, director or employee from competing with the business of the company will benefit from the terms of the certificate. Article 5(b) provides that the certificate will also apply where a vendor who has retained at least 10 per cent of the shares in the company is prevented from competing with the business, soliciting customers and/or employees of the business for a period of up to two years from any future sale of such shares.

Generally speaking, for a non-compete restriction on a shareholder to be enforceable, the shareholding must be substantial and must not constitute an artificial arrangement formed for the purposes of circumventing the requirements of the Competition Acts relating to non-compete restrictions or be held only for investment purposes.

3.9   Signing and Completion of Share Purchase Agreement

3.9.1   INTRODUCTION

One of the common practical issues of difficulty which arises with share purchase agreements is the concept of the signing of a share purchase agreement and the concept of completion of such an agreement. While the distinction between these two seems to be a matter which may be difficult to grasp, from a lawyer's point of view it is similar to the concept, which arises in a property transaction, where a contract is signed on one day and a couple of weeks later there is a completion. However, in many share purchase transactions, and particularly where no pre-conditions are involved, the signing will take place virtually contemporaneously with completion.

3.9.2   SIGNING

The central feature of signing for a share purchase agreement is to ensure that the commercial details of all of the contract documents are agreed. This would cover not only the share purchase agreement but also ancillary documents such as the disclosure letter, a deed of indemnity and documents dealing with other issues such as distribution agreements, employment agreements etc. Usually at the time of signing, the share purchase agreement and the disclosure letter are signed by the parties. It is more standard that the other documents such as a deed of indemnity and the ancillary documents mentioned above would be in agreed form at the time of signing but would not in fact be signed until completion takes place.

3.9.3   COMPLETION

If completion of a transaction is to be delayed for some time, there are a number of matters with which the purchaser and, to a lesser extent, the vendor must concern themselves, in particular the following.

3.9.3.1 Completion date

A firm completion date must be set or, alternatively, a date by which completion must take place. If this is not met, it is usually provided that either party may walk away from the transaction. This is important for the reasons outlined in more detail under pre-conditions at **3.4.4** above as the parties would not want to be bound to a course of action forever while waiting for pre-conditions to be fulfilled.

3.9.3.2 Business between signing and completion

If there is to be a gap between signing and completion, it is critical from the purchaser's point of view that the target company is run between signing and completion only on the basis of acting strictly in the ordinary course. Consequently the purchaser will usually seek to insert a clause insisting that it should agree any course of action other than trading in the normal course. These clauses would usually prohibit the target company on matters such as issuing new shares, payment of dividends, making acquisitions or disposals, hiring and firing an employee, granting mortgages, incurring significant capital expenditure and a number of other unusual types of transactions. The inclusion of such a clause is important from the point of view of a purchaser as, if the owners of the target company are free to take all manner of actions between signing and completion, the purchaser may find that the target company has radically changed over a short period of time.

3.9.3.3 Repetition of warranties

If there is to be a gap between signing and completion, it is critical from the purchaser's point of view that the warranties should be repeated at completion. If the vendor accepts this, the vendor is likely to want the ability to add extra disclosure items to the disclosure letter as obviously matters could happen between signing and completion which, if they had arisen before signing, would have been included in the disclosure letter. If this is agreed by the purchaser, it is usually on the basis that they have the right to walk away from the transaction should they not like the particular additional disclosures. This is a matter which should always be considered when there is to be a gap between signing and completion.

3.9.4 FORMALITIES OF COMPLETION

The essence of completion is that the purchaser will arrive at a completion meeting with a cheque or bank draft for the purchase price and the vendor will arrive at the meeting with a set of papers, which are handed over to the purchaser.

The set of papers which is required will vary from transaction to transaction but will include the following:

(a) Share transfers of the shares in the target company and the appropriate share certificates (if a share certificate is lost an indemnity in place of the lost certificate will usually suffice).

(b) If there is a group of companies involved in the target, all shares in subsidiaries which are not owned by other group companies should be covered by a share transfer and appropriate share certificate.

(c) A copy duly executed by the vendor and the target company of ancillary documents such as the deed of indemnity and ancillary contracts.

(d) The statutory books and registers of the target company.

(e) The directors' minute book of the target company.

(f) The seal of the target company.

(g) The certificate of incorporation of the target company.

(h) Title documents to any properties owned by the target company (although if these are mortgaged to a bank and the mortgage is being left in place, they may well not be presented at a completion).

(i) A certificate of title in relation to properties if this has been agreed.

(j) Any letters of consent required from third parties such as grant-aiding authorities, banks, mergers consent etc. These are discussed in more detail in pre-conditions above.

(k) CG50A clearance if this is required.

(l) A certified copy of the memorandum and articles of association of each target company.

(m) It is usual to get copies of bank mandates in place for the target company. These may be required to be changed at completion and having a copy of the mandates enables the necessary changes to be identified and made.

(n) Letters of resignation of the directors and secretary to the extent that it is agreed that they should resign. The letter of resignation should ideally include a confirmation from the director or secretary concerned that they have no outstanding claims against the target company. If this is not done, there is a danger from the purchaser's point of view that a claim could be asserted by such people.

(o) It is sometimes the case that the auditors will be asked to resign at completion. Resignation of the auditors is a matter to which some thought needs to be given under CA 1990, s. 185. A letter of resignation must either indicate that there are no circumstances connected with the resignation which should be brought to the notice of members or creditors or, alternatively, set out such circumstances. The notice of resignation is required to be filed with the Registrar of Companies and if there are circumstances connected with the resignation set out in the letter, it must be sent to persons entitled to receive the accounts.

(p) Repayment of loans between target company and the vendor/his associates.

(q) There are other documents which may be required depending on the circumstances but the above are the principal documents.

3.9.5 BOARD MEETING

A second important component of the completion of a transaction which needs to be organised by the vendor is the holding of board meetings of each target company. It is not sufficient to complete the transaction merely that the above documents be handed over. Some of them must be processed and approved by the board of the target company. In particular the following must be dealt with:

(a) Transfers must be approved for registration.

(b) Resignations of directors must be approved and new directors appointed.

(c) Resignation of the secretary must be approved and a new secretary appointed.

(d) The resignation of the auditors must be noted and new auditors appointed.

(e) Changes to the bank mandates should be effected.

(f) If the registered office is to be changed, a resolution to this effect must be adopted.

In connection with the transfer of shares, the board of the target company should satisfy itself that it has an absolute power to register the transfers without any consent being required from any shareholder. Alternatively, if shareholders have some form of pre-emption rights on the transfer of shares, these pre-emption rights should have been properly waived. In the context of the appointment of new directors, the target company should obtain the consent of the new directors in the form of the usual Companies Office form B10. (It is desirable but not strictly necessary to deal with this at completion.)

Once the various documents required are handed over to the purchaser and the board meetings are held, the purchaser then completes the transaction by formally handing the purchase price over to the vendor.

3.9.6   ITEMS TO BE ACTIONED POST COMPLETION

There are a number of matters which require to be attended to after completion takes place. In particular the following issues must be considered.

3.9.6.1   Stamping

All share transfers require to be stamped and presented for stamping within thirty days of completion of the transaction. Stamp duty is levied at the rate of 1 per cent of the consideration. Where the consideration consists of something other than cash or the transaction is not at arm's length, it may take some considerable time for the Stamps Adjudication Office to finalise the stamp duty. Generally, and in particular in those circumstances where stamping will take a long time, it is appropriate to include in the terms of the share purchase agreement a provision under which the vendor agrees to co-operate with the purchaser in voting the shares in whatever way the purchaser wishes. This is because it is not permissible to enter the name of the purchaser onto the register of members until stamping is completed. Thus, for example, if stamping is to take six months and an AGM of the target company takes place four months after completion, the persons strictly entitled to be represented at the AGM are the outgoing vendors and the purchaser should get sufficient powers of attorney under the share purchase agreement to enable itself to represent the vendor and control the votes on the shares.

3.9.6.2   Companies Office returns

Various returns to the Companies Registration Office need to be attended to. It is not necessary to return particulars of the new shareholders to the Companies Registration Office although this detail will in due course be included in the annual return. However, if there are new directors then particulars of the new directors should be filed within fourteen days from completion. A new bank mandate should be given to the bank as soon as possible.

3.9.6.3   Directors' interests

There is a requirement under Part IV of CA 1990 for directors and the secretary to notify the acquisition and disposal of shareholdings in a company of which they are officers to the company. This should be done within five business days of the acquisition or disposal occurring. If the vendor is a director or an entity controlled by a director, a notification should be given to the target company as to the disposal. If the purchaser is a director or a party connected with a director, a notice should also be given to the target company of the acquisition of the shareholding interest. The failure to give this notice in the case of an acquisition may result, pursuant to CA 1990, s. 58, in any right or interest of any kind in respect of the shares not being enforceable directly or indirectly by action or legal proceedings. It is also an offence to fail to comply with such a requirement.

3.9.6.4   Tax returns

The vendor may also be required to file a capital gains tax return following completion.

3.9.6.5   Name change

If a target company is a member of a group or has a name which identifies it with the vendor, it will almost certainly be provided in the agreement that the target company must change its name. Again this is a matter which requires to be actioned post completion. It is often the case that if this arises a special resolution providing for the change of name will be adopted at the time of completion and it is therefore a matter of processing this through the Companies Registration Office following completion.

3.9.6.6   Access to records

The vendor may need access to the records of the target company after completion and may seek the inclusion of such a clause in the share purchase agreement. This is in order for the purchaser, but should be subject to a stringent confidentiality obligation, which allows for disclosure of information obtained only if this is required by law.

3.10   Analysis of Typical Share Purchase Agreement

A typical share purchase agreement consists of the following components:

1. Parties.

2. Recitals.

3. Definitions.

4. Pre-conditions.

5. Consideration provision.

6. Warranties.

7. Restrictive and other covenants.

8. Completion.

9. Miscellaneous provisions

10. Schedules (including schedule of warranties).

3.10.1   PARTIES

It is standard to set out the names and addresses of the parties at the front of the document. If any of the parties are companies, it may be useful to list their registered numbers as no matter how many times a company changes its name, it can always be identified by reference to the registered number.

3.10.2   RECITALS

It is standard in a commercial contract such as a share purchase agreement to set out recitals. These broadly set out brief details of the target company including its registered number and issued share capital and then recite that the vendor has agreed to sell the shares and the purchaser has agreed to purchase the shares. Recitals are useful in that they set out the broad parameters of the target company up front and give an idea as to the broad subject matter of the agreement.

3.10.3   DEFINITIONS

It is conventional in a share purchase agreement as with other commercial documents that terms which are frequently used are defined for all purposes of the agreement. This section may appear in different parts of the agreement; most usually, however, as the opening section of the agreement. It is not, however, unknown that it would appear at the end of the main body of the agreement or sometimes in a schedule. A few terms, which are frequently included in this, are worth mentioning:

- Definitions will normally include a definition of the 'accounts'. The purchaser will want this to cover accounts of each company involved in a group and also to include a consolidated accounts for the group as a whole. This definition should also include the directors, and auditors' reports and notes thereto as these form a very important part of the accounts.

- Terms are sometimes defined for the purposes of restrictive covenants. It is extremely important in this context to clarify that the territory to which they extend and the business which is covered are commercially acceptable to the parties involved and that they do not infringe the principles of common law and the Competition Act applicable to restrictive covenants.

- If there is to be a difference between the vendors and the people who are giving the warranties, it is conventional to insert a separate definition of the term 'warrantors'.

3.10.4   PRE-CONDITIONS

This section of the agreement covers the matters which are referred to in detail in the section entitled 'Pre-conditions to Share Purchase Agreement' at **3.4**. Specifically the section will identify:

(a)   the substantive conditions precedent;

(b)   relevant 'negative' conditions precedent; and

(c)   an end date.

This section typically provides that the vendor and the purchaser will use their best efforts to secure the satisfaction of the conditions.

3.10.5   CONSIDERATION PROVISION

This clause is the operative provision, which provides that the purchaser will purchase and the vendor will sell the shares in question. It is important that the section provides that they are being sold free from all encumbrances and with the benefit of all rights attaching to them as otherwise there is a possibility that the purchaser will be deemed to have acquired the shares subject to whatever encumbrances may be attached to them such as equities, options, mortgages, charges, reservation of title etc.

This section also sets out the consideration, which is actually payable. This is fully discussed in 'Consideration Payable under Share Purchase Agreement' at **3.7**.

3.10.6 WARRANTIES

It is usual to include in a share purchase agreement the provisions which govern the detailed terms of the warranties. Typical items, which are included in this section, are as follows:

- A warranty that the parties have full power and authority to enter into and perform the share purchase agreement.

- A warranty that the shares being sold constitute all of the shares in the capital of the company and are not subject to encumbrance.

- A provision that the warrantors warrant as set out in a schedule to the document.

- A provision that the warrantors waive any rights which they may have to sue the target company or its employees or agents for any inaccurate information given to them in connection with the preparation of the disclosure letter. If this were not done, a warrantor on being sued by the purchaser might seek to join an employee or agent of the target company who in turn would probably have a right to join the target company. If this were to happen it would defeat the purpose of getting the warranty and the target company might end up funding the ultimate award to the purchaser.

- This section of the agreement will also usually contain the agreed limits on warranties. The types of provisions are reviewed in 'Limits on Warranties' at **3.5.7**.

3.10.7 RESTRICTIVE AND OTHER COVENANTS

A section of the agreement normally provides for restrictive covenants, which bind the vendor. The details of what would be included in these are discussed at **3.8.**

Such a section may also include other covenants such as covenants concerning a change of name of the target company or the vendor and covenants concerning ancillary agreements.

3.10.8 COMPLETION

A section of the agreement usually provides for the formalities of completion. This will include the list of documents to be handed over at completion, the agenda for the board meeting to take place at completion and a covenant that the purchaser will pay the purchase price on completion. If there is to be a gap between signing and completion, it may be appropriate at this point of the agreement to make provision to cover this.

The details of this are discussed in 'Signing and Completion of Share Purchase Agreement' at **3.9**. This section may also deal with matters to take place post completion such as stamping of share transfers.

3.10.9 MISCELLANEOUS PROVISIONS

It is usual that the last clause of a share purchase agreement consists of general provisions sometimes referred to as 'boiler plate clauses'. Matters typically dealt with in these clauses include a prohibition on the making of any public announcement except by agreement between the parties, a provision dealing with the assignment of warranties, a provision dealing with who will bear expenses and a provision dealing with the service of any notices required under the agreement. This usually provides for notices to be served by hand or by post and specifies a time limit after which they are deemed to have been given. It may sometimes also provide for methods of communication such as fax or e-mail.

There is usually a clause providing that a once-off waiver by a party of a liability will not be construed as a general waiver and further that an acquiescence in a breach will not be deemed to be a general waiver.

It is often provided, particularly where there are a number of parties involved, that the original agreement may be signed in more than one counterpart. This facilitates signing where parties are in a number of different locations.

It is sometimes provided that the share purchase agreement and identified ancillary documents constitute the entire agreement between the parties. This is helpful, particularly from a vendor's point of view, as it prevents a purchaser arguing that there are unwritten warranties which form the basis on which they entered into the agreement.

The general clauses at the end will usually deal with the governing law of the contract. If all of the parties are clearly located in Ireland, this should not give rise to a problem if it is omitted. However, if there are parties from different jurisdictions, the omission of a governing law clause may give rise to difficulties and consequently it is important that something should be included. For foreign parties, it may also be appropriate to include a clause under which they submit to the jurisdiction of an Irish court.

3.10.10 SCHEDULES

It is usual to include matters in schedules to cover the detail of items such as warranties, the members of the board of the target company and details of its properties.

CHAPTER 4

COMMERCIAL LENDING

4.1 Introduction

The array of legal issues which could arise in the giving of money on a temporary basis between businesses is potentially vast, but the issues which arise on a day-to-day basis tend to be predictable, if not always capable of precise determination. This chapter endeavours to highlight these common issues, some of the pitfalls for those unfamiliar with the lending process and the main registration matters without which the taking of security may become, in a legal sense, meaningless. The main focus is on companies borrowing from, and granting security to, lenders.

The ambition of the chapter is further limited by confining itself to situations where the lender of the money is a financial institution. Intra-group lending is common but tends to be surrounded by such informality that solicitors are often not part of the process. Nevertheless, issues of permissible borrowing (particularly in the context of financial assistance) may arise in the intra-group situation. Practitioners need to be alert to the legal consequences of proposed structures, even or perhaps particularly, when the client regards the matter as straightforward and internal.

The first part of this chapter deals with different types of borrower and a selection of financial facilities. The second part analyses different forms of security and the usual checks to be carried out when the borrower is a company incorporated under the Companies Acts 1963–1999. The third part deals with registration issues. The fourth part examines the minefields of financial assistance and transactions, perhaps within Part III of the Companies Act 1990 ('CA 1990'). The fifth part outlines how company law may change, given the provisions of the Company Law Enforcement Bill 2000.

4.2 Who is the Borrower?

It may seem trite to emphasise that the legal characterisation of the borrower will be crucial in deciphering the legal requirements to ensure that effective security is achieved. This review examines individuals, partnerships, companies, corporate entities and State boards. Each is examined in terms of capacity, authorisation and applicable legislation.

4.2.1 INDIVIDUALS

4.2.1.1 Capacity

An individual may do anything unless prohibited by law. If the borrower is an individual the issues which may affect capacity are:

74

(a) Is the person 18 or older? If not, the law relating to infant contracts will have to be analysed to make sure that the terms of the loan agreement will be enforceable.

(b) Is the person a bankrupt or capable of being made a bankrupt? A search in the Bankruptcy Office and the Judgments Office will assist. If the transaction which is being funded is at less than market value, a declaration of solvency may be useful.

(c) Is the person mad? Insanity takes away capacity but there is no law searcher who can help you on this one!

4.2.1.2 Authorisation

Individuals may authorise others to act on their behalf. A power of attorney is usually required to prove the authorisation in any borrowing transaction. Some matters are peculiarly within the knowledge of the individual. Because of this most solicitors advising lenders would be very reluctant to accept, for example, a family home declaration made by an attorney.

4.2.1.3 Applicable law

As individuals may do anything unless prohibited by law, up until recently there was little to concern lenders in general applicable law. However, consumer legislation now means that dealing with individuals may often require more legal due diligence than needed when lending to a company.

The European Communities (Unfair Terms In Consumer Contracts) Regulations 1995 (SI 27/1995) and the Consumer Credit Act 1995 both circumscribe freedom of contract by imposing procedural and substantive obligations on a party dealing with a consumer, namely a person acting outside his trade, profession or business. Legal advisers to financial institutions lending to individuals constantly face the question of whether the individual borrower is a consumer.

If so, the consequences for the documentation are fundamental. Most financial institutions have standard consumer credit documents, but some which only deal with business lending (as they see it) may not be aware of the possible impact of the consumer legislation and rely on their legal advisers to highlight any difficulties.

General domestic legislation, such as the Family Home Protection Act 1976, may impact on commercial lending. Many sole traders live on the business premises, be it a farm, pub or shop. If the entire premises is given as security then issues of spousal consent, guarantees, independent legal advice and value on any forced sale will have to be considered. Splitting the premises so that only the business portion is captured is not always feasible. The Consumer Credit Act 1995 provisions in relation to housing loans would also require careful scrutiny in such a situation.

Given the reference to 'curtilage' in the Family Home Protection Act, any division of the property aimed at excluding the family home from the security is not guaranteed to be successful. If the loan is revolving (being drawn, repaid and drawn again), as will often be the case in small businesses where the loan is really filling cashflow gaps, the Supreme Court decision in *Bank of Ireland v Purcell* [1989] IR 327 necessitates ensuring family home and related legislation compliance each time the redrawing takes place. Each event is a new loan with new security amounting to a new conveyance for the purpose of this societal legislation.

There is one area where special rules have been created for individual borrowers. Floating charges are generally only available to companies. However, the Agricultural Credit Act 1978 allows individual farmers to create floating charges on agricultural stock. Farming income tends to be seasonal with a high capital requirement to acquire stock or buy seed and then income coming in during another part of the year. The stocking and restocking in particular would be cumbersome if security had to be taken each time, so the floating charge is useful.

4.2.2 PARTNERSHIPS

4.2.2.1 Capacity

While the partnership legislation provides a framework for entities to come together with a view to profit, the law does not recognise the partnership as having any legal personality which is separate from the partners. Therefore questions of capacity of partnerships are really questions about the capacity of each partner.

4.2.2.2 Authorisation

An analysis of the partnership deed and the partnership legislation will disclose who may act for the partnership. Often one partner may bind all, but in some circumstances the lender requires all partners to sign regardless so that there is no possibility of any subsequent dispute about authority.

4.2.2.3 Applicable law

The Partnership Act 1890 is enabling, not mandatory. Parties are free to depart from the parameters set out. No separate legal entity is created and limited liability is not granted, so the law is comfortable with the partners deciding themselves how to regulate their venture. The Partnership Act 1890 has provided a useful set of non-mandatory parameters for partnership activity.

Limited partnerships (under the Limited Partnerships Act 1907) may give rise to limited liability, but only for passive partners. The 1907 Act is in addition to the general partnership law. The Investment Limited Partnerships Act 1994 made some further changes, primarily to encourage collective investment schemes.

To avail of tax reliefs, partnerships became popular vehicles for investments in items as diverse as hotels, car parks, life policies and equipment. Successive Finance Acts have limited the tax efficacy of partnerships and so the frequency with which partnership structures will appear in financing transactions in the future has been substantially reduced.

4.2.3 COMPANIES

4.2.3.1 Capacity

Most commercial lending transactions involve companies borrowing. Most companies have been incorporated under the Companies Acts 1963–1999. As an artificial legal entity, a company may only do what the law permits. Before deciding what a company may do, the first question to answer is whether the company exists:

(a) The certificate of incorporation proves that the company was incorporated on a particular day—it does not guarantee ongoing existence. However, sometimes the promoters of a company seek to borrow before the company is incorporated, so checking that there is a certificate can be useful. The certificate will also confirm the company number. As a company may change its name, using the company number in documents such as a guarantee and a mortgage may assist in identifying the corporate borrower in spite of any subsequent name change.

(b) A company might be in legal limbo due to being struck off the register. The Companies Registration Office has been using its powers of strike off to encourage companies to file annual returns and accounts. Under the State Property Act 1954 the assets of a company which has been dissolved by strike off vest in the Minister for Finance. Section 12(6) of the Companies (Amendment) Act 1982 ('C(A)A 1982') permits the company, or indeed a creditor, to apply to the High Court for reinstatement of the company to the register. Once restored, the company is deemed by s. 12(6) to have continued in existence as if it had never been struck off. The Registrar may restore the company if application is made within one year of strike off.

(c)   A company may have been placed in receivership, under the protection of the court (examinership), or in liquidation.

A search in the Companies Registration Office is an important first step when dealing with a borrower which is a company. The information is not exhaustive or necessarily conclusive, but it may avoid subsequent embarrassment at completion if, for example, the company has been struck off.

The objects of the company are set out in the memorandum of association. Generally, borrowing and granting security are not regarded as objects but rather are powers to be used to further the objects of the company. Therefore, matching the borrowing to a permissible business objective is important. Often, the objects will have been sourced from standard company memoranda, which as a matter of luck may or may not have objects which match the actual business. It is a simple matter to amend the memorandum to introduce appropriate objects but if the deficiency is not spotted, the borrowing may be invalid and consequently the lender may be unable to recover the money lent.

Because incorporation as a limited company provides not only a separate legal entity but also limited liability, the legislation contains various protections so that this special privilege is not abused to the detriment of third parties. Two of the major issues which arise in this area, namely financial assistance and dealings with directors or connected persons, are considered in more detail below.

4.2.3.2   Authorisation

Because a company is an artificial entity it necessarily has to deal with the world through others. The articles of association set out how the internal management is regulated. Usually, the board of directors will have day-to-day control. Sometimes the shareholders/ members will have to consent, either because of a specific legislative requirement (e.g. CA 1990, s. 29 for substantial property transactions) or because of bank policy (e.g. where there is a potential conflict of interest between a director's own affairs and those of the company). It is vitally important in the lending context to ensure that regulation 79 of Table A has been excluded as otherwise the directors' authorisation to borrow will be rendered practically worthless.

In addition, a company may appoint an attorney, although this usually only arises for transactions abroad.

4.2.3.3   Applicable law

The Companies Acts 1963–1999 are undergoing extensive review. A Company Law Enforcement Bill is pending at the time of writing. The Company Law Review Group awaits statutory establishment.

4.2.4   OTHER CORPORATE ENTITIES

While much commercial activity is carried on through companies, partnerships and sole traders, other legal forms of business organisation also exist. Specific legislation deals with friendly societies and co-operatives. Foreign corporates may operate branches in Ireland rather than establishing separate subsidiaries. The co-operative movement has been particularly successful in Ireland in the agriculture and agribusiness areas.

4.2.4.1 Capacity

Sometimes the question of whether the co-op has the power to borrow, never mind how much it may borrow, may arise. As co-ops tend to have a large membership, changing the rules can be difficult and time consuming. Establishing the basic capacity of a co-op to enter into the proposed transaction has to be the first priority when dealing with a co-op borrower.

4.2.4.2 Authorisation

Likewise, on authorisation the committee may have to go to the members to approve borrowing or the granting of security. If this is needed there may be substantial notice periods required to convene a meeting of the members.

4.2.4.3 Applicable law

Currently the government is overhauling the legislation affecting co-operatives, and not before time. The Friendly Societies Act 1893 belongs to a different era both temporally and commercially.

4.2.5 STATE BOARDS

Many State commercial enterprises are incorporated under the Companies Acts 1963–1999, e.g. Aer Lingus and ICC Bank. However, others which have separate legal personality(ies) are creatures of a tailor-made statute, e.g. the Electricity Supply Board. In the latter category, one must check the specific legislation to ascertain whether the body may borrow, what protection third parties are given in relying on a decision of the board or whatever the body is called, and whether any third party consent (often the Minister for Finance) is needed for the transaction to be effective.

4.3 Lending to a Company

4.3.1 DOCUMENTS

The certificate of incorporation, the memorandum and articles of association, a list of directors and a search in the Companies Registration Office provide the starting point. A discussion with the lender about the purpose of the loan from the bank's perspective helps clarify whether the reason is a legitimate object of the company.

The facility letter/letter of offer is checked to make sure that the security may be put in place. Issues of independent advice may arise if a spousal guarantee is needed to take effective security. For example, a small business may not be able to offer sufficient security to satisfy the bank's requirements. The owner may be asked to give a personal guarantee backed by security on some personal assets, some of which may be in the joint names of that person and their spouse.

4.3.2 TYPES OF SECURITY

A company may create a fixed charge on property. A company may also create a floating charge on its general assets or a category of assets. A fixed charge would be the usual security on a building. A floating charge would be used for ancillary items or for categories where the items constantly change (e.g. the stock of the business). A fixed charge gives the best position to the bank as regards any consequences of enforcement. The main distinction with a floating charge is that the preferential creditors such as the Revenue Commissioners have priority before the floating charge but after the fixed charge.

Cashflow, the money being paid into a company by its customers, is very important to the financial health of a company. But these debts which are due to the company are constantly changing with new debts being created and old ones being paid off. Until the 1980s it was doubted whether a fixed charge could be taken on such receivables.

In *Re Keenan Brothers Ltd (in receivership)* [1985] IR 401, the Supreme Court decided that an appropriately worded security on receivables could qualify as fixed. The Revenue Commissioners responded by getting special priority status inserted into the following year's Finance Act (Finance Act 1986, s. 115). Subsequent Supreme Court decisions are difficult to reconcile, with practitioners being left with the unsatisfactory and dangerous task of trying to anticipate the conclusions of a court which is reluctant to overrule its previous decisions and yet which does not always seem to adhere to stare decisis.

4.3.3 ASSETS AVAILABLE FOR SECURITY

Title documents are needed for property security. Sometimes banks will accept certificates of title from the solicitor acting for the borrower. This may raise difficult questions of responsibility. If the solicitor knows something which might be relevant to a decision on credit rating, must he disclose it to the bank? Few solicitors endeavour to clarify the nature of the task they are performing when giving certificates even though arguably a duty of care is owed to the bank. As well as dealing with title and access matters, the identity of the property and the status of any authorisations, not just for the buildings and use but also for the business activity (such as an EPA integrated pollution control licence), are relevant to the bank. After all, there is little point in getting the title right if the business cannot function because of failure to comply with applicable regulatory requirements.

If stocks and shares are being given then the nature of the security should be clarified. Will the shares be transferred into the name of a nominee company of the bank? Who will have the benefit of dividends, bonus shares and voting rights? Are the shares represented by a share certificate or have they been 'dematerialised' as part of the CREST paperless trading system? If the shares are not quoted on a Stock Exchange how does the bank expect to trade them? If there are restrictions in the articles of association on trading shares, can these be amended to enable the bank to sell without reference to the board of the company?

Sometimes confusion arises as to who is checking the insurance position. Banks will normally want their interest noted on property policies and to ensure that appropriate levels of business risk insurance (e.g. for employer liability and public liability) are in place. Some banks insist on being named as recipients of any insurance proceeds in property policies to be certain that the proceeds of any claim come to the bank. The business risk policies may not seem relevant but a claim could wreck the financial viability of the borrower. The bank would prefer that the loan was repaid rather than having to enforce the security.

If any life policy is to be put in place, then early application by the assured is advisable. Occasionally, the due diligence, which the life assurance company does, turns up some factor requiring further investigation (e.g. a family history of a medical problem). Even having to do a medical examination may lead to unforeseen delays and tension if this is the only matter holding up drawdown of the facility.

A life policy in simple terms is a promise by the life assurance company to pay if a death occurs. The bank takes security by having the person entitled to the policy (not necessarily but usually the life assured) execute a security assignment to the bank. The bank (or its legal adviser) should:

(a) notify the life company of the security interest; and

(b) seek confirmation that no prior notices have been received, that the life company does not have any claim and that the policy will not be terminated without giving the bank notice (between fourteen and thirty days) so that the bank could try to keep the policy in force (e.g. by paying outstanding premiums).

4.4 Types of Facilities

4.4.1 OVERDRAFTS

Overdrafts are usually negotiated for a period of up to one year and are repayable on demand. These facilities are most suitable for customers with frequent fluctuation between debit and credit balances. Often the bank will require that an account with the benefit of an overdraft nevertheless has a credit balance for a minimum aggregate period (e.g. a month) during the year. If the customer cannot achieve this then a longer term loan may be more appropriate.

4.4.2 TERM LOAN

Term loans comprise loans which are repayable by negotiated amounts over a period. As these loans are not repayable on demand (unlike overdrafts), the events of default which enable the bank to require early repayment are important. Term loan facilities usually require regular disclosure of financial information (whether in the form of management accounts or audited accounts or both) as well as ongoing covenants to ensure that the business continues to be run on a sound financial basis.

4.4.3 REVOLVING CREDIT FACILITIES

Revolving loans comprise loans which are rolled over after specified periods with an original or renegotiated maturity. A typical money market revolving credit facility envisages the borrowing/rolling over of borrowings by a company for interest periods to be selected by the company subject to a bank veto. For example, a company will elect to borrow £100,000 for a period of six months. At the end of that period the company may renew the loan for another period as selected by the company and agreed by the bank.

The bank borrows the money on the inter-bank market and then lends it on to the company with a margin for its profit together with certain expenses. These revolving credit facilities may be quasi-overdrafts or may be term loans. They may be demand facilities, without events of default, or may be term loans with events of default.

4.4.4 PROVISION OF GUARANTEES TO THIRD PARTIES

Financial institutions may provide guarantees/indemnities/undertakings to third parties at the request of a company. A typical example of such a guarantee would be a performance bond on a building contract or on a planning permission condition. The bank issues an undertaking to a third party such as the employer of the builder on a building contract or the local authority imposing conditions in a planning permission. If specified events occur (e.g. failure to complete the development permitted by a planning permission) then the bank must pay the specified sum of money. The bank will require a counter-indemnity from the company so that the bank can clearly recover from the company any such payments.

4.4.5 FACTORING

Factoring, strictly speaking, does not constitute a lending service by banks. However, companies that factor their debts to banks usually see factoring as a financial facility comparable to borrowing. Factoring, in practical terms, constitutes the offering by a company to a lender of an option whereby the lender may acquire the debts invoiced by the company for particular sums of money and those debts are paid to the lender rather than to the company. Effectively the debts are sold in advance of their being paid. Factoring in the ordinary course of business is exempt from stamp duty.

4.4.6 LEASING

Leasing, again, whilst not constituting the giving by a bank of a loan, nonetheless enables companies to acquire assets by making periodic payments tapering down to nominal payments. The bank buys an asset and leases it for a primary leasing period which may be anything from two to seven years. After the expiry of the primary leasing period, a secondary leasing period for an indeterminate time proceeds, at the start of which the rental payment is reduced to a nominal amount. To all commercial intents and purposes (and from an accounting point of view) the asset then becomes the property of the lessee/company. Legally, however, it remains the property of the lender.

With the deregulation of commercial hire purchase on the enactment of the Consumer Credit Act 1995, the legal need to avoid the option to purchase on the completion of the primary leasing period disappeared. As a result, many such transactions are now characterised as commercial hire purchases with the lessee having the option to buy the asset for a nominal amount at the end of the primary period.

4.5 Types of Security

Why do banks require security? What do the buzzwords mean? What types of security are sought?

4.5.1 PURPOSE—PRIORITY ON INSOLVENCY

The purpose of a bank taking security is to ensure a quicker and more assured payout in the event that a company goes into receivership, examinership or liquidation. The priority set by CA 1963, ss. 285 and 98 as amended is as follows:

(a) Creditors secured by a fixed charge.

(b) Preferential creditors (e.g. certain taxes, rates, redundancy payments, payments due to employees which rank pari passu).

(c) Creditors secured by a floating charge.

(d) Ordinary creditors.

(e) Subordinated creditors (e.g. participators' loans specifically subordinated, e.g. for the purpose of obtaining an IDA grant).

(f) (Sometimes) preferential shareholders.

(g) Ordinary shareholders.

(h) (Occasionally) deferred shareholders.

4.5.2 LEGAL TERMINOLOGY

4.5.2.1 Debenture

Debenture has three meanings:

(a) 'An instrument usually under seal, issued by a company or public body as evidence of a debt or as a security for a loan of a fixed sum of money, at interest. It contains a promise to pay the amount mentioned in it and is usually called a debenture on the face of it': *Osborn's Concise Law Dictionary*.

(b) In the context of borrowing by a company the word debenture usually means a document which contains a covenant by the company to pay all sums due or to become due by the company to the lender and which contains a charge (fixed and/ or floating) in favour of the lender.

(c) On the money markets, a debenture usually means a debt security (whether secured or unsecured). Section 2(1) of CA 1963 states that 'debenture' includes debenture stock, bonds and other securities of a company whether constituting a charge on the assets of the company or not.

4.5.2.2 Mortgage

(a) A legal mortgage is a transfer of a legal estate or interest in land or other property for the purpose of securing the repayment of a debt. In the real property context, a mortgage transfers the land interest to the mortgagee. Mortgages are used for Registry of Deeds property.

(b) An equitable mortgage is one which passes only an equitable estate or interest, either because the form of transfer or conveyance used is an equitable one, i.e. operates only as between the parties to it and those who have notice of it (such as an equitable mortgage by deposit of title deeds or an equitable mortgage of shares by deposit of the share certificates) or because the mortgagor's estate or interest is equitable, that is, it consists merely of the right to obtain a conveyance of the legal estate.

4.5.2.3 Charge

A charge is the form of security for the repayment of a debt or performance of an obligation consisting of the right of a creditor to receive payment out of some specific fund or out of the proceeds of the realisation of specific property. In the real property context, a charge is taken on Land Registry property and is registered as a burden on the folio.

4.5.2.4 Pledge

A pledge arises where goods, or documents of title for goods, are delivered by the pledgor to the pledgee to be held as security for the payment of a debt or for the discharge of some other obligation. The subject matter of the pledge will be restored to the pledgor as soon as the debt or other obligation is discharged. Where a definite time for payment has been fixed, the pledgee has an implied power of sale upon default. If there is no stipulated time for payment, the pledgee may demand payment and in default thereof may exercise the power of sale after giving notice to the pledgor.

In the case of a pledge delivery of possession may be actual or constructive. A pledgor of goods has only a 'special property' in them while a mortgagee has an absolute title to the goods subject to the right of redemption. A further distinction between a pledge and a mortgage is that a pledgee (unlike a mortgagee) cannot obtain a foreclosure but only has a right to sell the goods. A pledge is the transfer of possession—but not ownership—of a chattel as security for the payment of a debt or performance of an obligation. The chattel may be sold if the owner defaults.

This form of security is relevant in the case of items the ownership of which may be transferred by delivery.

4.5.2.5 Hypothecation

Hypothecation is the creation of a charge on a chattel as security for payment of a sum of money where the property remains in the possession of the debtor.

4.5.2.6 Lien

A possessory lien is the right to retain that which is in the possession of the person claiming the lien until the claim is satisfied. Possession is essential to the effective creation of a lien. The person claiming the lien must have acquired possession rightfully and possession must be continuous.

A lien is the right to hold the property of another as security for the performance of an obligation. A particular lien exists only as a security for the particular debt incurred (e.g. a garage holding on to a car pending payment of a repair bill) while a general lien is available as a security for all debts arising out of similar transactions between the parties (e.g. a solicitor having a lien on his client's papers to secure his costs).

A possessory lien (whether particular or general) is lost where the claimant loses possession of the goods, the amount claimed is paid, alternative security is taken or the lien is abandoned. A lien may be enforced only by right of retention. No claim may be made for storage or for any other expense to which the person exercising the lien may be put. There is no general right of sale.

Notwithstanding the old law that solicitors have a general lien, there has been an increasing tendency for solicitors being required to prove a particular lien. Sections 125 and 180 of CA 1990 have removed a solicitor's lien in so far as it relates to corporate books, documents and records, if the company is in liquidation or under court protection.

Common carriers have a lien in respect of the freight on goods carried. Innkeepers have a lien on most of the luggage and other property brought in to the inn. A person who, at the request of the owner, has done work and expended money on a chattel has a particular lien in respect of his claim.

4.5.2.7 Principal securities delivered by companies

Floating charge over undertaking

A floating charge constitutes a charge over all the assets of the borrower company as acquired from time to time. The company remains free to deal with its assets in the ordinary course of its business. The charge only becomes a fixed charge upon crystallisation. On the appointment of a receiver or liquidator, the floating charge is fixed on all assets in the ownership of the company at that time.

The main elements of charges include:

(a) The covenant to pay. This usually extends to cover all sums due or to become due whether as principal or as surety, whether alone or jointly with any person, company or other entity.

(b) The charging clause or provision. This will usually be a charge on 'all the undertaking property and assets of the company whatsoever and wheresoever present and future including its uncalled capital for the time being and goodwill'.

(c) Negative pledge/restrictions on other charges. There will usually be a restriction on the company creating any other charge ranking pari passu (equal) with or in priority to the floating charge. In the absence of such a provision the company could create a fixed

mortgage or charge on particular property in favour of another lender. This restriction should be included on the Form 47 so that any subsequent lender searching in the Companies Office would be made aware, not only of the existing floating charge, but also of the negative pledge restriction.

(d) Continuing security/the rule in Clayton's Case. The rule in *Clayton's Case* (1816) 1 Mer 572, stated that sums paid into a borrower's account go to reduce or extinguish the liability on foot of a security whilst subsequent payments out of the account create new advances not caught by the security. Therefore this rule is specifically excluded if the charge is to constitute continuing security and is not to be satisfied by any interim repayments.

(e) Further assurance and power of attorney. The company will undertake to deliver such further documents as the lender may require to ensure that the charge created continues to be valid. It is usual also for the security document to contain a power of attorney by way of security whereby the lender is authorised to do whatever is necessary in order to perfect the security and do other things in the name of the company.

(f) Events of default and power to appoint receiver. Events of default are essential in a term facility. The power to appoint a receiver is the most important practical power that a lender has to enforce its security.

Mortgage/charge/equitable mortgage over land

A mortgage is created on unregistered property subject to the Registry of Deeds and a charge created on registered property which is registered in the Land Registry. A charge on registered land constitutes a mortgage by deed for the purposes of the Conveyancing and Law of Property Act 1881 (by virtue of the Registration of Title Act 1964). Therefore the holder of such a charge is entitled to exercise the statutory powers of sale set out in the Conveyancing Acts.

An equitable mortgage is created by the deposit on behalf of the company of relevant documents of title to property. Unusually, an equitable mortgage may be created by deed if the interest being mortgaged by the borrower company is an equitable interest only.

Mortgage of plant and machinery

It is possible for a company to create a specific mortgage over its plant and machinery (as well as charging such plant and machinery in the general sense by way of floating charge). Frequently, such a document is described as a 'chattel mortgage'. This expression should not be confused with a chattel mortgage under the Agricultural Credit Act 1978.

Chattel mortgage under Agricultural Credit Act 1978

It is possible for an individual, a company (or for that matter any other entity) to create a chattel mortgage in favour of a 'recognised lender' (most of the Irish licensed banks are recognised lenders) of 'stock' under the Agricultural Credit Act 1978. Stock is agricultural produce or machinery used in processing or distributing it. This is dealt with in greater detail below. The chattel mortgage may include fixed and/or floating charges over such stock.

4.5.3   PARTICULAR ASSETS

4.5.3.1   Land including licensed premises

When taking security over land, it is usual for the memorandum of association of the company to be checked to see that the company has authority in its objects clause to acquire, hold, mortgage and dispose of land. The conveyancing procedures involved in taking a mortgage of land from a company do not differ greatly from those followed when an individual is creating a mortgage over land although there are extra registration requirements per the Form 47 which is referred to later. Formalities required for the purpose of taking mortgages over land are dealt with in the Conveyancing module of the Professional Course to which you should cross-refer for necessary materials.

A company is entitled to hold a licence for the sale of intoxicating liquor although it has to be said that many district judges are happier to see a company's licence held in the name of an individual nominee of a company. The licence to sell intoxicating liquor is not a transferable asset.

Instead, it is usual for a collateral deed of covenant to be delivered by the licence holder, be it the company or the individual nominee. The covenantor undertakes to do everything to preserve the licence and to do everything necessary so as to vest the licence in the bank's nominee should the occasion arise on an enforcement of security.

4.5.3.2   Stock-in-trade

It is usual for the stock-in-trade to be charged by the floating charge in a debenture but not by any fixed charge. It is technically possible for stock to be charged by way of fixed charge but then such assets would cease to be 'stock-in-trade' in the accepted sense as a specific release would be required every time the particular stock was sold. When representing a lender it is worth finding out how much stock-in-trade is subject to reservation of title. Any receiver put in by the lender could not dispose of such property for the benefit of the company unless agreed by the owner retaining title.

4.5.3.3   Plant and machinery

Plant and machinery, if they are movable or if they are not substantial, will often be charged simply by the floating charge provisions of a debenture. However, in cases of substantial machinery, e.g. valuable printing machines or packing machines, fixed charges, sometimes separately in the form of a chattel mortgage, will be taken. It is important that details of the make or the manufacturer or supplier are obtained, together with a precise description of the items and details of the serial numbers. Sufficient information should be included in the mortgage clearly to identify the property.

Most importantly, a lender will have to satisfy itself that the items are not subject to any hire purchase or leasing agreements and that any reservation of title clauses in the contracts of supply have been waived. Alternatively, an auditor's certificate to this effect would be sought, or a letter from the supplier.

.5.3.4   Ships

Ship mortgages are a particular discipline and art form in themselves. They must conform to a particular format and, when delivered, there is usually a collateral deed of covenant between mortgagor and lender. Fishing vessels are frequently mortgaged as security and appropriate specific covenants should be included in the deed of covenant.

.5.3.5   Aircraft

Aircraft may be mortgaged by chattel mortgage in the same way as plant and machinery save that such chattel mortgages are likelier to be more 'big ticket' (in other words of greater monetary value) than plant and machinery chattel mortgages. Section 122 of CA 1990 clarified that mortgages of aircraft or shares in an aircraft and ships must be registered under CA 1963, s. 99. Charges on ships or shares in a ship were registrable under s. 99. Section 122 of CA 1990 included, for the first time, an aircraft or share in an aircraft.

4.5.3.6   'Stock' (Agricultural Credit Act 1978)

Stock is defined by the Agricultural Credit Act 1978, as including:

(a)   animals and birds of every kind and the progeny and produce of such animals and birds;

(b)   insects and fish of every kind and the progeny and produce of such insects and fish;

(c)   agricultural crops (whether growing on or severed from the land);

(d)   trees (whether growing on or severed from the land);

(e)   any product derived from any of the foregoing;

(f)   machinery, implements, vehicles, fixtures, fittings and materials used in or for the production, manufacture, processing, preparation for sale or marketing of any agricultural or fishery produce.

Agribusiness is exceedingly important in Ireland and it is conceivable that all of the assets of a company, other than its land, could constitute 'stock' within the meaning of the Agricultural Credit Act. It may be worthwhile for a lender to put in place this form of security rather than a standard debenture and charge. There are certain powers given to a chattel mortgagee such as the right of inspection, making of an inventory and the possibility of crystallising a floating charge before the appointment of a receiver, specifically under the terms of the Agricultural Credit Act.

4.5.3.7   Shares and debentures

It is common for lenders to take security over stocks and shares. More often than not, security will be taken over quoted shares and debentures which are securities of public companies. Security over shares in unquoted companies is less attractive because of the lack of a ready market for sale and, in private companies, restrictions on transferability. Shares may be fully or partly paid up but it is unusual for partly-paid shares to be offered as security for a loan or for that matter to be accepted by lenders as security. The three principal categories of shares and debentures to be considered in the context of taking security are:

(a) Bearer shares/debentures

The title to bearer securities passes by delivery and share warrants are fully negotiable instruments.

(b) Registered shares/debentures

Most securities are 'registered', i.e. the names and addresses of the holders are entered in a register which shows the amount of stock or the number of shares which they hold. As proof of such registration, a share certificate or stock certificate is issued. However, the advent of the CREST system of dematerialised shares has changed this for certain quoted companies.

(c) Inscribed shares/debentures

Inscribed stock involves the persons named being entered in the inscription books of the registration authority. No certificate is supplied but instead a stock receipt or certificate of inscription is issued. This stock receipt (unlike a stock certificate) does not require to be produced when the stock is sold. The stock is transferable in the books of the registration authority on the personal attendance of the holder or of a duly appointed attorney, who is normally a solicitor or banker.

Therefore the transfer of them to a lending institution would require personal attendance with the registration authority. This kind of stock is common enough on the continent but is rare in Ireland. However, the advent of the CREST system of dematerialised shares has changed this. CREST allows for the helpless ownership and trading of shares, which are listed on certain Stock Exchanges.

The usual forms of securities offered as security to lenders are as follows:

(i)   Debenture stock. A loan to the company which may or may not be secured on the assets.

(ii) Preference shares/stock. These will usually rank before the ordinary shares with regard to payment of dividend and capital.

(iii) Ordinary shares/equity capital. These shares constitute the 'real' ownership of a company.

(iv) Deferred shares. These are rarely issued these days and would rank last for payment of dividend and capital.

Stocks and shares in quoted companies have certain advantages as security:

(a)   they are easy to value;

(b)   there are few formalities when transferring them;

(c)   they may easily be sold; and

(d)   full negotiability in the case of bearer securities.

Unquoted shares have their own disadvantages. There may be difficulty in valuing the shares or in finding a purchaser. Even if the bank finds a purchaser, it may be that the directors in the exercise of the power conferred on them by the articles may decline to register a transfer in the lender's favour or in favour of the lender's nominee or purchaser. In certain cases the articles of association may prevent the bank taking a legal mortgage over the shares in the first place.

CREST (uncertified securities)

The Companies Act 1990 (Uncertified Securities) Regulations 1996 (SI 68/1996) came into effect on 24 January 1997. The Regulations provide for the holding of shares of a class in uncertificated form if they are to be a 'participating security' for the purposes of the Regulations. On a voluntary basis publicly quoted companies may apply to CRESTCO Limited (a company established under the Regulations to operate the CREST system in Ireland) for admission of their shares as participating security.

It is not possible to take an equitable deposit over uncertificated marketable shares (because there are no share certificates).

4.5.3.8   Cash, debts receivable

It is possible to take a fixed charge over credit balances at a bank or to take fixed charges over debts receivable.

In the case of charges over cash, the House of Lords in *Morris v Agrichemicals* [1997] 3 WLR 909 has confirmed that it is possible for a bank to obtain a charge over a credit balance of a borrower with itself. The bank will often look to obtain rights of set-off against that deposit as well in addition to the banker's right of set-off.

As to fixed charges on book debts, the provisions of Finance Act 1986, s. 115 (as amended by Finance Act 1995, s. 174) require careful consideration. Section 115 was introduced to defeat the priority that fixed charges over book debts were obtaining ahead of the Revenue Commissioners as a preferential creditor. The provisions enable the Revenue Commissioners to serve notice on the holder of a fixed charge over book debts requiring that holder to pay to the Revenue sums received on foot of any security subject to certain rules. The amendment effected by s. 174 gives limited protection to lenders if a copy of the Form 47 is sent to the Collector General (currently at Sarsfield House, Limerick) within twenty-one days of the creation of the charge.

4.5.3.9 Goods and bills of lading

In the case of exports of goods a bank may be required to open a letter of credit to facilitate the transaction. The bank will take a pledge of the relevant goods upon receipt of the documents of title to those goods which, in certain contracts, will typically be an invoice, an insurance policy and a bill of lading.

A bill of lading is a document signed by the ship's owner or by the master or other agent of the ship's owner which states that certain goods have been shipped on a particular ship and sets out the terms on which those goods have been delivered to and received by the ship's owner. It is generally used when the goods shipped form part only of the intended cargo of the ship (a charterparty being employed if the goods form the complete cargo). On its being signed, it is handed to the shipper. A bill of lading has three purposes which are that:

(a) it is a receipt for the goods shipped containing the terms on which they have been received;

(b) it is evidence of the contract for the carriage of the goods; and

(c) it is a document of title to the goods.

Therefore, security over such goods would be created by a pledge of the bill of lading.

From a strict legal point of view there is no necessity for any written evidence of a pledge. In practice, however, a pledgee usually obtains the pledgor's signature to a document called a 'letter of pledge'. A separate letter of pledge may be executed in respect of each transaction of a pledgor or the pledgor may be asked to execute a general letter of pledge. A general letter of pledge will contain clauses such as:

(i) A clause providing that the pledgee will have a pledge upon all goods delivered by the pledgor or by his agent into the possession of the pledgee and upon all bills of lading and other documents of title deposited by the pledgor or his agents with the pledgee or its agents.

(ii) The pledgor will agree that the goods and documents of title are pledged as a continuing security for the payment of all sums owed by the pledgor either solely or jointly with any other person or persons, whether on balance of account or on guarantees or in respect of bills of exchange and including interest and other banking charges.

(iii) The pledgor will agree that in the case of a default on demand, the pledgor may sell the goods or any part thereof.

(iv) The pledgor will agree to keep the goods fully insured in such office as the bank may approve.

(v) The pledgor will undertake to pay all rent and other expenses incidental to the warehousing of the goods.

(vi) The pledgee will look for an indemnity from the pledgor in respect of any default or neglect by any agent of the pledgor.

4.5.4 SUPPORTING SECURITY

4.5.4.1 Guarantee

Meaning

A contract of guarantee is a contract by one person to be answerable for the debt or default of another. Under the Statute of Frauds (Ireland) 1695, a guarantee must be in writing.

There are three parties concerned and two contracts.

(a) The first contract involves the principal creditor ('lender') and the principal debtor ('borrower').

(b) The contract of guarantee involves the principal creditor (lender) and the guarantor or surety. The guarantee is a collateral security and there must be primary liability in some person other than the guarantor, the guarantor being liable only secondarily, i.e. if the principal debtor (borrower) does not pay.

An indemnity is different from a guarantee in that the person giving the indemnity is primarily liable on foot of the indemnity and there is no secondary liability.

An indemnity is a much harder bond than a guarantee. Even though the principal may escape, the indemnifier remains liable. One distinction between a guarantee and indemnity is that, whereas a guarantee must be in writing, an indemnity need not be.

It must be stated that frequently in a guarantee document, there is an indemnity to require payment by the guarantor if the guarantee provisions in the guarantee fail.

As with other contracts the guarantee must be supported by consideration, unless under seal, but the consideration does not have to be expressed in the guarantee.

Invariably, however, consideration is expressed in the guarantee and lenders are generally not happy to accept a guarantee without some consideration being expressed in it, even if it is under seal.

Termination of liability of guarantor

The guarantor is a favoured debtor and may insist on rigid adherence to the terms of the guarantee. A guarantor's liability does not arise until the principal debtor has made default. Although only secondarily liable for the debt, it is not necessary for the creditor to request the debtor to pay or to sue the debtor before taking proceedings against the guarantor. It has been held that, in the absence of a specific provision to the contrary, a guarantor is discharged from liability under a guarantee in the following circumstances:

(a) If the transaction is void as between the principal debtor and the creditor.

(b) If the principal debtor is discharged or if the creditor releases the principal debtor from liability.

(c) If there is any material variation of the terms of the contract between the creditor and the principal, e.g. allowing the principal debtor extra time to pay.

(d) Any change in the constitution of the persons to or for whom the guarantee was given (e.g. changes in partnerships). This rule was embodied as far as partnerships were concerned in the Partnership Act 1890, s. 18.

Usual clauses found in guarantees

Most guarantees contain a clause permitting the creditor, without the consent of the guarantor, to vary the form of security, which it has in respect of the principal debtor's debt, and to grant the principal debtor extra time for payment.

The guarantee will also contain a clause whereby the guarantor undertakes not to protect himself by taking security from the principal debtor. The reason for this is to ensure that if the debtor becomes bankrupt and part of his liability is unsecured, his free assets will not be depleted to the detriment of the creditor as a result of charges created in favour of the guarantor.

The guarantee should also contain a clause indicating that the security will be a continuing security and that it will remain in full force until all obligations of the principal debtor have been discharged. This is inserted in order to exclude the operation of the rule in *Clayton's Case* (1816) 1 Mer 572. If the rule was not excluded each sum paid into the principal debtor's account, in the case of a bank after the execution of the guarantee, would reduce the guarantor's liability while each debit to the account would create a fresh advance for which the guarantor would not be liable.

The guarantor will be prohibited from suing the debtor in respect of any money paid on foot of the guarantee until such time as the entire debt due to the creditor has been discharged in full. If this clause were not included it could prejudicially affect the creditor. For example, a customer's account is overdrawn by £1,000 and the surety has guaranteed the repayment thereof with the limit up to £500. When the surety in response to a demand from the creditor pays the creditor the latter sum then, in the absence of agreement, the surety would be entitled to bring an action against the principal debtor for £500, thus reducing the assets available to satisfy the remainder of the creditor's debt.

The operative clause whereby the guarantor agrees to guarantee the debt usually contains a provision that the guarantor will pay the principal debt on demand. By inserting this provision, one may avoid the Statute of Limitations 1957 running until such time as demand is made. For example, where a debtor has a running account with the bank for a number of years, this could be relevant. The guarantee should also contain a provision as to what would constitute the service of the demand and this would usually be contained in a notice clause.

As stated above, it is usual for provisions to be incorporated into the guarantee permitting the creditor and the principal debtor to vary the contract, even if the liability of the guarantor is thereby increased.

Guarantees by partnerships

Unless it may be shown that the giving of guarantees is necessary for the carrying on of the business of a particular partnership in the ordinary way, one partner has no implied authority to bind the firm by executing a guarantee: Partnership Act 1890, s. 5. Therefore, unless it clearly appears from the partnership agreement that the giving of guarantees is part of the ordinary business of the firm, a creditor should either have the guarantees signed by all the partners on behalf of the firm or, alternatively, have a guarantee executed by one partner with the express written authority of the others.

Guarantees by limited companies

A company may not execute a guarantee unless it has the power to do so by virtue of its memorandum of association. One should look at the articles to check the provisions for proper execution. Unless there are provisions to the contrary, the guarantee may be executed under seal or under hand. Whichever method is followed, at the very least a board resolution should be passed.

4.5.4.2 Assignment of life policy

Life assurance policies are frequently taken out by companies on key personnel. These life policies may be mortgaged by the company that has taken out the insurance. More usually the particular key individuals take out policies for the purpose of a financial transaction. The life policies are assigned to the lender by means of a deed of assignment. Failure to get a life policy organised is often a cause of delays in completing a lending transaction. The usual delay would be awaiting the result of medical examinations and any necessary tests. If there is a life policy requirement, it should be acted on immediately. A lender will require to be satisfied that the policy details are in order. The main relevant points would include:

(a)   the life assured;

(b)   the beneficiary under the policy—often the same as the life assured, but may be the borrower company or a spouse of the life assured. The assignment of the policy must come from the beneficiary of the policy;

(c)   the amount of the policy; and

(d)   the term of years of the assurance.

A life policy is a chose in action (property which cannot be reduced to physical possession). As with all charges over choses in action, the creditor/bank must protect its priority by giving notice of its security to the obligor, in this case the assurance company.

However, the rule that priority of an assignment is governed by the order of notice to the debtor is subject to the variation that the policy of assurance is equivalent to the title deeds of real property. Therefore, if the chargor is unable to produce the policy, this is a circumstance which puts the creditor/bank on enquiry. If the policy is held by an existing mortgagee, then failure to produce it would be constructive notice of the prior charge. A chargee with notice of a prior charge does not obtain priority even if he is the first to give notice to the debtor.

Just as in the case of stocks and shares, the charge over the policy may be either legal or equitable. However, notice to the assurance company is necessary in either case to preserve priority and protect the efficacy of the charge.

Life policies have certain advantages as security:

(a)   After a number of years certain life policies will generally acquire what is called a surrender value which value will increase from year-to-year.

(b)   A life policy may be easily realised, if the bank takes a legal mortgage of the policy. In this situation, the creditor is in a position to surrender the policy and obtain payment at the surrender value.

(c)   The policy retains a relatively stable and generally increasing value provided the premiums are paid.

As against this certain disadvantages should be borne in mind:

(i)   The risk that the policy holder may be unable to pay future premiums.

(ii)   There is a risk that the policy may be vitiated by the assured's non-disclosure of all facts and circumstances affecting the risk.

(iii) There is a risk that the policy holder may not have an insurable interest in the life assured (unlikely if the individual himself/herself has taken out the policy).

(iv)   Note medical exceptions on certain policies. Certain life assurance policies constitute accident policies only. Other types to be alert to include those which provide death benefit cover, and cover which reduces over time—mortgage protection policies.

A legal mortgage of a life policy is effected invariably by an assignment of the life policy. It is possible for an absolute assignment to be made of a life policy in favour of a lender. This may happen from time to time where the insurance policy itself has no surrender value. On completion of the relevant borrowing relationship the policy may simply be allowed to lapse.

However, usually there is a conditional assignment of the life policy, i.e. an assignment subject to redemption or repayment of the secured obligation. The deed of assignment contains an assignment of the assured's right to recover the policy money and notice of assignment is served on the assurance company. The notice to the assurance company binds the assurance company to pay the money on foot of the policy to the assignee. Notice also enables the creditor to acquire priority over earlier assignees who have not given notice to the assurance company, provided that the creditor had not received actual or constructive notice of the earlier assignment at the time when the creditor made the advance.

Non-production of the policy may amount to constructive notice of an earlier assignment and therefore the creditor should always insist upon production of the policy. The notice must be in writing. The notice must give the date and purport of the assignment and it must be addressed to the assurance company's principal place of business. It is usual practice to request the assurance company to acknowledge receipt of the notice by signing a duplicate notice sent to the company.

An equitable mortgage of a life policy is also possible but is not particularly common. Being a chose in action, no particular formality is necessary to create a mortgage of it. An equitable mortgage of a life policy may be created by an oral agreement between the parties or by a deposit of the policy accompanied by a written memorandum. A mortgage of this nature is perfectly valid as against the mortgagor's assignee or trustee in bankruptcy but it gives the mortgagee an equitable interest only. When the policy money becomes payable the company will require a discharge from the assured as well as from the mortgagee.

Equitable mortgages of life policies are rare but if a creditor is content with this security, the debtor's signature to a memorandum of deposit should be obtained containing clauses to the effect that the security will be a continuing security, that he/she will pay the premiums when they become due and that he/she will execute a legal mortgage when called upon.

Notice should be made to the assurance company of the equitable mortgage to protect the mortgagee's priority. If equitable mortgagees fail to give notice, their priorities are determined by the order of the dates of their respective equitable mortgages.

It will be unlikely that a second charge will be created over a life policy where the creditor holds the policy in its possession. However, where a second assignment is executed the assignee should give notice thereof to the creditor/bank.

4.5.4.3   Collateral issues

Frequently the controller of a company will create a charge over his/her individual property to support a guarantee or indemnity obligation. In these circumstances, it is important that the provisions of relevant family and consumer credit legislation are considered.

For example, if the managing director of a company is guaranteeing the company's borrowings and granting security over the family home his wife should obtain independent legal advice with regard to the transaction. The bank will need advice on whether this security amounts to a housing loan within the Consumer Credit Act 1995.

4.5.4.4   Set-off

We discussed earlier the matter of set-off in the context of the ability of a company to create a charge over a cash deposit with a bank in favour of that bank. It is usual in conjunction with the taking of security over companies (or for that matter on the opening of accounts of the companies in the case of certain banks) for 'Letters of Lien, Appropriation and Combination' to be signed on behalf of a borrowing company entitling the bank to combine accounts at will so that, particularly in the event of insolvency, it will be the net sum due by the company to the bank that must be repaid only, with any other sums due being written off against credit balances.

CA 1990 amended C(À)A 1990 to provide that in the case of court examinations, banks were not entitled to exercise rights of set-off. C(A)(No.2)A 1999 restored the former position so that exercise of set-off between accounts of the same company is allowed again.

4.6   Secretarial Considerations and Requirements

Set out below are company documents and procedures which a lender's adviser will examine concerning a borrowing company.

4.6.1   INCORPORATION

The fact of incorporation of the company must always be proven. 'Does the company (still) exist (under its supposed name)' may seem a very basic question but it is one which must always be addressed. Frequently an anticipated change of name may not have occurred, and occasionally an intending borrowing company has been struck off the register for failure to deliver annual returns. In view of the practice of the Companies Office whereby companies that do not deliver annual returns are struck off the Register, the fact of non-dissolution proved by an up-to-date company search will be required.

4.6.2   POWER OF THE COMPANY TO BORROW

A certified copy of the memorandum of association will be required, first so as to establish what the company's objects are and, secondly to ensure that there is a specific enabling power set out in the objects clause permitting the company to borrow money and, where relevant, to deliver security and/or to give guarantees in respect of the obligations of third parties such as subsidiary companies.

A typical sub-clause in the objects clause permitting borrowing would be:

> To raise or borrow or secure the payment of money in such manner and on such terms as the directors may deem expedient and in particular by the issue of bonds, debentures or debenture stock, perpetual or redeemable, or by mortgage, charge, lien or pledge upon the whole or any part of the undertaking, property, assets and rights of the company, present or future, including its uncalled capital for the time being and goodwill and generally in any other manner as the directors shall from time to time determine and any such debentures, debenture stock or other securities may be issued at a discount, premium or otherwise, and with any special privileges as to redemption, surrender, transfer, drawings, allotments of shares, attending and voting at general meetings of the company, appointment of directors or otherwise.

4.6.3   POWER OF THE COMPANY TO DELIVER SECURITY

It is usual for the sub-clause in the objects clause of the memorandum of association which authorises borrowing to deal also with the delivery of security, as in the above example.

4.6.4   POWER OF THE COMPANY TO GIVE GUARANTEES

It is usual for there to be a separate sub-clause in the objects clause of the memorandum of association which authorises the giving of guarantees. Here is an example:

> To become surety for and to guarantee, support or secure whether by personal covenant or indemnity or by mortgaging or charging all or any part of the undertaking property and assets (present and future) uncalled capital and goodwill of the Company or all or any of such methods, and either with or without the Company receiving any consideration therefor, the performance of the obligations or the repayment or payment of the principal amounts of and premiums interest and dividends on any loans, stocks, shares, debentures, debenture stocks, notes, bonds or other securities of any person, authority (whether supreme local municipal or

otherwise), firm or company, including (without prejudice to the generality of the foregoing) any body corporate which is for the time being the Company's holding company as defined by Section 155 of the Companies Act, 1963, or any statutory modification or re-enactment thereof or another subsidiary, as defined by the said Section, of the company's holding company or otherwise associated with the Company in business, including suppliers of goods to the Company, its holding company or any subsidiary thereof, as defined by the said Section.

4.6.5 DIRECTORS' POWERS TO EXERCISE THE COMPANY'S POWERS

The articles of association will be looked at especially to see if any amendment has been made to article 79 of Table A. Article 79 of Table A limits the amount that the directors may borrow to an amount equal to the nominal value of the issued share capital of the company, unless the company in general meeting authorises a higher amount of borrowing.

A typical article found in the articles of association of a private company, excluding article 79, would be as follows:

The Directors may exercise all the powers of the Company to borrow money, and to guarantee, support or secure (whether by guarantee indemnity or otherwise) the obligations of third parties, and to mortgage or charge all or any part of its undertaking, property and assets (present and future), uncalled capital and goodwill in connection with such borrowing or guaranteeing, and, subject to Section 20 of the Companies (Amendment) Act, 1983, to issue debentures, debenture stock and other securities whether outright or as security for any debt, liability or obligation of the Company or of any third party. Debentures, debenture stock and other securities may be made assignable free of any equities between the Company and the person to whom the same may be issued. Any debentures or debenture stock may be issued at a discount, premium or otherwise and with any special rights as to redemption, surrender, drawings, allotment of shares, attending and voting at general meetings of the Company, appointment of directors or otherwise.

In the case of public limited companies with a quote on one of the Stock Exchange markets, the articles disapply the provisions of Table A. There is, however, an article enabling the directors to borrow money but limiting the amount to a particular multiple (usually three times) of the aggregate of the nominal share capital of the company and the consolidated reserves of the company and its subsidiaries.

Occasionally a public limited company's auditors will be asked to confirm that such borrowing limits have not been exceeded in a particular transaction.

4.6.6 REQUIREMENT FOR ORDINARY OR SPECIAL RESOLUTION OF THE COMPANY IN GENERAL MEETING

An ordinary resolution approving borrowing, delivery of security or the giving of a guarantee is mandatory if the company's articles include regulation 79 of Table A and the amount to be borrowed or liability to be incurred exceeds the limits set out in that regulation, or if there is any similar restriction on the borrowing powers of the directors.

A special resolution approving borrowing, delivery of security or the giving of a guarantee will require to be passed by the company in general meeting if the provisions of CA 1963, s. 60 apply to the proposed borrowing, delivery of security or giving of a guarantee.

An ordinary resolution is usually required if CA 1990, s. 29 dealing with substantial non-cash asset transactions is relevant. Sometimes, in the case of transactions where a company is guaranteeing the obligations of third parties, lenders will seek the passing of a resolution of the company in general meeting noting that the giving of the guarantee is bona fide in the best interests of the company, noting some consideration received by the company for the giving of the guarantee, and resolving that the board of directors be authorised and directed to attend to the delivery of a guarantee. A typical resolution doing this would be as follows:

> A form of guarantee was produced to the meeting whereby the company would guarantee all sums due or to become due from [holding company] to [Bank] without limitation. It was resolved that the giving of such guarantee by the company would be bona fide in the best interests of the company as a whole, the company receiving administration services from [holding company] and for this and other reasons the meeting being unanimously of the opinion that the company would derive a benefit from the giving of the guarantee and such guarantee would be in connection with the obligations of [its holding company] and it was resolved that such guarantee as may be required by [Bank] be given and that the board of directors be and they are hereby authorised and directed to arrange for the execution and delivery of the proposed guarantee and any other matters arising in connection therewith.

4.6.7   RESOLUTION OF THE BOARD OF DIRECTORS

As a general rule it may be said that in transactions where a company is borrowing itself and the objects clause and directors' powers are satisfactory, a lender will look for a resolution of the board of directors whereby the directors resolve to borrow the money and, if relevant, deliver the relevant security in accordance with their powers. A typical resolution approving and accepting a facility letter would be as follows:

> That the facilities offered in facility letter from [Bank] dated [ ] be and they are hereby approved and accepted and that [ ] director and [ ] director be and they are hereby authorised to accept the said facility letter for and on behalf of the company.

Where a document is to be a deed, it will be sealed in accordance with the provisions of the articles of association. Most companies either adopt regulation 115 of Table A or an article in similar terms whereby the seal is to be affixed on documents only by the authority of a resolution of the board of directors with the relevant document being signed by a director and countersigned by another director, the secretary or some other person appointed by the directors for the purpose.

A typical resolution of a meeting of the board of directors approving the sealing of a debenture would be as follows:

> A Debenture (in duplicate) incorporating fixed and floating charges over the Company's property and assets by the Company in favour of [Bank] and a Memorial thereof were produced to the meeting the text of which had been agreed by the Company's Solicitors and the Solicitors for [Bank]. The Directors noted that this Debenture was to be given to the [Bank] to secure the present and future, actual and contingent obligations of the Company to [Bank] whether as principal or as surety and whether solely or jointly with any person. The Directors having been fully advised as to and having themselves considered and being aware of the terms of the said Debenture and the legal and commercial implications of the execution thereof, it was unanimously resolved:
>
> (a)   that the execution thereof was in the best interests of the Company;
>
> (b)   that the Debenture should be and was thereby approved;
>
> (c)   that the seal of the Company be affixed to each execution copy in accordance with the Company's Articles of Association;
>
> (d)   that any Director, the Secretary or any Solicitor representing the Company be and was thereby authorised and directed to sign the prescribed particulars of the Debenture in Form 47 for delivery to the Registrar of Companies; and

95

(e)   that the seal of the Company be affixed to the Memorial of the Debenture in accordance with the Company's Articles of Association.

Where a guarantee is to be executed a typical resolution passed by the board of directors of the guaranteeing company would be as follows:

It being noted that the company was authorised by its objects to deliver a guarantee to secure the obligations of any person [and it being further noted that the company in general meeting had authorised and directed the directors to attend to the execution and delivery of a guarantee in favour of [Bank] to secure the obligations of [holding company] it was resolved that the guarantee by the company to [Bank] to secure the obligations of [holding company] to [Bank] be and is hereby approved and that the seal of the company be affixed thereto in accordance with the Articles of Association of the Company.

Some lenders are satisfied if a guarantee is signed on behalf of a company rather than executed under the seal of the company. Since guarantees (whether sealed or under hand) are no longer stampable, stamp duty considerations no longer arise.

4.6.8   COMPLETION OF A BORROWING TRANSACTION—DOCUMENTS TABLED/HANDED OVER

4.6.8.1   Certificate of incorporation

The original certificate of incorporation, any certificate(s) of incorporation on change of name and, needless to say, an up-to-date Companies Office search will be required so as the continued incorporation of the company under its purported name is seen to subsist.

The original certificate of incorporation and any certificates of incorporation on change of name will be required in connection with delivery of any charge document to the Land Registry.

4.6.8.2   Memorandum of association

A copy of the memorandum and articles of association certified as being a true copy of the current document incorporating all amendments will be required. Authentication of such a document under the Companies Acts may be effected by a director or the secretary.

4.6.8.3   Members' resolutions

If CA 1963, s. 60 applies, a certified copy of the special resolution will be required together with evidence that the resolution has been delivered to the Companies Office for filing. Most importantly, a copy of the relevant statutory declaration made under the provisions of CA 1963, s. 60 will require to be furnished together with satisfactory proof that a copy of the declaration was delivered for filing to the Companies Office on the day that notices convening the EGM at which the special resolution was passed, were sent out.

In the event that regulation 79 or a comparable article applies, a certified copy of the ordinary resolution approving the borrowing will be required. Likewise, if an ordinary resolution is obtained for general purposes only, for example, in the case of a guarantee by a company with a minority shareholder.

If CA 1990, s. 29 is relevant, then a certified copy of the requisite resolution will be needed.

4.6.8.4   Director's resolution

A certified copy of the resolution of the meeting of the board of directors approving borrowing/delivery of security/giving of guarantee will be required. As a general rule, a certified copy resolution will be signed by either the chairman or the secretary although the chairman should be the signatory in view of CA 1963, s. 145(2).

4.6.8.5 Security documents

Additional documents may be needed, depending on the security:

debenture with floating charge

mortgage of land	all documents of title to land.
mortgage over plant and machinery	auditors' certificate as to no reservation of title/ HP or leasing
charge over shares	share warrant or share certificate, memorandum of deposit
assignment of life policy	original life policy, letter confirming no lapse or cancellation of life policy, birth certificate of life assured (if age not admitted on the policy)

guarantee

4.6.8.6 Form 47 for security documents containing charges

Prescribed particulars of charges must be delivered to the Registrar of Companies within twenty-one days of the creation of a charge. If the security includes a fixed charge on book debts then a copy should also be sent to the Collector General within the same twenty-one-day period.

4.6.8.7 Memorial of any security documents affecting any interest in land

If a mortgage of unregistered land is being created by a company, then a memorial of that mortgage will be needed. Even if a debenture contains merely a floating charge in general terms over the undertaking property and assets of the company a memorial of that debenture may be registered in the Registry of Deeds.

4.6.8.8 Certificate of company secretary as to certain corporate details

It is common on completion to obtain a certificate from the company secretary certifying the identity of the directors, the secretary, the location of the registered office, including confirmation that no other charges have been executed, certifying that no resolution has been circulated to put the company into receivership, liquidation or court examination and that no petition is pending to put the company into receivership, liquidation or court examination, that no judgment has been obtained capable of being converted into a judgment mortgage and that the company is not subject to any agreement, order or trust whereby its powers of borrowing or delivering security are in any way impaired. It is unclear what redress a lender will obtain from a secretary who misstated any of these facts, but it does at least provide some comfort that these matters have in fact been looked into.

4.6.8.9 Particulars of insurance

Frequently lenders will look for evidence of non-life insurance which is relevant for a borrower's business, e.g. insurance of particular key assets or buildings.

Generally lenders will require that their interest be noted on the insurance policies. At the very least a letter is sought from the insurers undertaking that they will not let the policies lapse or be cancelled without prior written notice to the lender. This will be so as to enable the lender to pay the premiums to preserve the insurance if the lender believed that that was important.

4.6.8.10 Searches

Searches with satisfactory explanations of acts appearing will be handed over.

Office	Will disclose
Companies Office	Charges, insolvency, dissolution of company, restriction and disqualification of directors
Judgments Office	Registered money judgments
Sheriffs Office	Unexecuted execution orders against goods, rates certificates
Revenue Sheriffs Office	Unexecuted Revenue certificates
Registry of Deeds	Documents affecting any interest in heritable property
Land Registry	Burdens on registered property, pending dealings

In certain cases searches on overseas registers will be required.

4.7 Post-Completion Procedures

4.7.1 STAMP ALL STAMPABLE DOCUMENTS

The rate of stamp duty payable on security documents such as mortgages is £1 per £1,000 secured subject to a maximum of £500 on a document. Collateral and counterpart documents are stamped at £10 each. It does not matter that the documents are under seal or otherwise. Note that documents transferring an interest in real or leasehold property and certain asset sale agreements must be stamped at various rates depending on the nature of the property and other factors. As stamp duty law in the residential sector is regularly amended, practitioners must be particularly careful to ensure documents have the relevant statutory certificates and sufficient money is held to pay applicable stamp duty.

If a promissory note is taken as part of the security package, an adhesive stamp of 7p is affixed.

4.7.2 REGISTRATION OF A CHARGE

4.7.2.1 Companies Office

When a company executes a charge, particulars of the charge must be delivered to the Registrar within twenty-one days from the date of its creation. Failure to do so renders the charge void against any liquidator or creditor. Registration for an Irish company is undertaken by lodging a Form 47. In the case of a foreign company, a similar procedure using a Form 8E is required, whether or not the company has registered on the External Register. If the applicant for registration is the company itself, the form must be verified by some person interested in the charge otherwise than on behalf of the company, setting out such interest. Generally, the solicitor for the lending institution will verify the particulars.

If particulars are not filed within the appropriate period application may be made to court under CA 1963, s. 106 for an order extending the time for registration or rectifying the error in the application. The court must be satisfied that the omission to register was accidental or by mistake.

If the charge becomes void under s. 99 by failure to register on time, the money secured immediately becomes payable and the lender may immediately sue for the debt.

A new security document may be executed and the appropriate particulars filed within the appropriate time. The difficulty which could arise here is in respect of CA 1963, s. 288 in that in the case of a floating charge, the charge could be rendered invalid if the borrower is wound up within twelve months of the creation of the charge as no cash is paid to the company at the time of, or in consideration for, the granting of the charge.

Note if a property subject to an existing mortgage is acquired by a company, the new purchasing company must file a Form 47(b), as the existing charge now represents a charge on its property. Note also the Irish Companies Office practice is to reject any Forms 47/ Forms 8E delivered outside the twenty-one-day period even if the Form 47/8E had been delivered originally within the period with inadvertent errors only.

Certain charges created by non-Irish companies over assets in Ireland are registered on the 'Slavenburg Register'. This has arisen because of the mismatch between CA 1963, s. 111 and Part XI of that Act. External companies having an established place of business in Ireland should have delivered appropriate particulars to the Companies Office so that a file may be opened in their name in the Companies Office to register charges. Section 111 applies the rules as to registration of charges to companies having an established place of business in Ireland whether or not they have so registered. The practice has developed therefore of delivering Forms 8E to the Companies Office of such companies and they are put on a (non-indexed) 'Slavenburg Register' (named after the case of that name which highlighted the issue in England).

4.7.2.2 Land Registry/Registry of Deeds

Normal registration in the Registry of Deeds and Land Registry proceeds where title is unregistered and registered land respectively.

In the case of registered land, debentures incorporating floating charges only are not ordinarily registered against folios although note that in 1986 an amendment to the Land Registry Rules 1972 was enacted making crystallised floating charges registrable charges under the provisions of the Registration of Title Act 1964.

4.7.2.3 County Registrar (Agricultural Credit Act chattel mortgages)

A charge over stock must be registered with the appropriate County Registrar under the Agricultural Credit Act 1978, within one month from the date of its creation. Note that the registration requirement arises wherever the 'land' of the borrower is situate. Land is defined as any land used for the purpose of the business of the company. Frequently registration has to be effected in more than one county. If more than one registration is to be effected, careful checking of each registrar's requirements is advisable. For example, is a stamped original required to be presented?

4.7.2.4 Port of ship

A mortgage on a ship must be registered at the port of registration of the ship.

4.7.2.5 Notification to other lending institutions

If there is a prior mortgage or charge and the security is to rank second, notice should be served on the first mortgagee that a second mortgage or charge is being created.

If there is a sharing arrangement between two or more banks, it should be evidenced in writing and agreed on by the various lenders setting out the sum of money in respect of each lender for which the security will be shared. Priority may be regulated in a priority agreement.

4.7.2.6   Notice to assurance company

When a life policy is assigned as security, notice must be served on the assurance company that the policy has been assigned. The notice should also request particulars of any prior notice of charge to the insurance company. A statutory fee of 25p may be payable but is rarely if ever required.

4.7.2.7   Obligations of company—filing requirements

Section 60 declaration

A copy section 60 declaration of solvency by the directors must be delivered to the Companies Office for filing on the date that notices are dispatched for an EGM at which it will be proposed as a special resolution that 'financial assistance' within the meaning of s. 60 be given.

Special resolutions

Generally under s. 141 special resolutions must be filed in the Companies Office within fifteen days.

Filing on a foreign companies or commercial register may be needed. For example, does a charge document charge assets in Northern Ireland or Great Britain? If there is any element of foreign law to be considered, whether because of the location of assets or the place of incorporation of the borrower, appropriate legal advice should be obtained from a lawyer qualified to practise in that jurisdiction.

Write up register of debenture holders

Section 91 of CA 1963 requires a company to keep a register of debenture holders. The register should be written up by the company secretary.

Have copy charge document available under s. 109

Section 109 of CA 1963 requires a company to have copies of documents creating charges available for inspection by creditors.

Put members'/directors' resolution in minute book pursuant to s. 145

Section 145 of CA 1963 requires the keeping of minute books. Appropriate minutes should be put in the appropriate books.

4.7.3   RELEASE OF SECURITY

4.7.3.1   Floating charge

A release of a floating charge would be effected by deed or by letter returning the original floating charge. If the floating charge has been registered in the Registry of Deeds then it is usual for there to be a deed of release and for a memorial to be furnished. In a conveyancing transaction a non-crystallisation letter is handed over.

4.7.3.2   Mortgage on real/leasehold property

A mortgage is released by a deed of release or by receipt under the Housing Act 1988.

4.7.3.3   Charge registered in the Land Registry

A charge registered in the Land Registry is released by means of a deed of discharge in the appropriate Land Registry Form—Form 71A or B.

4.7.3.4 Equitable mortgage by deposit of title deeds

An equitable mortgage by deposit of title deeds is released by a simple letter of release.

4.7.3.5 Notification of release

Unusually, it is the company which notifies the Companies Office that a charge has ceased to affect the company's property or that it has been discharged. A Form 49 or a Form 49A, as appropriate, is submitted to the Companies Office. The Registrar serves notice on the relevant lending institution that a form has been filed and the charge will be struck off within a certain period unless notice to the contrary is served by the lending institution on the Companies Office.

4.8 Financial Assistance in Connection with Purchases of and Subscriptions for Shares

4.8.1 THE LEGAL PROVISIONS

One of the most troublesome provisions of Irish company law is CA 1963, s. 60. The origins of this section go back to the English Companies Act 1929, s. 45 which was introduced on the recommendation of the Greene Committee which had reviewed English legislation. It outlawed the giving by a company of assistance for the purpose of, or in connection with, the purchase of (but not subscription for) its shares. The Committee's example of the sort of transaction that the section was ultimately aimed at was where a group of individuals acquired control of a company by buying shares out of borrowed money which, when they were appointed directors to the company, they would procure that the company would repay from its own assets. The company therefore provided money for the purchase of its shares.

The 1929 provision was re-enacted with amendments as in the English Companies Act 1948, s. 54, which prohibited financial assistance for the purpose of, or in connection with, the subscription for, as well as the purchase of, shares in the company concerned. This provision was enacted into Irish law by CA 1959, s. 3. The Jenkins Committee, which reported on the operation of the English Companies Acts in June 1962, proposed certain amendments and, as often happens in these circumstances, Ireland took heed of deliberations overseas. When consolidating companies legislation the Oireachtas enacted the provisions of the Companies Act 1959, s. 3, with some of the amendments as proposed in the Jenkins Report, as CA 1963, s. 60.

The motivation for the provision is to prevent the reduction of the share capital of the company and asset stripping. However, as we will see later, it has a wider effect than that anticipated. The Jenkins Committee had described the previous unqualified provision as 'an occasional embarrassment to the honest without being a serious inconvenience to the unscrupulous'. The same may be said of our s. 60.

The European Communities (Public Limited Companies Subsidiaries) Regulations 1997 (SI 67/1997) prohibit a subsidiary of a public limited company from financially assisting in the purchase of, or subscription for, shares in its parent public company.

4.8.2 WHAT IS FORBIDDEN BY S. 60

4.8.2.1 General

Section 60 prohibits:

Financial assistance:

- directly or indirectly

- by means of a loan

- by means of a guarantee

- by means of the provision of security

- or otherwise

for the purpose of or in connection with:

- a purchase made

- a purchase to be made

- a subscription made

- or subscription to be made

by any person of shares:

- in the company

- or in the company's holding company.

The following are examples of transactions that would be affected by s. 60:

'directly or indirectly'	If buyer company wishes to buy shares in a target company, the target company cannot lend money to the subsidiary of the buyer company so as the buyer company may be put in funds.
'by means of a loan'	A target company cannot lend money to a buyer company to enable it to buy the shares.
'by means of a guarantee'	A target company cannot guarantee the borrowings of a buyer of its shares.
'by means of . . . the provision of security'	This would be a corollary of the previous example where, for example, a target company would give security to a bank by way of a charge over its assets and a guarantee to secure borrowings of a buyer of its shares.
'otherwise'	Examples of other forms of financial assistance could include the purchase by a target company of an asset belonging to a subscriber or purchaser of its shares, a similar purchase by that company's subsidiary, or the placing of the target company's trading opportunities in the hands of a subscriber or purchaser of shares.

4.8.2.2 Has there been financial assistance?

Has the target company or any of its subsidiaries helped a buyer of shares in any way directly or indirectly?

Has the company whose shares are being subscribed for or transferred or any of its subsidiaries done anything to help the share subscription or share transfer happen?

4.8.2.3 Is there a connection?

While it is easy to establish where assistance has been given 'for the purpose of' a share purchase or subscription, it is less easy to establish where assistance has been given 'in connection with' such a transaction.

- Would the share purchase or subscription have proceeded in the absence of the transaction whose connection with the share purchase or subscription is in doubt?

- Would that transaction whose connection is in doubt have proceeded in the absence of the share purchase or subscription?

4.8.2.4 A word of warning

The extremely restrictive provisions of the English Companies Act 1948, s. 54 generated a jurisprudence which could be said to rely on benevolent interpretation of that section. The view of certain legal authors in relation to the replacement of those provisions which are now in the English Companies Act 1985, ss. 151–158, is that those replacement provisions will be construed more widely, as the sections provide a way out of the difficulties in certain circumstances, as does the Irish s. 60. Therefore, one cannot rely completely on cases interpreting the previous English law. In particular, many of the UK s. 54 cases are concerned with the legality or otherwise of the transactions being considered. In Ireland s. 60(14) is specifically concerned with this point.

The current English law refers to the 'acquisition' of shares rather than a 'purchase' or 'subscription'. This, along with the precedents (one pre-1948, interpreting their 1929 legislation, and another post-1948 but interpreting a section to do with prospectuses) has led some UK commentators to suggest that the previous law would not apply on a share-for-share exchange. However, it may be argued that if, but for this technicality, there was financial assistance, the directors would be in breach of their fiduciary duties to implement a transaction in which such financial assistance was present. There is no guarantee that an Irish court would not include a share exchange in the definition of 'purchase' or 'subscription'.

In the case of *Belmont Finance Corporation v Williams Furniture (No. 2)* [1980] 1 All ER 393 a company bought an asset at a fair market price from a purchaser of its shares so as to put the purchaser in funds to purchase the shares. The corresponding UK provisions were stated to have been breached. An arm's length transaction in the ordinary course of a company's business which serves to finance an acquisition of a company's shares may be caught by this section. However, in the English case of *Charterhouse Investment Trust Ltd v Tempest Diesels* [1986] BCLC 1 it is suggested that one should look at the commercial realities of the circumstances.

4.8.3 CONSEQUENCES OF CONTRAVENING S. 60

Making the statutory declaration without reasonable grounds for the opinion that the company will be able to pay its debts as they fall due may result in a fine and imprisonment on conviction. If a company acts in contravention of s. 60, every officer in default is liable to a fine and imprisonment.

Any transaction in breach of s. 60 is voidable at the instance of the company against any person (whether a party to the transaction or not) with notice of the facts which constitute the breach. In *Bank of Ireland Finance Ltd v Rockfield Ltd* [1979] IR 21 the Supreme Court held that the notice required was actual notice.

4.8.4 WHAT S. 60 DOES NOT PROHIBIT

The principal exception is for financial assistance given by a company (other than a public limited company or in relation to plc shares) under the authority of a special resolution where the procedure set out in s. 60(2)–(11) are complied with. Other transactions which are exempted include the payment of a dividend properly declared by a company (s. 60(12)), the discharge of a liability lawfully incurred by a company (s. 60(12)), the lending by a company of money in the ordinary course of its lending business (s. 60(13)(a)), the provision by a company of funding for an employee share scheme (s. 60(13)(b)) and the making by a company of loans to employees (other than directors) (s. 60(13)(c)) to enable such persons to purchase or subscribe for shares in the company.

Section 60 does not apply to the acquisition of non-convertible debentures or loan stock.

4.8.5 FINANCIAL ASSISTANCE COMPLIANCE

As the reason for the capital maintenance rules is to preserve the share capital of the company for the benefit of creditors and shareholders, it is not surprising that the procedure available to private companies to give financial assistance requires the safeguarding of these interests.

4.8.5.1 Creditor protection

Creditors are protected through a declaration of solvency by a majority of the directors of the company. This statutory declaration must be made at a meeting of the directors held not more than twenty-four days before a meeting of shareholders. Section 60(4) of CA 1963 is very specific about what the statutory declaration must contain. The declaration must state:

(a) the form the assistance will take;

(b) the persons to whom the assistance is to be given;

(c) the purpose for which the company intends those persons to use the assistance; and

(d) that the directors making the declaration have made full enquiries as to the affairs of the company and that having done so they have formed the opinion that the company, having carried out the transaction whereby such assistance is to be given, will be able to pay its debts in full as they become due.

The equivalent English legislation requires all the directors to make the declaration and also requires that an auditor's report reinforcing the opinion of the directors be obtained. Neither requirement exists under Irish law. However, in practice, directors often seek professional advice from the company auditors so that they will be able to confirm having made full enquiry into the financial condition of the company.

Under s. 60(5), the penalty for making a declaration without having reasonable grounds for the stated opinion is a criminal offence leading on conviction to the possibility of imprisonment and/or a fine. If the company is wound up within twelve months after the making of the declaration, and if the debts of the company are not paid within twelve months of the commencement of the winding-up, then there is a statutory presumption that directors did not have reasonable grounds for making the statutory declaration of solvency.

4.8.5.2 Shareholder protection

The shareholders are protected through being notified about the transaction in advance and being given the opportunity of considering it. Notice of the extraordinary general meeting at which the matter will be considered must be accompanied by a copy of the statutory declaration of solvency. Notice must be given to all shareholders regardless of whether or not under the articles of association they have the right to receive notice and to attend the special resolution meetings.

If all of those entitled to vote do actually vote in favour the transaction may proceed. Otherwise, if because of absence, abstention or voting against, there is not unanimity, there is a waiting period of thirty days during which a shareholder may apply to court to have the transaction blocked. Those who voted in favour of the resolution may not subsequently object: s. 60(10). Shareholders wishing to challenge the decision must have at least 10 per cent of the nominal value of the issued share capital or any class of issued share capital: s. 60(9). Any court challenge must be launched within twenty-eight days after the day on which the special resolution was passed: s. 60(11).

Often the validation procedure will be organised so that all members are consenting and, therefore, the extraordinary general meeting may be held on the same day as notices are issued. This may be achieved if all the members consent to the meeting being held at short notice and the auditors consent as well.

4.8.5.3 Filing requirements

It is of crucial importance that s. 60(2)(b) is strictly adhered to. A copy of the directors' declaration of solvency must be filed in the Companies Registration Office on the same day as the day on which notices of the extraordinary general meeting are sent out to shareholders. Failure to comply with this requirement means that the validation procedure is not applicable.

Strict compliance with the various procedural requirements of the section is necessary. For example in the case of *Re Northside Motor Co Ltd*, 24 June 1985, HC (unreported), efforts to comply with s. 60 were not made until after the financial assistance had been granted. In addition, Costello J considered that the special resolution which was in fact passed was inaccurate. On either ground the section would not have been complied with. Subsequently in the case of *Lombard & Ulster Banking Ltd v Bank of Ireland*, 2 June 1987, HC (unreported), Costello J emphasised that 'if the procedural requirements were not adopted the transaction is an illegal one'.

4.8.5.4 Consequences of breach

Any transaction in breach of s. 60 is voidable at the instance of the company against any person with notice of the facts which constitute the breach. It is important to note that it is notice of the facts and not notice of the legal consequence of the facts that is important here. Therefore, if anyone in the relevant organisation knows the circumstances but fails to appreciate the legal significance that will still constitute adequate notice to that organisation.

The most likely situation in which a company will endeavour to avoid such a transaction is where the company has been wound up and the liquidator is endeavouring to set aside security granted to a bank in relation to the transaction.

The Supreme Court has decided in *Bank of Ireland Finance Ltd v Rockfield Ltd* [1979] IR 21 that notice in this context means actual knowledge and not constructive notice. In the circumstances of that case, even though s. 60 had not been complied with, the bank security survived because the bank did not have actual notice of the relevant facts. Costello J went into further detail in the *Lombard & Ulster* case (on p. 11 of the unreported judgment):

> 'It must be shown that [the party] had "actual notice" of the facts which constitute the breach, that is (a) that they or their officials actually knew that the required procedures were not adopted or that they knew facts from which they must have inferred that the

company had failed to adopt the required procedures or (b) that an agent of theirs actually knew of the failure or knew facts from which he must have inferred that a failure had occurred.'

If a company contravenes s. 60 then every officer who is in default is liable on conviction to a fine or imprisonment or both.

4.8.5.5 Exceptions

Section 60(12) specifically states that s. 60 does not prohibit the payment of a dividend properly declared or the discharge of a liability lawfully incurred. Regulation 116 of Table A states that the company in general meeting may declare dividends. While under regulation 117 the directors may pay interim dividends it seems clear that the exception given by s. 60(12) applies only to final dividends as declared by the company in general meeting. One consequence of this interpretation would appear to be that interim dividends are not included within the exception.

There has been some debate about the limits on the concept of a liability lawfully incurred. In particular from time-to-time questions arise as to whether a transaction at an inflated value or on unusual terms would qualify. In the British case of *Belmont Finance Corporation v Williams Furniture Ltd (No. 2)* [1980] 1 All ER 393 the company acquired an asset at a fair price from a third party. The case was rather an extreme example because it seemed clear that the company had no need for the asset bought and that the sole reason for entering into the transaction was to put the other party in funds to buy the shares. The court decided that this was not a lawfully-incurred liability within the meaning of the equivalent English legislation. Specifically the court refused to give a view on a hypothetical situation where there was some commercial reason for the transaction and funding the potential share-holder was another reason.

In the case of *Charterhouse Investment Trust Ltd v Templest Diesels Limited* [1986] BCLC 1 the transaction under consideration was a management buyout. As the target company was in financial difficulties the vendor parent company agreed to improve the financial state of the company, including, for example, injecting £750,000 in cash into the company, making redundancy payments and rearranging intra-group debt terms all in exchange for the target company surrendering tax losses.

Hoffmann J (now Lord Hoffmann) decided that the transaction did not constitute financial assistance within the meaning of the equivalent English section. He stated that the transaction should be looked at as a whole to decide whether it constituted the giving of financial assistance. In this case, the target company was substantially better off after the transaction. The judge decided that the surrendering of the tax losses did not amount to financial assistance.

Various provisions of the judgment have been cited with approval by McCracken J in the case of *Re CH (Ireland) Inc*, 12 December 1997, HC (unreported). However, the focus on the purpose and overall effect of the transaction does not seem to give sufficient weight to the wording of the section which also allows for financial assistance to arise where the transaction is not for the purpose of, but is in connection with, a subscription or purchase of shares. Given that breach of the section may result in a criminal sanction, it is under-standable the judges have given narrow interpretations where there is room for doubt. McCracken J endorsed Hoffmann J's common sense approach that:

'The words have no technical meaning and their frame of reference is in my judgment the language of ordinary commerce. One must examine the commercial realities of the transaction and decide whether it can properly be described as the giving of financial assistance by the company, bearing in mind that the section is a penal one and should not be strained to cover transactions which are not fairly within it.'

The difficulty for the practitioner is forecasting whether in a subsequent case a judge will adopt a similarly purposive approach rather than a literal interpretation of how the section applies. Until the position is clarified by further legislation a cautious approach is probably the more prudent route to take.

4.8.5.6 Public company subsidiaries

The European Communities (Public Limited Companies Subsidiaries) Regulations 1997 restricted the circumstances in which certain companies could, among other things, provide financial assistance for the purchase of, or subscription for, shares in a parent public company. Until these regulations were introduced, the restrictions on public limited companies providing financial assistance could be avoided by having a subsidiary provide the assistance instead. While the provisions of the statutory instrument are quite difficult to decipher in so far as they relate to subsidiaries giving financial assistance, the starting point should always be to ascertain whether regulation 5 applies if assistance is being given in connection with a purchase of or subscription for shares in a plc.

4.8.5.7 Restricted director

If a director of the company is the subject of a restriction order pursuant to CA 1990, s. 150 then CA 1990, s. 155(2) stipulates that the company cannot avail of the validation procedures set out in CA 1963, s. 60(2)–(11). Therefore, if a company has a restricted director, the only financial assistance which may be given by that company is assistance within s. 60(12) and (13), which relate to properly declared dividends, lawfully incurred liabilities, lending money in the ordinary course of business and assisting employee share schemes.

4.8.6 TRANSACTIONS WITH DIRECTORS

Part III of CA 1990 placed extensive restrictions on transactions which could take place between the company, on the one hand, and directors or connected persons on the other hand. There was a concern that persons in positions of power could siphon off company assets, thereby depriving creditors and shareholders of items which should rightfully be kept by the company. In a sense the legislation was an extension of the capital maintenance rules, and in some ways created an asset maintenance rule. In practice the legislation has been difficult to interpret, has increased the costs of doing business and has not necessarily resulted in those disposed to improper activity refraining from such activity. The Company Law Enforcement Bill 2000 contains important amendments to the provisions of Part III.

4.8.6.1 Transactions

The legislation relates to loans, quasi-loans and credit transactions, as well as guarantees and security given in relation to loans, quasi-loans and credit transactions. Section 25(1) of CA 1990 confirms that the word 'guarantee' includes 'indemnity'.

A quasi-loan is defined by CA 1990, s. 25(2) as being a transaction under which the creditor pays a sum for the borrower or reimburses expenditure incurred on behalf of the borrower in circumstances where the borrower is to reimburse the creditor. Therefore, if the company pays a director's personal credit card bill, the company is acting as creditor and the director is a borrower from the company.

A credit transaction is defined by CA 1990, s. 25(3) as one in which the creditor supplies any goods or sells any land, enters into a hire purchase agreement or conditional sale agreement, leases or licenses the use of land, hires goods in return for periodical payments or otherwise disposes of land, or supplies goods or services on the understanding that payment is to be deferred. If a company leases a car to a director, the company is a creditor in a credit transaction.

4.8.6.2 Prohibitions on a company

Section 31 of CA 1990 provides that a company may not:

(a) make a loan or a quasi-loan to a director of a company or of its holding company or to a person connected with such a director;

(b) enter into a credit transaction as creditor for such a director or a person so connected; or

(c) enter into a guarantee or grant security in connection with a loan, quasi-loan or credit transaction to any other person for such a director or a person so connected.

4.8.6.3 Who are directors?

Section 27 of CA 1990 extends the meaning of 'director' to include shadow directors. These are persons in accordance with whose directions or instructions the appointed directors of the company are accustomed to act. There is an exception for professional advisers. Section 2(1) of CA 1963 defines a 'director' as including any person occupying the position of director by whatever name called.

4.8.6.4 Who is a connected person?

Who is a conncected person is a far more difficult question to answer. Section 26 of CA 1990 lists relevant persons as including the spouse, parent, brother, sister or child of the director. Note there is no age limitation in relation to the child. A person acting in his capacity as the trustee of any trust, the principal beneficiaries of which are the director, his spouse or any of his children or any corporate body which he controls is also a connected person. A partner of the director is a connected person but there is no guidance as to whether this refers to a business partner, a personal partner or both.

A body corporate is deemed to be connected with a director if it is controlled by that director. The section (in s. 26(3)) goes on to provide that a director is deemed to control a body corporate if, but only if, he is alone or together with the persons previously mentioned interested in more than one-half of the equity share capital of that body or entitled to exercise or control the exercise of more than one-half of the voting power at any general meeting of that body.

Under CA 1963, s. 155 equity capital means the issued share capital of the company excluding any part thereof which neither as respects dividends nor as respects capital carries any right to participate beyond a specified amount on a distribution. Therefore, to be excluded, the share capital must have participation rights, both in relation to dividends and capital, which are capped.

There has been some debate about the interaction of s. 26(2), which deems a body corporate to be connected with the director if it is controlled by that director, and s. 26(3) which sets out situations in which the body corporate is deemed to be controlled. Subsection (2) makes the body corporate a connected person if it is controlled by a director. Section 26(3) deems specified circumstances to amount to control. It is possible that a situation could arise where the facts do not amount to deemed control within s. 26(3) but could be equated with actual control, thereby falling within s. 26(2).

4.8.6.5 Exceptions

Minor transactions

Because various day-to-day transactions, such as the payment of personal expenses to be reimbursed in due course by the director, come within the s. 31 prohibition, s. 32 provides a threshold below which transactions do not infringe. If the net value of arrangements between a company and a director or a connected person are worth less than 10 per cent of the relevant assets of the company, then the exception applies.

Section 29(2) of CA 1990 defines 'relevant assets' as either the value of net assets determined by reference to the last set of statutory accounts laid before an annual general meeting or, if that has not happened, the amount of the called-up share capital. The range of the exception is further limited because it only applies where the company makes a loan or quasi-loan or enters into a credit transaction for the director or connected person. Granting a guarantee or providing security in respect of a loan, quasi-loan or credit transaction made for a director or connected person by a third party do not appear to be covered.

Furthermore, the utility of the s. 32 exception is further eroded because if the actual value of arrangements availing of s. 32 exceeds 10 per cent of the relevant assets for any reason, the arrangements must be reorganised within two months so that the 10 per cent level is not exceeded. Therefore, if the relevant asset value falls, for example, because the company is making losses, reorganisation of these arrangements may be needed. Because of this, s. 32 is only really of use for temporary arrangements.

A further impediment to s. 32 having any effective use is that s. 39 allows for unlimited personal liability to be imposed on a person who benefited from a s. 32 arrangement where a company being wound up is insolvent if the court concludes that the arrangements made a material contribution to the company's inability to pay its debts if they fell due. It is for the court to decide the extent of any personal liability on the basis of all the circumstances.

Intra-group

Section 34 provides a far more meaningful exception to the s. 31 prohibition. A company may make a loan or quasi-loan to another company in the same group. The company may also enter into a guarantee or provide security in connection with a loan or quasi-loan made by a third party to another company in the group. However, s. 34 does not cover all the eventualities prohibited by s. 34. In particular, a credit transaction or a guarantee or security in relation to a credit transaction is not mentioned in the exception. Care must be taken to ensure that s. 31 may be availed of and that the companies are actually in the same group within the meaning of CA 1963, s. 155. If the companies are merely associated or are controlled by the one individual without being in a group then s. 34 cannot apply.

Holding company

Section 35 allows a company to enter into a loan, quasi-loan or credit transaction and to guarantee and give security in relation to loans, quasi-loans or credit transactions in respect of its holding company. The combined effect of ss. 34 and 35 is that while a subsidiary may enter into any of the transactions prohibited by s. 31 for its holding company, a holding company may not do likewise (in respect of credit transactions) for its subsidiaries, and sister companies may not do likewise (in respect of credit transactions) for other sister companies.

Ordinary course of business

Section 37 enables transactions in the ordinary course of business on arm's length terms to take place without coming within the prohibitions set out in s. 31. The value of the transaction must not be greater, and the terms in which it is entered into must not be more beneficial for the person for whom the transaction is made, than that or those which the company ordinarily offers or it is reasonable to expect the company to have offered to a person of the same financial standing as the director or connected person. However, while the exception relates to loans, quasi-loans and credit transactions, it does not mention guarantees or security in relation to loans, quasi-loans and credit transactions.

8.6.6 Consequences of breach

Section 38 sets out civil remedies. The transaction is voidable at the instance of the company (which will include any liquidator). Purchasers for value without actual notice take precedence. The transaction will not be avoided if restitution is no longer possible or if the company has been indemnified for the loss or damage suffered by it. Furthermore, the benefiting director or connected person, along with every director who approved the transaction, is liable to the company for any gain made and must indemnify the company for any loss suffered by the company. Lack of actual notice of the circumstances which constitute the contravention is a good defence but, as with s. 60, the defence is lack of actual knowledge of the facts which give rise to the contravention rather than lack of actual knowledge of the legal consequences of those facts.

An offence is committed by an officer of the company who permits the contravention of s. 31. Likewise, a person who procures a company to enter into a transaction prohibited by s. 31 is also guilty of an offence.

4.8.6.7 Substantial property transactions

Less severe restrictions are placed on substantial property transactions. Nevertheless, compliance with the relevant provisions of CA 1990, s. 29 is equally important because the consequences likewise involve the transaction being voidable. If a director or connected person is acquiring a non-cash asset of a certain value then the transaction must be approved by an ordinary resolution of the company in general meeting and (if the person is a director or a person connected to a director of the holding company) a resolution in general meeting of the holding company.

A non-cash asset has the requisite value if the value is at least £1,000. Once that threshold has been met, the test to be applied is whether it is worth more than the lesser of £50,000 or 10 per cent of the net asset value, in accordance with the last statutory accounts laid before the annual general meeting or if there are no such accounts the amount of the called-up share capital.

Breach of s. 29 results in the transaction being voidable at the instance of the company (which would include a liquidator). Purchasers for value without notice, the provision of an indemnity for loss or damage suffered by the company, ratification by the company in general meeting within a reasonable period or the impossibility of restitution prevent avoidance being used.

However, the director, connected person and any director authorising the transaction will be made liable to account for any gain made and to indemnify the company for any loss or damage suffered by the company.

No ordinary resolution is required for substantial property transactions between a holding company and a wholly-owned subsidiary or between two wholly-owned subsidiaries of the one holding company.

4.8.6.8 Proposed changes

The Company Law Enforcement Bill 2000 will make very important changes to Part III of CA 1990. While it is always dangerous to speculate about draft legislation, this Bill, which also contains provisions in relation to company law enforcement generally, may be enacted during 2001.

If the legislation is passed in its current form then the burden imposed on practitioners by Part III of CA 1990 will be lessened. Instead of an outright prohibition with obscure exceptions, the regime will be one where a company will be allowed to guarantee and give security for obligations of directors and connected persons if:

(a) a declaration of solvency similar to that required by CA 1990, s. 60 and by CA 1963, s. 256 in relation to the members voluntary winding-up is made; and

(b) an independent person's report confirming that the company will be able to pay its debts as they fall due (made by the auditor or person qualified to be auditor) is available.

Unfortunately the Bill does not clarify the vagueness in the interaction between s. 26(2) and s. 26(3) in relation to control. However, clarification will be given in so far as 'partner' means being in partnership pursuant to the Partnership Act 1890 rather than any personal relationship.

The provisions of s. 32 will be made even less attractive because the consequence of not rearranging matters within two months of the 10 per cent threshold being breached will be that the arrangements will become voidable by the company. However, s. 35 will be made more clear and the current artificial distinction between transactions within a group will be removed so that any company in the group will be able to enter into a loan, quasi-loan or credit transaction or grant a guarantee or give security in relation to a loan, quasi-loan or credit transaction for any company.

CHAPTER 5

PARTNERSHIPS

5.1 Nature of Partnerships

5.1.1 IMPORTANCE OF PARTNERSHIP LAW

5.1.1.1 General

Partnerships occupy an important part of Irish business life for a number of reasons.

First, partnership is the default form of business organisation in the sense that any time two or more people carry on a business venture without forming a company, they will invariably be partners. This point is highlighted by the case of *Joyce v Morrissey* [1998] TLR 707 which involved *The Smiths*, the 1980's rock band. A dispute arose about the sharing of the band's profits between, on the one side, the lead singer (Morrissey) and lead guitar player (Johnnie Marr) and, on the other side, the drummer and bass guitarist. Although the four may never have thought that they were creating a partnership when they formed the band, it was held that they were carrying on business as partners and therefore the rules in the Partnership Act 1890 about the division of profits applied to them. In that case, it meant that all four were entitled to share the band's profits equally and the court rejected Morrissey's and Marr's claim that as they were the main creative force behind the band, they were entitled to a greater share of the profits. In most cases, any time two or more people carry on business together without doing it through the medium of a registered company, they constitute a partnership and are subject to partnership law. Indeed, even where two or more companies are involved in business together, they will be subject to partnership law if they do not form a special purpose joint venture company for the project.

The second reason partnerships form an integral part of Irish business life is because there is a large section of Irish business which is effectively required to use partnerships to operate. This is because professionals such as lawyers, doctors, dentists, vets and accountants are not allowed to incorporate. Thus, any time two or more such professionals carry on business together, they will invariably be partners.

The third and final reason why partnerships occupy an important role in Irish business life is because they provide significant tax, accounting and disclosure advantages over companies. For example, in a company both corporation tax and income tax are paid in respect of the profits of the enterprise, i.e. corporation tax is paid on the company's profits and income tax is paid on the company's dividends paid to shareholders. However, a partnership is 'see-through' for tax purposes and therefore there is only one point at which tax is payable on the enterprise's profits, i.e. income tax is paid by the partners on the share of the profits received by them and no tax is paid by the partnership. As regards disclosure and accounting advantages, partnerships do not generally have to publicly file their accounts while companies do and it is considerably easier and cheaper for partners to subscribe and withdraw capital from a partnership than it is for shareholders in a limited company, thus making partnerships popular venture capital vehicles.

112

For the foregoing reasons, it follows that a lawyer, whether having a large corporate practice or a general practice, will encounter clients who either consciously or unconsciously are in business partnerships and who will require advice on the applicable law. In addition, the solicitors themselves may be partners in a law firm, since approximately one out of every four solicitors is a partner in a law firm. Perhaps the most important aspect of partnership law is the fact that the Partnership Act 1890 implies standard terms into every partnership unless the parties agree otherwise. Since many of these implied terms are inappropriate for modern partnerships, it is imperative that every partner and his legal adviser be aware of those terms and have a written partnership agreement which replaces them with more appropriate terms.

5.1.1.2 Partnership versus company

It is useful at this juncture to compare partnerships with the main form of business association in Ireland, the registered company. A partnership, unlike a company, is not a separate legal entity from its members, thus explaining why a company is taxed separately while a partnership is not taxed but the partners are taxed. Similarly, it is to be noted that partnerships are not required to go through any registration process to be formed, while companies have to be registered in the Companies Office. On the other hand, the main advantage that limited companies have over partnerships is that the shareholders have limited liability while partners have unlimited liability. Yet it should be remembered that partners may themselves be limited liability companies and in this way have an effective cap on their liability. In addition, in many companies (particularly in small businesses), limited liability is largely illusory because of the common requirement for directors and often their spouses to provide personal guarantees to banks and other creditors.

In addition, as is noted hereunder (see **5.6** below), there are two other types of partnerships in which some of the partners have limited liability, namely the limited partnership and the investment limited partnership. In this section, however, we concentrate on ordinary partnerships.

5.1.1.3 Why is it important to determine whether a partnership exists?

In this section, we look at the rules for determining whether a partnership has come into existence as well as some of the formalities for the operation of partnerships. The question of whether a partnership exists is important because a partner is liable for the losses which his co-partner causes in carrying on the partnership business and this includes situations where he/she has defrauded clients of the business. On the other hand, a partner is also entitled to an equal share of the partnership profits and for this reason, in a profitable business, it would be an advantage to be a partner. Another situation where it is important to establish whether a partnership exists is where a potential plaintiff is faced with a penniless defendant. If the defendant is carrying on business with a richer business colleague, it would be useful to establish that his richer business colleague is his partner and therefore jointly liable for the damages suffered by the potential plaintiff. Clearly, in these types of situations the question of whether a partnership exists will be of importance.

.1.2 RELEVANT LAW

Much of the law relating to partnerships is to be found in the Partnership Act 1890 ('1890 Act'). The 1890 Act was a codification of the law of partnership as it had developed up to 1890. However, it is important to note that the Act does not provide a complete code of partnership law, and indeed s. 46 specifically provides that:

> *The rules of equity and of common law applicable to partnership shall continue in force except so far as they are inconsistent with the express provisions of this Act.*

Therefore regard must always be had to the case law from both before and after the 1890 Act.

5.1.3 DEFINITION OF PARTNERSHIP

5.1.3.1 General

The definition of a partnership is to be found in s. 1(1) of the 1890 Act which states: 'Partnership is the relation which subsists between persons carrying on a business in common with a view of profit'. Where people carry on business in common through the medium of a company, they are specifically excluded from being partners by s. 1(2) of the 1890 Act. It should be noted that a written partnership agreement is not a prerequisite for the existence of a partnership since the court will have regard to the true contract and intention of the parties as appearing from the whole facts of the case. To satisfy the definition of partnership two or more persons must be actually carrying on a business. It follows from this that an agreement to run a business in the future does not constitute an immediate partnership, nor does the taking of preliminary steps to enable a business to be run. Similarly, two or more people cannot agree that they were partners retrospectively unless they were actually carrying on business at the relevant time. In *Macken v Revenue Commissioners* [1962] IR 302, the parties signed a partnership agreement in the month of April, but it provided that the partnership 'shall be deemed to have commenced' in January of that same year. The High Court held that the partnership did not commence until the parties actually started carrying on business together which was in the month of April.

The definition of partnership in s. 1(1) also requires the parties to be carrying on business with a 'view of profit'. In *McCarthaigh v Daly* [1985] IR 73, the respondent, a prominent Cork based solicitor was involved in a rather clever tax loophole which has since been closed off by the Revenue Commissioners. Under that scheme Mr Daly agreed to contribute capital of £50 to a limited partnership connected with the Metropole Hotel in Cork in the tax year 1977–78. However, the arrangement was completely uneconomical and was clearly designed to make a loss, rather than a profit, which loss was to be used to reduce the income tax of Mr Daly on his personal income as a solicitor. Mr Daly sought to set off his share of the losses of the limited partnership which amounted to £2,000 against his personal income tax as a solicitor. O'Hanlon J in giving his decision was constrained by procedural rules. It is clear that if, it were not for the constraints of these procedural rules, O'Hanlon J would not have held that this arrangement constituted a partnership because of the absence of the 'view of profit'.

In addition to the definition of partnership in s. 1(1) of the 1890 Act, s. 2 of the 1890 Act lays down certain 'rules for determining the existence of a partnership'. These rules include the following:

- joint or common ownership of property 'does not of itself create a partnership' even where profits from the property are shared: s. 2(1);

- the sharing of gross returns does not of itself create a partnership: s. 2(2). The difference between gross returns and net profits is illustrated by the example of a person who sells goods on commission for another. Such a person will receive a percentage of the gross sales or gross returns of the business. However, if he was to receive a percentage of the profits, this would involve the additional step of calculating the costs and overheads which would have to be deducted from the gross returns to calculate the profits, if any, of the business. Thus, a percentage of the gross returns could be valuable while a percentage of the net profits might be nothing; and

- the receipt of a share of profits is prima facie evidence of partnership (s. 2(3)) but it does not of itself make the recipient a partner.

5.1.3.2 Distinction between partner and lender

At this juncture, it is appropriate to consider the distinction between a partner and a lender since it has been noted that s. 2(3) provides that a person who receives a share of the profits of a partnership is prima facie a partner. Obviously, this distinction is important in view of the unlimited liability of a partner for the debts of the partnership whereas the lender only stands to lose the money invested if the business fails. It is not unknown for some lenders/investors to wish to avoid the consequences of being a partner but at the same time share in the profits of the borrower's business. Subsections (a) to (e) of s. 2(3) of the 1890 Act provide for this and other such scenarios by stating that:

(a) a person does not become a partner merely because a debt is paid to him by instalments out of profits;

(b) an employee does not become a partner merely because his remuneration varies with profits;

(c) a widow or child of a partner is not a partner merely because a proportion of profits is paid to that person as an annuity;.

(d) a lender who receives a share of profits is not automatically a partner if the contract is in writing and signed by all the parties; and

(e) a vendor who receives payment for his business varying with profits is not automatically a partner.

However, there remains a risk that anyone who receives a share of profits may be held to be a partner and therefore personally liable for debts. For this reason, it is important for a lender who does not wish to take on the risk of unlimited liability to ensure that he does not become a partner, e.g. by avoiding any suggestion that he has a right to take part in management and by having a written agreement setting out the terms of his involvement with the firm as required by s. 2(3)(d). It will often occur that the same fact situation will fall within more than one of the subsections of s. 2(3). This was the case in *Re Borthwick* (1875) ILTR 155 which concerned the payment of a share of the profits of a partnership business to an employee, Kirkpatrick, who was also a lender to the business. In that case, Kirkpatrick advanced £800 to Borthwick, a general merchant in Belfast. This sum was to be used to purchase Irish flax for the business. Under the terms of their agreement, Kirkpatrick was to receive repayments of interest and principal at a rate of half of the profits derived from the sale of the flax. On the bankruptcy of Borthwick, it was alleged by his assignees in bankruptcy that Kirkpatrick was a partner of Borthwick's and therefore should have his debt deferred to the other creditors of Borthwick (see further in relation to the deferral of a partner's debts on the bankruptcy of his partner, Twomey: *Partnership Law* (Butterworths, 2000) paras 27.153 et seq.). Harrison J held that Kirkpatrick, although the recipient of a debt out of the profits of Borthwick's business, was not his partner but his employee.

5.1.4 NUMBER OF PARTNERS

The Companies Act 1963, s. 376 prescribes that the maximum number of persons who may be members of a partnership is twenty. However, pursuant to s. 13 of the Companies (Amendment) Act 1982 solicitors and accountants are not subject to this limitation.

5.1.5 CAPACITY

Like any other contract, any person including a minor (a person under 18 or an unmarried person) is legally capable of entering into a partnership contract. Yet, the minor will not, during his minority, incur liability to his co-partners or to third parties for the debts of the firm or the acts of his co-partners: *Lovell and Christmas v Beauchamp* [1894] AC 607. In addition the contract is voidable at the instance of the minor.

Companies as well as individuals may enter into a partnership with other companies or with individuals, assuming that the companies have the power to do so under their objects clause.

In marital disputes, it is sometimes overlooked that spouses may be partners in relation to a family business or investments. Thus, there is no reason why one spouse would not be able to rely on the terms of the 1890 Act regarding the equal division of profits and assets on a dissolution of the partnership, which dissolution will invariably occur on the breakdown of a marriage.

5.1.6 TYPES OF PARTNERSHIPS AND PARTNERS

Every partnership is either a partnership at will (informal partnership) or a formal partnership (or, as it is sometimes called, a fixed-term partnership). A partnership at will is one which may be dissolved by any one partner at any time by notice: see 1890 Act, ss 26(1) and 32(c). Every partnership is presumed to be a partnership at will unless there is an express or implicit agreement to the contrary between the partners: *Murphy v Power* [1923] 1 IR 68. Where there is an express or implicit agreement to exclude the right of a partner to dissolve the partnership by notice, the resulting partnership is known as a formal partnership (fixed-term partnership). The exclusion of this right is often achieved implicitly, e.g. by the agreement that the partnership will last for a fixed term and the majority of formal partnerships are such fixed-term partnerships.

In addition to there being different types of partnerships, there may also be different types of partners. Two types of partners are worthy of specific mention, i.e. a dormant partner and a salaried partner. A dormant partner is a partner who plays no active role in the business of the partnership. However, the term has no legal significance since a dormant partner has the same rights and liabilities as any other partner and so he is entitled to an equal share of the profits of the firm, he is equally liable for the losses of the firm and he is entitled to take part in the management of the firm.

The term 'salaried partner' is in fact a contradiction in terms, since he is not a partner but an employee. A salaried partner is a person who normally operates in the middle rank of professional partnerships between true partners and salaried employees. The salaried partner is held out to the world as a partner yet he receives a salary and sometimes a bonus by way of remuneration but he does not receive a share of the profits like a normal partner. In addition he is not entitled to the other rights of partnership, e.g. to vote at partners' meetings, to dissolve the firm etc. However, as regards outsiders who deal with the firm, the salaried partner is as good as a partner. This is because he is held out to be a 'partner' and thus will be liable to third parties who relied on the fact that he was a partner under the principle of holding out as a partner, which is considered below: see **5.3.4**. For this reason, it is advisable for a salaried partner to receive an indemnity from the partners in respect of such potential liabilities to third parties.

5.1.7 BUSINESS NAME OF PARTNERSHIP

Partnerships commonly trade under a name other than the names of the partners. This has implications under the Registration of Business Names Act 1963 since if the business of a partnership is carried on under a name which does not consist solely of the surnames of all the partners, then the firm must register this name as a business name (Business Names Act 1963, ss. 3(1)(a) and 4) and it must publish the true names of the partners on the stationery of the firm: Business Names Act 1963, s. 18. The case of *Macken v Revenue Commissioners* [1962] IR 302 highlights that although the filing in the register of business names may appear to be troublesome red tape, it may be important at a subsequent date in establishing that a certain person had become, or had ceased to be, a partner. There, the High Court held that no partnership existed between a father and his two children who traded under the name 'Patrick Macken & Son'. One of the factors in the court's decision that the children were not partners was that they had not registered that name as a business name. They would have had to do this if it was a partnership since the name 'Patrick Macken & Son' was not the name of the three purported partners.

5.1.8 WHY A WRITTEN PARTNERSHIP AGREEMENT IS ESSENTIAL

The effect of the 1890 Act for partnerships is like the effect of Table A of the Companies Act 1963 for companies. This is because, like Table A, the 1890 Act sets out certain basic terms of the partnership agreement which will apply to every partnership, save in so far as they are modified or excluded by the partners. In this sense, the 1890 Act may be viewed as a default partnership agreement whose terms apply to every partnership if they are not excluded. For this reason it is crucial for partners and their advisers to be aware of all of the rights and duties which are implied by the 1890 Act and then to decide which of them are appropriate for the partnership and which of them should be modified by the terms of the partnership agreement.

Unlike Table A, where the majority of the terms of Table A are appropriate for most companies, it is fair to say that the majority of the terms of the 1890 Act are wholly inappropriate for most partnerships. It is for this reason that it is crucial that most partnerships have a written partnership agreement and that such a partnership agreement expressly provides terms which are contrary to those contained in the 1890 Act. A few examples will illustrate how inappropriate the 1890 Act is for most partnerships:

(a) There is no right under the default partnership agreement to expel a partner. Thus, no matter how unprofessional or negligent or belligerent a partner is, his co-partners may not expel him from the partnership in the absence of a right of expulsion.

(b) In every partnership at will, regardless of the number of partners in the firm, be it two or thirty-two, any one partner in the firm may dissolve the partnership by simply arriving at a partners' meeting and giving notice orally that the firm is dissolved.

(c) If a partner dies, the firm will automatically dissolve under the terms of s. 33 of the 1890 Act and may be wound up at the wish of any one partner. There is no general right in law to acquire a deceased partner's share, so if the surviving partners want the firm to continue, they have to enter negotiations with the deceased partner's estate to purchase this share. Therefore, a written partnership agreement should provide that the death of a partner will not dissolve the firm but instead that the deceased partner's share may be purchased by the surviving partners pursuant to an agreed valuation mechanism.

(d) There is no general power to retire under partnership law. Thus, the only possibility for a partner who wishes to retire in the absence of a retirement provision is for him to dissolve the partnership. This is a drastic solution and accordingly it is important to have a provision allowing a partner to retire.

These are but four examples of why a carefully drafted partnership agreement is necessary to avoid the full rigours of the 1890 Act (see further Twomey: *Partnership Law*, paras 21.03 et seq.). The only way to ensure against these and other rights which may be inappropriate in a partnership is to have a carefully drafted provision in the partnership agreement excluding those rights.

Finally, in considering the application of the terms of a partnership agreement to the day-to-day running of a firm, it is important to bear in mind the terms of the 1890 Act, s. 19. Section 19 provides that the rights of partners may be varied by express or implied consent. For this reason, in some circumstances it may be prudent for a partner who is conducting himself contrary to his express rights under the partnership agreement to clarify in writing that such action is not to be construed as an implied variation of the terms of the partnership agreement.

5.2 Partners' Rights Inter Se

5.2.1 INTRODUCTION

Once it is established that a partnership is in existence, the next step is to determine the respective rights of the partners inter se, and in this section consideration is given to these rights. It has been noted that the 1890 Act operates for partnerships very much like Table A of the Companies Act 1963 operates for companies, since in the absence of any other agreement between the partners, the terms of their partnership agreement may be found in the 1890 Act. It has also been seen that some of these default rules are inappropriate for modern partnerships and therefore the partners may wish to have a written partnership agreement which excludes them. Reference has already been made to one of those default rules, namely the right of any one partner to dissolve the partnership by giving notice. Reference will now be made to the other important default rules in the 1890 Act regarding the internal operations of a partnership.

5.2.2 MANAGEMENT OF THE PARTNERSHIP

Section 24(5) of the 1890 Act states that, subject to contrary agreement, express or implied, '[e]very partner may take part in the management of the partnership business'. If the management structure of a particular partnership is to be different from the equality of partners presumed by s. 24(5), then express agreement should be made. For example, in the large professional partnerships, it is usual for the partnership agreement to provide for the management of the firm to be delegated to a management committee.

5.2.2.1 Decisions of the partners

Section 24(8) of the 1890 Act says that (subject to contrary agreement, express or implied)

[a]ny differences arising as to ordinary matters connected with the partnership business may be decided by a majority of the partners, but no change may be made in the nature of the partnership business without the consent of all the partners.

It should be noted that the expression 'majority of the partners' means a majority in number and not on the basis of capital contribution, profit-share or otherwise. It follows that under the default partnership agreement, a simple majority of the partners is required to take a decision regarding ordinary partnership matters. If the partners desire a different voting system, an express term must be put in the partnership agreement. In the case of *Highley v Walker* (1910) 26 TLR 685, the taking on of one of the partner's sons as an apprentice in the partnership business was regarded as an ordinary matter within the terms of s. 24 (8) and therefore it only required a decision of the majority of the partners and not a unanimous decision of the partners. If there is an equality of votes between the partners the law provides that a decision is deemed not to be taken and the status quo is preserved: *Clements v Norris* (1878) 8 Ch D 129.

5.2.2.2 Restrictions on majority rule

There are two main limitations imposed on the ability of the majority of the partners to bind the whole firm.

First, partners are under a fiduciary duty to each other and so must exercise their powers for the benefit of the firm as a whole. For example, in *Heslin v Fay (No. 1)* (1884) 15 LR Ir 431, the partnership agreement for a grocery store in North King Street in Dublin gave one partner, Fay, the power to increase the capital of the firm if it was necessary for carrying on the business of the firm. The agreement also entitled each partner to withdraw the amount of any surplus capital paid by him to the partnership. When one of the partners, Heslin, called on his co-partners to repay the surplus capital which he had paid to the firm, Fay responded by raising the capital of the firm, so as to reduce the amount of the surplus owed to Heslin. It was held that Fay had no right to use his power of increasing the capital for the purpose of resisting Heslin's demand for a return of his surplus capital and, for this reason, Heslin was granted a dissolution of the partnership. Thus, a partner owes a fiduciary duty to his fellow partners and an important aspect of this is the requirement to show the utmost good faith in his dealings with them much like the duty a trustee owes to a beneficiary, and this aspect of a partner's fiduciary duty is considered further below at **5.2.4**.

The second main type of limitation on the majority rule is to be found in the following provisions of the 1890 Act:

- Section 24(8) requires unanimity for a change in the partnership business. This is because a partner who has decided to invest in one particular type of business may not be forced to invest in something else against his wishes.

- Section 24(7) provides that: 'No person may be introduced as a partner without the consent of all the existing partners'. Such a rule is vital to the running of a small partnership where each partner will wish to ensure that his fellow partners cannot force him to go into partnership with someone of whom he disapproves. In large firms, it is common to exclude this default rule by allowing for a new partner to be admitted by a vote of 75 per cent or more of the partners.

- Section 25 prevents expulsion of a partner by a majority of the partners unless all the partners have expressly agreed to such a power being conferred. Since there is no right of expulsion under the default partnership agreement, one reason for having a written partnership agreement is to provide the partners with such a right.

Finally another limitation on majority rule in partnerships is the general common law principle that, like any contract, a partnership contract may not be amended without the consent of all the signatories, although it is possible for an amendment to the partnership agreement to be inferred from a course of dealings by all the partners.

5.2.3 OTHER PROVISIONS OF THE 1890 ACT AFFECTING PARTNERS' RIGHTS INTER SE

Other provisions of s. 24 which affect the relationship between the partners are as follows:

- Section 24(2) gives a partner a right to be indemnified by the firm in respect of payments made and personal liabilities incurred 'in the ordinary and proper conduct of the business of the firm or in or about anything necessarily done for the preservation of the business or property of the firm'.

- Section 24(9) gives all the partners a right to inspect and copy the partnership accounts.

5.2.4 A PARTNER'S FIDUCIARY DUTY TO HIS CO-PARTNERS

5.2.4.1 Generally

The existence of a partner's fiduciary duty to his co-partners has long been recognised by the courts. It is because they trust one another that they are partners in the first instance and therefore the partners are required not to abuse this trust and this duty between fiduciaries is the primary control of partners' behaviour inter se. In the case of *Williams v Harris*, 15 January 1980, HC (unreported) McWilliam J recognised the existence of a partner's fiduciary duty and he noted that 'the mere existence of a partnership creates a fiduciary relationship between the partners'. In addition to this general common law duty, the 1890 Act recognises a number of aspects of the duty in ss 28–30.

5.2.4.2 1890 Act, s. 28

Section 28 provides that:

> *Partners are bound to render true accounts and full information of all things affecting the partnership to any partner or his legal representative.*

The Scottish case of *Ferguson v MacKay* 1985 SLT 1994 provides a good example of this fiduciary duty. It concerned a solicitor who was retiring from his firm and who was negotiating the terms of his retirement package with his partners. Before finalising these terms, his partners failed to disclose that three substantial conveyancing instructions had been received by the firm. After the retirement package was agreed, the retiring partner discovered that his co-partners had been less than frank in relation to these lucrative instructions. The court held that his co-partners had breached their fiduciary duty to give him full information on all things affecting the partnership and granted damages to the retiring partner for this breach.

5.2.4.3 1890 Act, s. 29

Section 29 provides that a partner must account to the firm for any profits made from partnership property in the following terms:

> *(1) Every partner must account to the firm for any benefit derived by him without the consent of the other partners from any transaction concerning the partnership, or from any use by him of the partnership property, name or business connexion.*
>
> *(2) This section applies also to transactions undertaken after a partnership has been dissolved by the death of a partner, and before the affairs thereof have been completely wound up, either by any surviving, partner or by the representatives of the deceased partner.*

The principle in s. 29 to account for private profits made by partners applies also to 'partnership opportunities' so that if a transaction was entered into by a partner where the opportunity came to him as a result of the partnership and which might have been used to benefit the partnership, he will have to account to his partners for the benefit he derived therefrom unless his partners have consented to the transaction following full disclosure of the circumstances. The concept underlying this principle is that these opportunities are regarded as partnership property and therefore may not be appropriated by one partner for his exclusive benefit.

5.2.4.4 1890 Act, s. 30

Section 30 of the 1890 Act provides that:

> *If a partner, without the consent of the other partners, carries on any business of the same nature as and competing with that of the firm, he must account for and pay over to the firm all profits made by him in that business.*

In *Lock v Lynam* (1854) 4 Ir Ch R 188, the parties had agreed to enter a partnership for the purpose of obtaining contracts for the supply of meat to British troops based in Ireland. During the operation of this partnership, Lynam entered into similar arrangements with third persons, whereby he was to share in the profits of similar contracts, if obtained by them. Lock sought an account of the profits of these contracts which Lynam had with third parties. Lynam argued that there was no agreement with Lock that he would not enter into similar contracts with third parties. Nonetheless, Lord Chancellor Brady held that such conduct by Lynam was a breach of his duty of good faith to his partner and he ordered that an account of those contracts be taken.

It remains to be observed that there is overlap between s. 30 and s. 29(1), since a partner who continues as a partner but at the same time sets up a new business may be held accountable to his partners because he is competing with his firm *or* because he is using 'the partnership property name or business connection' for his own benefit.

120

5.2.4.5 No common law restriction on former partner competing with firm

A related issue concerns the position of a former partner. It should be noted that a partner's fiduciary duty to his co-partners does not prevent a *former* partner from competing with his former firm in the absence of an agreement to that effect. Thus, a party to a partnership agreement governed only by the default terms of the 1890 Act who leaves the partnership and sets up a competing business and who does not use the partnership property, name or business connection is not liable to his partners in any way under the 1890 Act. For this reason, it is common for written partnership agreements to have non-compete clauses. Any such restriction must however comply with the Competition Act 1991. In the Competition Authority decision in *Doyle/Moffit*, 10 June 1994 the agreement between two vets provided for Moffit to gradually acquire Doyle's partnership share over the life of the partnership and their partnership agreement restricted Doyle, for five years from the date of his retirement and within twenty miles of the practice, from acting as a vet for any clients of the firm. The Competition Authority held that in terms of geographic coverage (twenty miles) and subject matter (veterinary surgeon) the restriction was reasonable but in terms of duration (five years) it was excessive since, in general, non-compete clauses of more than two years are longer than necessary to secure the transfer of the goodwill and therefore offend against s. 4(1) of the Competition Act 1991.

5.2.5 FINANCIAL RIGHTS AND DUTIES OF PARTNERS

5.2.5.1 Capital

The capital of a partnership is the cause of more confusion than most other areas of partnership law. This is caused in part by the confusion between the assets or other property of a partnership on the one hand, and its capital on the other hand. This confusion will be avoided if the capital of a firm is thought of as the sum which is contributed by the partners to establish the firm. The capital of a partner may be contributed in the form of cash or in the form of property (including, for example, business premises or the goodwill of an existing business).

5.2.5.2 Division of profits and sharing of losses

Section 24 of the 1890 Act lays down a number of rules as to division of profits. These rules are default rules since they may be varied by an express or implied agreement of the partners. Nevertheless, even if the default rules are to apply, the partnership agreement should state the ratios in which profits and losses of income and profits and losses of capital are to be divided between the partners, in order to avoid any confusion. The main default provision is to be found in s. 24 (1) of the 1890 Act which provides that:

> *All the partners are entitled to share equally in the capital and profits of the business, and must contribute equally towards the losses whether of capital or otherwise sustained by the firm.*

Thus s. 24(1) provides as regards the sharing of profits that they are to be shared equally. The contribution of capital in unequal shares does not give rise to the implication that profits are not to be shared equally. If a partner is to receive more than an equal share of profits because of his capital contribution or the work he does or for any other reason, this must be specifically agreed to and should be expressly stated in the partnership agreement.

As regards the sharing of losses, s. 24(1) states that the default rule is that losses are shared equally. However, if the partners share profits unequally (because of an express or implied agreement to do so), then losses of capital or of income will also be shared in the same proportion unless there is an agreement to the contrary. This principle is clear from s. 44(a) and s. 44 (b)(4) of the 1890 Act and also from the case of *Robinson v Ashton* (1875) LR 20 Eq 25.

5.2.5.3 Redistribution of capital contributions and sharing of capital losses and profits

Section 24(1) states that 'all the partners are entitled to share equally in the capital'. Particular care should be taken with this phrase since it does not mean that the capital which was contributed unequally by partners is treated as an aggregate fund to be divided between the partners in equal shares. Rather, this reference to 'capital' must be read as being first subject to the requirement in s. 44(b)(3) of the 1890 Act that capital contributions are repaid to the partners rateably according to the amount of their respective contributions. The effect of this part of s. 24(1) is that once the capital contributions have been repaid, the partners share equally in the capital profit or divide the capital losses equally, unless they have agreed a different sharing ratio. If there is no specific agreement regarding capital profits and capital losses, then if the profits or losses of income have been agreed by the partners to be shared unequally, the profits and losses of capital, in the absence of a specific agreement, will be shared in that proportion: 1890 Act, s. 44(a) and (b)(4) and *Robinson v Ashton* (1875) LR 20 Eq 25. The partners are, of course, free to agree to any form of division they like and, for example, they may decide that capital profits should be divided in the same ratio as capital was contributed by the partners.

5.2.5.4 Interest on capital

Section 24(4) provides that in the absence of contrary agreement 'A partner is not entitled ... to interest on capital'. Where capital is contributed unequally it may be considered appropriate to make provision in the partnership agreement for interest on capital to be paid to the partners so as to compensate the partner who has contributed more. In such a case the partnership agreement should specify the rate of interest to be paid. At the end of the firm's financial year, the net profit of the firm is determined and the partners' first entitlement will be to interest on capital and then the remaining net profit will be allocated in accordance with the agreed profit-sharing ratio.

5.2.5.5 Interest on loans

Section 24(3) also provides a default rule in respect of loans by a partner to his firm. It provides that, in the absence of contrary agreement, a loan by a partner to the partnership carries interest at the rate of 5 per cent. It should be noted that this rate of interest is paid only on 'actual payments or advances'. Interest is not payable under s. 24(3) on a share of profits which is simply left in the business in the shape of undrawn profits of a partner. The partners are, of course, free to agree that interest will be paid on undrawn profits if they wish.

5.2.5.6 Remuneration of partners

Another important default rule regarding partners' financial rights and duties is contained in s. 24(6) which provides that: 'No partner shall be entitled to remuneration for acting in the partnership business'. In some partnerships it may be appropriate to override this default rule, e.g. where the division of work between the partners is unequal and the partners agree that some of them are to be paid compensation for the extra work which they do. As with interest on capital, such a sum payable to a partner is merely a preferential appropriation of profit. It is important not to confuse such a partner who receives a preferential appropriation of profit with a 'salaried partner'. The latter is simply an employee of the firm who is held out to the world as a partner. He is not a partner since he is not 'carrying on business in common' with the partners but is employed by them.

5.2.5.7 Drawings

The amount of money which represents a partner's share of the profits of the firm will not be known until the profit and loss account of the firm has been drawn up after the end of the partnership's financial year. For this reason, it is usual for a partnership agreement to provide that the partners have the right to take a specified amount of money on account of their anticipated profits, known as 'drawings'. If at the end of the year the partner has taken less than he was entitled to, he may draw the balance. If he has taken more than his entitlement, the partnership agreement should provide for him to pay back the excess to the firm. Sometimes, the partnership agreement may provide that each partner is to leave undrawn in the business a proportion of his entitlement to profit. This is because businesses normally need to retain funds to meet increased costs of trading and to fund any future expansion.

5.2.6 PARTNERSHIP PROPERTY

In every partnership, it is important to determine which property is owned by the partnership and which property, although it may be used by the partnership, is the property of a partner or partners individually or of some third party. This is because partnership property, unlike the personal property of a partner which is used by the firm, must be used for the purposes of the partnership and so, for example, any increase in its value will accrue to the firm and not to an individual partner. In the case of the personal property of a partner, that partner will be entitled to use it as he wishes and on the bankruptcy of the firm or on his bankruptcy, the property is available for the benefit of his separate creditors, in priority to the firm's creditors.

This crucial question of whether property is partnership property is determined by the agreement and intention of the partners, be that express or implied. If the partners intend that property is to be partnership property, then the fact that it happens to be vested in one partner's name will be irrelevant to a finding that the property belongs to the firm. For this reason, each case must be determined according to its own set of circumstances. However, the 1890 Act assists in this enquiry by providing two rebuttable presumptions regarding the status of property as partnership property. Thus, it is presumed that property which is acquired for the purposes and in the course of the partnership business is partnership property since s. 20(1) of the 1890 Act provides that:

> All property and rights and interests in property originally brought into the partnership stock or acquired, whether by purchase or otherwise, on account of the firm, or for the purposes and in the course of the partnership business, are called in this Act partnership property, and must be held and applied by the partners exclusively for the purposes of the partnership and in accordance with the partnership agreement.

It is also presumed that property which is purchased with partnership funds is partnership property, since s. 21 of the 1890 Act provides:

> Unless the contrary intention appears, property bought with money belonging to the firm is deemed to have been bought on account of the firm.

Yet, one must not lose sight of the overriding importance of the intentions of the partners and these presumptions may therefore be rebutted in appropriate circumstances. *Murtagh v Costello* (1881) 7 LR Ir 428 illustrates that courts do not take a restrictive approach to determining whether property was acquired 'for the purposes of and in the course of the partnership business' as required by s. 20(1) of the 1890 Act. In that case, the partnership agreement provided for the parties to become partners as flour merchants and 'in all other matters in which the majority of them should agree to trade or deal'. During the course of the partnership, the partners acquired two pieces of freehold land in Athlone, which were purchased using partnership money and were conveyed into the name of two of the partners in trust for the firm. One piece of land was farmed by one of the partners, and the second piece of land was occupied by tenants. The profits from the farming and the rent from the tenants were brought into the profit and loss account of the firm. It was argued that neither piece of land was partnership property since farming and renting of property were not part of the trade of flour merchants. This argument was rejected by Chatterton

V-C who held that both properties were partnership property since the improvements thereon were paid for out of partnership money; the profits therefrom were entered into the profit and loss account and the lands themselves were entered in the balance sheet. It is clear therefore that the term 'partnership business' as used in s. 20(1) of the 1890 Act is not to be interpreted restrictively but rather includes a situation where property is not strictly within the description of partnership business as set out in the partnership agreement, provided that it is held for the benefit or on behalf of the partnership business.

To avoid a situation where a court has to decide the intention and agreement of the partners regarding the status of property, the question of which property is partnership property should be clarified where practicable in the partnership agreement. Indeed, sometimes of equal importance is a provision indicating which property is not partnership property. In the High Court case of *Barr v Barr*, 29 July 1992, HC (unreported), a wholesale grocery partnership in Donegal stored some of its goods in a garage which adjoined the home of one of the defendant partners. The garage appeared in the balance sheet of the firm and was held to be partnership property. However, the other partners claimed that the defendant's home was also partnership property. While the report does not indicate what evidence supported such a claim, it was rejected by Carroll J. Such problems could have been avoided by a provision in the partnership agreement clearly delineating which property was and which property was not partnership property.

5.3 Relations Between Partners and Third Parties

5.3.1 INTRODUCTION

In the course of carrying on the partnership's business, the partners will invariably incur debts and other obligations. In this section, we look at the nature of the partners' liabilities for these obligations as well as the extent to which an individual partner may bind the partnership as a whole. We will then go on to look at whether it is possible for individuals who are not in fact partners at the time the debt or obligation was incurred to be liable for that debt or obligation (whether because they have been held out as partners or because they are admitted to the partnership subsequently).

5.3.2 NATURE OF LIABILITY OF PARTNERS TO THIRD PARTIES

Partners are liable for the debts and obligations of the partnership without limitation: 1890 Act: ss. 9 and 10. Their liability is joint in the case of contractual obligations and joint and several in the case of tortious obligations. However, the significance of this distinction between joint and joint and several obligations was much reduced by the Civil Liability Act 1961 which now allows proceedings to be brought successively against persons jointly liable even where there has been an earlier judgment against other persons who were jointly liable for that obligation. Where a firm is unable to pay its debts out of partnership property, the creditor of that firm is entitled to obtain payment from the private estates of the partners. Special rules apply in such cases, so as to attempt to do justice both to the creditors of the firm and to the separate creditors of the individual partners. These rules are contained in the Bankruptcy Act 1988, s. 34. It is not intended to deal with these rules in detail (see further Twomey: *Partnership Law*, paras 27.01 et seq.). However, they may be summarised as follows:

- partnership property is used to pay partnership creditors in priority to the personal creditors of each partner;

- personal property of each partner is used to pay his personal creditors in priority to partnership creditors;

- if the personal creditors of a particular partner are paid in full from his personal property, then the partnership creditors may resort to the balance of that partner's personal property; and

- if the partnership creditors are paid in full from partnership property, the personal creditors of a partner may resort to the balance of his share of the partnership property.

5.3.3 AUTHORITY OF PARTNER TO BIND FIRM

5.3.3.1 Generally

The relationship between partnership law and the law of agency is very close and some of the rules regulating the relationship between a partnership and the outside world may be explained purely in terms of particular applications of agency principles and, in particular, from examining the nature of a partner's authority to bind the firm. In general terms, the partnership as a whole is bound by a partner acting within the scope of his authority. This authority of a partner may arise in three ways, i.e. express authority, implied authority and ostensible authority.

- Express authority is where the authority of the partners is specifically agreed upon by the partners.

- Implied authority is implied either from a course of dealings between the partners (which amounts to an actual agreement) or because the authority is a natural consequence of an authority actually given to the partner.

- Ostensible authority arises from the fact that a person dealing with a partner is, in certain circumstances, entitled to assume that the partner has authority to bind the firm.

The first two types of authority are categories of actual authority (in the sense that the partner has in fact authority to do the act in question) which distinguishes them from ostensible authority where there is no actual authority but, for the protection of third parties, the partner is deemed to have authority to do the act in question.

5.3.3.2 Express authority

The scope of express authority depends on the agreement between the parties. The partnership agreement may specify what powers the partners individually are to have and may specify that some partners are to have greater powers than others. The extent of express authority is not, in practical terms, of great significance to a person dealing with a partner. This is because, whether or not there is express authority, the third party will usually be able to rely on the ostensible authority of the partner. The outsider need only rely on express authority where the partner has done something which the law does not consider to be within the ostensible authority of a partner.

5.3.3.3 Implied authority

It has been noted that the authority of a partner to do an act may be implied from a course of dealing involving the partners or because the authority is a natural consequence of an authority actually given to the partner. This is called implied authority. The implied powers of partners in a trading partnership are more extensive than the powers of partners in a non-trading partnership. This is because the court recognises the need of the partners and the persons dealing with them to rely on normal trading practices.

Examples of powers assumed to be available to partners in all partnerships include the power to:

(a) bring or defend legal proceedings in the firm name or the joint names of all of the partners;

125

(b) open a bank account in the name of the firm;

(c) sign cheques on behalf of the firm;

(d) enter contracts on behalf of the firm within the ordinary course of business of the firm;

(e) sell goods belonging to the firm; and

(f) take on employees for the purposes of the partnership business and dismiss such employees.

A partner in a trading partnership will be assumed to have all the above powers and also the power to grant security for borrowings and to draw, accept or endorse a bill of exchange or promissory note.

5.3.3.4 Ostensible authority

The scope of ostensible authority is not always easy to establish or describe. Such authority may be said to arise from the fact that the partner who is acting of behalf of a firm *appears* to have authority to bind the firm and it is, therefore, reasonable for the outsider to assume such authority. It is for this reason that it is sometimes referred to as apparent authority. The principle underlying ostensible authority is to be found in the 1890 Act, s. 5 which provides that:

> *Every partner is an agent for the firm and his other partners for the purpose of the business of the partnership; and the acts of every partner who does any act for carrying on in the usual way the business of the kind carried on by the firm of which he is a member bind the firm and his partners, unless the partner so acting has in fact no authority to act for the firm in the particular matter, and the person with whom he is dealing either knows that he has no authority, or does not know or believe him to be a partner.*

The easiest way to understand the scope of the section is to examine each of the qualifications on a partner's authority which the section recognises. First, it should be noted that the section does not say that *anything* which a partner does binds the firm; rather to bind the firm the following requirements must be satisfied:

(a) the act must be done by a partner;

(b) the act must be done qua partner; and

(c) the act must be within the ordinary course of business of the firm.

The first and second requirement are generally easy to establish, while the requirement that the act be within the firm's ordinary course of business has caused the most difficulty.

Act must be done by a partner

Before a firm is bound by the act of its partner, it is perhaps self-evident that the act must be that of a partner and the fact that the partner in question is a dormant partner or a junior partner does not in any way reduce his power to bind his partners: *Morans v Armstrong* (1840) Arm M & O 23. In cases where a partner in a firm does not have the authority to do acts within the ordinary course of business of a firm, the third party must believe that he is dealing with a partner. This is because, under s. 5 of the 1890 Act, if the partner does not have authority to do an act which is within the firm's ordinary business, the firm will nonetheless be bound by that act, *unless* the third party did not know or believe that he was a partner. Where the third party does not believe that he is dealing with a partner, he must then be taken to know that the first requirement for the firm to be bound has not been satisfied. If the partner is a partner with the authority but the third party does not know he is a partner then the firm will still be bound provided that each of the requirements above is satisfied.

Act must be done qua partner

The second requirement to be satisfied for a firm to be bound by the actions of a partner is that the act in question must be done by the partner qua partner. It is important to distinguish between this requirement and the fact that the act must be done within the ordinary course of business of the firm. Thus, the act of a partner in an accountancy firm who becomes a company director of his family company, may not be binding on his firm since, although done by a partner and constituting an act which is within the ordinary course of business of an accountancy firm, it may not have been done by him qua partner. A good example of a case in which a partner was held not to be acting qua partner is *British Homes Assurance Corporation Ltd v Paterson* [1902] 2 Ch 404. In that case, the plaintiff instructed a solicitor, Atkinson, to act on its behalf in relation to a mortgage. At that time, Atkinson practised under the name of Atkinson and Atkinson. Soon after he entered partnership with Paterson and he informed the plaintiff that he would in future carry on business under the name of Atkinson and Paterson. The plaintiff ignored this and continued to deal with the solicitor as Atkinson and Atkinson and, on completion of the transaction, sent a cheque to him in the name of 'Atkinson and Atkinson or order'. When Atkinson absconded with this money, the plaintiff sued Paterson for the return of the money. It was held that the defendant was not liable for the default since the plaintiff had intentionally contracted with Atkinson as an individual and not qua partner.

Act must be within the firm's ordinary course of business

The third and final condition to be satisfied for a firm to be bound by the acts of its partners is the one which has received the most attention from the courts, namely that the act be within the ordinary course of business of the firm. The classification of a particular act as being within the 'ordinary course of business of the firm' is crucial since in most cases the question of the liability of the firm for the acts of a partner is determined by this fact. For example, a firm of doctors would be liable for the damage caused by the negligent driving of one of the partners where he is involved in a car accident on the way to see a patient. This is because the negligent driving of the partner is an act which is committed by the partner while acting in the ordinary course of business of the firm. On the other hand, the firm of doctors will not generally be liable for the damage caused by one of the partners where, on his way to see a patient, he decides to take a detour and assault an innocent third party. This assault would not be regarded as being 'within the ordinary course of business of the firm' since the partner is acting in a completely unusual manner for his own purposes and not in order to benefit the firm.

In the context of the ordinary course of business of a solicitors' partnership, in *United Bank of Kuwait v Hammond* [1988] 1 WLR 1051 an undertaking given by a solicitor to the bank as security for a loan by the bank to his client was held to be within the ordinary course of business of a solicitor. Accordingly the firm in this case was held liable when the undertaking given by one of the partners was not honoured. In contrast, in the nineteenth century case of *Plumer v Gregory* (1874) LR 18 Eq 621, a partner borrowed money from a client without the knowledge of his co-partners saying to the client that the firm wanted it to lend to another client. The borrowing of money from a client for lending to another client was held not to be within the ordinary course of business of a solicitors' firm and the firm was held not to be liable for the loss to the client.

Finally, a partner who makes a contract with an outsider without authority will be personally liable to the outsider for breach of warranty of authority where the partnership as a whole is not made liable on the contract. However, where a contract made without authority is ratified by the partnership, it becomes binding on the partners as well as on the outsider. In addition, where the partner's authority to do acts within the ordinary course of business of the firm is restricted, section 8 of the 1890 Act provides that an outsider is not prejudiced since it provides that the third party is not affected by any restriction placed on the powers of the partner unless he has notice of it.

5.3.4 PERSONS HELD OUT AS PARTNERS

So far we have only considered the liability of actual partners vis à vis outsiders. A person who holds himself out as a partner or who ' knowingly suffers himself to be represented as a partner' is liable to anyone who 'on the faith of such representation' gives credit to the firm as if he were a partner: 1890 Act, s. 14. The most common example of the application of this rule is where a 'salaried partner' (who is in fact an employee of the firm, rather than a partner) allows his name to be used by the partnership (e.g. on notepaper) and it is worth noting that in the most recent Law Society survey, it was estimated that 8 per cent of law firms had salaried partners. In view of the potential liability under s. 14(1), it is advisable for salaried partners to obtain an indemnity from the 'true' partners in relation to this potential liability. A person cannot be held liable under s. 14(1) unless he has in some way contributed to the mistake made by the person giving credit to the firm, for example, by allowing his name to be given as a partner. This is illustrated by the English case of *Tower Cabinet Co Ltd v Ingram* [1949] 2 KB 397. In that case a partner retired from his firm and due to carelessness on his part omitted to destroy the headed notepaper of the firm which contained his name. It was held that this carelessness did not constitute him knowingly suffering himself to be held out as a partner, as he did not know that the notepaper was used by the firm after his retirement. Clearly, if he had known this fact, he would have been held to have knowingly suffered a holding out and would have been liable to the creditors who relied on him being a partner.

Section 14(1) only applies where 'credit is given' to the firm by the third party on the basis of the misrepresentation that a person was a partner in the firm. This term is construed widely so that, for example, the apparent partner is liable where goods are delivered, as well as where cash is lent to the firm. In *Nationwide Building Society v Lewis* [1998] 3 All ER 143 it was noted that, as s. 14(1) was simply an example of the wider doctrine of estoppel by conduct, the precise language of s. 14(1) ('given credit to the firm') was not important once there was a reliance or an acting on the faith of the representation.

5.3.5 LIABILITY OF NEW PARTNERS

Section 17(1) of the 1890 Act provides that 'a person who is admitted as a partner into an existing firm does not thereby become liable to the creditors of the firm for anything done before he became a partner'. This provision ensures that an incoming partner is not liable to the existing creditors of the firm merely because he has become a partner in a firm which has a large number of obligations and debts. As between himself and the existing partners the incoming partner may agree to pay a share of debts owed to existing creditors. This does not make him directly liable to the existing creditors as they are not privy to the contract. The new partner may become directly liable to existing creditors by a novation (that is, a tripartite contract between the old partners, the new partner and the creditor whereby the existing contract between the old partners and the creditor is discharged and replaced by a contract between the new firm, including the new partner, and the creditor). However, this will not be a regular occurrence in modern partnerships because it would necessitate an agreement between a partnership and its creditors every time a partner joins the firm.

5.3.6 LITIGATION INVOLVING PARTNERSHIPS

Order 14, r 1 of the Superior Court Rules (SI 15/1986) provides that a partnership may sue or be sued in its firm name. There is no need to set out in the proceedings the names of the individual partners since the use of the firm name means that the partners are sued individually as definitively as if they had their names set out. Order 14, r 1 states:

> *Any two or more persons claiming or being liable as co-partners and carrying on business within the jurisdiction, may sue or be sued in the name of the respective firms, if any, of which such persons were co-partners at the time of the accruing of the cause of action ....*

However, it is crucial to bear in mind that this procedural rule is simply that, i.e. a rule of procedure which allows partnership litigation to be conducted *as if* the firm was a separate legal entity. It does not alter the fundamental nature of a partnership as an aggregate of its members and this issue will remain of relevance in the conduct of any such litigation. A consequence of this aggregate nature of partnerships is the fact that although the same firm name may be used in litigation by or against a firm, with each change in the membership of the firm, a new partnership is created. It follows that one must 'look through' the firm name to see who is ultimately liable for the partnership obligation being litigated, namely those persons who were partners in the firm at the time of the accrual of the cause of action. It is for this reason, that the Rules of Court also allow a party in partnership litigation to apply to court for a statement of the names of the partners in the firm at the time of the accrual of the cause of action. It follows that parties to an action against a firm may not dispense with the need to identify the correct parties to their action, since it is only these parties against whom a judgment may be executed.

Where an action is brought against a partnership in the firm's name the proceedings may be served:

(a)   on any one or more partner, or

(b)   at the principal place of business of the partnership within the State, on the person having control or management of the partnership business there.

A person who has a judgment against a partner for the partner's personal liability may enforce that judgment against the partner's share of partnership property by means of 'a charging order': 1890 Act, s. 23(2). He may not enforce such a judgment against the partnership property by means of execution proceedings: s 23(1). Where a charging order is made the other partners may discharge it by paying off the judgment debt or, if a sale of the partner's interest in the firm is ordered, they may purchase that partner's interest. A charging order gives the other partners a right to dissolve the partnership if they wish: s 33(2).

5.3.7   GUARANTEES

Section 18 of the 1890 Act is a very important provision and one which should be borne in mind by lawyers acting for a bank receiving a guarantee from a partnership in respect of its loan. Section 18 provides that a continuing guarantee is revoked by any change in the firm whose liabilities are being guaranteed. Accordingly, it is very important to have a provision in such a guarantee to the effect that the terms of the guarantee will continue after any change in the firm. Otherwise s. 18 will ensure that the guarantee is automatically revoked by any retirement of a partner in the firm or any admission of a new partner into the firm.

.4   Actions Between Partners

.4.1   INTRODUCTION

Disputes between partners may involve a wide variety of potential actions ranging from a claim for damages to an application for the appointment of a receiver to the firm. However, regardless of the form of action, two important characteristics of the partnership relationship should be borne in mind as these two characteristics will commonly influence the outcome of the litigation. First, one of the grand characteristics of a partnership is the fact that it is not a separate legal entity, but an aggregate of all the partners. For this reason, the partners are not treated as debtors or creditors of the firm while the partnership continues, since to do so would involve the concept of a person owing himself a debt. It is only on a final settlement of accounts between the partners on the firm's dissolution that they are regarded as debtors and creditors. It is for this reason that the courts are reluctant to facilitate a partner in suing his co-partners in respect of a single partnership obligation. Instead, the courts lean in favour of all partnership obligations being determined as part of the general settlement of accounts on the dissolution of the firm.

The second important characteristic of the partnership contract is that it requires a high degree of confidence and trust between the partners. It is therefore understandable that the courts would be reluctant to compel an unwilling person to be another person's partner. For this reason, the specific performance of partnerships, while not unheard of, are certainly not granted as a matter of course. For the same reason, the courts favour granting other remedies such as injunctions and appointing receivers/managers as part of the dissolution of partnerships rather than during the life of partnerships. This judicial attitude may be easily justified since the very fact that a court application is being made in the first place indicates that the degree of trust and confidence necessary for the partnership to continue may be absent. Thus, any order which is intended to apply during the life of the partnership may turn out to be futile and clearly the court does not wish to involve itself in making such orders.

In this section we look at the remedies available to a partner which include dissolution of the partnership, appointment of a receiver and other remedies which may be available under the terms of the partnership agreement itself. (For further remedies, see Twomey: *Partnership Law*, paras 20.01 et seq.)

5.4.2   DISSOLUTION BY THE COURT

5.4.2.1   Generally

Dissolution of a partnership may occur automatically (e.g., on the death of a partner) by notice (e.g., any partner may give notice dissolving a partnership at will) or by court order (e.g., in the case of permanent incapacity of a partner). The various circumstances in which dissolution takes place are considered at **5.5**. In this section we intend to consider only those types of dissolution which provide a remedy in a dispute between partners, i.e. under s. 35(c) (order of dissolution where a partner is guilty of misconduct), s. 35(d) (order of dissolution where a partner breaches partnership agreement) or s. 35(f) (order of dissolution where it is just and equitable to dissolve the partnership).

In a formal partnership (i.e. where the partners have excluded the right of a partner to dissolve the partnership by notice) the partners usually agree to remain in partnership together for a fixed term (for this reason, they are sometimes referred to as fixed-term partnerships). It will often occur that some of the partners may wish to bring the partnership to a premature end for a variety of reasons ranging from personality clashes to the wrongful conduct of a partner. Unfortunately, there is no automatic right under the 1890 Act for the partners to expel a partner guilty of misconduct and for this reason, these types of situations often result in an application to court for a dissolution of the partnership under the 1890 Act, s. 35. The only other option open to the partner(s) wishing to end the partnership with a difficult partner is to attempt to terminate the partnership in breach of the partnership agreement which is obviously an unsatisfactory solution.

A number of general aspects of s. 35 are worthy of mention at this juncture. This section provides for the dissolution of a partnership in six separate instances (as to which see **5.5.2.4**). The court has an absolute discretion to order a dissolution in any of the six cases listed in s. 35. If for no other reason, this fact should encourage potential litigants to make every effort to resolve their differences amicably since there is no requirement on a court to order or not to order a dissolution, regardless of the conduct of the partners. However, since the courts generally lean against ordering the specific performance of a partnership agreement between unwilling partners, the result of an application to dissolve a partnership often, but not always, is a court dissolution. In addition, partnership disputes usually end up in dissolution because a court in a partnership dispute, unlike the situation in a company dispute, does not have a statutory power to order the expulsion of a partner or the sale of one partner's share to his co-partners. It follows that the parties to a partnership dispute have the added knowledge that a dissolution is more likely than not to result from an application to court under s. 35 with the likelihood that the practice or business of the partnership will have to be sold and the consequent loss of goodwill. In general terms therefore, there is a very great incentive for partners to attempt to agree to dissolve amicably without incurring the costs of going to court to obtain an order to dissolve the partnership.

Although s. 35 has six separate headings under which a dissolution of a partnership may be claimed, more often than not, a dissolution will be sought under s. 35(f) on the grounds that it is just and equitable for the court to order the dissolution of the partnership. Such an application obviates the need for the petitioner to satisfy the pre-conditions of the other subsections of s. 35 such as incapacity, breach of partnership agreement etc.

5.4.2.2 Conduct prejudicial to the business: s. 35(c)

Section 35(c) provides that a partner may apply to the court for dissolution

> *when a partner, other than the partner suing, has been guilty of such conduct as, in the opinion of the court, regard being had to the nature of the business, is calculated to prejudicially affect the carrying on of the business.*

This subsection may be relied upon even though the prejudicial conduct has nothing directly to do with the partnership. Thus, a partner's criminal actions may have been committed completely separate from his partnership, but yet may fall within the terms of s. 35(c). The use in s. 35(c) of the phrase 'guilty of such conduct ... as is calculated to prejudicially affect' connotes a strong degree of culpability on the part of the partner. Accordingly, it is thought that the conduct in question must be done with the intention of causing harm to the partnership and not simply that it has a possibility of harming the partnership business.

5.4.2.3 Breach of partnership agreement: s. 35(d)

Section 35(d) provides that a partner may apply to the court for dissolution

> *when a partner, other than the partner suing, wilfully or persistently commits a breach of the partnership agreement, or otherwise so conducts himself in matters relating to the partnership business that it is not reasonably practicable for the other partner or partners to carry on business in partnership with him.*

This subsection contemplates that the trust between partners has broken down. If this breakdown results from persistent breaches of the partnership agreement or conduct in relation to the business, then the court may order dissolution. *Heslin v Fay (No. 1)* (1884) 15 LR Ir 431 provides an example of a case where a dissolution order was made as a result of the wilful breach of the terms of the partnership agreement. There, the partnership deed for a grocery partnership in North King Street in Dublin provided that each partner was entitled to withdraw any surplus capital in the firm which had been advanced by him. When Heslin called on his partners to repay him his surplus capital, they refused to do so and instead falsely claimed that they had raised the capital of the firm by admitting another partner and this had the effect of swamping Heslin's surplus capital. Accordingly, it was held by the Irish Court of Appeal that the decision by the other partners to refuse to return the capital was a wilful breach of the partnership agreement which justified an order for the dissolution of the partnership.

5.4.2.4 Just and equitable dissolution: s. 35(f)

Section 35(f) provides that a partner may apply to the court for dissolution 'whenever in any case circumstances have arisen which in the opinion of the court render it just and equitable that the partnership be dissolved'. This provision is the equivalent of s. 213(f) of the Companies Act 1963 which applies only to companies but the cases decided under that section are likely to be relevant to s. 35(f). One such case is *Re Vehicle Buildings* [1986] ILRM 239 which concerned a quasi-partnership. (A quasi-partnership is an entity, which is in form a company, but in substance a partnership, such that it is appropriate to apply the principles of partnership law to it.) It involved a private company which was a partnership in all but name, since it was owned by a Ms Fitzpatrick and a Mr Howley in equal proportions and in which they were the sole directors. The relationship between the two broke down leading to a state of deadlock in the management of the company. Murphy J granted an order for the winding-up of the company on just and equitable grounds under s. 213(f) of the Companies Act 1963 on the basis that treating it as a partnership, it would be appropriate to dissolve it under s. 35(f) of the 1890 Act.

5.4.3 APPOINTMENT OF RECEIVER/MANAGER

The court may appoint a receiver or manager in all cases in which it appears to be just and convenient to so do on the application of any partner or other persons interested in the preservation of the firm's assets, such as the personal representative of a deceased partner. It is important to distinguish between the two officers: a receiver takes the assets of the partnership under his protection and in this way, the assets remain under the protection of the court; while a manager has the additional role of carrying on the partnership business under the direction of the court. For this reason, it is perhaps more useful for a manager to be appointed. However, it should be noted that the court is particularly reluctant to make an appointment of a manager or receiver in the case of a professional partnership in view of the damage to the professional reputation of the firm: *Floydd v Cheney* [1970] 2 WLR 314.

5.4.4 MEDIATION AND ARBITRATION

'Partnership actions always take a long time and, indeed, are one of the most expensive and unsatisfactory types of action which we have' per Kenny J in *O'Connor v Woods*, 22 January 1976, HC (unreported). This view of partnership disputes was reiterated by the Supreme Court, albeit in the context of quasi-partnerships, when Murphy J observed that they were similar to matrimonial proceedings in that:

> '[Partnership disputes and family law disputes] both involve an examination of the conduct of the parties over a period of years and usually a determination by them to assert rights rather than solve problems. It may well be that the disparate forms of litigation are frequently fuelled by a bitterness borne of rejection: matrimonial or commercial. In neither discipline can the courts persuade the parties that it is in their best interests to direct their attention to solving their problems rather than litigating them.' (*Re Murray Consultants Ltd* [1997] 3 IR 23)

By repeating the observations of the Irish judiciary on the subject of partnership disputes, it is hoped to persuade some partners and their legal advisers to try and solve their problems by mediation or other non-adversarial methods and in particular to include a compulsory mediation clause in their partnership agreement and, failing resolution by mediation, it is suggested that the parties seek to resolve their differences by arbitration. Any such clause should be wide enough to include disputes arising during dissolution. A clause along the following lines is recommended:

> 'All disputes and questions whatsoever which shall either during the term of the Partnership or afterwards arise between the Partners or their representatives or between any Partners or Partner and the representatives of any other deceased Partner touching this Indenture or

construction or application thereof or any clause or thing herein contained or any amount valuation or division of assets, debts or liabilities to be made hereunder or as to any act, deed or omission of any Partner relating to the Partnership or as to any other matter in any way relating to the Partnership business or the affairs thereof or the right duties or liabilities of any persons hereunder shall be referred first to a single mediator to be nominated by all the persons in dispute or in default of agreement by the President for the time being of the Law Society. Failing a resolution of the dispute through such mediation to the satisfaction of all the parties, the dispute shall be referred to a single arbitrator to be nominated by all the persons in dispute or in default of agreement by the President for the time being of the Law Society in accordance with and subject to the provisions of the Arbitration Acts, 1954 to 1998 or any statutory modification or re-enactment thereof for the time being in force.'

5.4.5 EXPULSION OF A PARTNER

We have seen in this section that it is possible for a partnership to be dissolved by the court as a way of giving the plaintiff partner a remedy against his co-partners. However, the circumstances of the dispute within the partnership may be such that some partners would prefer to get rid of one or more of their co-partners without fully dissolving the partnership and in this section it is proposed to consider the expulsion of a partner from a partnership.

5.4.5.1 Need to expressly provide for expulsion in partnership agreement

There is no right under the 1890 Act to expel a partner. Indeed, the contrary is expressly stated by s. 25 which reads 'no majority of the partners can expel any partner unless a power to do so has been conferred by express agreement between the partners'.

The absence of a right under general partnership law to expel a partner is an important reason for having a written partnership agreement incorporating such a right, since no matter how unprofessional, negligent or belligerent a partner becomes, the other partners are not entitled to expel him from the firm in the absence of such a right. The desire of the partners in a firm to expel their co-partner, in the absence of a right to expel, may lead to a general dissolution of that firm. This is because the only recourse for the 'innocent' partners is to apply to court under the 1890 Act, s. 35 for a general dissolution of the partnership on the grounds of the partner's misconduct.

Where an expulsion clause is included in the agreement it will normally state that specific activities (such as fraud) or breaches of certain terms of the partnership agreement (such as requiring a partner not to compete with the partnership or to devote the whole of his time to the business) will justify expulsion. As noted at **5.5.2.3** below, bankruptcy of a partner is a ground for the automatic dissolution of the whole partnership (under the default rules contained in s. 33(1) of the 1890 Act) but in order to avoid the consequences of dissolution it is common for the partnership agreement to override this default rule and provide that a bankruptcy of a partner will not cause dissolution, rather that it will justify expulsion.

.4.5.2 Exercise of expulsion clause

If an expulsion clause is included in the partnership agreement, then the power must be exercised strictly in accordance with the agreement and in a bona fide manner and for the benefit of the partnership as a whole: *Blisset v Daniel* (1853) 10 Hare 493. The exercise of a power of expulsion will have serious repercussions for the expelled partner and may often lead to a loss of livelihood. For this reason, a court will strictly construe the right to expel a partner and any conditions which have to be met to exercise that right. Yet the courts will take a practical approach to the interpretation of expulsion clauses, as is illustrated by *Hitchman v Crouch Butler Savage Associates* (1983) 127 SJ 441. There, an expulsion clause which required the senior partner in a firm to sign all expulsion notices, was interpreted by the English Court of Appeal as not requiring his signature, when it came to his own expulsion notice.

5.5   Dissolution of a Partnership

5.5.1   GENERAL DISSOLUTION VS TECHNICAL DISSOLUTION

An important distinction must be made between the general dissolution of a partnership and its technical dissolution. If a partnership is subject to a general dissolution, the partnership will come to an end and its business is wound up. A technical dissolution is where there is a change in the membership of the partnership but no winding-up of the 'old' partnership since the business of the partnership continues as before the change in membership, such as where a partner leaves the firm or a partner joins the firm. The same events lead to the technical and general dissolution of a partnership, thus the death of a partner 'dissolves' the partnership that existed between the partners and thereafter the surviving partners may continue the partnership business as before (in which case there would be a technical dissolution) or they may decide to sell the partnership assets and wind up the business (in which case there would be a general dissolution). In this section we consider the legal consequences of the occurrence of both a general and a technical dissolution since it is only with the benefit of hindsight (i.e. was the firm wound up or did it continue in business) that one may determine whether a particular event led to the general or the technical dissolution of the firm.

As noted below at **5.5.2.3**, unless the partnership agreement provides otherwise, the death or bankruptcy of a partner results in the automatic dissolution of the partnership (1890 Act, s. 33(1)) and at that stage any partner may demand that the partnership is wound up, in which case the partnership will go into general dissolution: 1890 Act, s. 39. General dissolution is such an extreme step that an important reason to have a written partnership agreement is to provide expressly that dissolution is *not* to occur automatically on the occurrence of the death or bankruptcy of a partner.

5.5.2   DISSOLUTION OF A PARTNERSHIP

5.5.2.1   Dissolution by notice

Under the 1890 Act, ss. 26 and 32(c) and in the absence of any express or implied contrary agreement, any one partner may, at any time, give notice to their fellow partners to dissolve the partnership. This notice takes effect from the date specified in the notice (subject to the fact that the date of dissolution may not be before the date of receipt). If the notice is silent on the point, it takes effect from the date when the notice is received. Once the firm is dissolved under ss. 26 or 32(c), any partner is entitled under s. 39 of the 1890 Act to demand the sale of the partnership assets in order for the liabilities of the firm to be paid off and in this way to force the general dissolution of the firm. In most cases, this will have disastrous consequences for the partnership business. It is important therefore to bear in mind that ss. 26 and 32(c) may be overridden if the partnership agreement contains provisions to the contrary. As a result many partnership agreements exclude these default rights completely or require a majority vote or a minimum period of notice to be given before the partnership is dissolved. Commonly the right of a partner to dissolve a partnership is excluded by implication, namely by an agreement between the partners that the partnership shall last for a fixed term.

5.5.2.2   Dissolution by agreement

The partnership agreement may specify circumstances which cause the partnership to be dissolved, such as the occurrence of a particular event. The agreement may also specify the manner in which the partnership will be dissolved.

5.5.2.3   Automatic dissolution

A number of events cause partnerships to dissolve automatically under the terms of the 1890 Act.

Bankruptcy or death

The death or bankruptcy of a partner causes the partnership to be automatically dissolved, unless the partnership agreement contains provisions to the contrary: 1890 Act, s. 33(1). A good example of the automatic dissolution of a partnership by death is provided by *McLeod v Dowling* (1927) 43 TLR 655. In that case, McLeod posted a notice of dissolution to his sole partner, Dowling, that as and from the date of the notice, namely 23 March, the partnership was dissolved. The notice was received by Dowling on 24 March at 10 am, but McLeod had died at 3 am on that same day. Accordingly, the English High Court held that the partnership was dissolved not on the purported effective date (23 March), nor at the time that it was received (at 10 am on 24 March), but at the time of death of McLeod, at 3 am on 24 March since a partnership is dissolved automatically on the death of a partner, in the absence of contrary agreement.

Dissolution is a serious matter as it allows any one partner to demand the general dissolution of the partnership under s. 39 and for this reason, many partnership agreements provide that, instead of causing automatic dissolution, the death or bankruptcy of a partner shall give rise to the same consequences as a retirement, i.e. the deceased partner's share or the bankrupt partner's share is sold to the continuing partners: see **5.5.4.1**. This highlights again the importance of having a well-drafted partnership agreement to override the default rules in the 1890 Act which are in many ways inappropriate for modern professional firms, since most firms intend to continue in spite of the death or bankruptcy of a partner.

Illegality

Partnerships formed to carry out an illegal activity or which are contrary to public policy are automatically dissolved. A change of circumstances (including a change in the law) may make illegal a partnership initially formed for a legal purpose. Section 34 of the 1890 Act provides that a partnership is dissolved on the happening of an event which makes the business unlawful (for example, the date the change in the law takes effect). A provision to the contrary in the partnership agreement will not override s. 34. Two illegal partnership cases are of particular interest to lawyers. The first is the case of *Hudgell Yeates & Co v Watson* [1978] 2 All ER 363 which concerned a partnership in breach of the English equivalent of s. 59 of the Solicitors Act 1954 (the provision that solicitors may only enter partnership with other solicitors). The case involved an action by the plaintiff law firm against one of its clients for unpaid fees. The defendant argued that the action against him should be struck out because of one partner's inadvertent failure to renew his solicitor's practising certificate for a period of seven months. On this basis, the defendant alleged that it was an illegal partnership and he claimed that the firm was automatically dissolved as required by s. 34 of the 1890 Act. Although the failure by the partner to renew his practising certificate was accidental, the Court of Appeal was left with no option but to uphold the defendant's claim that the firm was illegal and dissolved automatically on the failure of this partner to renew his practising certificate. This case highlights that professionals, who are prohibited by statute from acting in partnership with unqualified persons, should ensure that their practising certificates are renewed on a timely basis. The failure to do so will render their partnership automatically dissolved, even where the failure is inadvertent.

The second case is the eighteenth century decision in *Everet v Williams* (1893) 9 LQR 197. In this case, an account of partnership dealings by one partner against his co-partner was sought. However, despite the partners' best efforts to conceal the purpose of the partnership, the court rejected the application on the grounds that it was an illegal partnership. The bill in equity which was filed by the plaintiff stated that he was experienced in commodities such as rings and watches and that it was agreed that he and the defendant would provide the necessary tools of their proposed trade together, namely horses, saddles and weapons. They also agreed to share equally in the costs of the venture, i.e. the expenses involved in staying at inns, alehouses and taverns. The bill stated that they had successfully 'dealt with' a gentleman for a gold watch and other goods and the plaintiff sought an account of these dealings. The court surmised that the partnership was between highwaymen and the action was dismissed on the grounds that it was an illegal partnership. To add insult to injury, the costs were ordered to be paid by the counsel who signed the bill and the solicitor for the plaintiff was attached and fined.

By expiration

Under s. 32(a) and (b) of the 1890 Act, a partnership is dissolved:

(a)   if it was entered into for a fixed term, upon the expiration of that term; and

(b)   if it was entered into for a single adventure or undertaking, upon the completion of that adventure or undertaking.

A provision to the contrary in the partnership agreement overrides s. 32(a) and (b). If the agreement is silent and the partnership continues despite the expiry of the term or the completion of the adventure, the 1890 Act, s. 27 provides that a partnership at will, dissolvable by notice, is brought into existence. Such a partnership is subject to the terms of the original agreement to the extent that these terms do not conflict with the incidents of a partnership at will.

5.5.2.4   Dissolution by the court

Finally, a partner may apply to the court for dissolution of the partnership provided one of the statutory grounds for dissolution by the court exists. This is only really an option when an easier method of dissolution is not available, either under the 1890 Act or under any partnership agreement. Section 35 of the 1890 Act sets out grounds for dissolution by the court. Those grounds which give the partners a remedy in the event of a dispute between the partners (that is to say, s. 35(c), (d) and (f)) have been considered earlier at **5.4.2**. The full list of s. 35 grounds is as follows:

Partner of unsound mind: s. 35(a)

A court may dissolve a partnership under s. 35(a) when a partner is of permanently unsound mind. It seems that s. 35(a) must be interpreted as requiring not just mental incapacity of the partner, but also that the incapacitated partner is incapable of performing his part of the partnership contract. In most cases, this will be easy enough to establish. However, where the partner is a dormant partner, his mental incapacity may have no such consequence since he will have no duties to perform in the partnership. For this reason, it is contended that the mental incapacity of a dormant partner may not lead to the firm's dissolution. Support for this view is to be found in the Scottish case of *Eadie v McBean's Curator Bonis* (1885) 12 R 660. There, the court refused to order the dissolution of the partnership where the insane partner had no active duties in the management of the firm but had merely provided the capital and the curator bonis of the insane partner opposed the application.

Partner incapable of performing partnership contract: s. 35(b)

A partnership may be dissolved by the court when a partner, other than the partner suing, becomes permanently incapable of performing his part of the partnership contract. Whether or not a partner has become permanently incapable is a question of fact. In *Whitwell v Arthur* (1865) 35 Beav 140 an attack of paralysis prevented a partner from performing his partnership duties. However, since medical evidence indicated that the paralysis might only be temporary, the petition for the dissolution of the partnership was refused.

136

Partner's behaviour prejudicially affecting business: s. 35(c)

A court may dissolve a partnership when a partner, other than the partner suing, has been guilty of such conduct as, in the opinion of the court, regard being had to the nature of the business, is calculated to affect prejudicially the carrying on of the business: see **5.4.2.2**.

Partner in breach of partnership agreement: s. 35(d)

A court may dissolve a partnership when a partner, other than the partner suing, wilfully or persistently commits a breach of the partnership agreement, or otherwise so conducts himself in matters relating to the partnership business that it is not reasonably practicable for the other partner or partners to carry on the business in partnership with him: see **5.4.2.3**.

Business running at a loss: s. 35(e)

A court may dissolve a partnership when the business of the partnership can only be carried on at a loss. In order for s. 35(e) to be invoked, the circumstances must be such as to make it a practical impossibility for the partnership to make a profit. If the partners who find themselves in this position cannot agree to bring the partnership to an end, this may be a valuable right if a delay in terminating the partnership will increase the amount of the loss, for which all the partners will be personally liable.

Just and equitable: s. 35(f)

A court may dissolve a partnership whenever, in the opinion of the court, it is just and equitable that the partnership be dissolved: see **5.4.2.4**.

.5.3 CONSEQUENCES OF A DISSOLUTION

5.3.1 Generally

The occurrence of one of the events leading to the automatic dissolution of a partnership (see **5.5.2.3**) will cause the partnership to be 'dissolved'. Whether this results in the technical or general dissolution of the firm depends on whether the right to wind up the firm under s. 39 of the 1890 Act has been excluded by the partners and, if not, whether a partner wishes to force the general dissolution of the firm by exercising this right under s. 39 of the 1890 Act. Section 39 provides:

> *On the dissolution of a partnership every partner is entitled, as against the other partners in the firm, and all persons claiming through them in respect of their interests as partners, to have the property of the partnership applied in payment of the debts and liabilities of the firm, and to have the surplus assets after such payment applied in payment of what may be due to the partners respectively after deducting what may be due from them as partners to the firm; and for that purpose any partner or his representatives may on the termination of the partnership apply to the Court to wind up the business and affairs of the firm.*

The most common way in which the right under s. 39 is excluded is by the partners having a partnership agreement which provides that when a partner leaves the firm, his share shall be purchased by the continuing partner.

Where the firm goes into general dissolution, s. 38 provides that, after the dissolution, the authority of each partner to bind the firm (as well as the other rights and obligations of the partners) continues despite the dissolution but only to the extent necessary to wind up the affairs of the partnership, and to complete transactions begun but unfinished at the time of the dissolution.

5.5.3.2 Realisation of partnership assets on general dissolution

Once the firm has been dissolved and the general dissolution begins, the value of the assets owned by the partnership will be ascertained, as will the extent of the debts and liabilities owed to creditors. In so far as it is necessary, the assets will be sold to raise the funds to discharge the debts. These assets will include the 'goodwill' attaching to the business. Goodwill has been defined by Lord Macnaghten in *Trego v Hunt* [1896] AC 7 as:

> 'the whole advantage, whatever it may be, of the reputation and connection of the firm, which may have been built up by years of honest work or gained by lavish expenditure of money.'

Where goodwill is sold, the purchasers will want to protect their investment against the loss of custom arising from the former owners setting up in competition in the same vicinity. Accordingly, the purchaser may wish to include a restrictive covenant in the sale agreement to guard against this possibility: see **5.2.4.5**.

5.5.3.3 Distribution of partnership assets on general dissolution

Once the liabilities of the partnership have been met, any surplus is distributed to the partners. Section 44(b) of the 1890 Act provides that, in the absence of any contrary agreement, on a general dissolution, the assets of the firm shall be applied in the following order:

(a) debts of the firm to third parties;

(b) repayment of advances made by the partners to the firm;

(c) repayment of the capital contribution made by the partners to the firm; and

(d) balance is divided in the same manner as the profits are divided amongst the partners.

Section 44(a) of the 1890 Act provides that if the partnership has made losses (including losses of capital), in the absence of any contrary agreement, these shall be met on the general dissolution of the firm in the following order:

(i) from profits;

(ii) from capital; and

(iii) from the partners in the proportion in which profits are divisible.

Both parts of s. 44 are subject to contrary agreement. In particular the partners may agree to share surplus assets and to contribute to losses in a ratio different from their normal profit sharing. However, the requirement that creditors are paid off first is not subject to variation by the partners.

5.5.3.4 Sharing of losses on general dissolution

Under s. 44(a) and (b), any loss or residue, whether of capital or profits, will be shared between the partners in the proportion in which they share the profits, in the absence of contrary agreement. These subsections are traps for the unwary as this sharing of the capital losses or capital profits applies irrespective of the manner in which the partners have contributed to the capital of the firm but rather in proportion to the rate at which profits are shared. (See also 1890 Act, s. 24(1); *Ex parte Maude* (1867) 16 LT 577; *Re Weymouth Steam Packet Co* [1891] 1 Ch 66; and *Re Wakefield Rolling Stock Co* [1892] 3 Ch 165.) Therefore, a partner who contributes all the capital of the firm and shares the profits of the firm evenly with his partner, will, in the absence of any agreement to the contrary, share evenly in any capital profit or capital loss on the winding-up of the firm. In some cases, this may come as a surprise to the partner who contributes all the capital and accordingly the terms of the sharing of capital residues or losses require careful consideration in such partnerships.

An example will highlight this issue. A, B and C contributed capital of £2,000 in the following proportions: £1,000, £500 and £500 respectively, the partners sharing profits and losses equally. On a winding-up there is residual capital of only £1,000, thus leaving a capital loss of £1,000. Under the general rules governing the sharing of capital losses, these are shared in the same proportion as the profit shares (1890 Act, s. 44(a)) so that A, B and C are required to contribute a third each, i.e. each notionally contribute £333 giving a notional capital of £2,000. This is because such a shortfall in the capital is as much a loss as any other shortfall and is made up in the same way, namely by being shared between the partners. The notional capital is then repaid to the partners in accordance with their capital contributions, since s. 44(b) requires the capital to be repaid to partners 'rateably'. Therefore they will notionally receive the £2,000 divided in proportion to their capital contributions, i.e. 2:1:1 so that A will notionally receive his £1,000 back and B and C will receive back £500 each. To get the actual amount received by A, deduct his notional contribution of £333 from the notional amount of capital he should receive (£1,000) to give £667 which he actually receives. Similarly for B and C, deduct their notional contribution of £333 from the notional amount of capital, which they were to receive (£500), to give £167, which they will each receive. So, in respect of A's initial capital contribution of £1,000, he gets back £667, and thus he makes a loss of £333. While in respect of B's and C's capital contributions of £500, they get back £167 and thus they also make a loss of £333 each. The same result could have been achieved by dividing the capital loss of £1,000 equally between A, B and C.

5.5.3.5   Notification of the dissolution

Under s. 36(1) of the 1890 Act, outsiders dealing with the firm after a change in the membership of the firm are entitled to treat all apparent members of the firm as still being members until the outsider has notice of the change: see **5.5.4.3**. In order to protect themselves from liability for obligations incurred after the dissolution, the partners in the dissolved firm are entitled to publicly notify the fact of the dissolution (1890 Act, s. 37) and s. 36(2) of the 1890 Act provides that persons who had no dealings with a firm prior to a change in the membership of the firm are deemed to be on notice of a change in the firm which is advertised in *Iris Oifigiúil.*

Section 36(2) only provides that *new* customers of the firm are on notice of the change advertised in *Iris Oifigiúil*. It does not apply to existing customers of the firm. To obtain protection from liability for obligations incurred with *existing* customers after the dissolution, the former partners should give notice individually to each of these customers. In the case of a technical dissolution (i.e. where the business of the partnership continues after the departure of a partner) this will be an important issue since the partnership business will continue as before. In practice in larger firms, the former partner may opt to rely on an indemnity from the continuing partners in respect of such liabilities rather than attempting to notify all the clients of the firm that he is no longer a partner.

5.5.4   DEPARTURE OF A PARTNER FROM A FIRM

5.5.4.1   Generally

Partnership agreements can, and should, contain provisions dealing with the departure of a partner from the firm. This is because the 1890 Act does not specifically deal with retirement. Under the 1890 Act the only option available to a partner who wishes to leave a firm is to give notice to dissolve the partnership under s. 26, if it is a partnership at will. If a s. 26 notice is given the partnership will be dissolved (see **5.5.2.1**); the section does not permit a partner to depart, i.e. retire, without having to dissolve the partnership . To avoid this, suitable provisions must be included in the agreement entitling a partner to leave the firm and usually providing for the continuing partners to purchase his share in the partnership. This section considers the position of a former partner, regardless of how he leaves the firm, whether by retirement or expulsion. The position of a partner who dies is considered at **5.5.5**.

5.5.4.2 Obligations incurred before departure

The mere fact that a partner leaves a firm does not release him from obligations incurred by the firm while he was a partner. Section 17(2) of the 1890 Act provides that 'a partner who retires from a firm does not thereby cease to be liable for partnership debts or obligations incurred before his retirement'. For this reason, it is common for the former partner to be indemnified by the continuing partners. In the absence of such an indemnity, the former partner is fully liable for all obligations incurred while he was a partner, subject only to the relevant rules on the barring of claims under the Statute of Limitations.

5.5.4.3 Obligations incurred after departure

The general rule is that partners are only liable for debts incurred by the partnership while they are members of the firm. Therefore, ceasing to be a partner prevents the *former* partner becoming liable on future debts as the retirement terminates the agency relationship. However, this general rule is subject to the very important exception in s. 36(1) of the 1890 Act which is considered below.

Section 36(3)

Section 36(3) is in keeping with the general rule that a former partner is not liable for obligations incurred after his departure. This section provides that a deceased partner's estate, a bankrupt partner or a retiring partner (who was not known to have been a partner by the person dealing with the firm), is not liable for obligations incurred after the date of death, bankruptcy or retirement. The subsection was considered in *Tower Cabinet Co Ltd v Ingram* [1949] 2 KB 397. In that case, A and B were in partnership. A retired and B continued the business under the old name. After A's retirement, the business ordered goods from a new supplier and failed to pay. The supplier sought to enforce judgment against A. The only knowledge the supplier had of A's connection with the firm was that A's name appeared on headed notepaper which, contrary to A's express instructions, had not been destroyed. The court found that, as the customer had no knowledge prior to A's retirement that A was a partner in the firm, A was completely protected by s. 36(3). (A further question arose of A's possible liability under s. 14(1) which is considered at **5.3.4**.)

Section 36(1)

In cases where creditors know of the partner's connection with the firm before the former partner departs, s. 36(3) is of no assistance. In this regard, s. 36(1) provides the important exception to the general rule that a former partner is not liable for obligations incurred by a firm after his departure. It provides that

> where a person deals with a firm after a change in its constitution, he is entitled to treat all apparent members of the old firm as still being members of the firm until he has notice of the change.

It is important to note that s. 36(1) only applies to existing customers of the firm and not to those persons who only began dealing with the firm after the former partner departed.

If the former partner wishes to be absolutely protected from liability for future debts he should give the existing customers formal notification of his retirement. Although the matter is not beyond dispute, it is thought that actual notice is not required under s. 36(1). Thus, it is suggested that some reasonable limits will be placed by the courts on the requirement of notice and this is likely to be done by interpreting 'notice' as including situations where from all the circumstances the third party should have been aware that the former partner was no longer a partner in the firm, i.e. constructive notice (see further Twomey: *Partnership Law* (Butterworths, 2000) paras 11.62 et seq.).

Section 14(1)

A former partner may also be liable for obligations incurred after his departure from the firm under the doctrine of holding out. This concept applies to all persons (whether they are former partners or not) who allow themselves to be held out as partners in a firm when in fact they are not partners: see also **5.3.4**). Section 14(2) of the 1890 Act provides that:

> *Every one who by words spoken or written or by conduct represents himself, or who knowingly suffers himself to be represented, as a partner in a particular firm, is liable as a partner to any one who has on the faith of any such representation given credit to the firm, whether the representation has or has not been made or communicated to the person so giving credit by or with the knowledge of the apparent partner making the representation or suffering it to be made.*

Therefore, even if no liability arises under s. 36(1), the former partner may be liable to any person (whether they had previous dealings with the firm or not) who has given 'credit' to the firm on the faith of a representation that the former partner is still a partner. In *Tower Cabinet Co Ltd v Ingram* [1949] 2 KB 397, it was also alleged that the former partner had allowed himself to be held out as a partner. However, since the former partner had not authorised the use of the old notepaper, he had not 'knowingly' allowed himself to be held out as an 'apparent' partner and so no liability under s. 14(1) arose.

In order to reduce the likelihood of a former partner being liable for obligations incurred after his retirement, he should ensure that the partnership agreement is amended to reflect the fact that he is no longer a partner from the date of his departure, he should remove his name from the headed notepaper of the firm, from the firm's signs and from the register of business names (if the firm name is registered as a business name, see **5.1.7**). If there is a dispute about when he left the firm, these actions will have the additional benefit of supporting the claim that he left on a certain date and is not liable for liabilities incurred after that date.

5.5.4.4 Post-dissolution profits of a firm

Once a partner has left a firm, the partnership agreement should provide for his share in the firm to be purchased by the continuing partners. If there is no agreement, the default right in s. 39 of the 1890 Act will apply and the former partner may force the winding-up of the partnership under s. 39.

In addition, s. 42(1) of the 1890 Act provides for the situation where a member of a firm ceases to be a partner (including by death) and the continuing partners carry on the business of the firm without any final settlement of accounts as between the firm and the outgoing partner or his estate. Under this section, the outgoing partner or his estate is entitled, subject to contrary agreement, at the option of himself or his personal representatives to claim:

(a) such share of the profits made since the dissolution as the court may find to be attributable to the use of his share of the partnership assets; or

(b) interest at the rate of 5 per cent p.a. on the amount of his share of the partnership assets.

Thus, in either case, it is necessary to determine the former partner's share of the partnership assets. The approach to be taken in determining this issue was considered by the Supreme Court in *Meagher v Meagher* [1961] IR 96. The case involved three brothers, who carried on the business of buying houses, renovating them and selling them at a profit. On the death of one brother, the other two brothers continued to carry on the business. The value of the assets of the partnership had increased considerably since the date of death of the first brother, due to a general increase in property prices in Ireland at that time. In considering the deceased partner's estate's claim for his share of the profits made since the dissolution attributable to his share of the partnership assets under s. 42(1), the question arose as to whether the value of a deceased partner's share in the houses was to be calculated on the date of death or on the date these partnership assets were realised. The deceased's personal representative claimed that the deceased partner's share in the partnership should be valued on the basis of the prices received for the houses when they were sold, which was a number of years after the death. The Supreme Court held that the value of a partner's share of the partnership assets is the value of those assets on dissolution, but as a general rule, this is to be taken as the price realised on the sale of the assets, whenever that may be, unless there is a plausible case that the value at dissolution varied appreciably from that realised by sale. In this case, the post-dissolution profits were due primarily to an increase in the value of the partnership assets (i.e. houses) which had increased in value while they remained unsold. For this reason it seems that the Supreme Court did not make any attempt to ascertain what share of the post-dissolution profits were attributable to the use of the former partner's share of the partnership assets, but rather appears to have assumed that his share of the revalued partnership assets included his share of the post-dissolution profits.

Any amount due from the continuing partners to the former partner under this section is a debt accruing at the date of the death: 1890 Act, s. 43. Raising a large capital sum to pay a former partner or his estate will put a large financial strain on the resources of many partnerships. For this reason, it is common for the partnership agreement to provide a method for valuing the former partner's share in the firm and by providing for this capital sum to be paid by instalments.

5.5.5   DEATH

As noted at **5.5.2.3**, death causes the automatic dissolution of a partnership. In order to avoid inconvenience to the surviving partners it is common to provide in the partnership agreement that, instead of leading to the general dissolution of the partnership, the surviving partners will continue the partnership business and usually the agreement provides for the deceased partner's share to be purchased by them. In this way, the right of a partner to wind up the partnership under the 1890 Act, s. 39 is excluded.

5.5.5.1   Liability of partner's estate for debts

It has already been noted that under the 1890 Act, s. 9 every partner is jointly liable for debts and obligations of the firm incurred while he is a partner. In addition, s. 9 provides that the estate of a deceased person is severally liable for such debts and obligations so far as they remain unsatisfied but subject to the prior payment of the deceased partner's personal debts. A partnership creditor may, therefore, proceed against the estate of a deceased partner in respect of partnership debts (even after obtaining a judgment against the other partners) provided some part of the debt is unsatisfied. However, partnership creditors are postponed to the deceased partner's own creditors. It has been noted at **5.5.4.3** that s. 36(3) of the 1890 Act provides that the deceased partner's estate is not liable for partnership debts contracted after the death.

5.6   Partnerships With Limited Liability

5.6.1   INTRODUCTION

The main type of partnership in Ireland is the ordinary partnership, which is the main focus of this text. However, there are two other types of partnership under Irish law, the limited partnership and the investment limited partnership, each of which will be considered in turn.

5.6.2 LIMITED PARTNERSHIPS

5.6.2.1 Generally

The legislation governing this type of partnership is the Limited Partnerships Act 1907 and this provides that the general law of partnership applies to limited partnerships save as provided by the express terms of the 1907 Act. Therefore all of the principles of general partnership law which we have considered heretofore are equally applicable to limited partnerships, unless inconsistent with the terms of the 1907 Act.

A limited partnership must consist of at least one general partner and at least one limited partner. The general partner has unlimited liability like a partner in an ordinary partnership. It is worth noting that there is nothing to stop a limited company being a general partner and in this way effectively limiting the liability of the general partner. The limited partner has limited liability since his liability is limited to the amount of capital contributed by him to the firm. In return for the Limited Partnerships Acts granting the limited partner the protection of limited liability, he forsakes the normal rights of a partner to take part in the management of the firm. In many ways, the role of the limited partner is like a shareholder in a limited company because his liability is limited to the capital he has contributed and he has no role in the management of the firm. Unlike an ordinary partnership a limited partnership must be registered in the Companies Office and only comes into existence on the issue of the certificate of registration.

5.6.2.2 Popularity of limited partnerships

Tax avoidance vehicles

Limited partnerships became popular tax avoidance vehicles during the 1970s because limited partnerships, like all partnerships, are tax-transparent in the sense that unlike a company (in which the company and its shareholders are two taxable entities) in a partnership, the partnership itself is not taxed but only the individual partners. Thus, instead of having two levels of tax (i.e. corporation tax on the company and income tax on the dividend received by the shareholders) the profits of an enterprise which is organised as a partnership are subject to just one level of tax, namely income tax on the profits paid to the partners. In addition, the limited partnership gives the added bonus of limited liability for the limited partners in the venture. Limited partnerships remain popular vehicles in tax-based ventures for these reasons (e.g. film financing). However, in the 1970s the limited partnership had the added bonus of facilitating the reduction of a partner's personal income tax bill by allowing him to use large losses in his role as a limited partner. As a see-through vehicle for tax purposes, the losses of the partnership were passed on to the limited partners and used by them to offset profits on their other income. If these losses were in excess of the amount of capital contributed by the limited partner, as they usually were, then the limited partner only lost his capital but was able to set off a much larger amount against his personal income tax. This practice has been eliminated by the Revenue which now restricts the amount which may be set off against a limited partner's personal income to the amount of capital which he has contributed to the partnership.

Venture capital vehicles

Limited partnerships are popular today as venture capital vehicles since they allow for the easy withdrawal of capital by investors in the limited partnership. The limited partners take no part in the management of the firm's money (which suits most venture capitalists) and instead the money invested in the partnership is managed by the general partners. The limited partnership structure has the advantage over limited companies of not requiring an application to be made to court for the capital of a limited partnership to be repaid to the investors.

5.6.2.3 Loss of limited liability by limited partner

The protection of limited liability for the limited partners may be lost in certain circumstances under the terms of the 1907 Act. Since the raison d'être for limited partnerships is, in many cases, the presence of limited liability for the limited partners, it is important to bear in mind that the protection of limited liability will be lost in a number of situations, including if the limited partner takes part in the management of the firm or if there is a failure to properly register the firm or any change in the details of the firm, e.g. as happened in the case of *McCarthaigh v Daly* [1985] IR 73. This case involved a prominent Cork solicitor in the tax loophole referred to already at **5.1.3.1** which has since been closed off by the Revenue Commissioners. The respondent agreed to contribute capital of £50 to a limited partnership formed for the purpose of leasing assets to the Metropole Hotel in Cork in the tax year 1977–78. He sought to set off his share of the losses of the limited partnership which amounted to £2,000 against his personal income tax as a solicitor. Mr Daly was successful in having this amount set off. However, s. 5 of the Limited Partnerships Act provides that if there is a failure to properly register a limited partnership in accordance with the terms of the Act then every limited partner is deemed to be a general partner with unlimited liability. In that case the limited partnership was formed in December 1977 and the following February the form LP1 (the form to be completed and filed for the registration of a limited partnership) was filed in the Companies Office containing details of the £50 contributed by the limited partners. The certificate of registration of the limited partnership was issued by the registrar of companies on 16 February 1978. It transpired that the £50 was not actually contributed by the limited partners until April 1978. For this reason, the form LP1 was incorrect when it stated that the limited partners had contributed £50. In the High Court, O'Hanlon J held that the limited partnership was an ordinary partnership since the partnership had not been properly registered. The lesson to be learnt from this case is that special care should be taken to ensure that any filings, which are required to be made under the 1907 Act, are accurately and properly made in order to avoid the intended limited partners failing to obtain limited liability.

5.6.3 INVESTMENT LIMITED PARTNERSHIPS ACT 1994

The third and final type of partnership under Irish law is the most recent creation. It is the investment limited partnership which was introduced into Irish law for the first time by the Investment Limited Partnerships Act 1994. It is important to bear in mind that although this is an investment 'limited' partnership, it is not governed by the Limited Partnerships Act 1907 but by the general principles of partnership law as set out by the Partnership Act 1890, the case law thereunder and by the Investment Limited Partnerships Act 1994 itself.

5.6.3.1 Purpose and nature of an investment limited partnership

In 1986, legislation was enacted in Ireland to encourage the establishment of an International Financial Services Centre in the Custom House Docks area. As the limited partnership is a popular investment vehicle in the US, it was decided to introduce this concept into the Irish funds industry in order to further encourage investment in the IFSC from other jurisdictions such as America, the Cayman Islands and Bermuda where such vehicles have been popular for many years.

The investment limited partnership is a collective investment scheme which has the Central Bank as its regulatory authority and the general partner must have a minimum paid-up share capital of £100,000. Section 5 of the Investment Limited Partnerships Act 1994 defines an investment limited partnership as a partnership consisting of at least one general partner and one limited partner having as its principal business the investment of its funds in property of all kinds. Like the position with limited partnerships formed under the Limited Partnerships Act 1907, a general partner in an investment limited partnership has unlimited liability for the debts and obligations of the firm, while a limited partner is not liable for the debts and obligations of the firm beyond the amount of his capital contribution. However, having one general partner and one limited partner is not sufficient for a partnership to constitute an investment limited partnership since an investment limited partnership is defined as 'a partnership which holds a certificate of authorisation' from the Central Bank. Thus, an investment limited partnership only comes into existence on the receipt of this certificate of authorisation. As these partnerships are only of interest to sophisticated investors in the Irish funds industry, it is not proposed to go into the detailed regulation of these partnerships, much of which is to be found in the Central Bank Notices issued pursuant to Investment Limited Partnerships Act 1994.

5.6.3.2 Limited partner

As with limited partnerships under the 1907 Act, a limited partner under the Investment Limited Partnerships Act is not liable for the debts or obligations of the investment partnership beyond the amount of capital which he has contributed. An individual, body corporate or a partnership may be a limited partner.

5.6.3.3 General partner

The general partner will normally be the fund manager and, like a partner in an ordinary partnership, he will be personally liable for all debts of the investment limited partnership. An individual and body corporate, and it seems a partnership, may be a general partner. Thus, there is nothing to stop a limited company being a general partner and in this way to effectively limit the liability of the general partner.

FURTHER READING

Twomey: *Partnership Law* (2000, Butterworths)

CHAPTER 6

INTELLECTUAL PROPERTY AND INFORMATION TECHNOLOGY

6.1 Introduction

6.1.1 GENERAL

Intellectual property is the bedrock of the information society and has a rapidly growing importance in every area of commercial life. It impinges on every aspect of business, indeed often it is the most valuable asset a business owns. As a result, it is exceedingly important that solicitors acquire at least a general knowledge of the area so as to recognise when their clients may require advice to protect this asset and so as to be able to give pragmatic and succinct advice.

6.1.2 WHAT IS INTELLECTUAL PROPERTY?

Intellectual property is that area of law which has evolved to protect what is essentially the fruit of creative endeavour. Legal rights have been introduced and developed to protect this intangible property, upon which many businesses rely and which, particularly in the information technology industry, may generate enormous profits for the proprietors of those businesses.

As with any piece of property, intangible or real or personal, intellectual property may be traded. It may be sold or assigned for monetary consideration. It may be licensed or bequeathed in a will. In short it may be exploited in precisely the same ways as any piece of real or personal property.

It is vital therefore that every business knows what intellectual property rights it owns, what should be done to achieve the best possible protection of those rights, whether those rights are being exploited as well as may be and what to do if those rights are infringed. The solicitor should be in a position to advise in relation to all of these matters.

6.1.3 CATEGORIES OF INTELLECTUAL PROPERTY

The principal areas of intellectual property are protected by statute. These statutes make provision for a scheme of registration of various rights in order to assist in the clearer identification of those rights and of their ownership. The statutes grant the owner of an intellectual property right a clear monopoly in the property protected, which may be exploited as the owner decides. Intellectual property rights include the following categories:

    (a)   patents which protect inventions;

(b) trade marks which protect names in the course of trade and in the provision of services;

(c) copyright and industrial design which protect the physical form of literary, dramatic, musical and artistic endeavour;

(d) passing-off which protects, in common law, the goodwill and reputation of a business; and

(e) confidential information in which under common law an obligation of confidentiality exists in relation to information imparted from one party to another.

It is extremely important that, when advising clients on each occasion, the specific statute should be carefully considered. Frequently cases in this area of the law fall to be decided on the precise wording of a particular section or subsection of the relevant Act.

6.1.4   INTELLECTUAL PROPERTY—CONTRACTUAL CONSIDERATIONS

All of the statutes and the common law which protect intellectual property allow the general rules to be changed by agreement between the parties concerned. It is, in almost every situation, prudent for a solicitor to advise the client that the intention of the parties should be clearly agreed and set out in writing, prior to any dealings between the parties relating to intellectual property rights. Thus, if one party has an idea, an invention which may be patentable, it is sensible for that person, prior to discussing the invention with anyone, to enter into an agreement in writing that the parties will keep any information exchanged confidential. The parties are therefore bound by contract not to reveal any information without consent.

Similarly, all of the relevant statutes and the common law provide rules in relation to the ownership of intellectual property in an employment contract. Nonetheless, it is sensible, for the avoidance of doubt to set out in writing what has been agreed between the parties to avoid arguments in the future.

Clearly, in any case where a person has an invention, or an author has written a book, a play or a film script, and wishes to agree with a third party to exploit that work in any way, it is essential, for the avoidance of argument in the future that the terms and the basis upon which the exploitation is to take place are clearly set out in writing prior to commencement of the exploitation. It is in these situations that the solicitor may be of vital assistance to the client.

6.1.5   INTELLECTUAL PROPERTY AND COMPETITION LAW

As intellectual property law allows the existence of a monopoly and competition law outlaws agreements whose object or effect is to prevent, restrict or distort competition, an obvious dichotomy may arise between the two areas of law. The Competition Act 1991 introduced into domestic Irish law provisions similar to articles 81 and 82 of the EC Treaty. Unlike the EC Treaty, there is no de minimus provision in the Competition Act.

Thus, the abuse of a dominant position is prohibited within the State. The provisions of the Competition Act 1991 are set out in detail in *Applied European Law*.

Patent, know-how and research and development licences are all covered by EU Commission block exemptions so that such agreements, which would generally infringe EU competition law, are permissible. There are at present no category certificates or category licences (the Irish equivalent of block exemptions) for licences of intellectual property under the Competition Act and so it may be necessary to make a notification to the Competition Authority. However, the same issues considered by the EU Commission will

147

be considered by the Competition Authority when granting its certificate. Care should be taken to ensure that protection under the Trade Marks Act 1996 or other intellectual property legislation should not be used as a vehicle for the operation of an anti-competitive agreement or to abuse a dominant position as such protection may be void.

Articles 28–30 of the EC Treaty prohibit measures which impose quantitative restrictions on imports from other Member States or have equivalent effect. The doctrine of exhaustion of rights has been developed to accommodate, on the one hand, the monopoly right granted in intellectual property law and, on the other hand, the European Union rules allowing free movement of goods within the Community.

A trader applying a trade mark to and selling goods in one part of the European Union cannot prevent the sale of those goods which have been placed on the market with his consent, being sold in another European Union country, even when the trade mark is registered in that other European Union country. The trade mark rights are exhausted when the goods have first been placed on the market for sale.

This doctrine of exhaustion of rights is generally thought not to apply to goods, which are imported from third countries outside the European Union. Thus, goods which are imported from, for example, the USA or the Far East, may not be sold in the European Union without the consent of the owner of the trade mark in the European Union. This is the case provided that the goods are clearly marked as being goods from a third country and preferably marked that consent is not given for their sale within the European Union. The case law is not altogether settled in this area and so the more clearly it is stated on goods that consent is not given for sale within the European Union the more likely it is that the courts will support the owner of the trade mark.

6.1.6   INFRINGEMENT REMEDIES

The remedies for infringement of intellectual property rights are in all cases damages, or an account of profits, an injunction to prohibit the infringement and delivery up and destruction of the infringing property.

Damages will be calculated by reference to a reasonable royalty rate or licence fee, but may take into account various matters in mitigation. For example, if a defendant could show that he was unaware of or had no reasonable grounds for suspecting that an intellectual property right existed, the plaintiff may be precluded from being awarded damages.

Certain of the statutes provide specific remedies for seizure of goods and orders for delivery up. Some of these remedies may be enforced by the Garda Síochána.

Further, infringement of copyright and of registered trade marks may constitute a criminal offence, the penalties for which are a fine and/or a term of imprisonment.

6.2   Patents

6.2.1   INTRODUCTION

The law relating to patents is governed by the Patents Act 1992 ('the 1992 Act') which has been in force since 1 August 1992. The Patent Rules were also enacted in 1992 to deal with the administration of patents by the Patents Office and with the powers of the Controller of Patents in relation to the regulation of the patent regime. A number of international Conventions also exist with the objective of streamlining patent application, filing and novelty search procedures throughout the world. These are the Paris Convention of 1883, the Patent Co-operation Treaty 1970, the European Patent Convention 1973 and the

Community Patent Convention. Solicitors generally do not become involved in the area of patents until issues arise for decision by the courts. This is an extremely specialised area of the law and patent agents who are trained in scientific and engineering matters are expert in the drafting and processing of patents. It is important, however, for a solicitor to have some knowledge of the patent process in order to be able to advise properly when the matter reaches the stage of court proceedings.

6.2.2   PATENTABILITY

A patent may be obtained for any patentable invention and will grant the owner of the patent a monopoly protection in the invention for either a ten- (short-term) or twenty-year period. An invention is patentable if it is susceptible of industrial application, is new and involves an inventive step: 1992 Act, s. 9(1). In the case of a short-term patent the invention must be new, susceptible of industrial application and must not clearly lack an inventive step: 1992 Act, s. 63(4). There is no definition in the 1992 Act of 'invention'. However, the following shall not be regarded as an invention:

(a)   a discovery;

(b)   a scientific theory;

(c)   a mathematical method;

(d)   an aesthetic creation;

(e)   a scheme, rule or method for performing a mental act, playing a game or doing business;

(f)   a computer program; and

(g)   the presentation of information.

It is also provided that a method for treatment of the human or animal body by surgery or therapy and a diagnostic method practised on the human or animal body shall not be regarded as an invention susceptible of industrial application: 1992 Act, s. 9(4). However, it is provided that this provision shall not apply to a product and, in particular, a substance or composition for use in any such method.

An invention shall be considered to be new if it does not form part of the state of the art. This comprises everything made available or disclosed to the public (whether in the State or elsewhere) in any way before the date of filing of the patent application: 1992 Act, s. 11. Disclosure of an invention will be discounted if it happened within six months before the filing of the patent application as a result of a breach of confidence or because the invention was displayed at an exhibition officially recognised under the Paris Convention on International Exhibitions 1928 and the application makes a declaration to that effect when applying: 1992 Act, s. 12.

The invention will be considered as involving an inventive step if, having regard to the state of the art, it is not obvious to a person skilled in the art: 1992 Act, s. 13.

An invention is considered as susceptible of industrial application if it may be made or used in any kind of industry. Industry in this context includes agriculture: 1992 Act, s. 14.

There are certain exceptions to patentability under the Patents Act: 1992 Act, s. 10. A patent will not be granted in respect of:

(a)   an invention, the publication or exploitation of which will be contrary to public order or morality, provided that the exploitation will not be deemed to be so contrary only because it is prohibited by law; and

(b)   a plant or animal variety or an essentially biological process for the production of plants or animals other than a microbiological process or the products thereof.

6.2.3   GRANT OF A PATENT

Patents are granted by the Patents Office to which a formal application is made. Of their nature such applications are extremely technical and the actual application will be made by a specialised patent agent. However, it is important for a solicitor to be able to give a client an idea of the procedure involved in obtaining protection.

6.2.3.1   Applications

A patent application may be made by any person alone or jointly with another person (1992 Act, s. 15) but the right to a patent belongs to the inventor (1992 Act, s. 16) who has a right to be mentioned in the application: 1992 Act, s. 17.

A patent application for a twenty-year patent must contain (1992 Act, s. 18):

(a)   a request for the grant of a patent;

(b)   a specification containing a description of the invention to which the application relates, one or more claims and any drawing referred to in the description or the claim; and

(c)   an abstract (a brief summary description).

The application must be accompanied by a filing fee (1992 Act, s. 18), must clearly disclose the invention to which it relates (s. 19) and the claim or claims must define the matter for which protection is sought and must be supported by the description (s. 20). The application must relate to one invention only or at least to a group of inventions, which are so linked as to form a single inventive concept: s. 21.

If application is being made for a short-term (10-year) patent, the specification must (1992 Act, s. 63(7)):

(i)   describe the invention and the best method of performing it, which is known to the applicant;

(ii)   incorporate one or more claims, which must not exceed five, defining the matter for which protection is sought; and

(iii)   be accompanied by any necessary drawings and an abstract.

A full-term (twenty-year) patent and a short-term patent may not co-exist for the same invention: 1992 Act, s. 64.

Under s. 23 of the 1992 Act the date of filing of a patent application is the earliest date upon which the applicant paid the filing fee and filed documents which contained:

(A)   an indication that a patent is sought;

(B)   information identifying the applicant; and

(C)   a description of the invention even though the description does not comply with the requirements of the Act or with any requirements that may be prescribed.

If an objection is raised at the time during which the application is being examined that the application relates to more than one invention the applicant may amend the specification or delete the claims. The applicant may also file another application for the extra invention. This is known as a 'divisional application' which is in respect of subject matter, which must not extend beyond the content of an earlier application as filed and complies with the relevant requirements. Such an application will be deemed to have been filed on the date of filing of the earlier application and will have the benefit of any right to priority: 1992 Act, s. 24.

It is also possible to file an application and claim the priority of an earlier application in respect of the same invention, which has been filed either in the State or abroad: 1992 Act, s. 25.

150

6.2.3.2   Priority

The date of priority is the date of filing of the patent application (1992 Act, s. 27) in the State or abroad. This is an important date as it fixes the time which is to be considered for the purpose of assessing whether the invention is new. It also fixes the date from which infringement proceedings may be taken. Often an inventor will instruct his patent agent to apply for a patent at the first opportunity. This is to ensure that no rivals make application for the same invention and to obtain as early as possible a priority date. A more detailed application may then be filed within a twelve-month period. Once the application is received at the Patents Office, it is inspected by one of the Controller of Patents' examiners to make sure that the application complies with the requirements of the 1992 Act. The applicant may request that a search be undertaken on behalf of the Controller in return for the appropriate fee to ensure that the invention complies with the requirement that it is new. Clearly, if the invention is not new, it is open to attack and will be invalid. The Controller must allow an applicant an opportunity to amend the application in light of the result of the search report within a prescribed period.

Alternatively, an applicant for a patent may submit a statement to the Controller to the effect that an application for a patent for the same invention has been made in a prescribed foreign State (UK or Germany) or under the provisions of any prescribed Convention or Treaty (the EPC or the PCT): 1992 Act, s. 30; Patent Rules 1992, r. 26. In this case the applicant must submit evidence either of the results of the search carried out on that application or of the grant of a patent in pursuance of the application. Where the applicant has submitted the results of a search, the Controller shall allow an opportunity to amend the application in light of that evidence.

The patent application must then be published in the official journal of the Patents Office, which is published every fortnight. Publication must be as soon as practicable after the expiry of eighteen months from the filing date or from the priority date, if claimed. If the applicant requests it may be published earlier: 1992 Act, s. 28. If no objections are received the patent proceeds to grant—it is sealed and issued.

6.2.4   PROTECTION CONFERRED BY A PATENT

6.2.4.1   Generally

While a patent is in force it confers upon the proprietor the right to prevent all third parties not having his consent from using the invention whether directly or indirectly: 1992 Act, s. 40. Direct use of the invention includes, for example, making, putting on the market or using a product which is the subject matter of the patent, or importing or stocking the product for those purposes: 1992 Act, s. 40. The prevention of indirect use of the invention means that a proprietor may also prevent all third parties not having his consent from supplying or offering to supply in the State someone, other than a party entitled to exploit the patented invention: 1992 Act, s. 41.

6.2.4.2   Exception to monopoly

The following provisions are imported from the Community Patent Convention. The rights conferred by a patent do not extend to acts done privately for non-commercial purposes, or acts done for experimental purposes. These acts may be done without infringing the patent holder's rights. Nor do they extend to the extemporaneous preparation for individual cases in a pharmacy, of a medicine in accordance with a medical prescription. They do not extend either to use of the patented product on board vessels or aircraft or land vehicles, when such temporarily or accidentally enter territorial waters of the State or the State itself: 1992 Act, s. 42. This provision is presumably designed to assist in ensuring the safety of such vessels—the invention must be used exclusively for the needs of the vessel.

6.2.4.3 Rights on application

A patent application provisionally confers upon the applicant the same protection as that conferred on a granted patent from the date of its publication: 1992 Act, s. 44. In turn, infringement proceedings may be brought after a patent has been granted in respect of infringing acts committed between the date of publication of the application and the date of grant: 1992 Act, s. 56.

6.2.4.4 Extent of protection

The extent of the protection conferred by the patent or patent application is to be determined by the terms of the claims. A description and drawing submitted will be used to interpret the claims: 1992 Act, s. 45.

6.2.4.5 Short-term patents

The protection conferred by a short-term patent is the same as for a twenty-year patent subject to the provisions of the 1992 Act, s. 66. This section attempts to strike a balance between the rights of a short-term patent holder and third parties. To this end it requires the holder of a short-term patent to request the Controller to establish a search report on the invention before he may initiate proceedings against a third party for alleged infringement of his patent. Any such proceedings may be brought in the circuit court irrespective of the amount of any claim.

6.2.5 OWNERSHIP

The owner of a patent is normally the inventor. In the case of joint inventors both parties may be named as the owners of the patent.

In the case of inventions made by an employee, these will belong to the employer if they are made in the course of the employee's employment. The Act does not specifically provide this, so contracts of employment should stipulate that the inventions belong to the employer. If not stipulated in the contract then the invention may still be deemed to belong to the employer if the court considers it should because the invention was invented during the course of the employment of the employee or in circumstances where the employee was employed for the purposes of inventing. Section 16 of the 1992 Act states that if the inventor is an employee the right to a patent shall be determined in accordance with the law of the State in which the employee is wholly or mainly employed.

6.2.6 SUPPLEMENTARY PROTECTION CERTIFICATES ('SPC')

Pharmaceuticals may not be sold to the public unless they have been granted a product authorisation. In order to obtain such an authorisation, the applicant must provide detailed technical information in relation to the testing of the product and its efficiency, all of which must be considered by the regulatory authorities, in Ireland, the Irish Medicines Board. The SPC was introduced at the behest of the pharmaceutical industry to compensate that industry for the lengthy regulatory delays which occur while a manufacturer of a new product is seeking approval for sale of it to the public. The EU Regulations EC1768/92 introducing the SPC, were incorporated into Irish law by the European Communities (Supplementary Protection Certificate) Regulations 1993 (SI 125/1993). The SPC has the effect of extending the twenty-year life of a pharmaceutical patent by a period, which gives protection for fifteen years from the date upon which it first received marketing approval in the European Union. The maximum extension allowed over and above the usual twenty-year patent is five years.

It is important to check whether an SPC exists in relation to a pharmaceutical product if the client is considering manufacturing the patented product as the patent may have been extended and the client might be exposed to an infringement action.

6.2.7 INFRINGEMENT

A patent is infringed by anyone who, in the State without the consent of the proprietor, makes, offers or puts on the market a product which is the subject matter of a patent or uses a process which is the subject matter of a patent knowing (or it is obvious to a reasonable person in the circumstances) that the use of the process is prohibited.

Civil proceedings may be brought by the proprietor or licensee of a patent for alleged infringement of a patent: 1992 Act, s. 47. He may seek:

(a) an injunction restraining the defendant from any apprehended act of infringement;

(b) an order requiring the defendant to deliver up or destroy any product protected by the patent in relation to which the patent is alleged to have been infringed or any article in which the product is inextricably comprised;

(c) damages in respect of the alleged infringement;

(d) in the alternative an account of profits derived by the defendant from the alleged infringement; and

(e) a declaration that the patent is valid and has been infringed by the defendant.

Damages will not be awarded nor will an order be made for an account of profits against a defendant who proves that, at the date of infringement, he was unaware of and had no reasonable grounds for supposing that the patent in question existed. However, he will be deemed to have been aware or to have had reasonable grounds for so supposing where the number of the relevant patent had been applied to a product: 1992 Act, s. 49.

6.2.8 GROUNDLESS THREATS

In the normal course, where a property right is being infringed the owner will instruct a solicitor to send a strong letter demanding that the infringement be stopped. This is known as a 'cease and desist' letter. In the case of patents it is important to note that a person who has been threatened with proceedings for infringement of a patent may bring his own proceedings to court for relief: 1992 Act, s. 53. He may seek:

(a) a declaration to the effect that the threats complained of were unjustifiable;

(b) an injunction against the continuance of the threats; and

(c) such damages if any as have been suffered.

It is for this reason that rather than the usual form of strongly-worded cease and desist letter being sent at the commencement of a patent action, a letter is sent simply drawing the attention of the alleged infringer to the existence of the patent. This is to avoid a claim for groundless threats being made against both the client and the solicitor.

6.2.9 REVOCATION

Any person may apply to the court or the Controller of Patents for revocation of a patent: 1992 Act, s. 57. The grounds for revocation are:

(a) the subject matter of the patent is not patentable;

(b) the specification of the patent does not properly disclose the invention so that it may be carried out by a person skilled in the art;

(c) the matter disclosed in the specification extends beyond that disclosed in the application which was filed;

(d) the protection conferred by the patent has been extended by an amendment of the patent or the specification of the patent; and

(e) the proprietor of the patent is not the person who is entitled to the patent: 1992 Act, s. 58.

Thus an employee who claims an invention is not his employer's might apply for revocation or the owner of an existing patent might apply if the new patent is an obvious improvement of his patent. In cases where a claim for infringement is made, one of the standard defences is to seek revocation of the plaintiff's patent on one or all of the grounds (a) to (e) above. The Controller has the power to revoke patents on his own initiative if it appears that the patent which has been granted formed part of the state of the art. In such a case, the proprietor of the patent will have an opportunity of making observations and amending this specification of the patent in order to preserve it: 1992 Act, s. 60. In the event that proceedings for revocation are brought before the court, the Controller must be given notice in writing by the plaintiff of those proceedings: 1992 Act, s. 62. Section 94 provides that a communication between a person or person acting on his behalf and a solicitor or patent agent or person acting on his behalf, or for the purpose of obtaining, or in response to a request for information which a person is seeking for the purpose of instructing the solicitor or patent agent in relation to any matter concerning the protection of an invention, patent, design or technical information, or any matter involving passing-off shall be privileged to the same extent as a communication between client and solicitor in any proceeding before a court in the State: 1992 Act, s. 94.

6.2.10 INTERNATIONAL CONVENTIONS

6.2.10.1 The Patent Co-operation Treaty

The main object of the Patent Co-operation Treaty ('the PCT') is the streamlining of patent application filing and novelty search procedures for an applicant wishing to obtain patent protection in a wide number of countries around the world. It was signed by Ireland in 1970 and has been ratified as a result of the Patents Act 1992.

Under the Treaty the procedure is that the applicant makes one central application, usually to their local patent office, designating the countries in which patent protection is required. A novelty search is then carried out by an international searching authority and this search is then furnished to the National Office of each country in which protection is sought. Further prosecution in each country is then in the hands of the local patent office in accordance with its normal procedure.

6.2.10.2 European Patent Convention

The European Patent Convention ('the EPC') is more advanced than the PCT in that searching and examination are centralised in the European Patent Office in Munich. The EPC was made effective in Ireland by the 1992 Act. The procedure under the EPC is that anyone seeking to protect an invention in several member countries of the Convention may do so by making just one application to the European Patent Office in Munich. The applicant must designate all of the countries in which protection is desired. This means he must specifically name the countries in which he seeks patent protection for his invention. Nationals of both member and non-member countries are entitled to take advantage of this arrangement. Under the Patents Act 1992 a European patent designating Ireland granted by the European Patent Office is treated as if it was granted by the Irish Office: 1992 Act,

s. 119. However, if the language of the specification of the European patent is not English, a translation in English of the specification must be filed with the Irish Patent Office and published here in order that the patent may have effect in Ireland: 1992 Act, s. 119(6), (7). Similarly, in the case of a European patent application designating Ireland, such an application must be treated as having the same legal status in Ireland as an application filed with the Irish Office: 1992 Act, s. 120.

Section 122 of the 1992 Act permits a European patent application designating Ireland, which has been deemed to be withdrawn, to be proceeded with as a national application under the 1992 Act, subject to certain conditions.

Section 123 of the 1992 Act provides that the High Court is given jurisdiction to determine questions as to the right to be granted a European patent and sets out the circumstances in which such jurisdiction is exercisable.

Section 124 of the 1992 Act provides for the recognition in Ireland of questions as to the right to a European patent determined by a court or competent authority of another Contracting State of the EPC, subject to certain conditions.

A decision as to whether to file a European patent application specifying those European countries in which patent protection is sought or individual national applications will depend on several factors. The European patent procedure is expensive, but if protection in several countries is required, it may still be cheaper than a corresponding series of individual applications. The examination procedure carried out by the European Patent Office is well respected, so that if a European patent is granted, it is likely that such a patent would be subsequently upheld in the national courts. Another factor is that under article 99 of the EPC, a European patent may be revoked in total only during the first nine months of grant; subsequently it may only be revoked country by country, by application to the appropriate national court. Section 127 of the 1992 Act allows Ireland to be designated in an international application. This section also provides that an international application designating the State, for example, by an American client, shall be deemed to be an application for a European patent (under the EPC) designating the State. This means that functions concerning international applications, which would otherwise have to be performed by the Irish Patents Office, may instead be performed by the European Patent Office. The applicant will eventually receive a grant by the European Patent Office of a European patent designating Ireland if he has availed of this procedure.

.2.10.3   Community Patent Convention

The Community Patent Convention ('the CPC') was signed in 1989 but has not yet come into force. The 1992 Act does not itself mention the CPC although it includes a general provision allowing the Minister for Public Enterprise to make an order enabling effect to be given to 'any international treaty, convention or agreement relating to patents to which the State is or proposes to become a party': 1992 Act, s. 128. As a result of the Eleventh Amendment of the Constitution Act 1992 whereby article 29.4 of the Constitution was amended by constitutional referendum held on 18 June 1992, it will now be possible for Ireland to implement the CPC.

The CPC may be regarded as a further extension to the European Patent Convention with the difference that instead of a bundle of individual patents in European countries being granted, there is obtained instead a single patent known as a Community patent throughout all those European countries which are also members of the European Union. Certain difficulties have arisen in relation to the mechanics of the CPC and it is likely to be completely redrafted. However, the principle of the grant of a single patent will remain.

6.3   Trade Marks, Counterfeit Goods and Passing-Off

6.3.1   INTRODUCTION

This section of the law developed to prevent the public being deceived by a trader alleging that he had an association with goods which, in fact, he did not enjoy. The first Trade Marks Act was introduced in 1875 and brought in a system of registration of trade marks. Currently this area is governed by the Trade Marks Act 1996 ('the 1996 Act') and the regulations made thereunder.

6.3.2   WHAT IS A TRADE MARK?

6.3.2.1   Generally

Section 6 of the 1996 Act says that a 'trade mark' means:

> *any sign capable of being represented graphically which is capable of distinguishing goods or services of one undertaking from those of other undertakings.*

The Act goes on to say that a trade mark may, in particular, consist of words (including personal names), designs, letters, numerals or the shape of goods or of their packaging.

Thus, a trade mark may be something as simple as a name written in a particular script or with a band of colour around it, or as complicated as any designer can imagine. It does not have to be a name at all. It may be three stripes, it may be the shape of a bottle, and it may even be a smell provided that the applicant has been able to represent the smell graphically and that it is distinguishable from other smells.

Once a trade mark has been registered under the 1996 Act, it is a property right and the proprietor of a registered trade mark is entitled to all the rights and remedies provided by the 1996 Act. A trade mark may be registered in one of forty-two classes. There are thirty-four separate classes for marks used in connection with goods and eight classes for marks used in connection with services. Often a business may make a trade mark application in several classes.

6.3.2.2   Marks which may be refused registration

Sections 8–10 of the 1996 Act govern marks which may be refused registration. Signs which do not satisfy the requirements described above, which are devoid of any distinctive character, or which consist of signs or indications which may serve, in trade, to designate the kind, quality, quantity, intended purpose, value, geographical origin, the time of production of goods or of rendering of services, or other characteristics of goods or services which consist exclusively of signs or indications which have become customary in the practice of the trade will not be registered as trade marks.

However, if any of those trade marks has in fact acquired a distinctive character as a result of the use made of it, then registration will be permitted (for example, the Waterford Glass Mark is a mark indicating geographical origin but is registered because of its distinctive character).

Pursuant to s. 8(2) of the 1996 Act a sign will not be registered as a trade mark if it consists exclusively of the shape which results from the nature of the goods themselves, or the shape of goods which is necessary to obtain a technical result, or the shape which gives substantial value to the goods.

Pursuant to s. 8(3) of the 1996 Act a trade mark will not be registered if it is contrary to public policy or morality or if it deceives the public, for example, as to the nature, quality or geographical origin of the goods or service.

A State emblem of Ireland, or one which resembles such an emblem, will not be registered unless the consent to its registration has been given by the Minister for Public Enterprise. The national flag of the State will not be registered if it would be misleading or grossly offensive and the Controller may refuse to register a mark which consists of any emblem of a public authority unless as provided in s. 9 of the 1996 Act 'such consent as is required by rules is obtained'.

Pursuant to s.10(2) of the 1996 Act a trade mark will not be registered if it is identical to or similar to an earlier trade mark and the goods or services are identical, or if there exists the likelihood of confusion, including the likelihood of association of the later trade mark with the earlier trade mark. Pursuant to s. 10(3) of the 1996 Act a trade mark will not be registered if it is identical to or similar to an earlier trade mark and it is to be registered for different goods or services from those protected by the earlier trade mark if the use of the later trade mark would take unfair advantage of the earlier mark. A trade mark will not be registered if its use in the State is liable to be prevented because it is passing itself off as an unregistered mark already used in the course of trade or if it would infringe the copyright, registered design, or any other law relating to a right to a name, a right of personal portrayal or an industrial property right unless the owner of the earlier trade mark consents. An 'earlier trade mark' is defined in the 1992 Act, s. 11.

Pursuant to s. 12 of the 1996 Act, however, if there has been what is called honest concurrent use of the trade mark, then the Controller is not allowed to refuse the application.

3.3 REGISTRATION OF A TRADE MARK

3.3.1 Application for a trade mark

Application for registration of a trade mark is made to the Controller of Trade Marks and is made in respect of particular goods or services or in respect of particular classes of goods or services in one of the forty-two separate classes or categories of goods and services. Each class or category is defined in relation to the nature or description of the goods or services.

The Controller examines the application to make sure that the requirements of the 1996 Act have been fulfilled and once the application for registration has been accepted, it is advertised in the official journal which is published fortnightly. Any person is entitled to give notice of opposition to the registration within one month of the advertisement and that period can be extended by two months. If the Controller receives no objection then he registers the trade mark, which lasts for ten years and may be renewed for further periods of ten years on payment of the requisite fee, forever.

Section 17 of the 1996 Act provides that a person who applies for registration of a trade mark may disclaim any right to the exclusive use of any part of the trade mark. Further, the Controller may refuse to accept the application unless the applicant agrees to make a disclaimer in respect of a particular element of the mark. The registration which subsequently occurs therefore is restricted accordingly: s.17.

3.3.2 Non-use

Pursuant to s. 51 of the 1996 Act, if a trade mark has not been put to genuine use in the State by or with the consent of the proprietor for a period of five years, then it may be revoked.

3.3.3 Community trade marks

The Community Trade Mark Office (Office for the Harmonisation of the Internal Market (OHIM)) opened in Alicante in Spain in April 1996 to give the applicants for trade marks the facility to apply to a Central Office for a trade mark in any European country. There is a right to claim priority for an application for a period of six months from the date of filing of the first convention application and any filing equivalent to a regular national filing shall be treated as giving rise to the right of priority: s. 40.

6.3.4   BUSINESS NAMES

It is possible to register a business name under the Business Names Act 1963 ('the 1963 Act'). However, registration does not confer an exclusive right to the name in the registered owner. The purpose of the 1963 Act is to provide a register of firms and individuals trading in the State under a name other than that of the person concerned. Thus no exclusive protection is granted to the owner of a business name by registration of it. There may be several registrations for the same name each owned by a different party.

6.3.5   COUNTERFEIT GOODS

There is a very useful procedure which was introduced initially by the European Communities (Counterfeit Goods) Regulations 1990 (SI 118/1990) whereby upon payment of a fee of £400 for each three-month period, a trade mark owner may register his trade mark with the customs section of the Revenue Commissioners.

The regulations were amended in 1996 to cover what are called 'pirated goods' which include not only infringing trade marks but also goods made without the consent of a copyright owner or owner of 'neighbouring rights' or the holder of a design right, whether or not registered under national law. A further amendment is on the way.

Each consignment of goods with the trade mark applied and which is imported from a third country outside the European Union will be inspected to ascertain whether the goods are genuine. The trade mark owner will be requested to inspect the goods and if they are found to be counterfeit, the customs authorities will seize them and they will ultimately be destroyed.

The importer has a right to oppose a seizure and must do so within one month. The procedure is very straightforward and, in comparison with the other remedy of court application for an injunction, is from a client's point of view just as effective and much more cost effective.

6.3.6   WHAT IS PASSING-OFF?

6.3.6.1   Meaning of passing-off

Passing-off is a tort actionable at common law. It recognises the right of a person to seek to protect the goodwill of his business from unfair trading. It prohibits a third party from selling goods or carrying on business under a name, mark, description or otherwise in such a manner as is likely to mislead the public or likely to deceive or confuse them into believing that the merchandise or business is that belonging to another person. The most succinct description of passing-off is that of Lord Parker in *A. G. Spalding & Brothers v A.W. Gamage Ltd* (1915) 32 RPC 273, a case which involved a stock of the plaintiff's footballs which they had discontinued and which the defendant bought and advertised for sale at very low prices as the latest model.

Lord Parker described the tort of passing-off as follows:

> 'Trader A cannot without infringing the rights of Trader B represent goods which are not B's goods or B's goods of a particular class or quality to be B's goods or B's goods of that particular class or quality'.

The right of protection which the plaintiff has is not just to protect a particular mark applied to goods or to protect a reputation but rather to give a trader a property right in the goodwill built up in the business. The courts have accepted that both the word 'trader' and the word 'goodwill' are very broad in meaning and whiskey and champagne makers, actors and writers have all been granted relief in passing-off. So, A cannot without infringing the rights of B represent goods, which are not B's goods, to be B's goods. This then is the essence of passing-off.

Passing-off is now regarded as having been categorically defined in the Advocaat Case: *Erven Warnink BV v J. Townsend & Sons (Hull) Ltd* [1979] AC 731. Lord Diplock in that case decreed that there were five characteristics, which must be present in order to create a valid cause of action for passing-off:

(a) a misrepresentation;

(b) made by a trader in the course of trade;

(c) to prospective customers of his or ultimate consumers of goods or services supplied by him;

(d) which is calculated to injure the business or goodwill or another trader (in the sense that this is a reasonably foreseeable consequence); and

(e) which causes actual damage to a business or goodwill of the trader by whom the action is brought; or (in a *quia timet* action) will probably do so.

6.3.6.2 A misrepresentation

It should be understood that passing-off does not confer a monopoly right in either the name in a trade mark or in the get-up of goods. The action may only succeed if use of any of those things is calculated to mislead or may mislead. The defendant may use any part of the plaintiff's property, provided that he does not do it in a way which will deceive. The basis of the action is that a false representation is made by the defendant so that an association with another person (the plaintiff) is made in the minds of the public. This representation must be material in that there must be a proper risk of damage to the plaintiff.

6.3.6.3 Made by a trader in the course of trade

Although the *Advocaat Case* expressly required the plaintiff to be a trader, this requirement is in fact an unnecessary one. If the plaintiff is not trading, then he cannot suffer damage to his business or to his goodwill. Having said that, what constitutes a trader is, as far as the law of passing-off is concerned, extremely wide. Basically, anyone who makes an income from the provision of goods or services may be said to be a trader. Trade associations have been successful in bringing actions for passing-off, including, for example, the BBC and the British Medical Association. Charities such as Dr Barnados Homes have been granted injunctions. In these cases the court accepted the contention that in spite of the fact that the BBC, British Medical Association and Dr Barnardos are non-profit-making organisations they could nonetheless be regarded as trading. On the other hand, a political party was not considered to be a trader on the basis that it was involved in non-commercial activities: *British Medical Association v Marsh* (1931) 48 RPC 565 and *Kean v McGivan* [1982] FSR 119.

6.3.6.4 To prospective customers of his

On the face of it evidence of actual deception will be useful examples to persuade a judge that a passing-off has occurred. However, at the end of the day, it is settled that the court's decision will not depend solely on the evaluation of such evidence and that 'the court must in the end trust to its own perception into the mind of the reasonable man'. This view has been approved by Laffoy J in the High Court in the interlocutory application in *Symonds Cider & English Wine Co Ltd v Showerings (Ireland) Ltd*, 10 January 1997, HC (unreported) when she did not take into account the surveys of the opinion of the public which had been carried out by both parties as to confusion. Laffoy J was strongly of the view that she was able to decide whether a passing-off had occurred without such survey evidence and that it was more appropriate that she should do so.

6.3.6.5 Business or goodwill

Goodwill is created by trading. Originally this meant that the plaintiff had to satisfy the court that his business was within the jurisdiction and that he had been trading for some time. However, over the past twenty years or so, the courts have accepted that goodwill may be created in different ways, aside from simply trading within the jurisdiction. In *C&A Modes Ltd v C&A Waterford Ltd* [1978] FSR 126 the court accepted that even though C&A had no store in the Republic of Ireland, there was a very regular custom from the south to the north of Ireland where C&A had a store in Belfast and a substantial amount of advertising was carried out by C&A in the Sunday magazine supplements and in women's magazines and on television, all of which was received in the Republic of Ireland. This was the first case where a court accepted that goodwill could be built up from foreign trading.

In *O'Neills Irish International Sports Co Ltd and Charles O'Neill & Co Ltd v O'Neill's Footwear Dryer Co Ltd*, 30 April 1997, HC (unreported) Barron J appears to have decided in favour of the plaintiff more on the basis of their reputation than the goodwill they had built up in the name O'Neill. The defendant was a company owned by Mr John O'Neill who had obtained a patent for an electrically-operated shoe dryer. As he could not find any support from sports manufacturers, including the plaintiffs, for his invention and not having sufficient financial resources to manufacture it himself, he decided he would import a similar product from the Far East with a view to encouraging interest from manufacturers in his own product. He sold the imported product in a box similar to a normal shoe box with pictures of different types of shoe and of the dryer on it. The label on the box said that the product was an O'Neills footwear dryer and referred to Celbridge Ireland and also said 'made in China'. The plaintiffs sought an injunction on the basis of passing-off, claiming that they had a reputation in the name O'Neills and that the defendant was trading on that reputation. It was held that the defendant was deliberately trading upon the plaintiff's reputation and the court found that the defendant was wrong in the belief that he could use his own name and market his product under that name. While a person may use his own name in the course of trade, this does not entitle him to use it in such a way as is calculated to lead others to believe his goods are those of another.

6.3.6.6 Damage

The plaintiff must satisfy the court that the action of a defendant has or is likely to cause the plaintiff damage. The first of these requirements, that is where the plaintiff has already suffered damage is straightforward, in that if confusion in the minds of the public may be proved as to ownership of the goods and it may be argued that the defendant's goods are inferior, then the court may be satisfied that both the goodwill and the reputation of the plaintiff are being damaged. The second category, that is that the action is likely to cause damage, is in practice generally not a difficult proof to overcome. If goodwill and reputation may be shown and if, which is almost always the case, the defendant's products or the services offered are inferior, the court will accept that damage is likely to be caused. In *Falcon Travel v Falcon Leisure Group* [1991] IHR 175 Murphy J took a novel approach to the issue of damage. The plaintiffs had been trading in Dublin for three or four years when Falcon Leisure, the UK tour operator, began trading as well. The plaintiffs were able to show that they were receiving numerous phone calls which should have been for the defendants and that they were losing business from people ringing the defendants when they intended to ring the plaintiffs. The defendants argued that there could be no likelihood of confusion to the public as they were a tour operator and the plaintiff was a travel agency. The defendant also argued that the plaintiff had actually benefited from the confusion rather than having suffered damage. Murphy J agreed that a passing-off had occurred and that the plaintiff's reputation had become entirely submerged with that of the defendant. The court found that goodwill, which was appropriated, could constitute damage in itself, without proof of loss of custom. In this case the court awarded damages to the plaintiffs rather than an injunction so that Falcon Travel could launch an advertising campaign to make sure that the public was aware of the difference between the plaintiffs and the defendants.

6.3.7   INFRINGEMENT

6.3.7.1   Generally

The proprietor of a registered trade mark has exclusive rights in the trade mark and those rights are infringed if someone else uses an identical trade mark in relation to the same goods or services or similar goods or services so that a likelihood of confusion may arise on the part of the public: 1996 Act, s. 14. 'Use' includes in particular:

(a)   affixing a sign to goods or the packaging thereof;

(b)   offering or exposing goods for sale, putting them on the market or stocking them for those purposes under the sign or offering or supplying services under the sign;

(c)   importing or exporting goods under the sign; or

(d)   using the sign on business papers or in advertising.

6.3.7.2   Exceptions to infringement

No one is prevented from using a registered trade mark to identify goods or services as those of the proprietor or licensee of that registered trade mark, but such use must be in accordance with honest practices. Otherwise it will be treated as infringing the registered trade mark if it takes unfair advantage of, or is detrimental to, the distinctive character or reputation of the trade mark.

A trade mark is not infringed by the use of a person of his own name or address or of indications concerning the kind, quality, quantity, intended purpose, value, geographical origin, time of production of goods or of rendering of the service or other characteristics of goods or services, or where it is necessary to indicate the intended purpose of the product or service, in particular as accessories or spare parts. However, all of these uses must be in accordance with honest practices, industrial and commercial matters: 1996 Act, s. 15(2).

A trade mark will not be infringed by its use on goods which have been put on the market in the European Economic Area by the proprietor of the trade mark or with his consent. This is referred to as the exhaustion of rights of a registered trade mark and stems from EC law, confirming that the owner of a trade mark has exclusive right to use the mark and protect himself against competitors wishing to take advantage of the trade mark while at the same time prohibiting the owner of the trade mark using his mark to limit the free movement of goods.

However, there may be grounds for preventing the goods being sold, if, for example, their condition has been changed or impaired after they have been put on the market: s.16. Further, a trade mark owner can prevent goods from outside the European Economic Area being sold without his consent even if he has affixed his trade mark to the goods.

6.3.7.3   Remedies

When a mark is infringed, the court has the power to grant an injunction prohibiting the infringement and order the payment of damages and may require the infringer to remove the offending sign or, if that is not possible, to destroy the goods, materials or articles in question: 1996 Act, ss. 18, 19.

Section 20 of the 1996 Act makes provision for the owner of a trade mark to apply for an order for the delivery up to him of infringing goods, materials or articles.

Section 23 of the 1996 Act says that the court may make an order destroying goods which have been seized under the 1996 Act, s. 20. No rules of court have been made as to the service of notice on the infringer of this application to destroy but, in practice, the court will generally require that the infringer be notified of the application.

6.3.7.4 Seizure orders

Section 25 of the 1996 Act gives the district court the power to request the Garda Síochána to seize goods, materials or articles and to bring them before the court. On proof to the district court that they are infringing goods, materials or articles the court may make an order delivering them up to the owner of the registered trade mark, ordering them to be destroyed or dealt with in such other way as the court thinks fit. This is an extremely useful remedy if the client's trade marks are being infringed by the sale of counterfeit goods at, for example, a street market or concert. This section also means that an application may be made to the district court ex parte, which provides a cheap and effective remedy for the client.

6.3.7.5 Groundless threats

Section 24 provides that if proceedings are threatened for an infringement of a registered trade mark when it is not in relation to the application of the mark to goods or the importation of goods to which the mark has been applied or the supply of services under the mark, then the person who receives the threat of the proceedings may seek a declaration that the threats are unjustifiable and may look for an injunction prohibiting the threat and for damages.

6.3.8 ASSIGNMENT AND CHARGES OF REGISTERED TRADE MARKS

Trade marks are transferable by assignment, testamentary disposition or operation of law in exactly the same way as any personal property may be transferred with either the goodwill of the business or independently. An unregistered trade mark may only be transferred with the benefit of the goodwill of a business. Any assignment must be in writing, signed by the assignor and sealed, if the assignor is a body corporate.

Registered trade marks may also be charged in the same way as any other personal property. Where a trade mark has been assigned or mortgaged, particulars of the transaction should be registered with the Controller of Trade Marks. If this is not done then the transaction is ineffective as against a third party acquiring a conflicting interest and being unaware of the transfer or mortgage and as against anyone who is a licensee of the trade mark: 1996 Act, s. 29. Furthermore, unless the application for registration is made within six months of the transaction, or at least as soon as is practicable, the assignee/mortgagee will not be entitled to damages or to an account of the profits in respect of any infringement of the mark occurring after the date of the transaction and before the application for registration of the prescribed participators is made.

6.3.9 LICENSING

Licences of registered trade marks may be granted but they must be in writing, signed by and on behalf of the grantor to be valid. It is wise also to put a notice of the licence on the Register of Trade Marks. If this is not done the owner of the trade mark may be exposed to a claim to expunge the trade mark for non-use.

6.4 Copyright and Designs

6.4.1 INTRODUCTION

Copyright subsists in the physical material of a wide variety of work. The protection does not extend to ideas or principles, which underlie any element of a work. Thus copyright is a negative right to prevent the reproduction, including copying, of physical material.

6.4.2 COPYRIGHT AND DESIGN PROTECTION

6.4.2.1 Statutory regulation

Copyright is now governed by the Copyright and Related Rights Act 2000 ('the 2000 Act') Designs are protected by the Industrial and Commercial Property (Protection Act) 1927 ('the 1927 Act'). The Industrial Designs Bill was published on 7 July 2000 and will repeal the 1927 Act. It is expected to become law during 2001.

6.4.2.2 Subsistence of copyright

Copyright is a property right, like any other, which permits the owner of the copyright to authorise third parties to do certain things in relation to a work which would, except for the existence of the 2000 Act, be prohibited or, to use the word used in the 2000 Act, restricted.

Copyright subsists in:

(a) original literary, dramatic, musical or artistic works;

(b) sound recordings, films, broadcasts or cable programs;

(c) the typographical arrangement of published editions; and

(d) original databases: s. 17(2).

6.4.2.3 Industrial designs

The Industrial and Commercial Property (Protection) Act 1927 which originally dealt with all the statutory areas of intellectual property has been repealed, apart from the sections which deal with industrial designs. It is to be replaced in 2001. The Act provides that the proprietor of any new or original design may apply for registration. The word 'design' means

> only the features of shape, configuration, pattern, or ornament applied to any article by any industrial process or means, whether manual, mechanical or chemical, separate or combined which, in the finished article, appeal to and are judged solely by the eye, but does not include any mode or principle of construction or anything which is in substance a mere mechanical device.

This means that in order for a design to be registrable it must be something which in effect has no function but is purely decorative.

The 1927 Act further provides that copyright shall not subsist in designs, which are registrable under Part 3 of the 1927 Act. Thus, if a design is registrable under the Act but the owner of the design does not register it, he can do nothing to protect his design against infringers. The register is divided into classes and the same design may be registered in more than one class. The period of protection for a design is initially five years from the date of registration with provision for two further periods of five years, making a total of fifteen in all. Section 78 of the 2000 Act provides that copyright in a work is not infringed by anything done pursuant to an assignment or licence from a person registered under the 1927 Act and in good faith and in reliance on such registration without notice of any proceedings for the cancellation of the registration.

Section 79 of the 2000 Act provides that the making of any object which is in three dimensions will not be an infringement of copyright in a two-dimensional work if the object would not appear to a person who is not an expert in relation to objects of that description to be a reproduction of it. Further, reproduction of a three-dimensional object will not be an infringement of a two-dimensional work (other than a work relating to a work of architecture) where (a) the lines, contours, colours, shape, texture and materials of the product itself or its ornamentation that appear in the work and are applied to the objects are wholly or substantially functional, and (b) the object is one of a number, in excess of fifty identical objects, which have been manufactured and made commercially available by the owner of the copyright or by a person authorised by him or her in that behalf. This is known as the 'spare parts' exception, designed to prevent what has been a perpetual monopoly in engineering drawings.

6.4.3 OWNERSHIP: MEANING OF AUTHOR

Section 21 of the 2000 Act defines the term author by reference to different circumstances. Author means the person who creates a work. In the case of a sound recording, this is the producer. In the case of a film the producer and the principal director are the authors. In the case of a broadcast the person making the broadcast is the author.

In the case of a cable program, the person providing the cable program service in which the program is included is the author.

In the case of a typographical arrangement or a published edition, the publisher is the author.

In the case of a work which is computer generated, the person by whom the arrangement necessary for the creation of the work is undertaken is the author. In the case of an original database, the individual or group of individuals who made the database are the author. In the case of a photograph, the photographer is the author: s. 21.

Section 23 provides that the author of the work is the first owner of the copyright. However, there are three exceptions to this rule:

(a) where the work is made by an employee in the course of employment, the employer is the first owner of any copyright in the work subject to any agreement to the contrary;

(b) where the work is the subject of government or oireachtas copyright then the author is not regarded as the first owner. If the work is the subject of the copyright of a prescribed international organisation or the copyright in the work is conferred on some other person by an enactment then the author will not be the first owner of the copyright; and

(c) where a work except a computer program is made by an author in the course of employment by the proprietor of a newspaper or periodicals, the author may use the work for any purpose except for making it available to newspapers or periodicals without infringing the copyright.

6.4.4 DURATION OF COPYRIGHT

6.4.4.1 Literary, dramatic, musical or artistic work

Section 24 of the 2000 Act provides that copyright in a literary, dramatic, musical or artistic work or in an original database lasts for seventy years after the death of the author. In the case of such a work which is anonymous or pseudonymous copyright will expire seventy years after the date on which the work is first lawfully made available to the public. Where the author becomes known during that seventy-year period, copyright will expire seventy years after the death of that author.

6.4.4.2 Films

The 2000 Act, s. 25 states that copyright in a film lasts for seventy years after the last of the following people dies, namely (a) the principal director of the film; (b) the author of the screenplay of the film; (c) the author of the dialogue of the film; or (d) the author of music specifically composed for use in the film.

In a case where a film is first made available to the public during the period of seventy years following the death of the last of these people, copyright will expire seventy years after the date of such making available.

6.4.4.3 Sound recordings

The 2000 Act, s. 26 states that copyright in a sound recording lasts for fifty years after the sound recording is made or, where it is first made available to the public during that fifty-year period, for fifty years from the date of such making available to the public.

6.4.4.4 Broadcasts

The 2000 Act, s. 27 provides that copyright in a broadcast lasts for fifty years after the broadcast is first lawfully transmitted. Copyright in every repeat broadcast expires at the same time as the original broadcast.

6.4.4.5 Cable program

The 2000 Act, s. 28 provides that copyright in a cable program will expire fifty years after the cable program is first lawfully included in a cable program service. Again, copyright in a repeat cable program expires at the same time as the original one.

6.4.4.6 Typographical arrangements

The 2000 Act, s. 29 provides that copyright in a typographical arrangement of a published edition lasts for fifty years from the date it is first made available to the public.

6.4.4.7 Computer-generated works

The 2000 Act, s. 30 provides that copyright in a work which is computer generated lasts for seventy years after the date on which the work is first lawfully made available.

6.4.4.8 Copyright in works in volumes, parts etc.

The 2000 Act, s. 31 provides that where a work is made available to the public in volumes, parts, instalments, issues or episodes and the copyright subsists from the date on which the work is so made available copyright subsists in each separate item.

6.4.4.9 Works not previously available

Where work is made available to the public for the first time after the expiration of the copyright the person who makes it available will have the same rights as the author, except for moral rights, for twenty-five years from the date the work is made available.

4.5 INFRINGEMENT

4.5.1 Rights restricted

Under the provisions of s. 37 of the 2000 Act the owner of copyright in a work has the exclusive right to undertake or authorise others to undertake all of the following acts, namely:

(a)   to copy the work;

(b)   to make available to the public the work; and

(c)   to make an adaptation of the work.

Each of those acts is called 'acts restricted by copyright'. Copyright is infringed if any of the acts restricted is done by any person without the consent of the owner/author of a copyright.

6.4.5.2   Secondary infringement

Secondary infringement comprises a number of dealings with a work without the permission of the copyright owner, including selling, importing, making or having in his or her possession, custody or control a copy of the work knowing it to be an infringing copy, or having an article specifically designed or adapted for making copies of that work knowing that it has been or is to be used to make infringing copies.

6.4.5.3   Acts permitted in relation to copyright works

Chapter 6 of the 2000 Act sets out certain acts which are exempted from infringement: 2000 Act, ss. 49–106.

These include such matters as fair dealing, that is making use of a work for a purpose and to an extent reasonably justified by the non-commercial purpose to be achieved. For example, fair dealing may be for research or for private study, for criticism or for review: 2000 Act, ss. 50, 51.

Copyright in a work is not infringed if it is copied in the course of educational instruction or in preparation for education and instruction: 2000 Act, s. 53.

Librarians or archivists are permitted to make copies of a work for various purposes, again of a non-commercial nature: 2000 Act, ss. 61–70.

Copyright is not infringed in a work by anything done for the purpose of parliamentary or judicial proceedings or for the purpose or reporting those proceedings, nor is it infringed for the purposes of a statutory enquiry: 2000 Act, s. 71.

Any material comprised in records, which are open to public inspection, may be copied and a copy may be supplied to anyone without infringing copyright: 2000 Act, s. 73.

A back-up copy of a computer program may be made without infringing copyright: 2000 Act, s. 80. Copyright is not infringed when anything is done for the purposes of reconstructing a building: 2000 Act, s. 96.

6.4.6   MORAL RIGHTS

The Berne Convention on copyright requires independently of the author's economic rights and even after transfer of the said rights, the author shall have the right to claim authorship of the work and to object to any distortion, mutilation or other modification of or other derogatory action in relation to the said work which 'would be prejudicial to his honour or reputation'. These are introduced into Irish law for the first time in the 2000 Act.

Section 107 of the 2000 Act provides the paternity right. This is the right of the author to be identified as such. There are certain exceptions to these rules, including where copyright in the work originally vested in an employer, where the work is made for the purposes of a newspaper or periodical or where government or Oireachtas copyright subsists in the work.

Section 109 of the 2000 Act recognises the integrity right. This is the right of the author of a work to object to any distortion, mutilation or other modification of or other derogatory action in relation to the work, which would prejudice his reputation.

The integrity right does not apply to a work made for the purpose of reporting current events or of a newspaper or periodical. The integrity right is qualified in respect of works in which the copyright originally vested in the author's employer.

Pursuant to the 2000 Act, s.116 moral rights may be waived. Moral rights are not capable of assignment or alienation: s. 118. Moral rights may be passed on the death of the person entitled to the right: s. 119.

5.4.7 PERFORMER'S RIGHTS

A performer is granted rights by the 2000 Act for the first time in Irish law. The rights granted under s. 203 are the exclusive right to authorise or to prohibit:

(a) the making of a recording of the whole or any substantial part of a qualifying performance directly from the live performance;

(b) the broadcasting live, or including live in a cable program service of the whole or any substantial part of a qualifying performance; or

(c) the making of a recording of the whole or any substantial part of a qualifying performance directly from a broadcast or a cable program including the live performance.

5.4.8 DELIVERY UP AND SEIZURE

Section 256 of the 2000 Act provides that the owner of rights in a recording of a performance may apply to the District Court for a seizure order addressed to the Garda Síochána to seize illicit recordings, articles used to make illicit recordings or protection-defeating devices, where such items are being hawked, carried about or marketed and, subsequently, for such items to be destroyed or delivered up to the rights owner. Hearsay evidence will be permitted in any such application and the witness will not be required to reveal the source of his information. However, the applicant exposes himself to a claim in damages if, at the end of the day, no infringement is established or the application was made maliciously.

Section 257 of the 2000 Act introduces a novel application allowing a rights owner to seize recordings, articles or devices without the protection of a court order where it is impractical to seek an order first and subsequently to seek and order for destruction or for delivery up. Notice must first be given to the Garda Síochána for the district and the items may not be seized at a permanent or regular place of business. The section is clearly designed to assist rights owners at concerts and similar occasions.

5.5 Confidential Information

5.5.1 INTRODUCTION

This branch of intellectual property law deals with the protection of 'know-how'. Know-how may be secret formulae, secret processes as used in the manufacture of a product or something as simple as the names of customers and other sales information which, if disclosed to the competing business, would cause significant harm to the owner.

In certain cases an employer will impose an obligation of confidentiality on an employee in relation to proprietary information rather than apply for patent protection for a secret invention. This may operate as a more effective protection, since a patent has to be published and put into the public domain. This gives competitors the opportunity to improve upon the invention to such an extent that they may produce the second generation of product or a product entirely different which is also patentable and does not infringe the first product. On the other hand, if employees are bound by contract to keep their employers' invention secret then it may never come into the public domain like, for example, the secret formula for the manufacture of Coca-Cola.

The court, in a case of confidential information, is being asked to enforce a moral obligation. An equitable principle is invoked, that a person to whom something was made known in confidence cannot use the knowledge to the detriment of the informant.

6.5.2   RELATIONSHIPS IMPOSING CONFIDENTIALITY

In order to assess whether a relationship is one which imposes confidentiality, the court must first decide whether there exists from the relationship between the parties an obligation of confidence regarding the information which had been imparted and it must then decide whether the information which was communicated could properly be regarded as confidential. Once it is established that an obligation of confidence exists and that the information is confidential, then the person to whom it is given has the duty to act in good faith and this means that he must use the information for the purpose for which it is imparted to him and cannot use it to the detriment of the informant. The explanation of what constitutes confidential information was given by Costello J in *House of Spring Gardens Ltd v Point Blank Ltd* [1984] IR 611. This case is the leading case in the area of confidential information in Ireland and largely follows the English dicta on the subject.

In general, the areas where an obligation of confidence would be imposed may be divided into two sections:

(a)   protection of trade secrets/confidential information in non-employment cases. Thus, for example, where a plaintiff has employed a third party company to carry out a project on the plaintiff's behalf, an obligation of confidence will be imposed upon that third party and upon the plaintiff, not to use the information without consent; and

(b)   protection of trade secrets in the master and servant situation. In the course of employment, an employee has a duty to do nothing which would conflict with the business interests of their employer. It is always safest, where at all possible, to avoid argument in this area and to insert in an employee's contract of employment in clear terms an obligation to keep information including trade secrets and skill and experience gained during the employment confidential.

Once the contract of employment has concluded and an employee has left his employment, there is none the less a duty not to use confidential information. The leading case in this area is *Faccenda Chicken Ltd v Fowler* [1986] 1 All ER 617. In this case Neill LJ found that there were three types of information acquired by a servant in the course of employment:

(i)   trivia/public information which is not protected;

(ii)   skill and experience which is not protected although it could be restricted by contract in restriction of trade clause: this type of information is protected during the course of the employment under the duty of fidelity owed by the employee to his employer. After the employment ends subject to any competitive restraints the employee is free to use his skills and experience elsewhere; and

(iii)   trade secrets so confidential that, even though they have been learned by heart, can not be used for anyone's benefit but that of the employer and are protected even after the employee leaves employment.

168

6.5.3   REMEDIES

The remedies for breach of confidential information are an injunction to restrain the breach of confidential information and damages or an account of profits. In *Nu glue Adhesives v Burgers Galvin*, 23 March 1982, HC (unreported) McWilliam J found that if there had been an abuse of confidential information, damages would be limited to an amount equal to six weeks' salary for a chemist. He considered that the defendants could have come up with the formula themselves within a six-week period.

Where the court is asked to award an injunction, that injunction must be capable of being framed with sufficient precision to enable the enjoined party to know what it is he may not do: *Lawrence David Ltd v Ashton* [1991] 1 All ER 385.

In *Terrapin v Builders' Supply Co (Hayes) Ltd* [1960] RPC 128 Roxburgh J defined what he called the 'springboard' formula. He said:

> 'As I understand it, the essence of this branch of the law, whatever the origin of it may be, is that a person who has obtained information in confidence is not allowed to use it as a spring-board for activities detrimental to the person who made the confidential communication, and spring-board it remains even when all the features have been published or can be ascertained by actual inspection by members of the public... . The processor of such information must be placed under a special disability in the field of competition in order to ensure that he does not get an unfair start'.

Roxburgh J granted the plaintiff an injunction.

The courts, however, have found difficulties with the 'springboard' doctrine and have in some instances suggested that rather than an injunction being granted, the correct course is to compensate the plaintiff in damages: *Coco v A. N. Clark (Engineers) Ltd* [1969] RPC 41.

In some cases, in order to overcome the advantage gained by an employee in using confidential information, the court will impose an injunction for a period of time that it considers sufficient to enable a member of the public to come up with the formula themselves.

Moreover, it should be noted that overall it is often extremely difficult to prove a plaintiff employer's case to a degree sufficient to persuade a court to grant an injunction and the importance of ensuring the employers put in place properly drafted and reasonable contractual terms dealing with confidential information cannot be over-emphasised.

CHAPTER 7

FRANCHISING

7.1 Introduction

7.1.1 GENERAL

In the practice of commercial law, franchising is an area which brings together many different aspects of the law. It involves the drafting of commercial agreements, consideration of real property arrangements, intellectual property requirements, competition law and employee considerations, to name but a few.

The term 'franchise' is generally taken to mean the legal arrangement whereby one party grants a licence to another for the purpose of retailing its goods or services, often in a specified area or territory. This type of franchise is usually called a 'business format' or 'turnkey' franchise. This is because the franchisor presents the franchisee with a model of how the business will operate, and imposes stringent controls on the franchisee in respect of that business.

7.1.2 LEGISLATIVE BACKGROUND

In Ireland, there is no direct legislation governing franchising. Accordingly, with the exception of the need to comply with competition law requirements, there are no specific legislative obstacles to be overcome before a franchisor or franchisee may commence carrying on business in the State. Competition law requirements, in so far as they relate to franchises, are dealt with in some detail later in this chapter. In the meantime, it is in the Category Certificate/Licence in respect of Agreement between Suppliers and Resellers issued by the Competition Authority on 4 December 1998 ('the Category Certificate/ Licence') that one finds a legal definition of a franchise. It is referred to as

> 'an agreement whereby one party grants to the other party the right to exploit a package of intellectual property rights relating to trade marks, trade names, shop signs, utility models, designs, copyrights, know-how or patents, for the resale of goods or the provision of services to end users' (paragraph 6 of the Introduction, of the Category Certificate, art. 2(c) and the Category Licence, art. 2(c)).

Another essential element of a franchise is 'know-how'. The Category Certificate/Licence defines this as

> 'a package of non-patented practical information, resulting from experience and testing by the franchisor, which is secret, substantial and identified' (paragraph 6 of the Introduction to the Category Certificate/Licence).

The combined elements of the package of intellectual property rights, and the know-how, are essential to make up the type of franchise that is the subject of this chapter.

170

7.1.3   ADVANTAGES OF FRANCHISING

For a business considering expansion, there are many reasons why franchising is a possibility. First, expanding a business by means of franchising offers the franchisor an opportunity to expand relatively quickly, and at a reduced cost. For example, once a franchisor has carried out all the necessary background work to set up the franchise, the blueprint developed is one which may certainly be applied very easily to many different locations, and indeed, in many cases, may be adopted with a few modifications to facilitate the development of the franchise in other jurisdictions. In franchising its business, a franchisor is passing on to the franchisee all the capital costs associated with expansion, including the costs of sourcing, buying and fitting out premises, and finding, employing and training employees, as well as the assumption of ongoing obligations in relation to these matters.

In addition, the more members there are of a franchise network, the greater the purchasing power that will be available to the franchisor. This will of course benefit the franchise system as a whole, and not just the franchisor.

From a franchisee's point of view, the possibility of becoming a franchisee gives many people the opportunity they would not otherwise have of becoming self-employed. An attractive aspect of many franchises is that a franchisee does not need to have had previous experience of the business he is proposing to franchise. In a well-run franchise, the franchisor will offer comprehensive training programmes to franchisees in the franchise system and will train its franchisees to the standard required by it.

It is also believed that by taking on an established brand, the lead-in time to establish a successful business is reduced. This does depend on the nature of the franchise chosen, and the amount of background research which has been carried out by the franchisee before taking on the franchise.

Another definite benefit for the franchisee is the ongoing advice and support, and the benefit of the know-how, that is available from the franchisor. So, in theory, instead of the franchisee making all the usual mistakes made in the start-up of a business, these should be lessened.

Finally, it is said that it is often easier to raise finance to buy a franchise than it is to raise finance to set up in business on one's own account. In many cases this is true, particularly for a well-known brand, and a well-run franchise. However, much does depend on the quality of the franchise itself, and the reputation of that franchise. Banks are very aware of the various franchises available in the marketplace, and are as reluctant to lend money to a franchisee for investment in a badly-run franchise as for any other speculative venture.

.1.4   DISADVANTAGES OF FRANCHISING

As with most commercial arrangements, there may be pitfalls with franchising and both parties need to be aware of these.

One particular disadvantage, for both parties, is the loss of control suffered. Take, for example, the franchisor who may have spent many years building up his business and who now decides to turn to franchising as a means of expansion. In order to do this, he must disclose to the franchisee all the know-how that he has built up over the years in developing that business. In the franchise agreement itself, he will seek to impose many obligations and limitations on the franchisee with the objective of protecting that know-how and all his goodwill, but the reality is that the franchisee is a third party who is in business on his own account, is liable for his own success or failure, and who may well be tempted at some stage during the franchise relationship to maximise his profit, quite possibly at the franchisor's expense.

This loss of control may also affect franchisees, particularly if they have not fully considered the nature of the legal relationship into which they are proposing to enter. Take, for example, the franchisee who has achieved his life's ambition of setting up in business for himself. Many individuals will resent the level of control imposed on them by the franchisor. The franchisee also has to pay a percentage of its turnover to the franchisor, even if it is not making a profit, and is also restricted in selling the business.

A franchisor also has to develop different skills in order to develop a successful franchise. It is sometimes difficult for a franchisor to make the distinction between managing its own business, and managing a third-party business for the benefit of the franchise network as a whole. However, if a franchise is to survive and prosper, this is really what needs to be done.

7.1.5   AVOIDING THE PITFALLS

Many of the difficulties which affect franchises, particularly in the early days, may be avoided if certain preliminary steps are taken before a prospective franchisee commits to a franchise.

In the first instance, the franchisee really needs to consider the entire nature of the franchise relationship and then consider whether he is prepared to undertake the commitment involved. Starting in business as a franchisee is just the same as starting any new business, and involves all the hard work, dedication and setbacks that arise along the way. The franchisee does have the benefit of the ongoing advice and support, and of the initial training that will be provided by the franchisor, but is he prepared to accept the dictates of the franchisor, even if they conflict with his own views? If he is to succeed as a franchisee, he must do this.

It is impossible to under-estimate the importance of advising the franchisee to properly research the franchise he is proposing to acquire. Ideally such research should have been undertaken by the franchisee before he first seeks legal advice, but certainly it should be carried out prior to entering into the franchise. For example, it is important to ascertain just how long the franchise has been operating, and how many franchises there are, as opposed to company owned and operated outlets. Any market research in the area relevant to the franchise should be reviewed, and in this regard there are a wealth of government agencies who are prepared to make available statistics and research information. Assuming the franchise has been operating for some time, the franchisee should take the time to personally visit a few franchisees and see how they are operating. He should speak to franchisees other than those nominated by the franchisor, or those who have been in business for a short period of time and who may still be in the 'honeymoon' period. The prospective franchisee should ascertain from those other franchisees whether the franchise has lived up to their expectations, whether they are generating the livelihood they expected, whether the franchisor is actually providing the ongoing advice and support that under the franchise agreement he is supposed to? Clients should also be wary if they are to take the first franchise in a new territory. A franchisor could have a very successful management structure in place in, for example, the UK or the USA, which supports the franchisees there very well. In practical terms, the franchisee needs to consider how the franchisor will provide the necessary ongoing advice and support in Ireland. Whatever the relative practicalities of providing that advice, support and assistance from say the UK, one would certainly need serious reassurance regarding advice and support from the USA or Australia.

It is often considered that becoming a franchisee is a cheap way of starting up in business on one's own account. In fact, the opposite is true. In addition to funding all the usual costs associated with starting a business, a franchisee will usually pay an initial fee to the franchisor for the privilege of being permitted to join the franchise network. Depending upon the popularity of the franchise system selected, fees may be quite substantial. In addition, a franchisee will usually have to pay the franchisor a proportion of its turnover, and it is important to remember that this fee will be payable, even if no profit is being made by the franchisee. All these additional costs need to be accounted for by the franchisee in addition to the costs normally associated with starting a business, such as the costs of acquiring premises, taking on employees, and paying suppliers. A properly-advised client will have factored in all these additional costs and will be prepared for them.

Notwithstanding these pitfalls, it would be a mistake to believe that franchising as a means of doing business is not worthwhile. For a franchise that is well managed, properly supported and controlled, and with the franchisor and the franchisee committed to working together for the mutual benefit of the franchise system, franchising can be a mutually rewarding experience. However, proceeding in haste and without conducting appropriate research will undoubtedly backfire sooner rather than later on both parties.

7.1.6 PRELIMINARY CONSIDERATIONS

7.1.6.1 Introduction

It is inevitable that at some stage in a solicitor's professional career he or she will be approached by a client who is either considering purchasing a franchise, and who wants the agreement reviewed on his behalf, or alternatively, a client who has a good business idea, which he is considering expanding using the vehicle of franchising.

Essentially, the same considerations arise in both circumstances, but in one case the solicitor will be considering the matter from the point of view of the franchisor, and in the second scenario, the solicitor will be concerned to protect the position of the franchisee. For the purposes of illustrating the concerns which arise, it is proposed to proceed in this chapter outlining the matters which need to be considered by a potential franchisor, but in highlighting issues, to remark on those matters of which a franchisee should be aware.

7.1.6.2 Pilot scheme

Let us assume that when consulted by the client, the solicitor establishes that the franchisor has only been operating the business himself for four months or so. Both the British Franchise Association and the Irish Franchise Association Codes of Ethics for Franchisors require that a franchisor has at least one year's experience itself in running a business before considering franchising. The reason for this is simple to understand—how may a franchisor have accumulated sufficient know-how which can be passed to the franchisee, if it is still on a learning curve itself in respect of the operation of the business? Also, from a franchisee's point of view, it is preferable to be able to look at a pilot operation, which has produced a set of audited accounts, and where it will be possible for the franchisee to try and evaluate the potential profitability of the business.

Accordingly, if the client has been operating himself for a relatively short period of time only, it is likely to be more appropriate for him to defer his plans to franchise the business in the short-term, and to focus instead on building up the business, to make it attractive for potential franchisees. However, even at this stage, there are a number of steps which may be undertaken by the franchisor in anticipation of franchising. Some of these will require legal assistance, and others will not.

7.1.6.3 Intellectual property considerations

On the client's initial visit, it will be important to consider the position regarding intellectual property. It should be borne in mind that the franchise agreement itself will confer on the franchisee 'a package of intellectual property rights'. If the franchisor's intellectual property rights have not already been protected, then their protection should be considered immediately.

7.1.6.4   Trade mark

If the client has a trade name or any distinguishing trade mark, then this may well be capable of registration. Since the coming into force of the Trade Marks Act 1996 ('the 1996 Act'), names or marks are registrable in respect of both goods and services. If there is any possibility that the franchise will extend beyond Ireland, it may be worthwhile at this preliminary stage to consider whether a Community trade mark should be registered, which will be effective in all EU countries. As part of the registration process, the franchisor will need to consider all the classes in which the mark is to be registered, with a view to ensuring the maximum protection for himself and his franchisees. Usually a mark will need to be registered in more than one class in order to maximise the protection available to the franchisor.

Section 6(1) of the 1996 Act defines a trade mark as being any sign capable of being represented graphically, which is capable of distinguishing the goods or services of one undertaking from those of other undertakings. It may consist of words (including personal names), designs, letters, numerals, or the shape of goods or their packaging: 1996 Act, s. 6(2).

Once a trade mark is registered, any franchisee will be granted a licence of the mark. This will usually occur in the franchise agreement. Sections 32–36 of the 1996 Act contain provisions regarding the licensing of registered trade marks. A licence may be exclusive or non-exclusive. If it is non-exclusive, it may be limited in the extent of the goods or services for which the trade mark is registered. Alternatively, it may be limited for use in a particular manner, or in the locality in which it may be used. A trade mark licence will not be effective unless it is in writing and signed by or on behalf of the grantor. Also, unless otherwise provided for in the licence agreement, the grant of the licence will be taken as binding on a successor in title to the grantor's interest.

The grant of a licence is a 'registrable transaction' under the 1996 Act (1996 Act, s. 29(2)(b)), and should be registered with the Office of the Controller of Patents, Trade Marks and Industrial Designs. Registration as a licensee confers certain benefits on a franchisee, for example, an entitlement to bring an infringement action in his own name, or to recover damages or an account of profits.

The holder of an exclusive trade mark licence has entitlements over and above those conferred on non-exclusive licence holders, but in order to avail of these advantages the exclusive licence must be registered.

7.1.6.5   Patents

If the franchise business proposed involves a potential design, then the patent must be registered. Generally, an invention will be patentable if it is susceptible of industrial application, is new, and involves an inventive step. The term of a patent will generally be twenty years, but, as a consequence the Patents Act 1992 it is possible to apply for a short-term patent. If granted, these subsist for ten years. Section 40 of the Patents Act 1992 confers upon the proprietor of a registered patent the right to prevent all third parties not having his consent from using the invention either directly or indirectly.

7.1.6.6   Copyright

The franchisor will need to protect the copyright of his designs, shop layout, operations manuals, plans and specification for the fit-out of the premises, as well as the copyright in any materials used or distributed through the franchise. Copyright arises automatically under the Copyright and Related Rights Act 2000. It subsists in original literary, dramatic, musical and artistic works from the time the work is recorded in writing or otherwise by or with the consent of the author (ss. 17, 18) provided certain qualification criteria are met in respect of the author or the work. The qualification criteria are set out in Chapter 18 of the Act. It should be noted that the definition of literary work includes computer programs.

Section 24 of the 2000 Act provides that copyright in the works mentioned above will expire seventy years after the death of the author.

There are no registration formalities for copyright protection to be claimed.

7.1.6.7 Registered designs

In some franchises, there may be a necessity for the franchisor to apply for registration of a 'design', where simply claiming copyright would not be sufficient. Section 3 of the Industrial and Commercial Property (Protection) Act 1927 ('the 1927 Act') defines the word 'design' to mean:

> only the features of shape, configuration, pattern, or ornament applied to any article by any industrial process or means, whether manual, mechanical or chemical, separate or combined, which, in the finished article appeal to and are judged solely by the eye, but does not include any mode or principle of construction, or anything which in substance is a mere mechanical device.

The proprietor of a design may apply for registration of the design to the Designs Branch of the Patents Office. To be registrable, a design must be 'new and original': 1927 Act, s. 64(1). It must not have been published or used in the State prior to the application for registration. Where some other party claims copyright in the artistic work defining a design, the design will not be registered without the consent of the owner of the copyright: 1927 Act, s. 64(2). A design may be registered in more than one class. This will be determined by the Controller of Patents, Trade Marks and Industrial Designs. A design will be registered for an initial period of five years, and the registration may be extended up to a maximum of fifteen years. There is no provision for extension beyond that period.

7.1.6.8 Registration of a company

In addition to registering a trade mark, it is also worthwhile for a franchisor to register a company with the trading name, principally to avoid anyone else incorporating a company with that name. The name should also be registered as a business name, pursuant to the Registration of Business Names Act 1963.

7.1.6.9 Preparation of operating manual

All the know-how which the franchisor has accumulated in the operation of the pilot scheme, that information which is 'secret, substantial and identified', needs to be reduced to writing so that it is available for franchisees. The document in which it is collected is commonly referred to as the 'operating manual' or simply the 'manual'. The manual is the blueprint for the operation of the franchise business. It is the document which will be issued to franchisees for use as a point of reference wherever there is uncertainty as to how the business should be conducted. It will cover the practical information required by the franchisee to operate the business and will include matters such as accounting systems, sales and service reporting requirements, equipment maintenance, preparation of products, sources of supply, qualitative requirements for products, details of layout of premises, staffing requirements, customer complaint procedures, and obligations in relation to advertising. Of its nature, a manual must be developed for each business. As it will contain all the know-how, it is quite usual for a franchisor not to produce it to the franchisee until there is a binding legal agreement in place between them. It is also usual to provide that the contents of the manual will be kept confidential by the franchisee, and will not be copied, or disclosed to third parties. The franchise agreement itself will also impose an obligation on the franchisee to conduct the business in accordance with the manual. It will reserve the right for the franchisor to update the manual during the term of the agreement and will require the franchisee to comply with such amendments. These provisions are necessary to ensure that the franchise keeps pace with developments in the area over its term. Indeed, in a well-managed franchise, a franchisor will be constantly reviewing the business to ensure that it is managed to an optimum level.

7.1.6.10 Franchise premises

Not all franchises are property based. Many operate as mobile franchises, for instance through the use of customised vans, and others may be operated from a franchisee's own home. In many cases, however, particularly for retail franchises, a premises will be required, and if that is the case, the franchisor will need to consider how important the location of the premises is in the development of the franchise network. If it is of major importance, he may wish to consider retaining control of the premises in some way, so that if the relationship with the franchisee breaks down, or the franchise is not renewed on expiry, the franchisor will retain control of the premises. He can then decide to either trade from the premises himself, or permit a new franchisee to operate from the premises.

All of this seems reasonable, until one considers the statutory background in Ireland. The provisions of the Landlord and Tenant (Amendment) Act 1980 as amended by the Landlord and Tenant (Amendment) Act 1994, mean that a tenant will acquire a statutory right to continue in possession of a property, once he has five years' continuous business occupation. These rights may be avoided or contracted out of only for premises which are used wholly and exclusively as offices, and generally franchised businesses will not fall into that category.

It may be possible to avoid the effect of the landlord and tenant legislation by granting a licence to the franchisee. In order to successfully achieve the grant of a licence, it would have to be clear that the franchisee's basis for occupation is a personal right only. It would be preferable that the franchisee not have exclusive possession of the premises, and also that the franchisee not be liable for repairs, maintenance or indeed the payment of rates or insurance premiums relating to the property. If there were any doubt, it would ultimately be up to the courts to adjudicate on the nature of the relationship created, and the fact that the parties themselves designate the legal arrangement as a licence and not a lease will be only one of the matters taken into account. A court will look at all the circumstances before deciding whether occupation had been on foot of a lease or a licence.

There are therefore some difficulties to be overcome by a franchisor who wants to retain control of a franchise premises, and the question as to whether it is even worthwhile for a franchisee to try and control a premises by either buying or leasing it himself needs to be considered carefully. One way in which these difficulties may be overcome is for the franchisor to include in the franchise agreement an entitlement for himself to buy the premises from the franchisee on the expiration or early termination of the term. Such a provision will generally require the franchisor to buy the franchisee's business, as a going concern, for the market value. It may provide a mechanism for ascertaining the market price if the parties themselves are unable to agree. This is the only reasonably secure manner for the franchisor to retain control of the premises it requires.

7.2 Drafting the Franchise Agreement

7.2.1 INTRODUCTION

Once the franchisor is in a position to commence offering franchises, he needs to consider the preparation of the franchise agreement. This document will license the franchisee to carry on the business, using the know-how, the trade name and the trade mark, in accordance with the manual.

It is important, when drafting a franchise agreement to adopt a reasonable approach, creating an agreement which includes all necessary protections for the franchisor, but at the same time constitutes a workable document for the franchisee. A uniform franchise agreement should be used throughout a franchise network, imposing the same controls on all franchisees, with the objective of maintaining the integrity of the franchise system as a whole.

The agreement will also need to comply with competition law requirements, which are dealt with later in this chapter.

Although each franchise agreement is drafted to meet the requirements of each franchise system, most agreements are reasonably standard, whether they originate in Ireland, the UK, or the US.

7.2.2   PARTIES

The usual parties to a franchise agreement are the franchisor and the franchisee. However, if a franchisee wishes to trade using the vehicle of a limited liability company, the franchisor will generally require the promoters of the company, its shareholders, to join in the agreement in order to ensure compliance by the franchisee with its obligations pursuant to the agreement. The agreement will often include a clause to the effect that the shares in the company may not be sold without the franchisor's consent. The reason for this is that the relationship between franchisor and franchisee is quite a personal one, and a franchisor will often have spent quite a long time selecting suitable franchisees. He will therefore not want to find that without his knowledge, the franchisee company has been sold, and he is dealing with another party, who is unacceptable to him, or who may even be a competitor. For this reason the franchisee agreement will contain these restrictions, and may also provide that the agreement itself may not be assigned without the franchisor's consent.

7.2.3   DEFINITIONS

The definitions section is one to which the drafter of the franchise agreement needs to give considerable attention. It is in this section that the precise nature of what is being licensed to the franchisee will be specified. This section will contain definitions of the 'business' (precisely what is being franchised); the 'know-how'; the 'manual'; the 'location' (from which the franchise will operate); the 'fees'; the 'trade mark'; the 'net turnover' (on the basis of which the fees payable will be calculated); the 'products' and the 'territory', as well as any other definitions deemed necessary for the proper interpretation of the agreement. In this section particularly, it is vital to be precise and unambiguous.

7.2.4   RECITALS

As in any commercial agreement, the recitals in a franchise agreement will detail the background to the grant of the agreement. If the franchisor derives its title to grant the franchise agreement from a master franchise, this should be recited. Similarly, if the franchisor is itself a registered user of the trade mark (for example, if the mark is owned by a parent company), this should be recited also. It is also to be recommended that if terms reached with a franchisee are particularly favourable, for example, if it is the first franchise granted, that this be recited.

7.2.5   OPERATIVE PART

As in any commercial agreement, the document will need to precisely grant the entitlement to the franchisee, and recite the consideration for the grant.

7.2.6   FEES

One usually finds that the consideration given by the franchisee for the grant of a franchise is threefold—the payment of an initial fee, the ongoing payment throughout the term of the management services fees/royalties, and an advertising contribution.

7.2.6.1 Initial fee

The initial fee is generally a substantial cash sum paid by the franchisee to the franchisor for the privilege of becoming a part of the franchise network. It generally includes a fee for the entitlement to use the trade mark, the franchisor's costs of approving the franchisee, approving the premises, providing initial training, providing the manual, as well as a certain level of advice and assistance in the early weeks of the operation of the franchise. The franchisee should be quite clear on what is included in the initial fee, and what will be payable for thereafter. It is also reasonable to ask a franchisor to produce a breakdown of the calculation of the amount of the initial fee, and the franchisee should be comfortable with this breakdown. Given that franchising is not regulated in Ireland, a franchisee needs to be satisfied that a franchisor is not more interested in selling new franchises than in providing ongoing advice and assistance to existing franchisees. If there is an excessive level of profit accruing to the franchisor from the sale of the franchises, the temptation may be to do just that.

7.2.6.2 Management services fees

Management services fees are generally calculated as a percentage of turnover, although in some product-based franchises the fee is included in the wholesale price of the product and no separate fee is levied. Generally, however, one finds that although the level of fee payable may be reduced where the franchisor is getting a mark-up on products, some kind of ongoing fee will still be payable.

As the ongoing fee payable is generally calculated as a percentage of turnover, the agreement will often need to define turnover. The precise definition needs to be drafted in the context of each particular franchise. The decision as to what percentage is payable is really a matter for the franchisor, bearing in mind the nature of the business, the services to be provided, and the capacity of the business to bear the payment of the franchise fee. There is likely to be little prospect of long-term success if the franchisee finds that he is in business only to pay the franchisor's ongoing fees, and is not making any profit for himself. In striking the level of fees payable, the franchisor needs to achieve a balance that will meet the needs of both the franchisor and the franchisee.

7.2.6.3 Advertising contribution

It is usual for a franchise agreement to provide that the franchisee will make a contribution towards the cost of brand advertising, and this contribution is again usually calculated as a percentage of turnover. Often, a franchisor will restrict a franchisee from carrying out any advertising itself, as it will want full control in this area. The franchisor will usually be amenable to putting the advertising contribution into a separate bank account, and to covenanting that the contributions paid will be used only for advertising. He will usually also agree to account for the disbursement of the contributions. Also this will provide comfort to the franchisee that the advertising contribution is not subsidising the franchisor's profits.

If acting for a client who is the first franchisee in the State, it is worthwhile trying to get a commitment from the franchisor to spend the advertising contribution within the State, where it will benefit the franchisee, rather than in, for example, the UK where the benefit to the franchisee is likely to be minimal.

Other than payment of the initial fee, which is usually required to be paid on the grant of the franchise agreement, the ongoing fees are usually payable either weekly or monthly, depending on the nature of the franchise business.

7.2.7 FRANCHISOR'S OBLIGATIONS

In a franchise agreement, the franchisor's obligations are usually divided into two categories, the obligations of the franchisor on the grant of the agreement, and the obligations of the franchisor to be performed on an ongoing basis during the term.

A franchisor's initial obligations are likely to relate to matters such as the fit-out of the premises, the provision of training and the provision of the manual.

A franchisor's continuing obligations during the term are likely to include matters such as a covenant to promote the brand using the advertising contribution, a covenant not to compete with the franchisee (if an exclusive territory has been granted), either by trading itself or granting other franchises, an obligation to provide ongoing advice and assistance to the franchisee during the term, an obligation to provide products, if the franchise is a product-based one, and an obligation to continually monitor and seek to improve the franchise system and to include any improvements in the manual, which will be updated as necessary.

7.2.8 FRANCHISEE'S OBLIGATIONS

The obligations undertaken by the franchisee may be divided into a number of areas imposing controls on the franchisee as set out below.

7.2.8.1 Control of the franchise premises

Control of the franchise premises will include the covenants by the franchisee to fit out the premises as directed by the franchisor, and will usually also include a covenant by the franchisee to keep the premises in a good state of repair during the term. They may, if appropriate, extend to the franchisee covenanting to keep open during certain specified minimum hours. It is in this section also that the franchisee will permit the franchisor to enter the franchise premises, for the purposes of carrying out inspections of the business. This entitlement is very important for the franchisor, as otherwise it has no authority to enter the franchise premises, unless invited to do so by the franchisee. Clearly this would not be sufficient for the franchisor to properly supervise the franchise business. If the franchise is not property based, but is operated from a vehicle, the agreement is likely to require comparable covenants from the franchisee in respect of the vehicle. The objective of all these covenants is to ensure that the franchisee by its actions does not adversely affect the goodwill of the franchise system as a whole.

7.2.8.2 Control of the franchise business

Control of the franchise business is where the franchisee covenants to comply with the terms of the manual, and agrees to operate the business in accordance with the franchisor's instructions. There will usually be an acknowledgement in this section of the necessity that all franchisees operate the system in conformity with each other, for the benefit of the system as a whole, and the protection of the goodwill attaching to the trade mark.

In this section also, the franchisee will covenant to attend for further training as necessary during the term.

Many franchisors require the franchisee to operate the business itself, and not simply to act as an investor. If that is the case, this part of the agreement will contain a covenant by the franchisee to devote his full time to the operation and management of the business, and to try and maximise the development of the business during the term.

7.2.8.3 Control of products

Where the franchise is of a type which requires the franchisee to use only the franchisor's products in the business, there will be a covenant by the franchisee to do just that, and not to use any competing products. In addition, the franchisor is entitled to require the franchisee to use only products which meet objective qualitative criteria, which will usually be set out in the manual. All clauses in respect of the control of products need to be considered in the light of competition law requirements.

7.2.8.4 Control of the trade mark

The franchise agreement will be quite specific in terms of the licence granted to the franchisee. In obtaining these covenants the franchisor will be seeking to reinforce his control, and to specify how, and in what circumstances, the mark may be used. The agreement will usually provide that the franchisee may not incorporate the mark in its corporate or business name, and may not use the mark on any products it may manufacture itself. It will provide that any goodwill generated by the franchisee in using the mark will accrue to the franchisor, and the franchisee will covenant to protect and promote the goodwill attached to the mark at all times. Finally, the franchisee will usually be required to enter into a registered user agreement, and to notify the franchisor of any infringement of the mark.

7.2.8.5 Payment of fees

There will usually be a section in the agreement in which the franchisee covenants to pay all fees required to be paid under the agreement, at the times and in the manner provided for payment.

7.2.8.6 Record-keeping

A franchise agreement will impose stringent requirements on the franchisee in respect of the records to be maintained, and the information to be furnished to the franchisor. Quite often all this detail will be set out in the manual, but the agreement itself will specify the reporting dates, and reinforce the requirement, in relation, for example, to the provision of weekly, monthly or quarterly management accounts and annual audited accounts. Quite often, particularly in a franchise where the franchisor is not supplying products, the financial reports will be the only means the franchisor has of calculating the amount of the ongoing franchise fees payable. A franchisor will often reserve the right to carry out its own audit of the figures, and reserve to itself the right to enter the premises and inspect all the financial records for that purpose. If a franchisee is found to be understating its turnover, this may well entitle the franchisor to terminate the agreement.

7.2.8.7 Confidentiality provisions

Important parts of every franchise agreement are the clauses obliging the franchisee to keep information confidential. When one considers the nature of a franchise, the rationale for this is quite clear. The know-how which the franchisor passes to the franchisee through the manual, and the ongoing advice and assistance given must be protected. It is therefore quite reasonable for the franchisee to be required to keep information concerning the business, the franchisor, the know-how, and the manual confidential. Such a provision subsists, even after the expiration of the agreement, for so long as the information has not come into the public domain.

7.2.8.8 Non-compete obligations

In a franchise agreement it is permissible to prevent a franchisee from competing with the franchise business during the term, and for a maximum period of one year afterwards. This

180

provision needs to be considered in the context of competition law requirements, which are dealt with in detail later in this chapter. This is one of the areas where there are now some differences between the requirements of Irish law and EU law.

A franchisee should be particularly careful to evaluate fully the consequences of the non-compete provision. For example, if the premises consist of a retail shop, will the obligation prevent the franchisee continuing to trade as a shop, offering similar goods, after termination? Care needs to be taken in the drafting of this clause, and the full implications of a non-compete covenant should be evaluated and explained to the franchisee.

7.2.8.9　Insurance and indemnity

It is very important for a franchisor to ensure that the franchisee maintains in force a full range of insurance cover throughout the term. It is quite possible that the franchisor could find itself being sued because of the default of the franchisee, and in those circumstances the franchisor will be relying on the indemnity provided by the franchisee and contained in the franchise agreement. The range of cover necessary needs to be evaluated in the context of each particular franchise, perhaps in consultation with the franchisor's insurance broker, and the franchisor may well wish to provide that he be notified before any policy is to lapse.

7.2.9　ASSIGNMENT

As mentioned previously, a franchise agreement is not freely assignable, and indeed this is one of the areas which causes some conflict between franchisors and franchisees in practice. For reasons already given, a franchisor will want absolute control over the identity of the proposed assignee, and may not be willing to accept the person who has made the highest offer to acquire the franchise business from the franchisee.

The agreement will usually provide that if the agreement is to be assigned, the assignment shall be for the unexpired residue of the term, and be subject to the assignee entering into a new franchise agreement with the franchisor for that period, either on the same terms as in the franchise agreement of the selling franchisee or on the terms contained in the then current form of franchise agreement in use by the franchisor. The franchisor may require payment of a proportion of the purchase price, or alternatively a fee for dealing with the assignment, and will usually require the new franchisee to attend for training.

Sometimes the assignment clause will include an entitlement for the franchisor to buy the business on the same terms and conditions as are offered by the third-party purchaser. Whether or nor the agreement includes such a provision depends on the franchisor's requirements in each case.

The agreement will also usually specify that the franchisor is free to dispose of his interest in the agreement without reference to the franchisee.

7.2.10　DEATH OF A FRANCHISEE

One of the advantages in a franchise is that if some misfortune occurs to the franchisee, resulting either in death or incapacity, there is at least the support and assistance of the franchisor to fall back on. In such circumstances, the franchisor will often agree to lend management support and staff so that the business can continue to operate, although this will be at the cost of the franchisee. In many circumstances the franchisor may be willing to consent to the business being passed to a family member, subject to that person undergoing any necessary training. Naturally, a franchisor will not want such an interim situation to persist for too long, as it is possible that if the business is not being operated at optimum levels, it could detract from the goodwill of the franchise system as a whole. Therefore, the agreement may provide that if the business has not been transferred or sold within a particular period, the franchisor will be entitled to terminate the agreement. Alternatively, he may wish to exercise a right to buy the business. Again, each franchisor will develop the provisions required, taking into account the individual franchise system.

7.2.11 TERMINATION PROVISIONS

At first sight the provisions contained in a franchise agreement appear to be drafted very much in favour of the franchisor. The agreement will often specify a number of events, which, if they occur, will entitle the franchisor to terminate the agreement immediately. Occurrences which fall into this category include, for example, receivership or liquidation of the franchisee, failure to pay fees, release of confidential information, or the franchisee operating the business in such a way that it brings the trade mark and/or the franchise system into disrepute. Again, in each franchise, the franchisor needs to consider whether there are any circumstances, which could occur, which would lead him to feel that he must terminate the franchise with immediate effect. Obviously such circumstances would need to be quite serious, and this is not a step which the franchisor should threaten or implement lightly.

The agreement will then usually provide for a separate series of occurrences or events, breach of which may be notified to the franchisee, along with a specified time period within which such breaches must be remedied. If the franchisee fails to remedy these breaches, or is being repeatedly called upon by the franchisor to remedy minor breaches, such conduct or cumulative conduct may entitle the franchisor to terminate. In all circumstances the concern of the franchisor will be to protect and improve the integrity of the franchise system and the goodwill attaching to the trade mark.

The franchise agreement may or may not entitle the franchisee to terminate the agreement if there is default by the franchisor. In many cases such a provision will not be included.

Finally, in respect of termination provisions, it would be usual to provide that the termination of the agreement would not prejudice the entitlement of either party to proceed against the other in respect of any antecedent breach of the contract.

7.2.12 CONSEQUENCES OF TERMINATION

A franchise agreement will spell out the steps which need to be taken by the franchisee where the agreement is either terminated during the term for a breach, or expires by effluxion of time, and is not being renewed.

In those circumstances the franchisor will want to ensure that the franchisee ceases carrying on the business, and is no longer capable of being identified with the franchise. He will need to return the manual to the franchisor, cease using the trade mark and may well require to undertake either redecoration or alterations to the franchise premises so that there is no danger of the premises being mistaken for the franchise outlet. Compliance with these requirements may well involve the franchisee in considerable expenditure, of which it should be aware.

If the franchisor has an option to purchase, this will obviously affect the provisions of this clause, as if it is to be exercised, it is unlikely to be necessary for the franchisee to debrand the premises.

7.2.13 RENEWAL OPTION

A franchise agreement will usually provide that a franchisee is entitled to renew the agreement for a further term, on giving appropriate notice to the franchisor prior to the expiration of the term. This entitlement will usually only arise if the franchisee has been in compliance with the terms and conditions of the franchise prior to that date, and on the basis that the franchisee will sign up the then current form of franchise agreement being used by the franchisor for the extended term.

The franchise may require a fee to be paid for the renewal, but this will not usually be as significant as the initial fee, as quite a number of the services included in the initial fee will not be required, such as, for example, the approval of the fit-out of the premises, or the provision of initial training.

Some franchisees may have a difficulty covenanting to agree to sign an agreement, in perhaps five or ten years time, which they will not have had an opportunity to review. This concern must be balanced with the need which the franchisor has to be able to ensure that the franchise system continues to keep up to date, and improve, with such improvements embodied in the franchise agreement. Essentially the franchisor must be able to control the development of the system and must be able to maintain control of the system.

However, the decision to include an entitlement to renew needs to be considered in the context of EU law, as a direct result of the implementation of the 1999 Vertical Restraints Regulation, which is dealt with at **7.3.2.6 ff** below. That regulation prohibits any direct or indirect non-compete provisions in excess of five years' duration. It is likely that a renewal clause would be regarded as an indirect extension of the non-compete provisions. It therefore seems necessary to exclude such entitlements from agreements with an EU dimension.

.2.14 ACKNOWLEDGEMENTS BY FRANCHISEE

Franchise agreements generally contain a series of acknowledgements by a franchisee. These cover such matters as an acknowledgement of the franchisor's title to grant a licence of the trade mark, an acknowledgement that the franchisee is not relying on any representations made by the franchisor in respect of the profitability of the business, that the franchisee has been recommended to take independent legal and accounting advice, and that he has not been induced to enter into the agreement by the franchisor. This provision will usually acknowledge also that the restrictions contained in the agreement are reasonable and necessary, and finally, a provision that any grant not specifically included in the agreement is reserved to the franchisor.

.2.15 NO AGENCY

One important provision in a franchise agreement is a confirmation by both parties that they are separate and independent legal entities, and that in particular the relationship of principal and agent, partners or joint venturers does not exist between them. The franchisee is therefore not entitled to act as agent of the franchisor, bind him in any way, or pledge his credit.

2.16 MISCELLANEOUS CLAUSES

As with many types of commercial agreements, there are a series of 'boiler plate' clauses found in franchise agreements.

These include a force majeure clause, releasing the parties from their respective obligations in specified circumstances.

Another such clause is a severance clause, which will provide that if any part of the agreement is found to be unenforceable it will be severed. However, in the context of franchise agreements, and particularly non-compete obligations, a franchisor may wish to reserve the right to terminate the agreement if certain key clauses are found to be unenforceable. In general, one finds that agreements are drafted in compliance with all legal requirements, particularly competition law requirements. In some cases, however, perhaps because of the market share of one or the other parties to the agreement, it may be necessary to provide that the agreement be notified to either the Competition Authority in Ireland for a licence, or to the EU Commission for an exemption pursuant to article 81(3) EC Treaty. In such circumstances, it would be appropriate to provide that the anti-competitive provisions being notified to the relevant authority do not come into force until licensed or exempted, and also to provide that if the provisions are not approved, the parties will negotiate in good faith with each other to achieve modifications which are acceptable to the relevant authority.

In such circumstances, however, the franchisor is likely to want to reserve the right to terminate the agreement if the only solution acceptable to such authority is unacceptable to the franchisor. Provisions such as these will usually be negotiated between the parties, taking into account the particular circumstances of each case.

7.2.17 WHOLE AGREEMENT

The agreement will generally provide that the franchise agreement contains the entire agreement between the parties. Naturally, if this is not the case, for example, if concessions have been made which are comprised in a side letter, then reference to this needs to be made in this clause.

7.2.18 GOVERNING LAW AND JURISDICTION

If one is preparing a franchise agreement in Ireland, the governing law and jurisdiction will be that of Ireland. If the agreement is to be used in another jurisdiction, then it needs to be amended to take account of legal requirements in that jurisdiction, even if it is intended to retain the governing law and jurisdiction as that of Ireland.

7.2.19 NOTICES

The agreement will set out provisions dealing with service of notices, manner of service, and relevant time limits.

7.2.20 HEADINGS

Finally, the agreement will usually provide that the headings are for reference only, and are not to be used in construction of the agreement, or the provisions below them.

7.3 Competition Law Aspects of Franchising

7.3.1 INTRODUCTION

Virtually every franchise agreement has by its nature the potential to infringe both EU and Irish competition law. Franchise agreements generally contain restrictions on the type of business a franchisee may conduct, the products he may sell, the premises from which he may conduct that business, and often limit the area in which the business permitted may be

184

carried out. Franchisees are also usually subjected to post-term restrictions on competing with the franchise business. Similarly, franchisors are prevented from carrying on franchised businesses in exclusive territories granted. Clauses such as these are essential to franchise agreements. They allow franchisors to control the development of the franchise and protect know-how and intellectual property. They also protect the franchisee from unfair competition.

Essentially therefore the effect of many of the standard clauses found in franchise agreements is to 'prevent, restrict or distort' competition in goods or services and, as such, these clauses infringe both article 81(1) of the EC Treaty and s. 4(1) of the Competition Act 1991. Notwithstanding, it has been recognised both by the European Commission and by the Irish Competition Authority that franchise agreements confer economic benefits both on the parties to the agreements, and on the public as a whole. As such the anti-competitive clauses and effects are acceptable, provided the restrictions they seek to impose fall within certain parameters.

7.3.2 EUROPEAN UNION LAW

7.3.2.1 EC Treaty

The typical starting point in any analysis of the competition law aspects of franchising is the Treaty of Rome. Article 81 of the Treaty (formerly article 85) renders certain anti-competitive agreements and arrangements void. From a practical point of view, article 81, and the subsequent treatment by the EC Commission of franchising arrangements, is very relevant in the Irish context, principally because the Irish Competition Authority originally adopted substantially the same approach as the Commission. However, there have been some material developments recently both in Europe and in Ireland, the consequence of which is that there are now some significant differences between Irish and European competition law in relation to a number of vertical arrangements, including franchises.

7.3.2.2 EC Regulations

Recognising the economic advantages of franchising arrangements, the European Commission adopted a regulation granting a block exemption to categories of franchise agreements which fell within its scope. This regulation, Regulation (EEC) 4087/88 ('the Old Regulation') came into force on 1 February 1989. As a consequence of a new block exemption regulation adopted on 22 December 1999, Regulation (EC) 2790/1999 ('the 1999 Vertical Restraints Regulation'), the Old Regulation expired on 31 May 2000. The provisions of the Old Regulation will become academic in time, but existing franchise agreements which comply with the Old Regulation will continue to be exempt from article 81(1) until 31 December 2001. It is therefore, for the immediate future, necessary to be aware of the terms and requirements of the Old Regulation, until that date has passed. Thereafter franchise agreements will have to comply with the terms of the 1999 Vertical Restraints Regulation, or be notified for an individual approval to the Commission.

7.3.2.3 De minimis exemption

Another aspect of EU law which is relevant is the de minimis exemption which as of now (subject to compliance with certain conditions) entitles franchisors with a market share of less than 10 per cent to an exemption from the provisions of article 81(1) EC. This is provided for in the Commission Notice on Agreements of Minor Importance issued on 9 December 1997.

7.3.2.4 Drafting a franchise agreement

Since 1988, and the introduction of the Old Regulation, most franchise agreements have been drafted in order to comply with the Old Regulation, even though for many practitioners, franchising arrangements encountered will not have any EU competition law dimension at all. That is because, in the first place, article 81 EC only applies to agreements affecting trade between Member States. If an agreement only has an effect within a single Member State, then it is unlikely that any infringement of article 81 will arise. Having said that, in Ireland, many master franchise agreements granted are for territories covering both Northern Ireland and Ireland and, as such, affect trade between Member States. Secondly, even if the agreement has the potential to affect trade between Member States, there is a strong possibility that the franchisor will have a market share of less than 10 per cent and accordingly benefit from the provisions contained in the Notice on Agreements of Minor Importance, and so the provisions of article 81(1) EC will not apply.

If one has an agreement which has an effect on trade between Member States then it is necessary to consider EU law. At this time, the starting point for such consideration must be the Old Regulation, but any agreements in effect from 1 June 2000 must comply with the terms of the 1999 Vertical Restraints Regulation. When reviewing a franchise agreement which was in force on 31 May 2000 but which will expire on or before 31 December 2001, it is sufficient for that franchise agreement to comply with the Old Regulation, and if it does, it will be exempt from the provisions of article 81(1) EC. As mentioned above, if the agreement is to remain in force after 31 December 2001 then it will need to comply with the terms of the 1999 Vertical Restraints Regulation, or be notified to the EC Commission for a particular exemption.

7.3.2.5 The Old Regulation: summary

In view of the fact that the benefit of the Old Regulation will expire on 31 December 2001, this paragraph simply summarises the terms of the Old Regulation.

The approach of the European Commission under the Old Regulation was to look at standard types of franchise arrangements, and then to isolate particular types of clauses within franchise agreements. In respect of these clauses the Commission then set down a series of rules, and if the franchise agreement was to benefit from the Old Regulation, it needed to comply with those rules.

The rules effectively comprised clusters of clauses, as follows:

(a) Franchise agreements could contain a range of specified clauses, such as, for example, a restriction on the franchisor granting franchise agreements to others within a defined territory, or itself trading in the territory, or an obligation on the franchisee to exploit the franchise only from the franchise premises; these clauses are contained in article 2 of the Old Regulation.

(b) Franchise agreements could contain a further range of clauses, specified in article 3 of the Old Regulation, but these could only be included to the extent necessary to protect the franchisor's industrial or intellectual property, or to maintain the common identity and reputation of the franchised network. These include clauses such as an agreement to sell only the franchisor's goods, or to sell goods matching minimum objective quality specifications laid down by the franchisor, and an obligation not to compete in a similar or competing business to the franchisee within the territory, or not to compete with the franchisee within the territory for a maximum period of one year after termination.

The clauses, set out in articles 2 and 3 of the Old Regulation, are generally referred to as the 'whitelist' clauses;

(c) Franchise agreements had to contain the clauses set out in article 4 of the Old Regulation—if they did not, the exemption afforded to agreements by article 1 of the Old Regulation would not apply. These included, for example, an entitlement for the franchisee to be free to obtain the goods that are the subject matter of the franchise from other franchisees, or from authorised distributors where such had been appointed.

(d) Finally, article 5 of the Old Regulation sets out a series of clauses which, if included, will result in the franchise agreement losing the benefit of the Old Regulation. These include restrictions on the franchisee setting resale prices, or any prohibition on the franchisee meeting an unsolicited order received from outside the territory granted to the franchisee. The clauses set out in article 5 of the Old Regulation are often called the 'blacklist' clauses.

As the benefit of the Old Regulation will continue to apply to agreements in force on 31 May 2000, and will benefit such agreements until 31 December 2001, it is important to be aware of its terms in respect of such agreements.

7.3.2.6   Vertical arrangements

For agreements which came into effect on or after 1 June 2000 and for agreements in effect on 1 June 2000 but which will continue to operate after 31 December 2001, the terms of the 1999 Vertical Restraints Regulation (EC Regulation 2790/1999) ('the 1999 Regulation') are relevant. In adopting the 1999 Regulation, the European Commission has changed its approach completely, from an evaluation of the specific terms of agreements, such as has been seen in the analysis of the Old Regulation, to a broader overview of the economic effects of specific vertical arrangements. So, instead of dealing with franchise agreements in isolation, the 1999 Regulation covers a range of vertical agreements. The rationale for the change in approach is found in the recitals to the 1999 Regulation. Recital 7 acknowledges the likelihood that efficiency-enhancing effects will outweigh any anti-competitive effects due to restrictions contained in vertical agreements depending on the degree of market power of the undertakings concerned. This in turn depends on the extent to which these undertakings face competition from other suppliers of goods or services regarded by the buyer as interchangeable or substitutable for one another, by reason of the products, their characteristics, prices, and intended use.

The key points to note about the 1999 Vertical Restraints Regulation are:

(a) it is only available to franchisors with a market share of less than 30 per cent;

(b) it applies to both exclusive and non-exclusive arrangements;

(c) services and goods are included;

(d) multi-party agreements are covered (i.e. more than two parties);

(e) some vertical arrangements between competitors will be exempt; and

(f) franchisors may impose maximum price restrictions on their franchisees (but not price maintenance).

.3.2.7   Guidelines

On 24 May 2000, the Commission issued a Notice containing Guidelines outlining its policy on the interpretation of the 1999 Regulation. These Guidelines are very detailed and are crucial to a full interpretation of the 1999 Regulation. The Commission has indicated that it regards itself as bound by the terms of the Guidelines—although competition authorities in Member States will not be bound by them. The Commission's objective in issuing the Guidelines is to help companies make their own assessment of vertical agreements under the EU competition rules. The Commission has indicated that it will apply the Guidelines reasonably and flexibly. Therefore, in practice, when considering any EU competition law aspects of franchising, it is important to ensure that the Guidelines are also considered. The

Guidelines are available on the European Commission's website at http://www.euro-pa.eu.int/comm/dg04/antitrust/legislation/vertical_restraints/guidelines_en.pdf.

7.3.2.8 Meaning of vertical agreement

The 1999 Regulation does not specifically mention franchises, but applies to

> *agreements or concerted practices entered into between two or more undertakings each of which operates, for the purposes of the agreement, at a different level of the production or distribution chain, and relating to the conditions under which the parties may purchase, sell or resell certain goods or services ('vertical agreements')'* (1999 Vertical Restraints Regulation, art. 2.1).

This definition of vertical agreements incorporates not only franchise agreements, but also exclusive purchase agreements, selective and exclusive distribution agreements, and what are described in the Guidelines as 'non-genuine' agency agreements. The 1999 Regulation provides that article 81(1) of the EC Treaty will not apply to such vertical agreements where certain conditions are met. The conditions which are relevant to franchises are as follows:

(a) the market share held by the supplier does not exceed 30 per cent of the relevant market on which it sells the contract goods or services (1999 Regulation, art. 3.1);

(b) the vertical agreement must not have as its object any restriction on the buyer's ability to determine its sale price, without prejudice to the possibility of the supplier imposing a maximum sale price or recommending a sale price provided that they do not amount to a fixed or minimum sale price as a result of pressure from or incentives offered by any of the parties (1999 Regulation, art. 4(a));

(c) the vertical agreement must not have as its object any restriction of the territory into which, or of the customers to whom, the buyer may sell the contract goods or services, except the restriction of active sales into the exclusive territory or to an exclusive customer group reserved to the supplier or allocated by the supplier to another buyer, where such a restriction does not limit sales by the customers of the buyer (1999 Regulation, art. 4(b));

(d) the vertical agreement must not contain any direct or indirect non-compete obligation the duration of which is indefinite or exceeds five years, provided such limitation does not apply where the contract goods or services are sold by the buyer from premises and land owned by the supplier or leased by the supplier from third parties not connected with the buyer, in which case the duration of the non-compete obligation cannot exceed the period of occupancy of the premises and land by the buyer (1999 Regulation, art. 5(a)); and

(e) the vertical agreement must not contain any direct or indirect obligation causing the buyer, after termination of the agreement, not to manufacture, purchase, sell or resell goods or services unless such obligation:

  (i) relates to goods or services which compete with the contract goods or services;

  (ii) is limited to the premises and land from which the buyer has operated during the contract period;

  (iii) is indispensable to protect the know-how transferred by the supplier to the buyer; and

  (iv) is of a duration of limited to a period of one year after termination of the agreement (1999 Regulation, art. 5(b)).

The introduction of the 1999 Regulation has thrown up some interesting differences between EU and Irish competition law, and these are discussed in greater detail at **7.3.3.6** below.

7.3.2.9 Market share

One of the greatest practical difficulties facing lawyers in advising clients is in advising on the calculation of the market share. The Commission has given some consideration to this, and article 9 of the 1999 Regulation gives some assistance as to how the market share of 30 per cent provided for in article 3(1) of the 1999 Regulation is to be calculated. Article 9(1) specifies that market share

> shall be calculated on the basis of the market sales value of the contract goods or services and other goods or services sold by the supplier which are regarded as interchangeable or substitutable by the buyer, by reason of the products characteristics, their prices and their intended use.

For the purposes of ascertaining the market share article 9.2(a) of the 1999 Regulation provides that the market share is to be calculated on the basis of data relating to the preceding calendar year. The 1999 Regulation also contains provisions covering temporary increases of the market share threshold above 30 per cent. In addition the Guidelines go into some detail on market definition and market share calculation issues (Part V of the Guidelines, paragraphs 88–99).

The 1999 Regulation came into force on 1 June 2000 and expires on 31 May 2010.

7.3.3 IRISH COMPETITION LAW

7.3.3.1 Competition Act 1991

Section 4 of the Competition Act 1991 ('the 1991 Act') introduced into Irish law provisions which are substantially similar to those now contained in article 81(1) EC. Under the 1991 Act, s. 4(4) the Competition Authority established by the Act has the power, upon application, to issue a certificate to the effect that a particular agreement or arrangement does not infringe s. 4(1). It also has the power under s. 4(2) to license an agreement or arrangement, notwithstanding that it does infringe the provisions of s. 4(1). A certificate or licence of the Competition Authority may be amended or revoked by the High Court on appeal: s. 9(1).

7.3.3.2 Category Certificate/Licence

Following the approach taken by the European Commission, and having considered a number of notified franchise agreements, the Competition Authority issued a Category Licence for Franchise Agreements on 17 November 1994 (Decision no. 372: 'the Category Licence'). That Category Licence remained in force until 31 December 1999, and applied to all franchise agreements entered into on or before 31 December 1998.

In anticipation of the expiry of the Category Licence the Competition Authority, on 4 December 1998, issued a further Category Certificate/Licence which applies to Agreements between Suppliers and Resellers ('the 1998 Category/Certificate Licence': Decision no. 528). The 1998 Category Certificate/Licence replaced the 1994 Category Licence in respect of franchise agreements, and applies not only to franchise agreements, but also to exclusive distribution agreements, exclusive purchase agreements and, for the first time, selective distribution agreements—typical examples of agreements between suppliers and resellers of goods and services.

7.3.3.3 Objectives

To a large extent, in adopting the 1998 Category Certificate/Licence, the Competition Authority was anticipating the 1999 Vertical Restraints Regulation. The introduction of the new Category Certificate/Licence represented a significant change in approach by the Authority. Instead of focusing on the legal form of an agreement and issuing a licence particular to a category of agreements, the Authority took a much broader approach, looking at the economic consequences of the vertical arrangement analysed on a 'rule of reason' basis. The Authority's expressed objectives in introducing the 1998 Category Certificate/Licence were to:

(a) simplify the rules for business in respect of such agreements;

(b) reduce the need for notification of individual agreements;

(c) ensure greater consistency by focusing on economic effects rather than on legal form; and

(d) enable the Authority to focus its attention on those cases which are detrimental to economic welfare.

The focus of the Authority was to look at the possible existence of market power in a relevant market, to look at the actual effects on competition in the relevant market and, finally, to look at indicators of efficiency in the relevant market.

The 1998 Category Certificate/Licence issued by the Authority therefore included:

(i) a category certificate which provided that vertical agreements will not be deemed to be anti-competitive where neither the supplier nor the reseller has a market share in excess of 20 per cent (Certificate, art. 4); and

(ii) a category licence which provides that such agreements are anti-competitive, but permissible, where either the supplier or the reseller have a market share of between 20 per cent and 40 per cent (Licence, art. 2).

7.3.3.4 Restrictions prohibited

In order to avail of the benefit of the 1998 Category Certificate/Licence certain restrictive provisions are not permissible in any circumstances, regardless of market share. These are as follows:

(a) any restriction on the freedom of the reseller to determine his own resale prices, although the Authority does permit recommending of resale prices (Certificate, art. 5(a); Licence, art. 3(a)). If resale prices are to be recommended, and for the benefit of the 1998 Category Certificate/Licence to apply, the recommendation must:

   (i) inform the reseller that he is free to set his own prices;

   (ii) contain no reference to the margins resulting from applying any recommended price;

   (iii) involve no requirement to display any recommended price; and

   (iv) provide that no inducements are offered to secure compliance with the recommended price.

In the 1998 Category Certificate/Licence the Authority did consider the validity of the arguments that suppliers should be allowed to impose maximum resale prices. It concluded, however, that maximum resale price maintenance could be anti-competitive in certain circumstances, and was therefore unable to conclude that, in general, it did not contravene s. 4(1) of the 1991 Act. This position now conflicts with EU law, as the 1999 Vertical Restraints Regulation entitles a franchisor to specify a maximum sale price, provided it does not amount to a fixed or minimum sale price, as a result of pressure from or incentives offered by any of the parties (1999 Vertical Restraints Regulation, art. 4(a));

(b) any provision or combination of provisions which prevent resellers outside a particular territory from supplying customers in that territory in response to requests from such customers; and

(c) any non-compete restrictions which apply after termination of the agreement, other than the keeping of confidential and secret business information save that in respect of franchise agreements it is permissible to include post-term non-compete restrictions provided they do not exceed one year after the termination of the agreement.

7.3.3.5 Application of Certificate/Licence

In effect therefore, to take advantage of the 1998 Category Certificate/Licence, a party to the agreement will need to be able to determine, first of all, what is the relevant market, and secondly, its exact share of that market. The fact that the market share will vary from time to time will also complicate matters. From the legal practitioner's point of view, the shift in focus to economic effect means that it is difficult to advise clients as to whether or not they benefit from the 1998 Category Certificate/Licence. Unless a client is absolutely certain as to the relevant market, and its share in that market, it will be operating in an environment of substantially increased legal uncertainty. Some assistance in this regard has now been rendered by the adoption of the 1999 Vertical Restraints Regulation and the accompanying Guidelines, which indicate the economic principles which should be applied to determine the legality of restrictions applied, although it is by no means certain that the Irish Competition Authority will adopt a similar approach. It is quite possible that agreements will continue to be notified to the Competition Authority so that the Authority itself may declare that the agreements benefit from the 1998 Category Certificate/Licence. Many clients may decline to take the risk of assuming that the Authority or a court will accept its interpretation of the 'relevant market', and its share in that market, as such a decision may well leave an undertaking exposed to a claim for damages by an aggrieved party, if the assumptions are found to be incorrect.

Notwithstanding this, a franchisor should have good reason if it is intended to include anti-competitive provisions which fall outside the parameters set out in the 1998 Category Certificate/Licence. If an agreement does fall outside the 1998 Category Certificate/Licence then such an agreement, to be valid, must be notified to the Competition Authority for a licence pursuant to the Act. If no licence is sought, the consequence is that at the very least the anti-competitive provisions will be void and unenforceable, and quite possibly, depending on how intrinsic those anti-competitive provisions are to the remainder of the agreement, the agreement as a whole could be unenforceable. The franchisor may also be liable for damages, including exemplary damages: 1991 Act, s. 6.

7.3.3.6 EU law distinguished

The relative certainty which prevailed in competition law has now been upset by the introduction of the 1999 Vertical Restraints Regulation. There are now some material areas where the legal position differs significantly between Irish and European law. These areas are set out below.

The market share test under the 1999 Vertical Restraints Regulation is applied to the supplier only (in respect of franchise agreements) whereas under the 1998 Category Certificate/Licence it is applied both to the supplier and the buyer/reseller;

The market share thresholds are different, with the EU maximum now being 30 per cent, and the Irish maximum being 40 per cent, of the 'relevant market'.

Under the EU regime there is a 'de minimis' exemption for suppliers with a market share of less than 10 per cent and at the moment such suppliers may include in their agreements with franchisees the prohibited clauses (although this may be subject to review). Under Irish law, there is no 'de minimis' as such, but the 1998 Category Certificate/Licence does provide that where the parties have a market share of less than 20 per cent they may avail of the category certificate—they may not, however, include any of the prohibited clauses.

The 1999 Vertical Restraints Regulation modifies the legal position regarding the grant of exclusive territories, whereas the 1998 Category Certificate/Licence implicitly acknowledges that these are part of many vertical arrangements. The 1998 Category Certificate/Licence prohibits any clauses conferring absolute territorial protection, i.e. which prevent passive sales, but the grant of an exclusive territory is permitted. Under EU law the position now is that a buyer may be prevented from actively selling into an exclusive territory allocated to another buyer or exclusively reserved to the supplier. Previous block exemption regulations entitled a franchisor to impose a blanket active sales ban. This is not now acceptable, and such an active sales ban may only be imposed where the supplier has granted, will grant, or has reserved to itself an exclusive territory. In other words, if the supplier is allowing more than one reseller to operate in direct competition in a territory, there can be no legitimate reason to prevent active sales there by resellers from other territories.

The 1999 Vertical Restraints Regulation limits post-term restrictions to the premises from which the franchisee operated during the contract for a maximum of one year, whereas the 1998 Category Certificate/Licence limits post-term restrictions for a maximum of one year also, but does not limit the extent of its availability. Also, for the restriction to apply, the 1999 Vertical Restraints Regulation requires that the non-compete obligation must be indispensable to protect the know-how transferred by the supplier to the buyer.

As already indicated, under the 1999 Vertical Restraints Regulation, a supplier may specify maximum resale prices, but the 1998 Category Certificate/Licence does not permit this.

Under the 1999 Vertical Restraints Agreement, direct or indirect non-compete obligations must be limited in time and may not exceed a maximum period of five years. Hitherto, under EU law there has not been any limitation on the validity of non-compete obligations. Such a provision affects the type of clause, typically found in a franchise agreement, where the franchisee covenants not to sell competing goods for the duration of the agreement. As a consequence, most franchisors with agreements to which EU law applies will probably prefer to provide for the termination of the entire agreement after the expiration of a five-year period and allow for a new agreement to be concluded with a new non-compete obligation. This provision in the 1999 Vertical Restraints Regulation also means that a franchisee's entitlement to renew an agreement on expiration, also usually included in franchise agreements, cannot now be included, as the effect of the 1999 Vertical Restraints Regulation is that any non-compete obligations that are 'tacitly renewable' beyond five years are invalid, and indeed it seems that an express statement in renewable contracts that the non-competition obligation will not be renewed is required.

7.3.3.7   Practical considerations

What does this mean in practice? Is it now necessary to run a dual test on agreements, one to take account of the 1999 Vertical Restraints Regulation and one to take account of the 1998 Category Certificate/Licence? What is the position where there is an agreement which has an effect both on trade in the State, and between Member States? In many respects, this latter scenario may be easier to deal with—in recital 17 of the 1999 Vertical Restraints Regulation, the Commission emphasises the principle of the primacy of Community law and states that no measure taken pursuant to national laws on competition should prejudice the uniform application throughout the common market of the Community competition rules or the full effect of any measures adopted in implementation of those rules, including the 1999 Vertical Restraints Regulation. This would lead one to believe that in such circumstances the provisions of the 1999 Regulation will prevail over the terms of the 1998 Category Certificate/Licence. The Guidelines issued by the Commission make no comments in this regard, but do provide, at paragraph 4, that they are without prejudice to the interpretation that may be given by the Court of First Instance and the Court of Justice of the European Communities in relation to the application of article 81 to vertical agreements. One can see that the situation could develop where one party could have an agreement which is affected by article 81(1) EC, and that agreement could, for example, contain provision for maximum resale prices, and another party could have an agreement, effective only within the State, where such a clause is not permitted at all. Similarly, a franchisor may enter into an agreement, effective only with the State, with a renewable non-compete obligation on the franchisee for a period of say, ten years, but have another franchisee, subject to an agreement which affects trade between Member States, where the duration of the non-compete obligation cannot exceed five years. This really seems to be an anomalous situation, which will give rise to great uncertainty, and great difficulty from a practical point of view in advising clients. Other jurisdictions have cured the potential for such an anomalous situation to develop by legislative intervention. For example, s. 10 of the UK Competition Act 1998 provides that an agreement will enjoy parallel exemption if it would otherwise meet the criteria of an EU block exemption, but is simply lacking the effect on trade between Member States. Such an approach would guarantee that certainty would prevail. At present, however, it does not prevail in Ireland, leading to, for the immediate future, some uncertainty and inequality between franchisors and franchisees.

CHAPTER 8

AGENCY AND DISTRIBUTION AGREEMENTS

8.1 Introduction

This chapter deals with the application of Irish and EU law to agency and distribution agreements. The object of these types of agreements is to provide a contractual framework for the co-operation of independent undertakings at different levels in the chain of supply in bringing the goods or services of one of the parties to the marketplace.

8.2 Agency Agreements

8.2.1 INTRODUCTION

Agency agreements are arrangements whereby an agent concludes sales between a principal and customers, earning commission depending upon the volume of the goods sold. Title to the goods does not pass to the agent at any stage and he does not carry the risk in the goods. As a consequence any loss suffered due to non-payment for the goods is suffered by the principal and not the agent. Most agency situations involve economically a much closer relationship than might be the case for distributors. An agent typically functions as the marketing resource of the manufacturer and frequently sees little of, and has little responsibility for, the products for whose sale he is responsible. Through an agent, the principal may exert greater control over how its products are sold. Such control may be extensive since the legal responsibility is, in effect, between supplier and customer with the agent as intermediary and the terms of the supply, including the price, are in the supplier's control.

8.2.2 DEFINITION OF COMMERCIAL AGENT

Many commercial agents enjoy the benefit of the provisions of the European Communities (Commercial Agents) Regulations 1994 (SI 33/1994) ('the Regulations') and 1997 ('the 1997 Regulations')(SI 31/1997) which transpose into Irish law Council Directive 86/653/EEC of 18 December 1986 on the co-ordination of the laws of Member States relating to self-employed commercial agents ('the Directive'). The Regulations define a commercial agent as

> a self-employed intermediary who has continuing authority to negotiate the sale or purchase of goods on behalf of another person, hereinafter called 'the principal', or to negotiate and conclude such transactions on behalf of and in the name of the principal (reg. 2(1)).

The following points about the definition should be noted:

(a) Some commentators have been misled by the words 'self-employed' to conclude that the Regulations do not apply to companies acting as agents. This view is incorrect. In earlier drafts of the Directive, provision was expressly allowed for the exclusion of certain of the agent's rights where the paid-up share capital of the agent exceeded a given figure.

(b) The definition seems to exclude intermediaries who do not have continuing authority but who merely have a once-off authority to negotiate the sale or purchase of goods.

(c) The definition only applies to commercial agents for the sale of goods and not for the supply of services. This raises the question of the status of an agent who deals in both goods and services. The author's view is that the reference to goods is merely a matter of defining the status of the commercial agent and that, unless his activities in relation to services render his activities as an agent in respect of the sale of goods secondary, the Regulations will apply.

The Regulations also set out a list of exclusions from the definition of commercial agent, as follows:

(i) a person who, in the capacity of an officer of a company or association, is empowered to enter into commitments binding on that company or association (reg. 2(1)(a));

(ii) a partner who is lawfully authorised to enter into commitments binding on the partners (reg. 2(1)(b));

(iii) a receiver, a receiver and manager, a liquidator or an examiner, as defined in the Companies Acts 1963–1999, or a trustee in bankruptcy (reg. 2(1)(c));

(iv) a commercial agent whose activities are unpaid (reg. 2(1)(d));

(v) a commercial agent operating on commodity exchanges or in the commodity market (reg. 2(1)(e)); and

(vi) a consumer credit agent or a mail order catalogue agent for consumer goods, whose activities are considered secondary (reg. 2(1)(f)). The activities of such agents are presumed, unless the contrary is established, to be secondary for the purpose of the Regulations (reg. 2(2)).

The relationship of principal and agent for agency agreements to which the Regulations do not apply is governed by the general principles of common law.

3.2.3 CONCLUSION OF THE CONTRACT

The agency contract shall not be valid unless evidenced in writing: reg. 5. Commercial agency agreements not governed by the Regulations are subject to ordinary contract rules and may be made orally or in writing.

3.2.4 DUTIES OF THE PARTIES

3.2.4.1 Principal's duties

The principal's duties set out in article 4 of the Directive are to:

(a) act dutifully and in good faith (art. 4(1));

(b) provide his commercial agent with the necessary documentation relating to the goods concerned (art. 4(2)(a)). The nature of the necessary documentation is likely to vary on a case-by-case basis;

195

(c) obtain for his commercial agent the information necessary for the performance of the agency contract (art. 4(2)(b));

(d) notify the commercial agent within a reasonable period once he anticipates that the volume of commercial transactions will be significantly lower than that which the commercial agent could normally have expected (art. 4(2)(b));

(e) inform the commercial agent within a reasonable period of his acceptance, refusal and of any non-execution of a commercial transaction which the commercial agent has procured for the principal (art. 4(3)). As regards principals outside the scope of the Regulations, they are not under any similar duty under Irish law.

8.2.4.2 Commercial agent's duties

The commercial agent's duties set out in article 3 of the Directive are to:

(a) look after his principal's interests and act dutifully and in good faith (art. 3(1));

(b) make proper efforts to negotiate and, where appropriate, conclude the transactions he is instructed to take care of (art. 3(2)(a));

(c) communicate to his principal all necessary information available to him (art. 3(2)(b));

(d) comply with reasonable instructions given by his principal (art. 3(2)(c)).

The parties must not derogate from their duties outlined above: art. 5.

8.2.5 COMMISSION

8.2.5.1 Commission in the absence of agreement

In the absence of any agreement on remuneration between the parties, a commercial agent shall be entitled:

(a) to the remuneration that commercial agents appointed for the goods forming the subject of his agency contract are customarily allowed in the place where he carries on his activities; or

(b) if there is no such customary practice, to reasonable remuneration taking into account all the aspects of the transaction (art. 6(1)).

8.2.5.2 Entitlement to commission during the term of the contract

A commercial agent shall be entitled to commission on commercial transactions concluded during the period covered by the agency contract where:

(a) the transaction has been concluded as a result of his action (art. 7(1)(a));

(b) the transaction is concluded with a third party whom he has previously acquired as a customer for transactions of the same kind (art. 7(1)(b)); or

(c) the agent has an exclusive right to a specific geographical area or group of customers and where the transaction has been entered into with a customer belonging to that area or group (reg. 4). This is the case even when the customers were not acquired by the agent.

8.2.5.3 Entitlement to commission on transactions concluded after termination

A commercial agent shall be entitled to commission on commercial transactions concluded after the agency contract has terminated if:

(a) the transaction is mainly attributable to the agent (art. 8(a)); and

(b) the transaction was entered into within a reasonable period after the contract terminated (art. 8(a)); or

(c) the order of the third party reached the principal or the commercial agent before the contract terminated (art. 8(b)).

3.2.5.4 Sharing commission between incoming and outgoing agents

The incoming agent is not entitled to commission unless it is equitable for the commission to be shared.

3.2.5.5 When commission is due

The commission becomes due as soon as one of the following circumstances occurs:

(a) the principal has executed the transaction (art. 10(1)(a)); or

(b) the principal should, according to his agreement with the third party, have executed the transaction (art. 10(1)(b)); or

(c) the third party has executed the transaction (art. 10(1)(c)).

Commission becomes due at the latest when the customer has executed his part of the transaction or should have done so if the principal had executed its part of the transaction as it should have: art. 10(2). This mandatory final due date will mean that in the majority of cases, commission does not become due until the customer has paid. However, if the customer does not pay, or pays late, as a result of some failure or inability to perform on the part of the principal, then commission will become due when the customer would, if it had not been for that failure to perform, have paid. Thus, for instance, if the principal is in breach of its obligations to the customer or supplies defective goods and, as a result, the customer does not pay, then the principal still has to pay commission to the agent.

3.2.5.6 Time for payment

The commission must be paid not later than on the last day of the month following the quarter in which it becomes due (art. 10(3)). If the parties have agreed an earlier date for payment, that agreement will prevail. Any agreement to derogate from this provision to the detriment of the commercial agent shall not be permitted (art. 10(4)).

3.2.5.7 Extinction of right to commission

The right to commission may be extinguished only if and to the extent that:

(a) it is established that the contract between the third party and the principal will not be executed; and

(b) that fact is due to a reason for which the principal is not to blame (art. 11(1)).

The phrase *'it is established'* merits further comment. If the contract provides for the reference of a matter to an expert, for instance, and the resolution of that dispute takes several years, then seemingly the principal will have to pay commission and will only have a right to a refund of it at some time in the future if the matter is resolved in his favour. Thus, the principal could have paid substantial funds to the agent long before the principal receives any payment from the customer.

The words *'due to a reason for which the principal is not to blame'* clearly encompass breach of contract by the customer and customer insolvency. But it is not clear whether the words apply to the full range of events which could have caused the principal to fail to perform his obligations under the agency agreement. For example, if goods are not delivered by the

197

principal by the due date, then the principal may be in breach of contract. However, if this is the fault of a transport contractor, for instance, then, although the principal is in breach, is it appropriate to say that the principal is to blame? The author's view is that the words should properly be viewed as relating to breach of contract, and not *'blame'* in a causative sense. If this interpretation is correct, a suitably-worded force majeure provision in the principal's contract with the customer should protect the principal and entitle him to reclaim commission paid in the event that the contract does not proceed by reason of a force majeure event.

Any commission which the commercial agent has already received shall be refunded if the right to it is extinguished (art. 11(2)).

The principal must supply his agent with a statement of commission due not later than the last day of the month following the quarter in which the commission has become due (art. 12(1)). Such statement must set out the main components used in calculating the amount of commission. The main components are, presumably, the commission rate and the value of the contract upon which commission is payable. The commercial agent is entitled to demand that he shall be provided with all the information which is available to his principal and which he, the agent, needs in order to check the amount of commission due to him (art. 12(2)). This is stated in particular to include an extract from the principal's books. Article 12 does not impose any obligation of confidentiality on the agent as regards information it obtains from the principal's books. Such an obligation may be implied by the common law and/or as part of the duties imposed on the agent under article 3. This point may be covered by the inclusion of an express confidentiality provision in the agency contract.

8.2.6 NON-COMPETITION

Post-term non-compete clauses which prevent the agent competing with the principal after the agency agreement has terminated shall be valid only if and to the extent that they:

(a) do not extend beyond two years after termination of the contract (art. 20(3));

(b) are concluded in writing (art. 20(2)(a));

(c) relate to the geographical area or the group of customers and the geographical area entrusted to the commercial agent; and

(d) relate to the kind of goods covered by his agency under the contract.

8.2.7 TERM AND TERMINATION

8.2.7.1 Term

The term of the agency contract is a matter for agreement between the parties.

An agency contract for a fixed period which continues to be performed by both parties after that period has expired shall be deemed to be converted into an agency contract for an indefinite period (art. 14).

8.2.7.2 Termination

Where an agency contract is concluded for an indefinite period, either party may terminate it by notice (art. 15(1)). The period of notice shall be one month for the first year of the contract, two months for the second year, and three months for subsequent years. The parties may not agree on shorter periods of notice (art. 15(1)). If the parties agree on longer periods, the period of notice to be observed by the principal must not be shorter than that to be observed by the commercial agent (art. 15(4)). Unless otherwise agreed by the parties,

198

the end of the period of notice must coincide with the end of a calendar month (art. 15(5)). Nothing in the Directive affects the application of Irish law where Irish law provides for the immediate termination of the agency contract:

(a) because of the failure of one party to carry out all or part of his obligations (art. 16(a)); or

(b) where exceptional circumstances arise (art. 16(b)).

Various criticisms have been raised against the termination provisions of the Directive:

(i) there is no provision for compensation in lieu of notice;

(ii) there is no provision for reasonable notice;

(iii) it is unclear what happens if the proper periods of notice are not observed.

Regulation 2 of the 1997 Regulations provides that a commercial agent shall, after termination of the agency agreement, be entitled to be compensated for the damage he suffers as a result of the termination of his relations with the principal. The Directive provides that such damage shall be deemed to occur particularly where the termination takes place in circumstances:

(a) depriving the commercial agent of the commission which proper performance of the agency contract would have procured him while providing the principal with substantial benefits due to the commercial agent's activities; and/or

(b) which have not enabled the commercial agent to amortise the costs and expenses that he had incurred for the performance of the agency contract on the principal's advice; or

(c) where the agency contract is terminated as a result of the commercial agent's death (art. 17(4)).

The level of compensation payable will depend upon the 'damage' suffered by the agent as a result of termination of the agreement.

The commercial agent shall lose his entitlement to compensation for damage if, within one year following termination of the contract, he has not notified the principal that he intends pursuing his entitlement.

The compensation shall not be payable:

(1) where the principal has terminated the agency contract because of default attributable to the commercial agent which would justify immediate termination of the agency contract (art. 18(a));

(2) where the commercial agent has terminated the agency contract, unless such termination is justified by circumstances attributable to the principal or on grounds of age, infirmity or illness of the commercial agent in consequence of which he cannot reasonably be required to continue his activities (art. 18(b));

(3) where, with the agreement of the principal, the commercial agent assigns his rights and duties under the agency contract to another person (art. 18(c)).

Neither the principal nor the commercial agent may derogate from the terms of articles 17 and 18 to the detriment of the commercial agent before the agency contract expires.

For agency arrangements not governed by the Regulations and the 1997 Regulations, termination depends on the relevant contractual provisions.

2.8 CHOICE OF LAW

The Regulations do not specify whether they apply to agents operating outside Ireland. It is unclear from the text of the Regulations as to whether the Regulations may be avoided by the agreement being governed by the law of another member state of the European Union.

It may be, if the matter was challenged before an Irish court, that the court would take the view that, given the universal application of the Directive to each member state of the EU, that, if the governing law chosen was that of another member state, such governing law should be upheld (on the basis that the agent would be able to avail of the protection of the Directive by virtue of that member state's legislation implementing the Directive). It may be, on the other hand, that an Irish court would regard the provisions of the Irish implementing Regulations to be mandatory provisions which cannot be avoided by the parties choosing the law of another country.

The Contractual Obligations (Applicable Law) Act 1991 also provides for the general rule that a contract shall be governed by the law chosen by the parties (Sch. 1, art. 3(1)). The Act, however, provides (at Sch. 1, art. 3(3)) that

> *the fact that the parties have chosen a foreign law, whether or not accompanied by the choice of a foreign tribunal, shall not, where all the other elements relevant to the situation at the time of the choice are connected with one country only, prejudice the application of rules of the law of that country which cannot be derogated from by contract (hereinafter called 'mandatory rules').*

If it could be shown that the Irish implementing Regulations constituted 'mandatory rules' for the above purposes, then in a given case the Irish courts might well apply the protection of the Regulations to agents, irrespective of the choice of law outlined in the contract. One issue which has arisen is where an agency contract is stated to be governed by the laws of England. Given that the relevant UK implementing legislation (the Commercial Agents (Council Directive) Regulations 1993) only applies to activities of commercial agents in the UK, the question is whether an Irish agent appointed under a contract governed by UK law to conduct agency activities in Ireland would be able to benefit from the Regulations. The position is not clear from the text of the Regulations.

8.2.9 CONCLUSION

Agency agreements are arrangements whereby an agent concludes sales between a principal and customers, earning commission depending upon the volume of goods sold.

Many commercial agents enjoy the benefit of the Regulations.

To benefit from the Regulations, the agency contract must be evidenced in writing.

The Directive sets out mandatory duties of the principal and agency from which one may not derogate.

A commercial agent shall be entitled to commission on commercial transactions concluded during the period covered by the agency contract where the transaction has been concluded as a result of his action, or the transaction is concluded with a third party whom he has previously acquired as a customer for transactions of the same kind, or the agent has an exclusive right to a specific geographical area or group of customers and where the transaction has been entered into with a customer belonging to that area or group.

Agency agreements covered by the Regulations may contain post-term non-compete clauses which prevent the agent competing with the principal after the agency agreement has terminated provided that the clause is concluded in writing, does not extend beyond two years from the termination of the agreement, relates to the geographical area or the group of customers entrusted to the commercial agent and to the kind of goods covered under the agency contract.

Where an agency contract is concluded for an indefinite period either party may terminate it by notice. The period of notice shall be one month for the first year of the contract, two months for the second year and three months for subsequent years.

A commercial agent shall, after termination of the agency agreement, be entitled to be compensated for the damage he suffers as a result of the termination of his relations with the principal.

8.3 Distribution Agreements

8.3.1 INTRODUCTION

Distribution agreements are agreements between manufacturers or suppliers of goods and independent marketing companies which purchase the supplier's goods for resale. They reflect a specialisation of function between a manufacturer or supplier and an undertaking, the responsibility of which is to create and satisfy a demand for the products often in a specified geographical area. The supplier will commonly agree to appoint only one distributor for a given territory. The relationship between the supplier and the distributor is governed by the ordinary principles of contract law. As a distribution agreement is primarily a contract for the sale and purchase of goods or the provision of services, the Sale of Goods Act 1893, as amended by the Sale of Goods and Supply of Services Act 1980 ('the 1980 Act'), which is applicable to all contracts for the sale of goods and/or supply of services applies to distribution agreements. A distribution agreement may be made verbally or in writing.

8.3.2 TYPES OF DISTRIBUTION AGREEMENTS

8.3.2.1 Exclusive distribution

In an exclusive distribution agreement the supplier agrees with the reseller to supply only him with goods or services for resale within a defined area.

8.3.2.2 Non-exclusive distribution

In a non-exclusive distribution agreement the supplier agrees with the reseller to supply goods or services for resale within a defined area to the reseller but without any restriction on the supplier supplying other resellers within that area.

8.3.2.3 Selective distribution

In a selective distribution agreement the supplier agrees to supply goods and services only to those resellers satisfying certain professional or technical requirements, while the reseller agrees not to purchase such goods from, or sell them to, wholesalers or retailers outside the territory. Such agreements may include quantitative limits on the numbers of resellers to be appointed.

8.3.3 THE SUPPLIER'S DUTIES

The supplier's duties are governed by the terms of the contract in accordance with the general principles of contract law.

8.3.3.1 Sale of goods

The 1980 Act imposes the following obligations on the supplier of goods which, subject to the terms of the contract, are implied:

(a) that the supplier has the right to the goods at the time property in the goods is to pass (s. 12(1)(a));

(b) that the goods are and will remain free, until the time when the property is to pass, from any encumbrance (s. 12(1)(b));

(c) that where the goods are sold by description the goods will comply with the description (s. 13);

(d)   that the goods supplied under the contract are of merchantable quality (s. 14(2));

(e)   if the distributor makes known to the seller the particular purpose for which the goods are being bought, that the goods supplied under the contract are reasonably fit for that purpose (s. 14(4));

(f)   if the contract is for a sale by sample, that:

    (i)   the bulk shall correspond with the sample in quality;

    (ii)   the buyer shall have a reasonable opportunity of comparing the bulk with the sample;

    (iii)   the goods shall be free from any defect, rendering them unmerchantable, which would not be apparent on reasonable examination of the sample (s. 15(1)).

However, save that the condition referred to in s. 12(1)(a) and the warranty referred to in s. 12(1)(b) cannot be negatived, any of the other implied conditions or warranties above as between supplier and distributor may be negatived or varied by:

(i)   express agreement;

(ii)   course of dealing between the parties; or

(iii)   usage if the usage is such as to bind both parties to the contract (s. 55).

In addition, in relation to *a contract for the international sale of goods*, nothing in the 1980 Act prevents the parties to a contract from negativing or varying any right, duty or liability which is imposed by ss. 12–15 (s. 61(6)). *A contract for the international sale of goods* means a contract for the sale of goods made by parties whose places of business (or, if they have none, habitual residences) are in the territories of different States and in the case of which one of the following conditions is satisfied:

(a)   the contract involves the sale of goods which are at the time of the conclusion of the contract in the course of carriage or will be carried from the territory of one State to the territory of another; or

(b)   the acts constituting offer and acceptance have been effected in the territories of different States; or

(c)   delivery of the goods is to be made in the territory of a State other than that within whose territory the acts constituting the offer and the acceptance have been effected.

Consequently, in relation to distribution agreements between an Irish distributor and a foreign supplier/manufacturer, there is the right to vary substantially the implied conditions and warranties in relation to the quality of the goods supplied.

8.3.3.2   Supply of services

In every contract for the supply of services where the supplier is acting in the course of a business, the following terms are implied:

(a)   that the supplier has the necessary skill to render the service;

(b)   that he will supply the service with due skill, care and diligence;

(c)   that, where materials are used they will be sound and reasonably fit for the purpose for which they are required; and

(d)   that, where goods are supplied under the contract, they will be of merchantable quality (1980 Act, s. 39).

However, any term of a contract implied by virtue of s. 39 may be negatived or varied by:

(i)   an express term of the contract;

(ii)   course of dealing between the parties; or

(iii)   usage, if the usage be such as to bind parties to the contract (1980 Act, s. 40).

8.3.4   THE DISTRIBUTOR'S DUTIES

Distributors' duties are governed by the terms of the contract in accordance with the general principles of contract law.

8.3.5   LIABILITY OF THE PARTIES

8.3.5.1   The supplier as against the distributor

The supplier has the right to sue the distributor for any breach of the terms of the contract in accordance with the general principles of contract law.

8.3.5.2   The supplier as against third parties

The supplier is liable as the manufacturer of the goods in accordance with the general law of negligence to the user of the goods.

8.3.5.3   The distributor as against the supplier

The distributor has the right to sue the supplier for any breach of the terms of the contract in accordance with the general principles of contract law. The 1980 Act is the only legislation which imposes obligations on the supplier.

8.3.5.4   The distributor as against third parties

The distributor will be liable to third parties in accordance with the general law of contract. In addition, where a third party *deals* with the distributor *as a consumer,* any variation to the implied conditions and warranties under ss. 12–15 of the Act is void and in any other case the variation must be *fair and reasonable* in order to be enforceable.

A party to a contract 'deals as a consumer' if:

(a)   he neither makes the contract in the course of a business nor holds himself out as doing so;

(b)   the other party makes the contract in the course of a business; and

(c)   the goods or services supplied under or in pursuance of the contract are of a type ordinarily supplied for private use or consumption.

In relation to what is fair and reasonable, regard shall be had to the circumstances which were, or ought reasonably to have been, known to or in the contemplation of the parties when the contract was made. In particular, regard is to be had to the following:

(i)   the strength of the bargaining positions of the parties relative to each other;

(ii)   whether the customer received an inducement to agree to the term, or in accepting it had an opportunity of entering into a similar contract with other persons, but without having to accept a similar term;

(iii)   whether the customer knew or ought reasonably to have known of the existence of the term; and

(iv)   whether any goods involved were manufactured, processed or adapted to the special order of the customer.

8.3.6 COMPETITION LAW

Exclusive distribution and selective distribution agreements are covered by the Competition Authority's Certificate/Licence of 4 December 1998 in respect of agreements between suppliers and resellers (Competition Authority Decision no. 528). European Commission Regulation no. 2790/1999 on the application of article 81(3) of the EC Treaty to categories of vertical agreements and concerted practices provides a block exemption for vertical agreements where certain criteria are met. Full details are set out in Chapter 7: Franchising at **7.3.2.6 – 7.3.2.9**.

8.3.7 DURATION AND TERMINATION

Provisions on duration and termination are a matter for contractual agreement between the parties.

8.3.8 STANDARD TERMS OF A DISTRIBUTION AGREEMENT

8.3.8.1 Appointment of the distributor

A distributor is usually granted rights to purchase products *for resale* in a particular territory subject to the terms and conditions of the distribution agreement.

8.3.8.2 Appointment of agents

The agreement would typically provide that the distributor will be entitled (with the consent of the manufacturer) to appoint agents to assist the distributor and, in some instances, to appoint sub-distributors.

8.3.8.3 Exclusivity

The agreement should make it clear as to whether or not the distributor is being appointed as an 'exclusive' or 'non-exclusive' distributor.

8.3.8.4 Territory

The agreement should set out the territory in which the distributor is entitled to resell products. If the territory includes other EU countries, then the Regulation and the local competition laws of the other EU countries should be considered when drafting the exclusive distribution agreement.

8.3.8.5 Priority

It may be important for a manufacturer to provide in the agreement that a distributor is not entitled to any priority of supply of products as against the manufacturer's other distributors or customers. This will protect the manufacturer if he is unable to meet the orders of all his distributors at the same time.

8.3.8.6 Sale of minimum quantities

It may be provided that the distributor shall purchase a minimum quantity of products each year, and that failing such sales, the agreement will be terminable upon notice to the distributor.

8.3.8.7 Parallel trading

It is contrary to EU law if either party to a distribution agreement makes it difficult for intermediaries or users to obtain the products from other dealers within the EU or, in so far as no alternative source of supplies is available in the EU, from outside the EU.

8.3.8.8 Manufacturer's responsibility to supply products

Depending on the commercial terms of the distribution arrangement, the manufacturer may or may not be obliged to use its best endeavours to supply products to the distributor. On the other hand, it may be that the manufacturer will be entitled not to accept any order from the distributor. Manufacturers often insist that they will be entitled to make any alterations and specifications to the product as they think fit.

8.3.8.9 Distributor's responsibilities

The agreement should provide that the distributor is responsible for providing all necessary information in order for manufacturers to fulfil orders. The manufacturer will usually require the distributor to give a specified period of notice of the distributor's requirements for products and the agreement should set out the requirements regarding delivery date of the product.

8.3.8.10 Title and risk

The passing of risk is a matter for contractual negotiation and will usually depend on who is responsible for shipping the product. For example, it may be that risk passes to the distributor from the time the manufacturer notifies the distributor that the products are available for collection at the manufacturer's premises. Obviously the distributor should then insure the product.

8.3.8.11 Basis of supply

The agreement should set out the basis of supply, namely:

(a) where the goods will be available for collection;

(b) whether or not the manufacturer will transport the goods to the distributor's premises; and

(c) who should be responsible for risk in transit.

8.3.8.12 Price and payment

The agreement should make it clear as to whether or not the price includes transport and insurance and whether or not the price includes any applicable value added or other sales tax.

The agreement should provide for the time and method of payment.

The agreement should also include the consequences upon non-payment of the price. Care should be taken that the contract provides for the payment of interest. If the interest is of a penal nature, then the clause may be void.

8.3.8.13 Marketing

The provisions in relation to marketing are a matter of negotiation between the parties. It is necessary to determine who decides marketing policies, carries them out and who pays for the marketing.

The requirements of the Competition Authority's Category Certificate/Licence in respect of agreements between suppliers and resellers should be considered when determining promotion and marketing activities. In particular, the distributor must be given a free hand to determine the price at which it sells products to its customers and the supplier may not impose any restrictions on the reseller's freedom to choose customers.

In connection with promotion and marketing, the manufacturer may require further reporting requirements, maintenance of stock, compliance with legal requirements, consultation requirements, input into sales aids, catalogues, brochures, advertising and promotional material, the maintenance of a suitable sales force and any other relevant ongoing matters depending on the products being sold.

8.3.8.14 Support and training

It may be that the manufacturer will provide support and training services to the distributor. The agreement should set out the level of support and who will pay for this support and training.

8.3.8.15 Intellectual property

Depending on the commercial terms agreed between the parties the distribution agreement may provide for an authorisation from the manufacturer to the distributor to use its trade marks in the territory in respect of the products. It may also include further conditions relating to the trade marks and, in certain circumstances, prohibitions and modifications to the products and trade marks. It is important that the agreement provide that rights and goodwill in the trade mark remain with the manufacturer and do not pass to the distributor. Where appropriate, further protection regarding trade marks and intellectual property rights should also be included in the agreement.

8.3.8.16 Confidentiality

The agreement should include a clause relating to confidentiality. Although the Competition Authority Category Certificate/Licence in respect of agreements between suppliers and resellers does not apply where the supplier imposes restrictions on the distributor which will apply after the date of termination of the agreement, a permitted exception to this is a prohibition upon the use or disclosure of confidential information (provided such prohibition does not prevent or restrict the distributor from competing with the manufacturer after termination).

The agreement should contain provisions regarding confidentiality and information which is to be regarded as confidential and information which should not be used other than for the purposes of the performance of the agreement.

8.3.8.17 Warranties and liability

The distributor may require the manufacturer to warrant that products are of merchantable quality and fit for their purpose. The manufacturer may specify a limit on its liability (e.g. to the purchase price paid for the products or to replacement of the products). The manufacturer may not (pursuant to the Liability for Defective Products Act 1991) contract out of liability for death or personal injury caused by the negligence of the manufacturer. Otherwise, the manufacturer may wish to contract out of any liability to the distributor for any express or implied warranties or conditions and for any consequential loss.

8.3.8.18 Duration and termination

The agreement should set out specifically the duration of the agreement and set out the rights of either party to terminate the agreement prematurely. The agreement should also set out the consequences on termination relating to outstanding stock, orders, unpaid invoices, marketing etc.

8.3.9 SELECTIVE DISTRIBUTION

8.3.9.1 Definition

Selective distribution enables a manufacturer to control the type of outlet at which his product is sold. Typically selective distribution systems are used by manufacturers of technically advanced products or products of prestige in order to limit the outlets at which such products are available so as to maintain the actual or perceived quality of the product to the consumer at the point of sale.

These systems usually share the following characteristics:

(a) The supplier designates a limited number of selected exclusive distributors. Each distributor is allotted a main sales territory in which it must try to ensure the best possible distribution of the supplier's products.

(b) Within the allotted territory only the distributor may set up additional distribution points.

(c) A distributor may do business outside its main territory but may not establish any branch in the territory of another distributor.

(d) The supplier employs specially trained staff to give training courses at the distributor's premises and to carry out regular inspections of those premises.

8.3.9.2 The supplier's duties

The supplier's duties are:

(a) to guarantee the integrity of its selective distribution system;

(b) in the event of a large network, the supplier may undertake to organise a trustee responsible for answering enquiries as to whether particular distributors are members of the network; and

(c) to supply the distributor with products of high quality.

8.3.9.3 The distributor's duties

The distributor's duties are:

(a) to use its best endeavours to secure the widest possible distribution of the supplier's products;

(b) to carry out sales promotions by visiting customers and sending out circulars and advertising material;

(c) to have adequately qualified and trained staff capable of instructing, advising and generally looking after the purchasers of the supplier's products;

(d) to maintain complete stocks of the supplier's products large enough to enable all orders to be filled promptly;

(e) to be able to display a representative cross-section of the supplier's products;

(f) to check goods before selling them to the public;

(g) to promote the trade mark via publicity, advertising and other customary means; and

(h) to provide an after-sales service (replacement of articles and provision of advice to customers).

8.3.10   CONCLUSION

Distribution agreements are agreements between manufacturers or suppliers of goods and independent marketing companies which purchase the supplier's goods for resale.

As a distribution agreement is primarily a contract for the sale and purchase of goods or the provision of services, the 1980 Act applies to distribution agreements.

Exclusive and selective distribution agreements are also covered by the Competition Authority's Category Certificate/Licence in respect of agreements between suppliers and resellers and the European Commission Regulation on the application of article 81(3) of the EC Treaty to categories of vertical agreements and concerted practices.

CHAPTER 9

COMMERCIAL ARBITRATION

9.1   Introduction

9.1.1   GENERAL

Arbitration is a method of resolving disputes. It is an alternative to litigation. Unlike litigation, its use requires the consent of all parties to the dispute.

With the exception of certain statutory arbitrations (see **9.1.2** below), the basis of all arbitration is the agreement to arbitrate. If the parties to a dispute do not agree to arbitrate there can be no arbitration.

Arbitration is often chosen by parties to commercial agreements because of the potential advantages of arbitration over litigation. The advantages can be the following.

9.1.1.1   Advantages of arbitration

(a) Confidentiality

Arbitration proceedings are held in private and remain private unless there is an issue in the proceedings which becomes the subject of a reference to the courts.

(b) Specialist knowledge of arbitrator

Where the dispute requires specialist knowledge or experience to understand, the parties may feel more comfortable having the dispute adjudicated by a person with the particular specialist knowledge or experience. In arbitration the parties may choose the person whom they wish to act as arbitrator or, if they are unable to agree on the person to be selected, the method by which the arbitrator will be appointed.

(c) Flexibility of procedure

The conduct of the arbitration is not tied to any defined procedure. The parties are able to choose whatever procedure they feel is best suited to the resolution of their dispute.

(d) Costs

Because they have control over how the arbitration is to be conducted, the parties have control over the arbitration costs.

(e) Speed

Because the parties have control over the arbitration procedure they have control, subject to the co-operation of the arbitrator, over the speed at which the arbitration will be conducted and the time within which they may have a ruling on their dispute.

(f) Finality of the arbitrator's award

An arbitrator's award is final and binding on the parties. It cannot be the subject of an appeal other than under one of the limited headings for appeal permitted by the Arbitration Acts.

(g) Enforcement abroad

The enforcement of court judgments abroad can be difficult. Certain international Conventions make arbitration awards much easier to enforce in countries which have subscribed to the Conventions.

9.1.1.2 Disadvantages of arbitration

The advantages have, however, to be weighed against the following:

(i) Costs

The costs for which the parties are responsible in an arbitration will include the fees and expenses of the arbitrator. This is a cost not borne by parties in litigation who are not responsible for the costs of the judge.

(ii) Assorted disputes

An arbitrator does not have any jurisdiction either over persons who are not parties to the arbitration agreement or over issues which are not the subject of the reference to arbitration. Disputes between the parties involving other issues or involving third parties will, unless all of the parties concerned agree otherwise, have to be the subject of separate proceedings.

(iii) Sanctions

An arbitrator does not have all the powers of a judge to impose sanctions on a defaulting party. An arbitrator does not, for example, have power to strike out arbitration proceedings for want of prosecution.

9.1.2 IRISH ARBITRATION LAW

9.1.2.1 The Arbitration Acts

Irish arbitration law is governed by the Arbitration Act 1954 ('the 1954 Act'), the Arbitration Act 1980 ('the 1980 Act') and the Arbitration (International Commercial) Act 1998 ('the 1998 Act'), together referred to as 'the Arbitration Acts'.

Certain kinds of dispute may, however, be governed by the provisions of a particular statute which requires the dispute to be resolved in accordance with the provisions of an arbitration system established by the statute. This is commonly known as statutory arbitration. An example is the arbitration system established by the Acquisition of Land (Assessment of Compensation) Act 1919 which provides for the compensation payable to a landowner whose land has been acquired under a compulsory purchase order to be determined by arbitration by one of two statutory arbitrators appointed for the purpose under the Act.

Two kinds of arbitration are specifically excluded from the application of the Arbitration Acts.

9.1.2.2 Unwritten arbitration agreements

An arbitration agreement is defined by the 1954 Act, s. 2(1) as meaning 'a written agreement to refer present or future differences to arbitration, whether an arbitrator is named therein or not'. Although arbitration agreements are almost always in writing, this does not mean that an oral arbitration agreement is invalid but rather that it will not be governed by the provisions of the Arbitration Acts. This could be very important when it comes to the enforcement of the arbitration award because an award under the Arbitration Acts may be enforced, by leave of the High Court, in the same manner as a court judgment or order to the same effect.

9.1.2.3 Arbitrations relating to employment

Section 5 of the 1954 Act states that notwithstanding anything contained in the 1954 Act, the 1954 Act

does not apply to:

(a) *an arbitration under an agreement providing for the reference to, or the settlement by, arbitration of any question relating to the terms or conditions of employment or the remuneration of any employees, including persons employed by or under the State or Local Authorities, or*

(b) *an arbitration under Section 70 of the Industrial Relations Act, 1946 (No. 26 of 1946).*

The purpose of excluding such employment arbitrations from the provisions of the Arbitration Acts was to allow these to be dealt with by tribunals established to deal specifically with employment disputes (e.g. the Employment Appeals Tribunal).

9.1.3 MATTERS WHICH MAY BE REFERRED TO ARBITRATION

There is no clear distinction to be drawn between disputes which may be settled by arbitration and those which may not.

The general rule is that any dispute or claim concerning legal rights which may be the subject of an enforceable award is capable of being settled by arbitration. This general principle must be qualified as follows:

(a) under article 34.3.1 of the Constitution, the High Court has original jurisdiction in and power to determine all matters and questions, whether of law or of fact, civil or criminal;

(b) certain kinds of arbitration are governed by special statute (see **9.1.2** above);

(c) public policy requires that certain issues be dealt with by the courts or some other statutory tribunal;

(d) illegality may render an arbitration agreement unenforceable;

(e) by virtue of the 1954 Act, s. 26 an arbitrator does not have power to order specific performance of any contract relating to land or any interest in land.

9.2 Arbitration Agreements

9.2.1 TYPES OF ARBITRATION AGREEMENT

There are two basic types of arbitration agreement:

(a) the first is the agreement to submit existing disputes to arbitration which is often referred to as a 'submission agreement'; and

(b) the second is the agreement to submit future disputes to arbitration which usually takes the form of an arbitration clause in a more substantial agreement.

While a submission agreement has the same basic objective as an arbitration clause, there is nevertheless a fundamental difference in the way a submission agreement and an arbitration clause are approached.

When a submission agreement is being drafted the dispute has actually arisen. The parties are in a position to tailor the submission agreement to fit the particular dispute. This, of course, necessitates co-operation between the parties which may not be achievable.

This situation is quite different from the friendly relationship which normally exists when the parties are entering into a contract and are simply providing for the resolution of a possible dispute in the future. The arbitration provisions in such a contract do not normally go into too much detail as the parties do not know at the time what kind of disputes (if any) are likely to arise and, if they do, how best they should be handled.

Arbitration clauses may be found in a wide variety of contracts ranging from the once-off commercial contract, which has been the subject of detailed paragraph by paragraph negotiation, to the Law Society's General Conditions of Sale, and the standard conditions of many building contracts, insurance policies and travel booking forms.

9.2.2 DRAFTING THE ARBITRATION CLAUSE

9.2.2.1 General

The importance of a properly worded arbitration clause cannot be over emphasised. All too often agreements contain arbitration clauses which are poorly drafted and are either inadequate as a basis for the intended arbitration or are ill-suited to the kind of dispute which the arbitration is intended to resolve.

The following specimen arbitration clauses are attached at **9.18** below:

Schedule 1	Short form arbitration clause recommended by the Law Society
Schedule 2	Submission agreement
Schedule 3	Agreed arbitration clause for Arbitration Scheme arranged by the Chartered Institute of Arbitrators–Irish Branch on behalf of tour operators who are members of the Irish Travel Agents Association and which is to be included in their booking conditions
Schedule 4	Arbitration clause in Agreement and Schedule of Conditions of Building Contract issued by the Royal Institute of the Architects of Ireland (1996 Edition) with pre-condition for prior reference to conciliation
Schedule 5	Recommended arbitration clause—International Chamber of Commerce
Schedule 6	Model Arbitration Clause—United Nations Commission on International Trade Law (UNCITRAL)

There are many issues to be taken into account by the parties when drafting the arbitration agreement. Some of these are less easy to determine in relation to disputes arising in the future than in relation to those already in existence.

The following issues should be considered.

9.2.2.2 Number of arbitrators

It is a matter for the parties to decide when drawing up their arbitration agreement whether they wish to have one or more arbitrators. The general practice in Ireland is for

212

arbitration clauses in relation to commercial disputes to provide for the appointment of one arbitrator.

9.2.2.3 Qualifications of arbitrator

Generally speaking, any person may be chosen to act as an arbitrator if he has legal capacity.

Unless it is very clear what the nature of the dispute is going to be, it is often best left to those empowered to appoint the arbitrator, when the dispute has arisen, to choose an arbitrator appropriately qualified to deal with the dispute.

The arbitration rules of some institutions stipulate specific criteria and qualifications and, accordingly, if these rules apply to the arbitration, then the arbitrator appointed will have to meet the criteria and qualifications required.

9.2.2.4 Replacement of arbitrator

If the original arbitrator dies, refuses or is unable to act or if he becomes disqualified as a result of a successful challenge, the parties may wish to appoint a substitute. If the arbitration clause does not provide for the appointment of a substitute then application will have to be made to the High Court for a substitute to be appointed pursuant to the 1954 Act, s. 18.

9.3 Staying Proceedings in Litigation

Section 5(1) of the 1980 Act provides that if any party to an arbitration agreement commences legal proceedings against another party to the agreement in respect of any matter agreed to be referred to arbitration, any party to those proceedings may at any time after an appearance has been entered but before delivering any pleadings, or taking any other steps in the proceedings, apply to the court for the proceedings to be stayed. The court is bound to grant the stay unless it is satisfied that the arbitration agreement is null and void, inoperative or incapable of being performed or that there is not in fact any dispute between the parties with regard to the matter agreed to be referred.

The following three points should be noted:

(a) An application for a stay may only be made after an appearance has been entered. A premature application for a stay will be refused.

(b) 'Taking any other steps in the proceedings' has been held to mean conduct by the applicant which shows a decision on his part to use the proceedings already commenced to advance his case against the other party. In *O'Flynn v An Bord Gais Eireann* [1982] ILRM 324 Finlay P reviewed the question of what was or was not a step in the proceedings and stated the criterion to be whether the step taken involved costs which would be lost were the stay to be granted and the matter referred to arbitration. In that case, the defendant's solicitor wrote to the plaintiff's solicitor seeking an extension of time to file the defence. The court held that that was not a step in the proceedings which would preclude a stay.

(c) In *Administratia Asigurarilor de Stat v Insurance Corporation of Ireland plc* [1990] ILRM 159 it was held that the High Court has an overriding jurisdiction to refuse a stay where there are bona fide allegations of fraud.

9.4 Appointing the Arbitrator

9.4.1 GENERAL

It is very much in the claimant's interest, when a dispute arises and there is an agreement to arbitrate, to ensure that the arbitrator is appointed without delay. This is because:

(a) no orders may be made or other procedural steps taken until the arbitrator has been appointed;

(b) most claims must be made within certain time limits and failure to adhere to the time limits may be fatal, and

(c) although a successful party may be awarded the costs which he has incurred in having to arbitrate a dispute it is unlikely that he will recover legal or other costs incurred before the arbitration proceedings are commenced.

Arbitrators may be appointed in a number of different ways. The most usual are the following.

9.4.2 AGREEMENT OF THE PARTIES

Most arbitration clauses require the parties to try to agree on an arbitrator before any other method of appointing an arbitrator is adopted. Generally, the claimant will suggest a few names to the respondent who will either accept one of them or suggest some alternatives. If agreement cannot be reached then the procedure for the appointment of an arbitrator in default of agreement, which will be set out in the arbitration clause if properly drafted, will have to be invoked. This, for example, may require the arbitrator to be appointed by the president of some named institution. If there is no specified procedure, the party seeking the appointment will have to consider whether the High Court has the power under the 1954 Act to make the appointment.

Naming a specific arbitrator in an arbitration clause relating to a possible future dispute, where there is no guarantee that the person designated in the agreement to act as arbitrator will be willing and able to do so, is to be avoided.

Naming an arbitrator in a submission agreement entered into after the dispute has arisen, when the kind of person required as arbitrator is readily identifiable, may be more readily justifiable.

It is not, of course, sufficient for the parties merely to agree on the arbitrator. The person chosen must also consent to the appointment.

9.4.3 PROFESSIONAL INSTITUTIONS

Many arbitration agreements provide that in the event that the parties cannot agree on an arbitrator, the appointment may be made on the application of either party by the president for the time being of a named institution.

Most institutions nowadays have established their own guidelines for such appointments. As a general rule, they will charge a nominal administration fee before considering any application for an appointment and will require the following basic information to be submitted to the president before any appointment is made:

(a) a certified copy of the arbitration agreement;

(b) the names and addresses of the parties involved;

(c) details of the nature of the dispute;

(d) an estimate of the value of the claim in dispute;

(e) the names and addresses of any parties who for one reason or another should not be considered for appointment as arbitrator;

(f) evidence that the parties have failed to agree upon the appointment of an arbitrator.

The purpose of obtaining this information is because the president, before he may make the appointment, will have to:

(i) satisfy himself that he has the power to make the appointment and that any preconditions to the making of the appointment have been complied with; and

(ii) have sufficient information about the nature of the dispute and the parties to enable him to choose an appropriate arbitrator.

Normally, once he has made his appointment, the president will have no further powers in relation to the arbitration. Accordingly, if the arbitrator appointed by him subsequently refuses to act or is incapable of acting or dies, the parties, in the absence of any special provision in the arbitration clause, may be left with no alternative but to consider an application to the High Court under the Arbitration Acts for a substitute appointment to be made.

For this reason, it is recommended that an arbitration clause which gives a third party the power to appoint an arbitrator in the event of dispute should also give him the power to nominate a substitute arbitrator in the event that the original arbitrator refuses to act, or is incapable of acting, or dies.

.4.4 ARBITRATION INSTITUTIONS

Institutions have been established nationally and internationally to promote arbitration. These institutions invariably have model clauses which they recommend to parties whose wish it is when entering into an arbitration agreement to have the arbitration governed by their rules.

It is, however, always open to the parties to expand or modify the clauses to meet their own requirements. Some arbitration institutions (for example, the Chartered Institute of Arbitrators and the International Chamber of Commerce) have their own specific rules dealing with the conduct of the arbitration while others may adopt a standard set of rules with or without amendment.

.4.5 TRADE ASSOCIATIONS

Many arbitrations are governed by the regulations of trade associations whose standard conditions of trade provide for all disputes arising with members of the trade to be resolved by an arbitration system established by the particular trade.

.4.6 HIGH COURT

Section 18 of the 1954 Act confers on the High Court the power to appoint an arbitrator in cases where the parties have chosen arbitration as the method by which they wish their dispute to be resolved and have either not agreed on the manner in which the arbitrator is to be appointed or the arbitrator, or the authority chosen by them to appoint the arbitrator, is for whatever reason unwilling or unable to act.

9.5 Limitation Periods

The Statute of Limitations 1957 applies to arbitrations as it applies to actions in the High Court. Accordingly, an arbitration may be time-barred if the arbitration proceedings are not initiated in time.

Section 74 of the Statute deems an arbitration to have commenced

> when one party to the arbitration agreement serves on the other party or parties a written notice requiring him or them to appoint or concur in appointing an arbitrator or, where the arbitration agreement provides that the reference shall be to a person named or designated in the agreement, requiring him or them to submit the dispute to the person so named or designated.

Quite apart from the limitation period imposed by the statute, the arbitration agreement may itself impose a limitation period for the commencement of any arbitration proceedings, the conduct of the arbitration or the publication of the arbitrator's award.

However, the 1954 Act, s. 45 empowers the court to extend any time limit for such period as it thinks proper if it is of opinion that in the circumstances of the case undue hardship would otherwise be caused. What matters should be taken into account in determining if there would be undue hardship was considered in *Walsh v Shield Insurance Co Ltd* [1977] ILRM 218 where the court held that while there had been inexcusable delay on the part of the applicant in commencing arbitration proceedings under the terms of an insurance policy, the respondent had not been prejudiced by such delay and accordingly the court agreed to extend the time limit for appointing the arbitrator beyond that specified in the policy.

9.6 Preliminary Meeting

Except in the case of minor arbitrations, a preliminary meeting is probably the most important procedural step if the potential advantages of arbitration are to be achieved.

The preliminary meeting should be convened by the arbitrator as soon as possible after his appointment. The primary objective of the preliminary meeting is to establish the future conduct of the arbitration with a view to having the dispute resolved in the most efficient and economical way. On this, the arbitrator should seek to get the agreement of the parties but, in the absence of agreement, he is fully empowered to fix the procedure subject to any special provisions in the arbitration clause and subject to the general principles of natural justice.

A draft agenda of matters to be discussed at the preliminary meeting is included in Schedule 7 at **9.18.7**. The arbitrator may, however, decide to exclude from the agenda matters relating to the conduct of the arbitration hearing and postpone these for consideration to another meeting to be convened when the exchange of pleadings has been concluded.

As a general rule, before an arbitrator will agree to proceed with the arbitration, he will require one, or preferably both, of the parties to sign a Form of Appointment of Arbitrator on the lines of the draft set out in Schedule 8 at **9.18.8**. The arbitrator's purpose in requiring such a form to be completed is to give him a contractual right against at least one of the parties to recover any fees or expenses incurred by him in relation to the arbitration. An arbitrator may be left high and dry, having done a considerable amount of work in relation to the arbitration, if the parties settle their dispute and do so without reference to him.

Immediately following the preliminary meeting, the arbitrator will normally issue an order for directions which will encompass formal directions from the arbitrator on the future conduct of the arbitration by reference to what has been agreed or fixed at the preliminary meeting.

9.7 Powers of the Arbitrator

An arbitrator is appointed to determine a dispute which has arisen between the parties. It is important that the arbitrator identifies all of the elements of the dispute and that he takes all reasonable steps to conduct the arbitration, having at all times regard to the wishes and interests of both parties, in a fair, efficient and economic way.

Subject to any terms contained in the arbitration agreement, an arbitrator has a wide discretion as to how the arbitration is to be conducted. He must, however, have regard at all times to the overriding principles of natural justice.

Apart from any specific powers conferred upon him by the arbitration agreement, an arbitrator has powers conferred upon him by statute. The principal statutory powers are the following:

(a) Section 19 of the 1954 Act provides that every arbitration agreement (unless a contrary intention is expressed in the agreement and subject to any legal objection) shall be deemed to contain the following provisions:

    (i) that the parties to the reference and all persons claiming through them shall submit to be examined by the arbitrator on oath or affirmation;

    (ii) that any witnesses shall, if the arbitrator thinks fit, be examined on oath or affirmation;

    (iii) that the arbitrator will have power to administer oaths or to take the affirmation of any such person;

    (iv) that the parties to the reference and all persons claiming through them shall produce before the arbitrator or umpire all documents (other than documents the production of which could not be compelled on the trial of an action) within their possession or power respectively which may be required or called for; and

    (v) that the parties to the reference and all persons claiming through them shall do all such other things which during the arbitration proceedings the arbitrator may require.

(b) Section 23 of the 1954 Act gives the arbitrator power to make an award at any time.

(c) Section 25 of the 1954 Act gives the arbitrator power to make an interim award.

(d) Section 26 of the 1954 Act gives the arbitrator the same power as the High Court to order specific performance of any contract other than a contract relating to land or any interest in land.

(e) Section 28 of the 1954 Act gives the arbitrator power to correct in an award any clerical mistake or error arising from any accidental slip or omission.

(f) Section 29 of the 1954 Act gives the arbitrator power to order to and by whom and in what manner the costs of the reference and of the award are to be paid including, with the consent of the parties, power to tax or settle the amount of those costs.

(g) Section 35 of the 1954 Act gives the arbitrator power to state any question of law arising in the course of the reference or any award or any part of the award in the form of a special case for the decision of the High Court (see **9.9**).

(h) Section 17 of the Arbitration (International Commercial) Act, 1998 amends the 1954 Act, s. 34 and gives the arbitrator power to award interest at whatever rate he feels meets the justice of the case on all or part of any amount awarded by him both up to the date of the award and from the date of the award up to the date of actual payment (see **9.14.2** below).

217

Unless the arbitration agreement provides otherwise, an arbitrator does not have the following powers:

   (i)   power to order security for the amount claimed;

   (ii)   power to order security for costs;

   (iii) power to grant injunctions; and

   (iv) power to strike out arbitration proceedings for want of prosecution.

9.8   Protective Measures

Section 22 of the 1954 Act gives the High Court in relation to arbitration proceedings the same power as it has in relation to court proceedings of making orders in respect of the following:

   (a)   security for costs;

   (b)   discovery and inspection of documents and interrogatories;

   (c)   the giving of evidence by affidavit;

   (d)   examination on oath of any witness before an officer of the court;

   (e)   the preservation, interim custody or sale of any goods which are the subject matter of the arbitration;

   (f)   securing the amount in dispute;

   (g)   the detention, preservation or inspection of any property or thing which is the subject of the reference; and

   (h)   interim injunctions or the appointment of a receiver.

Section 22, however, states that the fact that the High Court is given these specific powers is not to be taken to prejudice any power which may be vested in an arbitrator of making such order.

9.9   Special Case

If an arbitrator is in doubt about the law, he is empowered under the 1954 Act, s. 35 to refer any question of law arising in the course of the reference in the form of a special case for the decision of the High Court. Further, if one of the parties in the course of the proceedings, but before the award has been published, requests the arbitrator to state a case to the High Court on a point of law, the arbitrator is obliged, in the absence of good reason, to do so. What may or may not be good reason was considered by the court in *Corporation of Dublin v MacGinley*, 22 January 1986, HC (unreported). In that case Murphy J stated that a point of law without substance or which authority adequately covers would constitute good reasons for not stating a case.

In *Mizen Hotel Co v Capwell Investments Ltd*, 30 June 1981, HC (unreported) the court held that the power of the arbitrator under s. 35 extends to questions of law only and not to questions of fact.

9.10   Removal of the Arbitrator

Section 24 of the 1954 Act empowers the High Court to remove an arbitrator who fails to use all reasonable dispatch in entering on and proceeding with the reference in making an award. An arbitrator who is removed by the High Court in such circumstances is not entitled to receive any remuneration for his services.

The High Court may also remove an arbitrator under the 1954 Act, s. 37 where the arbitrator has been guilty of misconduct. In the context of arbitration, the word 'misconduct' has been held to mean that the arbitrator exceeded his jurisdiction, or did not act impartially or has acted in a way which might 'reasonably give rise in the mind of an unprejudiced onlooker to the suspicion that justice was not being done': *State (Hegarty) v Winters* [1956] IR 336. It does not necessarily mean that the arbitrator has acted in any dishonest way.

9.11   Documents Only Arbitrations

While the general practice is for a formal arbitration hearing to be convened, the parties may agree that the matter in dispute may be satisfactorily determined by the arbitrator on the basis of written submissions being made to him. This could involve a substantial saving in costs.

In Ireland, the vast majority of arbitrations involve an arbitration hearing but in small straightforward arbitrations, having the dispute determined by written submission may make more economic sense. The general principle is that if all parties to the arbitration wish the arbitrator to proceed by way of written submission only then the arbitrator should accede to this request but if any party objects then an oral hearing should be held.

9.12   Arbitration Hearing

9.12.1   PRE-HEARING REVIEW

If there is to be an arbitration hearing the arbitrator may well decide, unless the arbitration is very straightforward, to hold a pre-hearing meeting with the parties or their representatives when the pleadings have been closed. The purpose of such a meeting would be:

(a) to check whether all of the directions given at the preliminary meeting have been complied with and whether any further directions are required;

(b) to review the issues in dispute and to encourage the parties, where possible, to agree figures, documents, photographs, plans or other exhibits with a view to avoiding unnecessary proofs at the hearing;

(c) to review and fix the format of the arbitration hearing; and

(d) to check that the facilities and other requirements necessary for the proper conduct of the arbitration hearing are in order.

9.12.2   ARBITRATION HEARING

When all of the pleadings have been exchanged and any pre-hearing review has taken place, the arbitrator will, in consultation with the parties, seek to fix a mutually convenient date, time and place for the hearing. If he cannot agree these with the parties then he is at liberty to fix them himself. In fixing them, he must, of course, have regard to any reasonable representations made by any party.

The arbitrator must conduct the arbitration hearing in accordance with the arbitration agreement. Within the constraints of natural justice, he has full power to decide on how the case will be heard and what procedure will be followed. This is, however, likely to have been agreed or fixed at the preliminary meeting or the pre-hearing review. It is a matter for the parties whether they wish to conduct their own case or be represented by solicitors or counsel. However, where one party is being represented by a solicitor or counsel, it is proper for the arbitrator to ensure that the other party has an equal opportunity to be so represented.

The conduct of the hearing, depending on the nature and size of the arbitration involved, may vary from being a mirror image of a court hearing, on the one hand, to extreme informality on the other. Whatever is agreed or determined, the underlying principle is that each party should be treated fairly and should have a reasonable opportunity to present his own case and to controvert his opponent's case.

It was held in *Grangeford Structures Ltd (in liquidation) v S.H. Ltd* [1990] ILRM 277 that an arbitrator is entitled to proceed with a hearing without one of the parties being in attendance if the arbitrator has given that party a reasonable opportunity to attend.

9.12.3 EVIDENCE

Evidence may either be written or oral (unless, of course, it is a documents only arbitration when all submissions will be written).

Unless the parties have agreed otherwise, the arbitrator is bound by the same rules of evidence as the courts. He must allow each party reasonable opportunity to present all his evidence and, if he fails to do so, his award may be set aside.

It is also important that the arbitrator decide only on the evidence before him and not on any knowledge or expertise of his own unless he openly expresses his views arising from that knowledge or expertise and allows the parties ample opportunity to comment on them.

As far as witnesses are concerned, an arbitrator has power under the 1954 Act, s. 19(1), unless the arbitration agreement provides otherwise, to examine on oath or affirmation the parties and witnesses to the reference. A witness who refuses to attend and give evidence at the hearing may be summoned to do so by the issue of a sub poena. The arbitrator has also an implied power under s. 19(1) to order discovery.

Where there are expert witnesses who have produced written reports, it is recommended that these be exchanged before the arbitration hearing and the arbitrator will frequently encourage the expert witnesses to distil their reports in advance of the hearing with a view to establishing the exact differences between them and thereby helping to identify for the arbitrator the precise issues in dispute.

9.13   Sealed Offers

There is no equivalent in arbitration to the lodgement system which exists in litigation. Offers which have been made by one party to the other prior to the arbitration hearing, and which the party making the offer wishes the arbitrator to take into account in any award which he is making on costs, are normally communicated to the arbitrator in a sealed envelope prior to the conclusion of the arbitration hearing. In case it influences his decision, the arbitrator should not open the sealed envelope until he has made his award on the substantive issue in dispute. The arbitrator will then make his award on costs having regard to whether or not the amount of the offer exceeds the amount of the award.

9.14 The Award

9.14.1 KINDS OF AWARD

There are two kinds of award:

(a) an interim award; and

(b) a final award.

An arbitrator may only make one final award. Accordingly, once he has made that award, his jurisdiction in relation to the arbitration to all intents and purposes ends.

Section 25 of the 1954 Act provides that, unless a contrary intention is expressed in the arbitration agreement, the arbitration agreement shall be deemed to contain a provision that the arbitrator may, if he thinks fit, make an interim award. The right to make an interim award allows the arbitrator to deal initially with some issues without having to deal with others. This may be very important if there is a preliminary issue involved, a decision on which may determine the outcome of the whole dispute without any other issues having to be decided upon.

If an issue of law arises on which the arbitrator requires a decision of the High Court, the arbitrator may give his award in the form of a special case. In such circumstances, the arbitrator will generally issue two or more alternative awards to cover the possible decisions which the High Court may give.

Unless the arbitration agreement provides otherwise, an award is not required to be in any particular form. If, however, it is to be enforceable, it should be in writing, signed by the arbitrator and dated.

As far as the contents of the award are concerned, the High Court will not enforce an award by an arbitrator unless it contains a clear and unambiguous adjudication on all of the matters referred to him. In this regard, it is not essential that each and every issue in dispute is dealt with separately but simply that the arbitrator has not left any issues referred to him, and over which he has jurisdiction, outstanding.

The practice in Ireland is for the arbitrator not to give reasons for his award unless he is specifically required by the parties to do so. In *David Manning v John R. Shackleton and Cork County Council* [1994] 1 ILRM 346 the applicant instituted High Court proceedings by way of judicial review seeking, inter alia, reasons for the arbitrator's award. Barron J refused to give the applicant relief in respect of the arbitrator's refusal to provide reasons for his award, and his judgment on this issue was confirmed on appeal by the Supreme Court, which held that the requirement that justice should appear to be done does not require that an arbitrator's award should incorporate anything in the nature of a reasoned judgment.

9.14.2 INTEREST

Under the 1954 Act, s. 34 a sum directed to be paid by an award, unless the award otherwise directs, carries interest from the date of the award at the same rate as a judgment debt. Section 34 did not, however, confer on an arbitrator power to award interest on any sums due up to the date of the arbitrator's award.

Section 17 of the 1998 Act amends s. 34 and gives the arbitrator power to award interest at whatever rate he feels meets the justice of the case on all or part of any amount awarded by him both up to the date of the award and from the date of the award up to the date of actual payment.

Section 17 applies only to arbitration agreements entered into after the day on which the 1998 Act came into operation (20 May 1998) unless the parties to the arbitration agreement agree otherwise.

9.14.3   COSTS

In arbitration, costs are divided into two categories:

(a)   the costs of the reference which are all the costs and expenses which a party has incurred in bringing his case to arbitration, and

(b)   the costs of the award which are the arbitrator's own fees and expenses.

Section 29 of the 1954 Act states that, unless the arbitration agreement provides otherwise, it shall be deemed to include a provision that the costs of both the reference and the award shall be in the discretion of the arbitrator who may direct to and by whom and in what manner those costs or any part of them shall be paid. The arbitrator is also empowered with the consent of the parties to tax and settle the amount of costs to be so paid.

Section 29 goes on to state that where an award directs any costs to be paid then, unless the arbitrator, with the consent of the parties, taxes or settles the amount to be paid by each party then the costs shall, in default of agreement between the parties, be taxed and ascertained by a taxing master.

Section 33 of the 1954 Act provides that if an arbitrator refuses to deliver his award until the fees demanded by him have been paid, the High Court may order that the arbitrator deliver the award to the applicant on payment into the High Court by the applicant of the fees demanded and the arbitrator's entitlement shall be such as the taxing master may in due course determine on taxation.

The following points should, however, be noted:

(a) Agreement as to costs

In dealing with the issue of costs, the arbitrator must observe the provisions of the arbitration agreement. Under the 1954 Act, s. 30 any provision in an arbitration agreement to the effect that any party shall pay all or any part of his own costs of the reference or award shall be void. This provision, however, does not apply to an agreement to submit to arbitration a dispute which has arisen before the making of that agreement.

(b) Award of costs

Under the 1954 Act, s. 31 if the arbitrator does not deal in his award with the liability for costs, any party to the reference may, within fourteen days of the publication of the award or such extended time as the High Court may allow, apply to the arbitrator for an order directing by and to whom those costs shall be paid. In such event, the arbitrator shall, after hearing any party who may desire to be heard, amend his award by adding such directions as he may think proper in relation to the payment of costs.

(c) Arbitrator's discretion

While an arbitrator has a discretion over who shall bear the costs of both the award and the reference and the manner in which those costs shall be paid, it has been held that that discretion must be exercised judicially. It is, therefore, unwise for an arbitrator to depart without good reason from the well-established judicial principle that 'costs follow the event'.

9.14.4   PAYMENT OF COSTS OF THE AWARD

As a matter of practice, an arbitrator will not issue his award until he has been paid his fees and expenses in full. The party who believes himself to be the successful party is more likely to be taking up the award. It is frequently the party who is ultimately not liable for the arbitrator's fees and expenses who therefore pays them in the first instance. Accordingly, while it may be self-evident, the award will often provide that in the event that the costs of the award are paid by the party not responsible for them, that party is entitled to recover those costs from the other.

9.14.5 PUBLICATION OF AWARD

When an arbitrator has made his award, it is generally said to be 'published'. However, the time limits for challenging the award are usually determined by reference to the date when there was publication or delivery of the award to the parties.

9.14.6 CHALLENGING THE AWARD

The High Court has power under the 1954 Act to remit or to set aside an award. The distinction between remission and setting aside is that in the case of remission the award is referred back to the arbitrator for his reconsideration, whereas when an award is set aside, the whole arbitration is made null and void.

Section 36 of the 1954 Act gives the High Court power to refer to an arbitrator for reconsideration any issues on which he has made an award, and provides that unless the court order directs otherwise, the arbitrator shall make his further award within three months after the date of the order.

Section 38 of the 1954 Act enables the High Court to set aside the award where:

(a) the arbitrator has been guilty of misconduct, or

(b) the arbitration or award has been improperly procured.

The High Court also has a general power under the 1954 Act, s. 39 to give relief where the arbitrator is not impartial or the dispute referred to arbitration involves a question of fraud.

Overall the grounds on which an award may be challenged are limited.

An application to the High Court to remit or set aside an award must be made within six weeks after the award has been made and published to the parties or within such further time as the High Court may allow.

9.14.7 ENFORCING THE AWARD

Under the 1954 Act, s. 41 an award on an arbitration agreement may, by leave of the High Court, be enforced in the same manner as a judgment or order to the same effect.

While a High Court judgment is directly enforceable, application has to be made to the High Court for the enforcement of an arbitration award. This is done by way of special summons pursuant to the provisions of Rule 4 of Order 56 of the Rules of the Superior Courts (SI 15/1986).

9.15 International Arbitrations

9.15.1 INTERNATIONAL ARBITRATIONS GENERALLY

International arbitration arises from disputes in international trade and as international trade increases so does international arbitration.

The facts which give rise to local or national disputes are normally no different from those which give rise to international disputes save for the fact that the disputing parties are of different nationalities, or the subject matter of the dispute, or the place where the obligation of the parties is to be performed is outside the State in which the parties have their places of business.

With the enormous increase in trade between Ireland and other members of the European Union, more and more disputes are falling within the category of international dispute.

Because litigation in an international contract is, in most cases, complex, slow, expensive and unpredictable and because the New York Convention 1958 on the Recognition and Enforcement of Foreign Arbitral Awards provides the means for enforcing awards in countries who have subscribed to the Convention, arbitration has become a primary method of resolving international commercial disputes.

9.15.2 NEW YORK CONVENTION 1958

A successful award is essentially valueless unless there is a means of enforcing it and a claimant, before embarking on any arbitration proceedings, should always consider whether, if his claim in the arbitration is successful, it may be readily enforced against the respondent.

The enforcement of an arbitration award is the prerogative of the courts in the country where enforcement is being sought. While in general their power to review awards is limited, the courts will only assist an enforcement if they are satisfied that the award has been made in a proper way. This applies as much in domestic arbitrations as it does in international arbitrations.

The 1958 New York Convention on the Recognition and Enforcement of Foreign Arbitral Awards was drafted with a view to simplifying the enforcement procedure. Essentially, this Convention sets out internationally accepted rules for the recognition and enforcement of arbitral awards, but while the Convention has considerably simplified the procedure for enforcement, the enforcement procedure is only available in those countries which have adopted the Convention. It was given legislative effect in Ireland by the 1980 Act.

Section 8 of the 1980 Act requires any person seeking to enforce an award to which the New York Convention applies to produce the duly authenticated original award or a duly certified copy, the original arbitration agreement or a duly certified copy and a certified translation if either of these is in a language other than English or Irish.

Section 9 of the 1980 Act details the limited grounds on which enforcement may be refused.

9.15.3 INTERNATIONAL ARBITRATION INSTITUTIONS

There are many international arbitration institutions. The principal institutions as far as Ireland is concerned are the following:

9.15.3.1 The International Chamber of Commerce

The ICC was founded in 1919 and is based in Paris where it established its Court of Arbitration in 1923. The court does not itself settle disputes. This is the task of the arbitrators appointed. It does, however, supervise each case, including the appointment of the arbitral tribunal, the conduct of the proceedings and the validity of the award.

The arbitration clause recommended for adoption by the ICC is set out in Schedule 5 at **9.18.5**.

.15.3.2 The London Court of International Arbitration

The LCIA was originally founded in 1892 as the London Chamber of Arbitration. It provides rules and facilities for international arbitrations and is supervised by a joint committee of management composed of representatives of the Chartered Institute of Arbitrators, the Corporation of the City of London and the London Chamber of Commerce and Industry. The membership of the LCIA comprises twenty-four leading international arbitrators drawn from different countries throughout the world.

.15.3.3 The International Centre for the Settlement of Investment Disputes

The ICSID was established in 1966 pursuant to the 1965 Washington Convention on the Settlement of Investment Disputes between States and Nationals of Other States and was given effect in Ireland by the 1980 Act. It operates under the auspices of the World Bank and is based in Washington.

ICSID arbitration is applicable only where at least one party to the dispute is a State which has ratified the Convention.

Most international institutions charge substantial fees for the services they provide.

.15.4 THE 1998 ACT

The 1954 Act and the 1980 Act did not draw any distinction between domestic arbitrations and international arbitrations. This was regarded as unsatisfactory in the context of international commercial arbitration. Parties involved in international commercial transactions who choose arbitration as a means of resolving their disputes do so as a general rule to avoid the difficulties which might otherwise be involved in litigation. The fact that the 1954 Act allowed for reference to the courts under the special case procedure was accordingly unattractive in the context of international commercial arbitration.

The 1998 Act adopted, with a few amendments, the United Nations Commission on International Trade Law (UNCITRAL) Model Law on International Commercial Arbitration. The text of the Model Law is set out in full in a Schedule to the 1998 Act. The Model Law was drafted by UNCITRAL in an effort to bring some harmony to the settlement of disputes in international trade. Under the Model Law there are very limited rights of access to the courts. Since its adoption, many countries have enacted legislation based on the Model Law.

The effect of the 1998 Act is that Irish law now draws a distinction between domestic arbitrations and international arbitrations.

.16 Attitude of Irish Courts to Arbitration

Recent decisions of the superior courts confirm that, apart from providing procedural assistance in arbitrations or dealing with points of law specifically referred to them for determination, the courts will not interfere with the arbitral process unless patent injustice or error requires them to do so. In the case of *Hogan v St Kevin's Co* [1986] IR 80 Murphy J. expressed the law as follows at p. 88:

> 'It seems to me that where parties refer disputes between them to the decision of an arbitrator chosen by them, perhaps for his particular qualifications in comprehending technical issues involved in the dispute or perhaps for reasons relating to expedition, privacy or costs, it is obviously and manifestly their intention that the issue between them should be decided and decided finally, by the person selected by them to adjudicate

upon the matter. . . . Thus it seems to me that at the end of the day both parties were content to have the important point of law determined not by the courts but by the arbitrator and that notwithstanding the fact that he himself possessed no legal qualification. Having adopted that course it seems to me that it would be unfair and unjust to permit the unsuccessful party to assert a right to have a decision of the High Court substituted for that of the arbitrator'.

That view was endorsed unanimously by the five judges of the Supreme Court in *Keenan v Shield Insurance Co Ltd* [1988] IR 89 all of whom subscribed to the views expressed in recent years by different High Court judges in many cases that arbitral awards ought to be regarded as final in all respects and should only be interfered with if an error in law is so fundamental that it cannot be allowed to stand.

9.17 Arbitrators vs Experts

Some agreements provide for disputes to be resolved by an arbitrator while others provide for resolution by an expert. Rent review clauses are a notable example of disputes where experts may be required.

Where an arbitrator is appointed both he and the parties involved are governed by the provisions of the Arbitration Acts. These provisions include the grant of certain rights on the one hand and the imposition of certain controls on the other. In particular, an arbitrator in reaching his conclusion is only entitled to take into account the evidence presented by both parties to him. He is not entitled to draw on his own knowledge without making it clear to the parties that he is doing so and allowing the parties time to make any appropriate representations to him.

While the expert may adopt a similar procedure to that of the arbitrator, the Arbitration Acts do not apply. The expert does not therefore have the controls imposed upon an arbitrator by the Arbitration Acts nor do the parties to the dispute have the benefit of the rights conferred by the Arbitration Acts on the parties to an arbitration.

Unlike an arbitrator, an expert will invariably make his own investigations and rely on his own knowledge and experience in making his decision.

Most agreements which provide for the appointment of an expert provide also that the expert's costs are equally shared between the parties.

9.18   Specimen Arbitration Clauses

9.18.1

SCHEDULE 1

Short Form Arbitration Clause Recommended by the Law Society

'All disputes which arise between the parties in connection with this Agreement, or the subject matter of this Agreement, shall be decided by an arbitrator agreed by the parties or, in default of agreement, appointed by the President for the time being of the Law Society of Ireland or in the event of his being unwilling or unable to do so by the next senior officer of the Society who is willing and able to make the appointment provided always that these provisions shall apply also to the appointment (whether by agreement or otherwise) of any replacement arbitrator where the original arbitrator (or any replacement) has been removed by order of the High Court, or refuses to act, or is incapable of acting or dies'.

9.18.2

SCHEDULE 2

Submission Agreement

This Agreement is made the   day of   20   between
[

                     ]

of [

                     ] ('the Claimant') of the one part and

[

                     ]

of [

                     ] ('the Respondent') of the other part.

W H E R E A S:–

1. [Recital of Agreement between Claimant and Respondent]

2. Disputes have arisen between the Claimant and the Respondent arising out of the said

COMMERCIAL ARBITRATION

Agreement and the Claimant and the Respondent wish to resolve all such disputes by arbitration.

Accordingly, the Claimant and the Respondent hereby agree to refer all of the said disputes to **[named arbitrator]** or should he be unable or unwilling to accept the appointment, to an arbitrator to be agreed by the Claimant and the Respondent or, in default of agreement, to be appointed by the President for the time being of the Law Society of Ireland or, in the event of his being unwilling or unable to do so, by the next Senior Officer of the Society who is willing and able to make the appointment **PROVIDED ALWAYS** that these provisions shall apply also to the appointment (whether by agreement or otherwise) of any replacement arbitrator where the original arbitrator (or any replacement) has been removed by order of the High Court or refuses to act, or is incapable of acting or dies.

9.18.3

SCHEDULE 3

Agreed Arbitration Clause for Arbitration Scheme arranged by the Chartered Institute of Arbitrators – Irish Branch on behalf of Tour Operators who are members of the Irish Travel Agents Association and which is to be included in their Booking Conditions

'Any dispute or difference of any kind whatsoever which arises or occurs between any of the parties hereto in relation to any thing or matter arising under, out of or in connection with this Contract shall be referred to arbitration under the Arbitration Rules of the Chartered Institute of Arbitrators – Irish Branch'.

9.18.4

SCHEDULE 4

Arbitration Clause in Agreement and Schedule of Conditions of Building Contract issued by the Royal Institute of the Architects of Ireland (1996 Edition) with pre-condition for prior reference to conciliation

'Clause 38(a) – If a dispute arises between the parties with regard to any of the provisions of the contract such dispute shall be referred to conciliation in accordance with the Conciliation Procedures published by the Royal Institute of the Architects of Ireland in agreement with the Society of Chartered Surveyors and the Construction Industry Federation.

If a settlement of the dispute is not reached under the conciliation procedures either party may refer the dispute to arbitration in accordance with Clause 38(b).

Clause 38(b) – Provided always that in case any dispute or difference shall arise between the Employer or the Architect on his behalf and the Contractor, either during the progress of the Works or after the determination of the employment of the Contractor under the Contract or the abandonment or breach of the Contract, as to the construction of the Contract or as to any matter or thing arising thereunder or as to the withholding by the Architect of any certificate to which the Contractor may claim to be entitled, then either party shall forthwith give to the other notice of such dispute or difference and such dispute or difference shall be and is hereby referred to the arbitration and final decision of such person as the parties hereunto may agree to appoint as Arbitrator or, failing agreement, as may be nominated on the request of either party by the President for the time being of the Royal Institute of the Architects of Ireland after consultation with the President of the Construction Industry Federation and the award of such Arbitrator shall be final and binding on the parties. Such reference, except on Article 3 or Article 4 of the Articles of Agreement or on the question of certificates, shall not be opened until after the Practical Completion or alleged Practical Completion of the Works or determination or alleged determination of the Contractor's employment under this Contract, unless with the written consent of the Employer or of the Architect on his behalf and the Contractor. The Arbitrator shall have power to open up, review and revise any opinion, decision, requisition or notice, and to determine all matters in dispute which shall be submitted to him and of which notice shall have been given as aforesaid in the same manner as if no such opinion, decision, requisition or notice had been given. Every or any such reference shall be deemed to be a submission to arbitration within the meaning of the Arbitration Act 1954 (No. 26 of 1954), or the Arbitration Act (Northern Ireland) 1957 (as the case may be) or any act amending the same or either of them'.

SCHEDULE 5

9.18.5

Recommended Arbitration Clause – International Chamber of Commerce

'All disputes arising in connection with the present Contract shall be finally settled under the Rules of Conciliation and Arbitration of the International Chamber of Commerce by one or more arbitrators appointed in accordance with the said Rules'.

SCHEDULE 6

9.18.6

Model Arbitration Clause —
United Nations Commission on International Trade Law (UNCITRAL)

'Any dispute, controversy or claim arising out of or relating to this Contract or the breach, termination or invalidity thereof, shall be settled by arbitration in accordance with the UNCITRAL Arbitration Rules as at present in force'.

[**NOTE:** UNCITRAL state that the parties may wish to consider adding:–

(a)   the appointing authority shall be .... (name of institution or person);

(b)   the number of arbitrators shall be .... (one or three);

(c)   the place of arbitration shall be .... (town or country);

(d)   the language(s) to be used in the arbitral proceedings shall be ....]

9.18.7   **SCHEDULE 7**

Draft Agenda for Preliminary Meeting

[NOTE: If the arbitrator intends to have a pre-hearing review with the parties, he may well confine the Agenda for the Preliminary Meeting to matters dealing with the conduct of the arbitration other than the hearing on the basis that the Agenda for the pre-hearing review will cover all matters pertaining to the conduct of the hearing.]

1. Review of Arbitration Agreement.

2. Check on any pre-conditions to be complied with before commencement of arbitration proceedings or appointment of arbitrator.

3. Validity of appointment of arbitrator.

4. Identification of parties in dispute.

5. Outline of dispute:

    (i)   subject matter of dispute;

    (ii)   approximate amount of claim;

    (iii) details of any counterclaim;

    (iv) approximate amount of any counterclaim.

6. Representatives of the parties and whether Counsel are being briefed.

7. Rules of procedure.

8. Any preliminary issues to be determined.

9. Pleadings:

    (i)   points of claim;

    (ii)   points of defence (and counterclaim, if any);

    (iii) points of reply (and defence to counterclaim);

    (iv) reply to defence to counterclaim;

    (v)   close of pleadings.

10. Evidence:

    (i)   witnesses of fact;

    (ii)   expert witnesses;

    (iii) extent to which expert reports and other evidence can be exchanged and agreed.

11. Discovery:

    (i)   extent to which discovery is required;

    (ii)   arrangements to be made.

12. Hearing:

    (i)   need for hearing;

    (ii)   estimated duration of hearing;

    (iii) venue;

    (iv) provisional date;

    (v)   need for transcript;

    (vi) arrangements to be made and responsibility therefor.

13. Inspection:

    (i)   need for inspection of any property or items involved in the dispute;

    (ii)   date of inspection;

    (iii) arrangements to be made;

    (iv) persons to be present.

14. Award:

    (i)   need for any interim award;

    (ii)   final award;

    (iii) procedure in relation to sealed offer.

15. Costs of the award:

    (i)   basis of arbitrator's charges;

    (ii)   joint and several liability;

    (iii) time and method of payment.

16. General directions:

    (i)   all communications by any party to the arbitrator (except for the purpose of fixing dates) to be simultaneously copied to the other party and to be noted on the correspondence accordingly;

    (ii)   exhibits, photographs and plans to be agreed where possible;

    (iii) reports and other evidence to be agreed where possible;

(iv)   figures to be agreed as figures where possible;

(v)   what documents to be submitted to the arbitrator and when;

(vi)   liberty to apply.

17. Any other business.

9.18.8   **SCHEDULE 8**

Draft Form of Appointment of Arbitrator

**IN THE MATTER OF THE ARBITRATION ACTS 1954–1998
AND IN THE MATTER OF AN ARBITRATION**

BETWEEN/

_____

Claimant

_____

Respondent

TO:

In consideration of your agreement to act as Arbitrator in the disputes or differences which have arisen between us relating to the matter detailed in the First Schedule hereto, which disputes and differences are hereby referred to you, we jointly and severally agree:-

(i)   to pay your fees, costs and expenses in connection with the Arbitration whether or not the Arbitration shall be carried to a conclusion and an Award made or published;

(ii)   to take up any Award within ten days from receipt by you of a Notice making the Award; and

(iii)   that your fees, costs and expenses shall be charged at the rate quoted in the Second Schedule hereto.

First Schedule

(Details of Contract in Dispute)

Second Schedule

(Fees, Costs and Expenses)

(a)   Minimum fee (for up to 2 hours)   £

(b)   Fee for each hour or part hour
      in excess of 2 hours   £

(c)   Expenses incurred (e.g. hire of
      room, hotel and travelling expenses,
      document copying)   at cost

(d)   Fees and costs of Advisers or
      Assessors (if any)   at cost

(e)   Value Added Tax on the above items   rate current
                                               at time of charge.

DATED THIS   DAY OF [MONTH] [YEAR]

SIGNED for and on behalf of

_____

in the presence of:–

SIGNED for and on behalf of

_____

in the presence of:–

CHAPTER 10

CONSUMER LAW

10.1 Introduction

10.1.1 GENERAL

Irish consumer protection law is by and large a recent development. Initially it reflected legislative developments in the United Kingdom but after 1980 the principal influence has been the steady stream of EU directives which were required to be implemented by Ireland as by other EU Member States. Sometimes this has been done by statutory instrument and at other times by primary legislation. While it may be regrettable that purely domestic inspiration has not been very evident over that period, at least it may be said that, because Irish consumer law throughout its short history has been shaped by outside forces, its standards reflect those of larger, more sophisticated economies where the needs of consumers have been taken seriously for some time.

10.1.2 LEGISLATION

The legislation to be examined is as follows:

- Merchandise Marks Acts 1887–1970

- Sale of Goods Act 1893

- Consumer Information Act 1978

- Sale of Goods and Supply of Services Act 1980

- European Communities (Misleading Advertising) Regulations 1988 (SI 134/1988)

- European Communities (Cancellation of Contracts Negotiated Away from Business Premises) Regulations 1989 (SI 224/1989)

- Liability for Defective Products Act 1991

- European Communities (Unfair Terms in Consumer Contracts) Regulations 1995 (SI 27/1995)

- Consumer Credit Act 1995

- Package Holiday and Travel Trade Act 1995

- European Communities (General Product Safety) Regulations, 1997 (SI 197/1997).

Neither the Merchandise Marks Acts nor the Sale of Goods Act are particularly consumer measures at all: they apply to all transactions in their ambit whether involving a consumer transaction or one between traders only. However, they have both been amended by more recent legislation in the last twenty years or so and this amending legislation has given them a particular relevance in consumer transactions in that the amendments made have given them a bias towards consumers in their dealings with traders.

10.1.3 CASE LAW

As one commentator has remarked:

'Judges in Ireland have developed aspects of the law in favour of the consumer in much the same way as in the UK; Irish judges are not bound by the precedents of their colleagues in the UK but will always consider UK judicial authority.' (Donelan: 'Consumer Protection Law in the Irish Republic' (1981) 131 NLJ 1086).

Thus the celebrated Scottish decision of the House of Lords in *Donoghue v Stevenson* [1932] AC 562 was considered by an Irish court in *Kirby v Burke* [1944] IR 207 where jam, when consumed, caused illness. Although the famous House of Lords' decision was not actually followed in *Kirby v Burke*, the principle that manufacturers owe a duty of care to consumers of their products has been accepted in Irish law and *Donoghue v Stevenson* has since been adopted by Irish courts.

However, it should be noted at the onset that there are few reported cases on the subject of Irish consumer legislation, largely because most claims involving consumers are for quite low amounts. Given that the value of products and services they would be litigating on as consumers would normally not come within the thresholds of the High Court, consumer claims are usually dealt with either in the small claims court, the district court or, at most, the circuit court, few of whose decisions—none in the case of the small claims court—are reported or even written down so as to be available in transcripts. This is understandable since the largest item of expenditure of a consumer apart from a home is likely to be a car; often the items at issue will be of considerably lower value. For this reason there is very little reported Irish case law available to illustrate the legislation covered in this chapter and often recourse has to be had to reported English cases on equivalent—but not necessarily identical—provisions of consumer legislation in that jurisdiction.

10.1.4 INDIRECT MEASURES

Although until 1978 there was no legislation in existence in Ireland specifically intended to protect consumers, there were laws in existence dealing with such matters as weights and measures and public health which had this effect indirectly. Under the Prices Acts 1958–1972 Ministers had power to intervene in the market by fixing maximum prices and charges for a large range of goods and services. While this power was used during the oil crisis of the early 1970s to fix maximum prices for the sale of petrol, for example, government policy more recently has been to allow market forces and competition to decide prices of goods and services.

The Industrial Research and Standards Act 1961 was intended to facilitate the setting of safety standards for a variety of products, and ministerial orders made under it prohibit the assembly, manufacture or sale of specific products (at first mostly toys and electrical products) in breach of its standards. Provision is made for testing and analysing products on sale to the public. Another example is the legislation dating back to the 1930s regulating preparation of agricultural produce such as dairy products and meat. This has more recently been greatly supplemented by a myriad of statutory instruments implementing EU directives concerned with food production and safety so that 'food law', covering the preparation of foodstuffs 'from farm to fork', has now become a speciality in its own right in some Irish law firms and is certain to be of even more importance in the future.

10.1.5 EU INFLUENCE

The foregoing legislation was either inherited from the time when Ireland was part of the UK or else is a domestic product, usually influenced by corresponding UK legislation. Later legislation has been EU-led, inspired by EU directives which required implementation in Ireland as in other Member States. In the case of statutory instruments, these were made under the European Communities Act 1972 and may be recognised by the inclusion of the words 'European Communities' at the beginning of the titles of the instruments concerned. It may be noted that there is no common definition of 'consumer' shared by the different pieces of legislation: the definition tends to vary from one measure to the next, sometimes quite markedly.

10.1.6 MISCELLANEOUS

Apart from the above legislation there are other provisions dealing with consumer protection which again are EU-driven. Thus, the labelling requirements for most foods have been set out in regulations implementing EU directives relating to the labelling, presentation and advertising of foodstuffs for sale to the ultimate consumer. Another example is the European Communities (Safety of Toys) Regulations 1990 (Si 32/1990) which implemented EC Council Directive 88/378/EEC on the approximation of the laws of the Member States concerning the safety of toys.

Two other statutes enacted in 1980 of relevance to consumers were the Pyramid Selling Act 1980 and the Trading Stamp Act 1980 which were intended to regulate abuses in the areas implied by the names of those Acts and were influenced by UK measures. These Acts were not reflecting EU legislation.

The rest of this chapter examines the principal consumer protection measures in some detail, in the order in which they came into law.

10.2 Consumer Information Act 1978

10.2.1 INTRODUCTORY OVERVIEW

The Consumer Information Act 1978 ('the 1978 Act') is the first Irish primary legislation specifically aimed at consumer protection. It provided for an increase in the level of accuracy required in relation to the supply of goods and the provision of services, establishing the office of Director of Consumer Affairs to supervise the Act and to ensure compliance with its provisions. The Act amended the Merchandise Marks Acts 1887–1970 which countered false descriptions and advertisements. These Acts applied to transactions between traders as much as to those between traders and the public and so does the 1978 Act although the latter is particularly designed to protect consumers.

Under the earlier legislation as amended by the 1978 Act any person who in the course of any trade, business or profession applies any false or misleading trade description to goods is guilty of an offence, as is any person who sells or exposes for sale, or has in his possession for sale in the course of any trade, business or profession any goods to which a false or misleading trade description is applied.

The 1978 Act greatly extended the definition of 'trade description' and included provisions to encourage truthfulness in describing services as well. The Act modified the defences in the original 1887 Act so that mens rea is no longer necessary for offences relating to trade description of goods and innocent intent is no longer a defence; the defences available are similar to those under the UK's Trade Descriptions Act 1968 from which a number of provisions relating to trade descriptions were taken. Effectively the 1978 Act imposes a positive duty of care on traders; the burden of proof is reversed in cases where the truth of a trade description is at issue so that the defence must prove that it is correct on the balance of probabilities.

As is often the case with legislation in Ireland, the draftsmen of the Consumer Information Act 1978 had the advantage of being able to see how the earlier corresponding UK legislation had worked in practice over several years and were sometimes able to improve on it thus making prosecutions easier to obtain.

10.2.2 THE ACT IN DETAIL

10.2.2.1 General

The Consumer Information Act 1978 established the office of Director of Consumer Affairs and cast the Director in the role of consumers' watchdog with the main responsibility for its overall supervision and the power to compel compliance with its provisions. He is empowered by the Act to apply to the High Court for banning orders to curtail misleading practices in the field of advertising and the provision of information to consumers and is able to prosecute offences referred to in the Act.

10.2.2.2 Office and functions

Section 9 of the Act established the statutory office of Director of Consumer Affairs as a position in the Civil Service, the holder of the office to be independent in the performance of his functions: s. 9(5). The functions of the Director were set out in s. 9(6) and may be summarised as follows:

(a) to keep under general review practices or proposed practices relating to the advertising of, and the provision to members of the public of information in relation to and descriptions of, goods, services, accommodation and facilities;

(b) to carry out examinations of any such practices or proposed practices where the Minister for Enterprise, Trade and Employment ('the Minister') requests him to do so or where the Director considers that, in the public interest, such examinations are proper;

(c) to request persons engaging in or proposing to engage in such practices that are, or are likely to be, misleading to members of the public in a material matter to discontinue or refrain from such practices and to institute proceedings in the High Court for orders requiring persons engaging or proposing to engage in such practices to discontinue or refrain from such practices;

(d) to request an increase in the precision of, or the amount of information contained in, the expressions that are, or are proposed to be, used in or in connection with such practices;

(e) to encourage and promote the establishment and adoption of codes of standards in relation to such practices;

(f) to publicise any legislation providing for the protection of consumers that, in his opinion, should be brought to the attention of the public; and

(g) to prosecute offences under the Merchandise Marks Acts 1887–1970 or under the Consumer Information Act itself.

10.2.2.3 Amendment

Section 55(1) of the Sale of Goods and Supply of Services Act 1980 extended the Director's review functions and gave the Director new prosecution functions for certain limited offences under the Act but, in the main, that Act was concerned with updating the civil law and issues of civil law involve matters to be resolved between the parties themselves so that the Director has little function in that regard.

10.2.2.4   Principal effect

The Consumer Information Act 1978 provided for an increase in the level of accuracy required and information given in relation to the supply of goods and the provision of services. It amended the Merchandise Marks Acts 1887–1970 and under the Acts as amended:

(a)   any person who in the course of any trade, business or profession applies any false or misleading trade description to goods, or causes another to apply such a trade description, is guilty of an offence and, in addition,

(b)   any person who sells or who exposes for sale, or has in his possession for sale in the course of any trade, business, or profession, any goods to which a false or misleading trade description is applied also commits an offence: Merchandise Marks Act 1887, s. 2 as amended by the Consumer Information Act 1978, ss. 3, 4.

The section thus comprises two separate offences:

(i)   the application of a false or misleading trade description to goods, and

(ii)   the sale of goods to which such a trade description has been applied already.

An offence is only committed by a person acting in the course of a trade, business or profession so that private persons are exempt. This change was inserted by the 1978 Act, s. 4(1) amending the 1887 Act, s. 2(1)(d).

A person is deemed to apply a trade description to goods if:

(a)   he affixes or annexes it to them or in any manner marks it on or incorporates it with:

(i)   the goods themselves or

(ii)   anything in, on or with which the goods are sold; or

(b)   he places the goods in, on or with anything to, on or with which the trade description has been affixed, annexed, marked or incorporated or places any such thing with the goods: 1978 Act, s. 4(3) amending the 1887 Act, s. 5.

The definition of 'trade description' was extended by the Consumer Information Act so that it is given a very wide meaning and includes any description, statement or other indication, direct or indirect, as to such a wide range of characteristics of goods that nearly all descriptions or indications of goods could come within the definition.

Three observations may be made in particular:

(a)   an oral statement may amount to a trade description (1978 Act, s. 4(3)(d));

(b)   the 1978 Act broadened the definition of 'false' so as to include 'misleading' and to commit an offence the false trade description must be false or misleading 'to a material degree' (1887 Act, s. 3(1) as amended by the 1978 Act, s. 2(2)) instead of 'in a material respect' as before; and

(c)   where the truthfulness of a trade description is in issue the burden of proof is reversed: the maker of the statement must establish that it is true on the balance of probabilities (1978 Act, s. 20).

There is hardly any Irish case law on the 1978 Act or on the Merchandise Marks Act which it amends. Most of the relevant case law consists of English cases under the UK's Trade Descriptions Act 1968 from which many provisions of the 1978 Act are borrowed.

10.2.2.5 Defences

Section 3 of the 1978 Act removed defences set out in the Merchandise Marks Acts 1887–1970 with the result that innocent intent is no longer a defence. Mens rea is no longer necessary for offences relating to trade descriptions of goods and the Act in effect imposes a positive duty of care on persons applying trade descriptions to goods or dealing with goods to which trade descriptions have been applied. It is a defence that:

(a) contravention was due to a mistake, or to reliance on information supplied to him, or to the act or default of another person, or to an accident or other cause beyond the defendant's control; and

(b) that he took all reasonable precautions and exercised all due diligence to avoid the commission of such an offence by himself or any other person under his control (s. 22(1)).

This defence is in the same terms as that in s. 4 of the UK's Trade Descriptions Act 1968, the operation of which was illustrated in *Tesco v Natrass* [1972] AC 153.

10.2.2.6 Application to services

A new departure in the 1978 Act was the inclusion of provisions relating to services, to the effect that persons making certain statements about services in the course of a business, trade or profession must have adequate grounds for believing those statements to be true (s. 6). Only statements which relate to specific aspects of the service are covered, e.g.:

(a) statements as to the provision of the service;

(b) the nature, effect or fitness for purpose of the service;

(c) the time, place or manner in which the service is provided; or

(d) the person by whom the service is provided.

The term 'statement' is not defined but it includes anything likely to be taken as a statement. Effectively the section appears wide enough to include most types of false or misleading indications of fact relating to services.

10.2.2.7 Proof of mens rea

The offences under s. 6 relate to false statements as to services made recklessly or in the knowledge that they are false, i.e. mens rea must be proved: the absence of an intent to deceive will be a defence, as will the absence of recklessness. A statement made regardless of whether it is true or false is deemed to be made recklessly unless the person making it had adequate grounds for believing that it was true. 'False' means false to a material degree.

Under the 1978 Act it is an offence to give a false or misleading indication of prices or charges for any goods, services or accommodation supplied (s. 7). It is also an offence to publish, or cause to be published, an advertisement for goods, services, or facilities if it is likely to mislead and thereby cause loss, damage or injury to members of the public to a material degree (s. 8). It is up to the defence to show that a particular advertisement is true, on the balance of probabilities. 'Advertisement' is defined as including a catalogue, a circular and a price list (1978 Act, s. 1(1)).

10.2.2.8 Compensation

As stated earlier, the 1978 Act took a number of its provisions in relation to trade descriptions from the UK's Trade Descriptions Act 1968 but provides by contrast that a court may, on imposing a fine for a specified offence, order that the whole or a part of the fine should be paid as compensation to a consumer witness for the prosecution who suffers a personal injury, loss or damage as a result of the offence except where the injured person takes civil proceedings (s. 17(3)). This means that the aggrieved consumer can be compensated without instituting a separate civil action.

10.2.2.9 Company officers

When a company commits an offence under the 1978 Act with the consent or connivance of its controlling authority—usually a director, manager or company secretary—the latter is also guilty of the offence (s. 19).

10.2.2.10 Authorised officers

Section 16 of the 1978 Act sets out the powers of the 'authorised officers' of the Director. For the purpose of obtaining information which may be required in order to enable the Director to exercise his functions under the Merchandise Marks Acts or the 1978 Act itself, an authorised officer is given powers of entry and inspection and may require information. These powers may apparently be exercised without there having to be reason to suspect that an offence may have been committed. A person who obstructs or impedes an authorised officer in the exercise of a power or does not comply with a requirement under s. 16 commits an offence.

10.2.2.11 Earlier legislation

Under earlier competition legislation (the Restrictive Practices Act 1972, repealed by the Competition Act 1991), there had existed a separate office, that of the Examiner of Restrictive Practices, who was empowered to investigate conditions obtaining, and complaints arising, in regard to the supply and distribution of goods or the supply of services with a view to controlling restrictive trading practices. The office of the Examiner lasted only briefly before being abolished by the Restrictive Practices (Amendment) Act 1987 which amended and temporarily extended, inter alia, the 1972 Act and the Consumer Information Act itself and increased the Director's duties and powers, bringing about a temporary transition in title from the 'Director of Consumer Affairs' to the 'Director of Consumer Affairs and Fair Trade', an office which amalgamated most of the functions of the Examiner of Restrictive Practices with those of the old Director of Consumer Affairs.

The functions of the Director of Consumer Affairs and Fair Trade in relation to competition were essentially those of the former Examiner of Restrictive Practices and included the enforcement of restrictive practices orders made under the Restrictive Practices Act 1972, only one of which—the Groceries Order 1987—had any real relevance by 1991. The Competition Act 1991 replaced the bulk of the existing legislation with effect from 1 October 1991 but retained the Groceries Order and the relevant provisions of the 1972 Act and the 1987 Act to enable enforcement of that Order; however, the Director's title was shortened to that of 'Director of Consumer Affairs' once again. The Director's powers in relation to consumer affairs were unaffected but the responsibilities of the Director in relation to matters of fair trade and competition were transferred to the new Competition Authority established under the Competition Act 1991, apart from the role he retained and still retains with regard to the enforcement of the Groceries Order, the continued existence of which is currently under debate.

10.2.2.12 More powers

Later legislation has extended the powers of the Director of Consumer Affairs bestowing new roles in consumer protection on that office. For example, another weapon was added to the Director's armoury with the advent of the European Communities (Misleading Advertising) Regulations 1988 (see **10.4** below) which implemented EC Council Directive 84/450/EEC of 10 September 1984 on misleading advertising. Whereas the Consumer Information Act requires that advertising or trade description must be misleading to a material degree, under the 1988 Regulations it seems that the Director may effectively exercise his discretion and decide for himself whether the advertising is likely to mislead.

More powers were conferred on the Director by the European Communities (Unfair Terms in Consumer Contracts) Regulations 1995, the Consumer Credit Act 1995 and the Package Holiday and Travel Trade Act 1995, for example. All of these measures are considered later in this chapter.

10.2.2.13 Annual reports

The Director is required to make a report to the Minister each year in relation to the performance of his functions during the previous year: Consumer Information Act 1978, s. 9(12) as amended. The report is later published and may be purchased by the public. The reports give an insight into the Director's role and the powers given to that office by different pieces of legislation. One point that became apparent in the 1990s is his growing responsibility in the matter of enforcing EU directives as implemented in Irish law.

While prosecutions may be a more visible sign of the Director's activity, the annual reports make clear that co-operation with traders and trade associations is an important part of the Director's job, and arguably preferable to conflict. Negotiation is often preferable to litigation and the encouragement of voluntary self-regulation by trade associations is part of the Director's role; the threat of prosecution is just one of the weapons at his disposal. In fact the Director's report for 1999 states that in that year there were only two successful prosecutions concluded.

10.3   Sale of Goods and Supply of Services Act 1980

10.3.1   INTRODUCTORY OVERVIEW

The Sale of Goods Act 1893 ('the 1893 Act') was enacted when Ireland was still part of the United Kingdom and although it has been repealed and replaced in that jurisdiction it is still law in Ireland although it has been amended by the later Sale of Goods and Supply of Services Act 1980 ('the 1980 Act') (see **10.3.2** below). It was enacted before the modern consumer boom and it reflected the basic caveat emptor principle of its era, perhaps particularly because it was a codifying statute reproducing case law which often went back many years and even centuries. The 1893 Act created no new law: as a codifying Act it made no changes to the existing common law position on sale of goods contracts but just embodied it in statutory form.

In its original form the Act made no reference to consumers at all and applied to all contracts for the sale of goods, both to purely commercial transactions between businesses and to consumer contracts alike, without differentiating between them. In 1893 the concept of 'consumerism' did not yet exist.

The 1893 Act became law at a time when the concept of freedom of contract was still dominant and did not set out to make a contract for the parties but merely set out what was to happen where a matter was not governed by express agreement between them. Under s. 55 in its original form any right, duty or liability arising by implication of law could be negatived or varied by express agreement between the parties or by the course of dealing between them and this was much exploited by drafters of exemption clauses who used it to exclude, inter alia, the implied conditions contained elsewhere in the Act itself, although the courts in Ireland have since ruled that where there is a breach of a fundamental term of a contract an exclusion or limitation clause cannot be relied on: *Clayton Love v B&I Steamship Co Ltd* (1970) 104 ILTR 157.

Section 55 was significantly restricted by the Sale of Goods and Supply of Services Act 1980 in the case of contracts involving consumers, who are given considerable protection from exemption clauses, particularly in the case of implied terms under the Act. Although the whole 1893 Act is capable of applying to consumer transactions for the sale of goods as to other such transactions, this chapter restricts itself to those sections of it expressly applied to consumer contracts by the later 1980 Act.

10.3.2   THE 1980 ACT

The 1980 Act amends and updates the Sale of Goods Act 1893. While it does not actually define the term 'consumer' it introduced into Ireland the concept of 'dealing as consumer' in statutory form and the rights of a purchaser under the Act may depend on whether he comes within this definition. It has been described as 'an attempt to cover in one step similar ground to that covered by perhaps six UK Acts enacted over a period of thirteen years (although not always in the same way or to the same effect)' (James Murray BL, in a paper delivered at a seminar of the Society of Young Solicitors in Wexford in 1980: SYS Lecture No. 129, p. 14; Mr Murray was the first Director of Consumer Affairs to be appointed).

The Act re-enacts with significant modifications the implied terms in the original Sale of Goods Act 1893 as to merchantable quality, fitness for purpose etc. and in consumer transactions these implied terms may not be excluded or varied. In other transactions they may only be excluded or varied to the extent that it is 'fair and reasonable' to do so, according to criteria set out in the Schedule to the Act. Contracts for services are also made subject to certain implied terms which may be excluded or varied but, in the case of consumer transactions, only if the exclusion or variation is brought to the attention of the consumer and it is fair and reasonable. These terms are:

(a)   the supplier has the necessary skill to render the service;

(b)   the service will be supplied with due skill, care and diligence; and

(c)   any material used or goods supplied will be of merchantable quality.

Part III of the 1980 Act also updated the law on hire purchase, which at the time was governed by the Hire Purchase Acts of 1946 and 1960. It extended the implied terms as to merchantable quality, fitness etc., mutatis mutandis, to hire purchase contracts. The Hire Purchase Acts have since been repealed by the Consumer Credit Act 1995, as has Part III of the 1980 Act.

The 1980 Act also contains provisions on a number of miscellaneous matters such as unsolicited goods and business directories although not all of these provisions have been brought into effect. The Act was well thought of at the time of its inception, one British commentary stating that 'by drawing freely on recent Commonwealth developments as well as indigenous ingenuity it offers a comprehensive range of solutions to many questions still unanswered in the United Kingdom' (Whincup, 'The Irish Sale of Goods and Supply of Services Act 1980' [1981] JBL 478).

10.3.3   THE 1980 ACT IN DETAIL

10.3.3.1   Introduction

The Sale of Goods and Supply of Services Act 1980 amends, updates and extends the Sale of Goods Act 1893. The main points about the 1980 Act are that:

(a)   The implied terms of merchantable quality, fitness for purpose etc. in the 1893 Act are re-enacted with modifications and, in consumer transactions, may not be excluded or varied unlike the situation under the original Act. In other transactions, i.e. in business-to-business transactions between traders where consumers are not involved, those terms may be excluded or varied only to the extent that it is 'fair and reasonable' to do so.

(b) Although the 1980 Act for the most part deals with civil law rights it does create various offences.

(c) In addition to the general implied terms mentioned above there is a condition implied in relation to certain transactions involving motor vehicles to the effect that the vehicle is free from any defects that would render it a danger to the public.

(d) There are special conditions on guarantees regulating the form of written guarantees.

(e) Contracts for services are subject to certain implied terms under the Act; these terms may be excluded or varied but, in the case of consumer transactions, only if the variation or exclusion is brought to the consumer's attention and if it is fair and reasonable.

(f) The law in relation to misrepresentation is amended by the Act along the lines of the UK's Misrepresentation Act 1967, although the amendments only apply to contracts with which the 1980 Act is concerned, i.e. those for the sale of goods or the supply of services or the letting of goods.

(g) Part III of the 1980 Act also originally implied certain terms into hire purchase contracts along the lines of those implied by the 1893 Act (as amended) into the sale of goods; however, Part III of the 1980 Act was repealed by the Consumer Credit Act 1995 (see **10.8** below).

10.3.3.2 'Dealing as consumer'

Section 3 of the 1980 Act defines the phrase 'deal as consumer' and the rights of a buyer under the Act may depend on whether or not he deals as a consumer. A party to a contract is said to deal as a consumer in relation to another party if:

(a) he neither makes the contract in the course of a business nor holds himself out as doing so, and

(b) the other party does make the contract in the course of a business, and

(c) the goods or services supplied under or in pursuance of the contract are of a type ordinarily supplied for private use or consumption.

Usually it will be for those claiming that a party does not deal as consumer to show that he does not do so (s. 3(3)). The definition is not expressly confined to a natural person. In a sale by competitive tender, or in relation to auctions of a type which can be defined by order, the buyer does not deal as a consumer (s. 3(2)).

10.3.3.3 Implied terms

Section 10 of the 1980 Act substitutes the provisions in the Sale of Goods Act 1893, ss. 12–15 which deal respectively with implied terms in relation to title, sale by description, quality or fitness, and sale by sample. The 1980 Act made important modifications to all but one of the implied terms in ss. 12–15.

10.3.3.4 Implied undertakings as to title

The new s. 12 deals with implied undertakings as to title and provides that in every contract for the sale of goods there is an implied condition that the seller has a right to sell and an implied warranty that there is no undisclosed encumbrance on the goods and that the purchaser will normally enjoy quiet possession of them. Accordingly, if the goods sold turn out to have been stolen, the buyer would normally be entitled to a refund of the purchase price. Section 12 may not be excluded by an exemption clause in any circumstances (s. 55(3), as inserted by the 1980 Act, s. 22).

10.3.3.5 Conditions

The terms in ss. 13–15 of the 1893 Act, as amended by the 1980 Act, are stated to be conditions rather than mere warranties so that a buyer is entitled to reject the goods if they fail to comply with them. These conditions may not be excluded by a clause in a contract where the buyer deals as consumer: any such exemption clause is void under s. 55(4), inserted by the 1980 Act, s. 22.

10.3.3.6 Sale by description

The new s. 13 reproduces the condition implied in the 1893 Act that goods should correspond with their description but enlarges the scope of the section so that, e.g. the selection of goods displayed on a supermarket shelf may be a sale by description and the markings on a package or label may form part of a description; even under the original s. 13 it was clear that there is a sale by description even though the buyer is buying something displayed before him on the counter or shelf, provided the article is sold as a thing corresponding to a description. The term 'description' is very wide and could cover such matters as ingredients, measurements, packing method and quantity. Most of the cases are English and concern the original s. 13 in the Sale of Goods Act 1893. It seems that liability under the section is strict.

In *Moore & Co v Landauer & Co* [1921] 2 KB 519 the buyers ordered 3,100 cases of peaches, to be packed in boxes of thirty tins each. In fact some of the boxes contained only twenty-four tins. The market value was found not to have been affected in any way but nevertheless it was held that the sellers were in breach of the condition in s. 13 and the buyers could reject the whole consignment.

In *Arcos v Ronaasen* [1933] AC 470 the buyers ordered wooden staves of a half-inch thickness but most of the staves delivered were between a half-inch and 9/16ths of an inch thick. It was held by the House of Lords that the buyers could reject the goods because 'half an inch' did not mean 'about half an inch'.

A sale of goods may still be a sale by description even where the buyer has seen the goods if they are sold as goods answering a description. In *Beale v Taylor* [1967] 3 All ER 253 the buyer read an advertisement offering a 1961 Triumph Herald 1200 for sale. When he went to inspect it he saw the figure '1200' on a metal disc on the rear of the car. After buying it he found that the car was actually made up of the rear half of a 1961 Herald 1200 welded to the front half of an earlier model, a Herald 948. The welding was inadequate and the car was not roadworthy. The Court of Appeal held that he had purchased the vehicle by reference to the description given and was entitled to damages for breach of s. 13 even though he had seen and inspected the vehicle.

Under the new s. 55, as substituted by the 1980 Act, s. 22, it is not possible to contract out of s. 13 where the buyer is a consumer. In a non-consumer sale contracting out is permitted to the extent that it is 'fair and reasonable'.

It is clear from the case law that the term 'sale by description' could cover at least three types of contract of sale, viz:

(a) all agreements to sell unascertained goods, i.e. purely generic goods (e.g. '100 bottles of beer') or goods not formally identified as the particular goods the subject of the contract;

(b) a contract for the sale of 'specific' goods (defined in the 1893 Act, s. 62 as 'goods identified and agreed upon at the time of a contract of sale') where the buyer has not seen them and is relying on the description; and

(c) a sale of specific goods seen by the buyer if the goods are sold not as specific goods but as goods answering a description.

10.3.3.7 Quality or fitness

The new s. 14 begins by repeating the general rule in its precursor that there is no implied term as to quality or fitness for any particular purpose of goods supplied under a contract of sale except as implied by statute thereby maintaining the old caveat emptor principle and then proceeds to deal with the implied terms that goods should be of merchantable quality and fit for the purpose or purposes for which they were bought. These implied terms only apply where the seller sells goods 'in the course of a business' (so private sales are not affected).

In sales of this kind, there is an implied condition of merchantable quality except as regards:

(a) defects specifically brought to the buyer's attention prior to the contract, or

(b) defects which ought to have been noticed in an examination of the goods by the buyer before the contract was made (s. 14(2)).

In *Thornett and Fehr v Beer & Sons Ltd* [1919] 1 KB 486, a case under the original s. 14(2), which was somewhat similar but not identical, a purchaser of barrels of glue made only a cursory examination, looking at the outside of the barrels only. If he had looked inside he would have noticed the defect, so he had no remedy. However, in *Wren v Holt* [1903] 1 KB 610, the purchaser of beer containing arsenic succeeded in his claim as no ordinary examination would have disclosed the defect.

Under the 1893 Act, s. 34 a buyer is not deemed to have accepted goods delivered to him unless and until he has had a reasonable opportunity of examining them for the purpose of ascertaining whether they are in conformity with the contract. This applies to all sale of goods contracts including those to which consumers are a party and could be relevant here (and to s. 15(2)(c)) at **10.3.3.10** below).

10.3.3.8 Merchantable quality defined

The term 'merchantable' was not defined in the 1893 Act. The dictionary definition is 'saleable, marketable'. It is a rather antiquated concept, decided by reference to the customs and attitudes of 'merchants' and their assessment of the saleability of goods. The 1893 Act at its inception was considered as a code for merchants and the main criterion was whether a merchant would buy the goods from another trader and be able to sell them on at around the same price he had paid for them ie. whether they were commercially saleable.

The new s. 14(3), for the first time, defines merchantable quality, as follows:

Goods are of merchantable quality if they are as fit for the purpose or purposes for which goods of that kind are commonly bought and as durable as it is reasonable to expect having regard to any description applied to them, the price (if relevant) and all the other relevant circumstances, and any reference in this Act to unmerchantable goods shall be construed accordingly.

The concept of durability was entirely new and did not exist in the corresponding UK legislation at that time (the Sale of Goods Act 1979, which had repealed and replaced the 1893 Act in that jurisdiction) although English decisions were beginning to include durability as an implicit element of merchantability, e.g. *Crowther v Shannon Motor Co* [1975] 1 All ER 139 where a car's engine seized up some three weeks after purchase and after over 2,000 miles of driving. In 1994 the UK amended their Sale of Goods Act 1979, replacing the concept of 'merchantable quality' by a new test of 'satisfactory quality', effectively throwing out many years of case law helping to define what was meant by the earlier term. These cases (and the cases which preceded the enactment of the codifying 1893 Act) are still of use to us in this jurisdiction although, now that we have the s. 14(3) definition, judicial interpretation of the term is not as vital as it may have been.

In *Bartlett v Sidney Marcus Ltd* [1965] 2 All ER 753 the seller of a second-hand car told the purchaser prior to the sale that the car's clutch was defective and would have to be repaired. The purchaser bought the car and drove it for several weeks covering up to 200–300 miles. When he took it to a garage he learned that the repair to the clutch was a larger and more expensive task than he or the seller had thought and sued the seller for breach of the original s. 14. The Court of Appeal rejected the claim, holding that a second-hand car is merchantable if it is capable of being driven in safety even if not perfect. Moreover, the defect had been brought to the purchaser's attention before entering into the contract and thus came within the statutory exception in s. 14(2)(a).

In *Business Application Specialists Ltd v Nationwide Credit Corporation Ltd* [1988] RTR 332 a second-hand car purchased for almost £15,000 needed repairs costing £635 but was held to be merchantable.

In *Bernstein v Pamson Motors (Golders Green) Ltd* [1987] 2 All ER 220, a new car broke down a month after purchase, having been driven for 140 miles. A day later the purchaser informed the sellers that he was rejecting the car as not being of merchantable quality. The sellers repaired the car but he refused to take it and sued under s. 14 of the UK's 1979 Act. It was held that the car was not of merchantable quality, the judge referring to *Bartlett* and the safety requirement there, but stating that the buyer of a *new* car is entitled to something more and that the fact that the car was capable of being repaired did not prevent it from being unmerchantable.

Rogers v Parish (Scarborough) Ltd [1987] QB 933 involved the sale of a faulty new car. It had leaking oil seals but was driven for several thousand miles before being repaired by the seller without charge. The Court of Appeal held that it was unmerchantable, disagreeing with the trial judge. The purchaser of a new car is entitled to drive it 'with the appropriate degree of comfort, ease of handling and reliability' and of pride in its appearance.

10.3.3.9 Fitness for purpose

Where the seller sells goods in the course of a business and the buyer, expressly or by implication, makes known to the seller any particular purpose for which the goods are being bought, there is an implied condition that the goods supplied under the contract are reasonably fit for that purpose, whether or not that is a purpose for which such goods are commonly supplied, except where the circumstances show that the buyer does not rely, or that it is unreasonable for him to rely, on the seller's skill or judgment (s. 14(4)).

Where the purpose is an obvious one (e.g. food is for eating, a car is for driving, a toy is for playing with) it is not necessary for the buyer to expressly inform the seller of it, but where goods are required for a particular purpose which is not obvious the seller will not be liable if not so informed. In *Griffiths v Peter Conway Ltd* [1939] 1 All ER 685 a woman who purchased a tweed coat failed to inform the seller that she had abnormally sensitive skin. When she contracted dermatitis she claimed damages under the original s. 14(1) of the 1893 Act but failed because of evidence adduced that if her skin had been of normal sensitivity the coat would not have caused the problem: it was held that she had not made her *particular* purpose known.

Normally reliance will be implied, at least in the case of sales to a consumer. When a customer enters a shop his reliance would usually be inferred because he presumes the retailer selected his stock with skill and judgment. When would 'reliance' be unreasonable? An example might be where the seller disclaims responsibility e.g. by saying that he is not familiar with a particular product or by indicating that he has no expertise in that area. Again, in a consumer sale the conditions in s. 14 may not be excluded by a term in the contract.

0.3.3.10 Sale by sample

Section 15 of the 1893 Act dealing with sales by sample is re-enacted without change in the 1980 Act but for convenience is included in the table in s. 10 of the latter Act along with the new ss. 13 and 14. Section 15(1) provides that a contract of sale is one by sample where there is a term in the contract, express or implied, to that effect. Section 15(2) provides that in the case of a contract for sale by sample:

(a)   there is an implied condition that the bulk will correspond with the sample in quality;

(b)   there is an implied condition that the buyer will have a reasonable opportunity of comparing the bulk with the sample; and

(c)   there is an implied condition that the goods will be free from any defect rendering them unmerchantable which would not be apparent on reasonable examination of the sample.

As regards (c), the words 'reasonable examination' mean a normal commercial examination and not, for example, a detailed laboratory-style analysis; the term means such an examination as is usually carried out in the trade concerned. This is clear from *Godley v Perry* [1960] 1 All ER 39 where a shopkeeper sold a plastic toy catapult, which had been displayed in the shop window, to a six-year-old boy. The catapult broke when the boy used it, causing him to lose the sight of one eye. The boy succeeded under ss. 13 and 14 but the wholesaler was held liable to the shopkeeper under s. 15 because, inter alia, the supply of catapults sold to the shopkeeper was a sale by sample, the bulk had a defect rendering it unmerchantable and this defect was not apparent on a *reasonable* examination—in this case, by pulling on the elastic.

It will be noted that this case involved breaches of ss. 13 and 14 as well as of s. 15. In fact many of the reported cases involve claims under more than one of the implied terms in ss. 13–15 and in practice claims are often made under two, or even all three, sections and a plaintiff may succeed under more than one of them. It may be that a claim under one of the sections may fail but that a claim under another section is successful. As all three sections imply a condition rather than a mere warranty, successful invocation of any of the sections is of equal value allowing the plaintiff to reject the goods and repudiate the contract as well as claiming damages.

For example, in *O'Connor v Donnelly* [1944] Ir Jur Rep 1 the plaintiff had purchased a tin of John West Middle Cut salmon for human consumption and after eating some of the salmon he and his family suffered illness. In claiming damages under the 1893 Act he alleged that he had made known the purpose for which the goods were being purchased and that he had relied on the defendant seller's skill and judgment, that the goods did not correspond with their description and that they were not of merchantable quality. While he failed on the ground of reliance (he was a former shopkeeper himself and had sold tins of salmon and sardines in that time and was adjudged by the court to be possessed of just as much skill and judgment as the defendant in relation to tinned salmon), it was held that the sale was by description and the goods supplied did not correspond with the description and were not of merchantable quality. He thus succeeded under the original ss. 13 and 14 of the 1893 Act.

In *McDowell v E.P. Sholedice & Co Ltd*, 31 July 1969, SC (unreported) a farmer selected 'Stuttgarter' onion seed suited to the Irish market. The defendant seed merchant, unable to supply this variety, offered 'Lyaskovaki' Bulgarian onion seed in its place and supplied a description of it on request by the plaintiff who did not know the latter type of seed. The plaintiff then consulted a number of horticultural specialists about 'Lyaskovaki' seed, without success, but the description given satisfied him that it had the characteristics of 'Stuttgarter' and he then ordered it. The onions it produced were unsuitable for the Irish market and were destroyed when they did not sell. The plaintiff's claim for damages succeeded, it being held that the sale of the seed was a sale by description and the goods did not correspond with the description and were not of merchantable quality, i.e. there was breach of both ss. 13 and 14.

Once again, under s. 55(4), as inserted by the 1980 Act, the condition in s. 15 may not be excluded in the case of a sale to a consumer.

10.3.3.11 Exclusion clauses

Section 55 of the Sale of Goods Act 1893 had dealt with exclusion clauses and provided that where any right, duty or liability would arise under a contract of sale of goods by implication of law it could be negatived or varied by express agreement or by the course of dealing between the parties, or by usage if the usage was such as to bind both parties to the contract. Section 22 of the 1980 Act substituted a new s. 55 into the 1893 Act. The new s. 55 repeats this provision of the 1893 Act but with important qualifications. The implied terms as to title and quiet possession in the 1893 Act, s. 12 as amended may not now be excluded and any term of a contract purporting to exclude such terms is void (1893 Act, s. 55(3) as amended).

In the case of a contract for the sale of goods, any term excluding the implied terms and conditions in ss. 13, 14 and 15 will be void where the buyer deals as consumer and, in any other case, will not be enforceable unless it is shown that it is fair and reasonable. This means that any exemption clause purporting to exclude the implied terms relating to quality and fitness for purpose or conformity with description or sample are void where the buyer deals as consumer (quite apart from the application of the European Communities (Unfair Terms in Consumer Contracts) Regulations 1995 (see **10.7** below)) and in any other case may not be enforced unless shown to be 'fair and reasonable'. The Schedule to the 1980 Act sets out criteria to be referred to in assessing what is 'fair and reasonable'. The test is that it should be fair and reasonable having regard to the circumstances which were, or ought reasonably to have been, known to or in contemplation of the parties when the contract was made. Regard is to be had in particular to, for example:

(a) the strength of the bargaining positions of the parties relative to each other;

(b) whether the customer receives an inducement to agree to the terms;

(c) whether the customer knew or ought reasonably to have known of the existence and extent of the term, having regard to any custom of the trade and any previous course of dealing between the parties; and

(d) whether any goods involved were manufactured to the special order of the parties.

10.3.3.12 Dealing as consumer

The 1980 Act contains a number of other provisions to protect consumers and the definition of the expression 'dealing as consumer' in the 1980 Act is relevant to other sections of the Act as well. For example, under the 1980 Act, s. 14, where goods are sold to a buyer dealing as consumer and in relation to the sale an agreement is entered into by the buyer with a finance house for the repayment to the latter of money paid by it to the seller in respect of the price of the goods, the finance house is deemed to be a party to the contract and liable for breach of the contract of sale. This provision led to two High Court cases in Ireland in the early 1980s on the issue of 'dealing as consumer' in s. 3, both decided by McWilliam J.

In *O'Callaghan v Hamilton Leasing (Ireland) Ltd* [1984] ILRM 146 the plaintiff, owner of a take-away food shop, bought a machine producing soft drinks containing crushed ice which he would dispense and serve to the customer. The purchase was by way of a leasing agreement with the defendant company. The machine was defective and the plaintiff sued for a refund of money paid and damages under s. 14. The plaintiff could only succeed under that section if he was a purchaser dealing as consumer. It was held that the contract was made in the course of the plaintiff's business and accordingly he did not 'deal as consumer'.

In *Cunningham v Woodchester Investments Ltd*, 16 November 1984, HC (unreported) another case under s. 14, the bursar of an agricultural college which had a large farm leased a defective telephone system from the defendant company, a finance house. He attempted to make the defendant liable for the breach of contract by the seller. It was held the goods were of a type not ordinarily supplied for private use and were to be used mainly in the course of the college's farming business; accordingly the plaintiff was not 'dealing as consumer' and his claim failed.

10.3.3.13 Failure to remedy breach of warranty

Where the buyer deals as consumer and is compelled to treat a breach of condition as a breach of warranty, if he complains promptly and the seller does not remedy the breach or replace the goods within a reasonable time the buyer may reject the goods and treat the contract as repudiated or have the goods repaired elsewhere and maintain an action against the seller for the cost (s. 53(2), as substituted by the 1980 Act, s. 21). Apart from this the general remedies set out in the old s. 53 of the 1893 Act are re-enacted without change in s. 22 of the newer Act.

10.3.3.14 Supply of services

The 1980 Act is the first Irish legislation to import implied terms into contracts for services. Part IV is the relevant part. These implied terms are set out in s. 39 as follows:

(a)   the supplier has the necessary skill to supply the service;

(b)   he will provide the service with due skill and diligence;

(c)   where materials are used they will be sound and reasonably fit for their purpose; and

(d)   where goods are supplied under the contract they will be of merchantable quality.

Under the new s. 40 these implied terms may be varied or excluded by an express term of the contract or by the course of dealing between the parties or by usage but where the recipient deals as a consumer they may only be varied or excluded to the extent that it is fair and reasonable to do so (again by reference to the Schedule) and only if the express term is brought specifically to the consumer's attention. No distinction is made in Part IV of the Act between conditions and warranties: the section just speaks of implied 'terms'.

10.3.3.15 Offence

Under s. 41 it is an offence to issue in writing any statement purporting to imply that the rights given in s. 39 of the Act are or may be excluded or restricted in contracts for services otherwise than as provided for under s. 40. Exceptions are made for particular services.

10.4   European Communities (Misleading Advertising) Regulations 1988

10.4.1   INTRODUCTORY OVERVIEW

The European Communities (Misleading Advertising) Regulations 1988 (SI 134/1988) ('the 1988 Regulations') implemented EC Council Directive 84/450/EEC of 10 September 1984 on the approximation of laws of the Member States relating to misleading advertising.

The 1988 Regulations give the Director of Consumer Affairs the power to request any person engaged in misleading advertising to discontinue or refrain from so doing. Any person, including the Director, may seek an injunction prohibiting advertising without having to prove actual loss or damage nor to show recklessness or negligence on the part of the advertiser. The regulations increased the powers of the Director giving him wide-ranging powers of search and inspection of companies' financial records in order to discharge his functions under the new legislation.

10.4.2 THE REGULATIONS IN DETAIL

10.4.2.1 Generally

The 1988 Regulations came into operation on 27 June 1988. Regulation 2 states that a word or expression used in the regulations and also used in the directive has, unless the contrary intention appears, the meaning in these regulations that it has in the Council directive. The regulations and the directive require to be read together; in fact regular reference must be made to the directive in practice in order to clarify and amplify the regulations themselves, which are quite brief.

Article 2(2) of the directive states:

> *Misleading advertising means any advertising which in any way, including its presentation, deceives or is likely to deceive the persons to whom it is addressed or whom it reaches and which, by reason of its deceptive nature, is likely to affect their economic behaviour or which, for those reasons, injures or is likely to injure a competitor.*

Regulation 3 provides that the Director, on a request being made to him in that behalf or on his own initiative, may request any person engaging or proposing to engage in any advertising which is misleading advertising to discontinue or refrain from such advertising.

Regulation 4(1) provides that any person—including the Director—may apply to the High Court for an order prohibiting the publication (or the further publication) of advertising which constitutes misleading advertising upon giving notice of the application to any person against whom such order is sought.

Where the Director has made a request under reg. 3 and that request has not been complied with the Director may apply to the High Court for an order prohibiting the publication (or the further publication) of advertising the publication of which is misleading advertising (reg. 4(2)).

In relation to an application by either the Director or any other person, such applicant is not required to prove either:

(a) actual loss or damage, or

(b) recklessness or negligence on the part of the advertiser.

While misleading advertising is also governed by the Consumer Information Act 1978 (see **10.2** above) that Act requires loss, damage or injury to members of the public to a material degree before an offence is committed.

To eliminate the continuing effects of misleading advertising the court may require publication of its decision in full or in part and in such form as it deems adequate and also require the publication of a corrective statement (reg. 4(4)).

Where an application is made the High Court may order an advertiser to provide evidence as to the accuracy of any factual claims made in any advertising if, taking into account the legitimate interest of the advertiser and any other party to the proceedings, this requirement appears appropriate in the particular case (reg. 4(5)(a)) and the court may deem any factual claim to be inaccurate if the evidence demanded is not provided or is deemed insufficient (reg. 4(5)(b)).

In deciding on applications made under reg. 4 the court is required to take account of all the interests involved and, in particular, the public interest.

Regulation 5 provides that in determining whether or not advertising is misleading the court should take account of all its features and in particular any information it contains concerning the measures set out in paragraphs (a) to (c) of article 3 of the directive. These matters are:

(a) the characteristics of goods or services, such as their availability, nature, execution, composition, method and date of manufacture or provision, fitness for purpose, uses, quantity, specification, geographical or commercial origin or the results to be expected from their use, or the results and material features of tests or checks carried out on the goods or services;

(b) the price or the manner in which the price is calculated, and the conditions on which the goods are supplied or the services provided; and

(c) the nature, attributes and rights of the advertiser, such as his identity and assets, his qualifications and ownership of industrial, commercial or intellectual property rights or his awards and distinctions.

10.4.2.2 Authorised officers

Under reg. 6(1) the term 'authorised officer' means a whole-time officer of the Minister authorised in writing by the Minister or the Director to exercise the powers conferred on such an officer for the purposes of the regulations. Every authorised officer is required to be issued with a warrant of his appointment as authorised officer and must when exercising any power conferred on him under the regulations produce the warrant if requested to do so (reg. 6(2)).

An authorised officer is given considerable powers to enable him to obtain information enabling the Director to discharge his functions under the regulations, e.g. he may:

(a) enter premises in which any trade or business or any activity in connection with the trade or business is carried on at all reasonable times and inspect the premises and any goods on the premises and may take any of the goods on paying or making tender of payment for them;

(b) require anyone who carries on any such trade, business or activity and any employee to produce to him books, documents or records and give him such information as he reasonably requires in regard to any entries therein;

(c) inspect and take copies from such documents;

(d) require any such person to give him any information he requires in regard to the persons carrying on the business or employed in connection with it; and

(e) require any such person to give him any other information which he may reasonably require in regard to such activity (reg. 6(3)).

Anyone obstructing or impeding the authorised officer in the exercise of his powers under reg. 6 is guilty of an offence and liable on summary conviction to a fine of up to £1,000; the offence may be prosecuted by the Director (reg. 6(4)).

The directive expressly does not preclude Member States from retaining or adopting provisions with a view to ensuring more extensive protection for consumers, persons carrying on trades and the general public (article 7 of the directive) nor does it exclude the voluntary control of misleading advertising by self-regulatory bodies.

In *Joseph O'Connor (Nenagh) Ltd v Powers Supermarkets Ltd*, 15 March 1993, HC (unreported) the regulations were successfully used. The case concerned an application for an injunction under reg. 4 restraining the defendant from publishing misleading advertisements concerning the supermarket businesses the plaintiffs carried on in Nenagh and Roscrea.

The case concerned the phenomenon of comparative advertising which was common at the time in the grocery trade. The defendants, who owned the Quinnsworth supermarket chain at the time, had published an advertisement comparing its prices with those of the plaintiffs, a rival in the area. They claimed that they were perfectly entitled to demonstrate that, over a range of goods which they selected, their prices were cheaper than the plaintiffs' prices. They had also distributed a handout in the Nenagh area some days later, making the same claims effectively as the advertisement but making five specific mis-statements as to the prices of the plaintiffs' goods, in each case making them appear significantly more expensive than their own. They denied the alleged errors. They also held a display of two shopping baskets on their premises with accompanying posters effectively replicating the claims made by them in the advertisements and the handout.

Keane J seemed disposed to accept on balance the advertisement but not the handout. He accepted the evidence on behalf of the plaintiffs that in relation to five items this misstated the plaintiffs' prices. The main problem was that the handout did not always compare like exactly with like, i.e. in three cases it gave the price of the same article but in a higher value category in the case of the plaintiffs, e.g. caster sugar rather than ordinary sugar, Knorr gourmet soups rather than the standard soups and a higher price brand of a particular fabric softener. Fresh foods were completely omitted from the comparison.

It was Keane J's view that the selection of goods did not fairly represent the spread of goods which the average shopper would buy in either store and given that fact it was incumbent on the defendants to ensure that they stated the prices accurately. Since they had failed to do so, the judge said, the accompanying list of prices 'could only lend a spurious authenticity to the claims made as the respective competitive positions of the two businesses in price terms'. Keane J emphasised that the order being granted in no sense restrained legitimate advertising by the defendants even if it took the form of price comparisons with a named competitor's products. They were perfectly entitled to mount such campaigns if they wished but 'if they elect to include comparisons with a named competitor, they must ensure that they are accurate, both in fairness to the competitor and in the public interest'. Strict accuracy in such comparisons is thus essential.

Realistically, the costs of a High Court application may deter the general public from using the regulations and it is likely that, apart from the Director, only business competitors would normally apply for an order under reg. 4.

10.5 European Communities (Cancellation of Contracts Negotiated Away From Business Premises) Regulations 1989

10.5.1 INTRODUCTORY OVERVIEW

The European Communities (Cancellation of Contracts Negotiated Away from Business Premises) Regulations 1989 (SI 224/1989) ('the 1989 Regulations') implemented EC Council Directive 85/577/EEC of 20 December 1985 to protect the consumer in respect of contracts negotiated away from business premises, and apply to contracts between a consumer and a trader when negotiations have been initiated away from business premises, e.g., by a door-to-door salesman, and offer protection to the consumer purchaser in such circumstances including the ability to withdraw from the contract during a certain period of time after entering into it.

10.5.2 THE 1989 REGULATIONS IN DETAIL

10.5.2.1 Introduction

The 1989 Regulations basically deal with what are known as 'doorstep sales' so that a consumer who buys certain goods or services from traders on his own doorstep, in his home or at his place of work (unless he has expressly requested the seller's visit) must be given a minimum of seven days' 'cooling-off' period within which he may withdraw from the contract without penalty.

10.5.2.2 Definitions

A 'consumer' is a natural person who in transactions covered by the regulations is acting for purposes which may be regarded as outside his trade or profession; 'trader' means a natural or legal person who, for the transaction in question, acts in his commercial or professional capacity, and anyone acting in the name or on behalf of a trader (reg. 2(1)).

This 'cooling-off' period is contrary to the traditional rules on contracts whereby persons who enter into a contract are normally bound by it immediately and may not normally escape from its terms after entry. The buyer must be given a statutory 'cancellation notice' and 'cancellation form' at the point of sale or the contract will not be enforceable against him (reg. 4).

Delivery or posting of the latter form to the trader renders the contract void (reg. 5(3)). When a contract is cancelled any sums paid by the consumer become due and owing by the trader (reg. 6(1)) and title in any goods sold vests in the consumer three months later (reg. 6(4)).

Not all types of contract come within the ambit of the regulations: e.g. insurance contracts are specifically excluded, as are contracts for the sale of securities and all contracts where the consideration is less than £40.

10.6 Liability for Defective Products Act 1991

10.6.1 INTRODUCTORY OVERVIEW

The Liability for Defective Products Act 1991 ('the 1991 Act') was enacted to give effect to EC Council Directive 85/374/EEC of 25 July 1985 on liability for defective products—the so-called Product Liability Directive. The Act's principal effect was to introduce into Irish law a remedy of damages based on the principle of no-fault or strict liability so that a producer is made liable for damage caused wholly or partly by a defect in his product, regardless of whether or not he was negligent. The new remedy exists alongside the usual civil remedies on product liability in both tort and contract. Under the Act the injured party need only prove the damage, the defect and the causal relationship between them, with no necessity to prove negligence. As it is a civil law measure the level of proof required to be discharged in any proceedings will be that of the 'balance of probabilities' rather than 'beyond reasonable doubt'. The Act contains a prohibition on the producer excluding or limiting his liability to an injured person.

10.6.2 THE ACT IN DETAIL

10.6.2.1 Generally

The 1991 Act gave belated effect to the so-called Product Liability Directive. The Act came into force on 6 December 1991. To comply with the terms of the directive Member States should have implemented it by 25 July 1988 and Ireland, along with some other Member States, was the subject of proceedings initiated against it by the EU Commission under article 169 (now article 226) of the EC Treaty for non-implementation within the time stipulated.

The Department of Industry and Commerce (since subsumed into the Department of Enterprise, Trade and Employment) issued an explanatory and discussion document concerning the directive and invited comments on the three options given to Member States in the way they implemented the provisions of the directive, requesting submissions to the Department.

Prior to the implementation of the directive by the 1991 Act the existing Irish law on product liability could be classified under two headings:

(a) contract law, and

(b) tort.

The Sale of Goods Act 1893, as amended, implies certain terms into contracts for the sale of goods incorporating two main implied conditions into every contract sale, namely:

(i)   that the product or goods are of merchantable quality, and

(ii) that they are reasonably fit for the purpose for which they were intended.

An action may be taken for damages for breach of contract where a purchaser of goods suffered loss or damage from them but there is a necessity to prove a contract between the injured party and the supplier or producer. If the injured party was not a party to the contract then he could not succeed in this way due to the doctrine of privity of contract.

Where no contractual remedy was available to a plaintiff injured by a defective product he could—and still can—sue in tort. Liability under tort arises where, because of a defect in a product arising from its faulty manufacture, damage is caused to a person or his property but to succeed in tort the plaintiff has to prove negligence.

The directive was not intended to replace existing law but rather to supplement it. It offers an alternative route to an injured plaintiff but the contractual and tortious remedies are still available to him. The effect of the 1991 Act implementing the directive is to introduce into Irish law the remedy for damages for negligence based on the principle of strict or no-fault liability. Liability is imposed on a producer for damage caused wholly or partly by a defect in his product irrespective of whether or not he was negligent.

10.6.2.2 Liability for damage caused by defective products

Section 2(1) imposes liability on a producer in damages in tort for damage caused wholly or partly by a defect in his product. Causation is the main criterion: the section creates a strict liability tort with no necessity to show negligence or fault on the producer's part.

10.6.2.3 Definition of 'product'

'Product' was originally defined in the 1991 Act, s. 1 (the interpretation section) as 'all movables with the exception of primary agricultural products which have not undergone initial processing'. The option of excepting such primary agricultural products from the definition of 'product' was offered to Member States by the directive and Ireland chose to do so in the Act. This option has now been removed by a later directive 99/34/EEC of 10 May 1999 amending the original Product Liability Directive so that such products are no longer outside the definition in section 1. This directive was implemented by the European Communities (Liability for Defective Products) Regulations 2000 (SI 401/2000).

The term product includes:

(a) movables even though incorporated into another product or into an immovable (e.g. bricks used in building a house), and

(b)   electricity (often deemed to be energy and not goods in other legislation) in respect of damage caused by a failure in generation.

10.6.2.4   Definition of 'producer'

Section 2(2) defines 'producer' as meaning:

(a)   the manufacturer or producer of a finished product, or

(b)   the manufacturer or producer of any raw material or the manufacturer or producer of a component part of a product, or

(c)   in the case of products of the soil, of stock-farming and of fisheries and game, which have undergone initial processing, the person who carried out such processing, or

(d)   any person who by putting his name, trade mark or other distinguishing feature on the product or using his name or any such mark or feature in relation to the product, has held himself out to be the producer of the product, or

(e)   any person who has imported the product into a Member State from a place outside the European Union in order, in the course of any business of his, to supply it to another, or

(f)   any person who is liable as producer of the product pursuant to s. 2(3).

Section 2(3) deems a supplier to be a producer of a product in certain circumstances, providing that, where damage is caused wholly or partly by a defect in a product, any person who supplied the product (whether to the person who suffered the damage, to the producer of any product in which the product is comprised, or to any other person) will, where the producer of the product cannot be identified by taking reasonable steps, be liable as the producer for the damage if:

(i)   the injured person requests the supplier to identify any person (whether still in existence or not) who comes within the definition of 'producer' in relation to the product;

(ii)   that request is made within a reasonable time after the damage occurs and at a time when it is not reasonably practicable for the injured person to identify all those persons, and

(iii)   the supplier fails within a reasonable time after receiving the request either to comply with the request or to identify the person who supplied the product to him.

Briefly stated this means that where the retailer ('any person who supplied the product') does not or cannot identify someone above him in the chain of distribution a plaintiff has a cause of action against the retailer as though he were the producer. There is no definition of what constitutes 'a reasonable time' so it would depend on the facts and circumstances of each particular case. Clearly the producer or manufacturer is the person to be sued in the first instance; other persons only where he cannot be identified.

10.6.2.5   Definition of damage

'Damage' is defined in the 1991 Act, s. 1 as:

(a)   death or personal injury, or

(b)   loss of, damage to, or destruction of, any item of property other than the defective product itself provided that the item of property

(i)   is of a type ordinarily intended for private use or consumption, and

(ii)   was used by the injured person mainly for his own private use or consumption.

10.6.2.6 Definition of defective product

Section 5(1) provides that a product is defective for the purposes of the Act if it fails to provide the safety which a person is entitled to expect, taking all circumstances into account, including:

(a) the presentation of the product (this could take in, e.g. advertising and labelling, presumably);

(b) the use to which it could reasonably be expected that the product will be put ('reasonably' is the operative word here), and

(c) the time when the product was put into circulation (in this connection see the 'state of the art' defence in s. 6 at **10.6.2.8** below).

These criteria are not exhaustive.

'Safety' is the crucial word in the section and indeed throughout the Act generally: products which are merely shoddy are not within the ambit of the Act (cf. Sale of Goods Act 1893, s. 14, as amended (*infra*), which speaks of 'merchantable quality' and 'fitness for purpose' which are clearly different concepts, although lack of safety could also constitute a breach of those conditions in many circumstances).

The subsection speaks of failure to provide the safety 'which *a* person is entitled to expect' (emphasis added): the test is clearly objective and not related to the expectations of the injured person himself alone or it would say *'the* person'.

Section 5(2) provides that a product should not be considered defective for the sole reason that a better product is subsequently put into circulation. This precludes the possibility of subsequent improvements to the product being used as a basis for holding the earlier version or model of it to be defective simply because it has since been improved upon. Were it not for this provision product development could be seriously hampered if not totally discouraged.

10.6.2.7 Proof of damage and defect

The onus is on the injured person concerned to prove the damage, the defect and the causal relationship between the defect and the damage (s. 4). All the injured person has to do is to prove that there was damage and that it was caused by the defect in the product, i.e. as stated earlier it is not necessary under the Act to adduce proof of fault on the producer's part.

10.6.2.8 Defences

Section 6 sets out several defences which a producer may put forward in any action against him. He will not be liable under the Act if he proves:

(a) that he did not put the product into circulation, or

(b) that, having regard to the circumstances, it is probable that the defect which caused the damage did not exist at the time when the product was put into circulation by him or that the defect came into being afterwards, or

(c) that the product was neither manufactured by him for sale or any form of distribution for an economic purpose nor manufactured or distributed by him in the course of his business, or

(d) that the defect concerned is due to compliance by the product with any requirement imposed by or under any enactment or any requirement of the law of the European Communities, or

(e) that the state of scientific and technical knowledge at the time when he put the product into circulation was not such as to enable the existence of the defect to be discovered, or

(f) in the case of a manufacturer of a component or the producer of a raw material, that the defect is attributable entirely to the design of the product in which the component has been fitted or the raw material has been incorporated or to the instructions given by the manufacturer of the product.

The defence at (b) above protects the producer from defects coming into being after the production process, e.g. in the course of distribution or at the hands of the injured party himself. It could create difficulties in the case of latent defects which only appear later on, e.g. the question might arise whether they were inherent in the product ab initio or developed later on. For instance, a particular model of a car may have a fault in the braking or steering system which only manifests itself after a year or when a certain mileage is reached but this defect may be held to have been present from the time it was put into circulation.

The defence at (c) above protects the non-commercial producer of a product and would cover many private transactions, e.g. gifts.

The defence at (e) above is known as the 'development risks' or 'state of the art' defence; it provides that if at the time of production a product is as safe as the current 'state of the art' permits then later improvements in safety in the production process may not be relied on to set the standard of safety. One question that arises is whether there are any geographical limits to the known 'state of the art', i.e. in the case of a product produced in Ireland is it enough that it complies with the state of scientific and technical knowledge in the industry in Ireland or must it comply with Europe-wide or even worldwide levels in that regard?

10.6.2.9 Limitation of actions

An action for the recovery of damages under the Act may not be brought after the expiration of three years from the date on which the cause of action accrued, or the date (if later) on which the plaintiff became aware, or should reasonably have become aware, of the damage, the defect and the identity of the producer (s. 7(1)). A right of action under the Act will be extinguished on the expiration of the period of ten years from the date on which the actual product which caused the damage was put into circulation by the producer unless the injured person has instituted proceedings against the producer in the meantime (s. 7(2)).

This ten-year cut-off period is a complete time bar to an action under the Act and is known as the 'long stop' provision. It seems totally arbitrary, too long in the case of, e.g. a loaf of bread, but too short in the case of, e.g. an airplane, and was apparently adopted as an average.

It could sometimes be difficult for an injured person to find out the date on which a product was put into circulation. Moreover, what is to happen in the case of a product which has a number of components, each put into circulation at a different time and thus each having different cut-off periods? However, in many circumstances the existence of a time bar would make product liability insurance easier for a producer to obtain and it was probably necessary from that point of view.

10.6.2.10 Prohibition on exclusion clauses

A producer may not limit or exclude his liability to an injured person under the Act by any contractual term, notice or any other provision, i.e. he cannot contract out of his liability under the Act (s. 10). This precludes small-print exemption clauses from being relied on by a producer against an injured person although it says nothing about others in the chain of supply, e.g. distributors or retailers.

10.6.2.11 Minimum threshold

The Act contains a de minimis provision of sorts. If damages awardable for a claim under the Act for loss of, or damage to, an item of property (other than the product itself) would not exceed £350 then no damages will be awarded (s. 3). The directive had also given Member States the option of placing an upper limit or ceiling on a producer's total liability for damage resulting from a death or personal injury and caused by identical items with the same defect, provided that the ceiling was not less than 70 million ECUs (article 16). Ireland did not exercise this option for the reason that this ceiling was so high that it was thought to be irrelevant or meaningless in practice.

10.6.2.12 Other rights of action

Section 11 makes clear that the Act will not affect any rights which an injured person may have under any enactment or under any rule of law, i.e. other rights of action are not precluded. This means in particular that rights under contract law or in tort are unaffected so that the injured person may sue under the Act, i.e. on strict liability principles, or they may proceed in the alternative in contract or in tort (which may be more appropriate avenues to relief in a particular case). In practice plaintiffs would usually sue under all these headings.

10.6.2.13 No retrospectivity

Under s. 13, the Act will not apply to any product put into circulation in a Member State before the commencement of the Act (on 16 December 1991), i.e. there will be no retrospective application of the legislation to products put into circulation prior to that date.

10.7 European Communities (Unfair Terms in Consumer Contracts) Regulations 1995

10.7.1 INTRODUCTORY OVERVIEW

The European Communities (Unfair Terms in Consumer Contracts) Regulations 1995 (SI 27/1995) ('the 1995 Regulations') implemented in Ireland EC Council Directive 93/13/EEC of 5 April 1993 on unfair terms in consumer contracts. The fundamental aim of the directive, and of the regulations implementing it, is to invalidate terms in consumer contracts for the supply of goods and services where the terms have not been individually negotiated and are unfair according to prescribed criteria. The Director of Consumer Affairs is given a role in enforcement of the regulations. He may apply to the High Court for an order prohibiting the use or continued use of any term in a contract which is adjudged by the court to be an unfair term, without prejudice to the right of a consumer to rely on the provisions of the regulations in any court.

10.7.2 THE REGULATIONS IN DETAIL

10.7.2.1 Introduction

The 1995 Regulations were made on 1 February 1995 and are stated to apply to all relevant contracts made after 31 December 1994.

The fundamental aim of the directive and of the Irish regulations implementing it is to invalidate terms in consumer contracts which have not been individually negotiated and are unfair according to criteria set out. The effect is that those engaged in business who deal with consumers should be careful about the terms and conditions which they offer to customers. The regulations considerably increase the rights of consumers. Although they are aimed mainly at contracts in writing, they could also have an impact on oral contracts and contracts partly written and partly oral.

10.7.2.2 Application

The title of the Irish regulations, and of the directive they implement, suggest that they apply to all consumer contracts. In fact, they are limited just to contracts for the sale of goods and contracts for the supply of services. Regulation 3(1) of the Irish regulations provides that the regulations apply to any term in a contract concluded between a seller of goods or a supplier of services and a consumer which has not been individually negotiated, apart from the exceptions in Schedule 1.

Schedule 1 expressly excludes certain contracts and particular terms from the scope of the regulations, so that they do not apply to:

(a)   contracts of employment;

(b)   contracts relating to succession rights;

(c)   contracts relating to rights under family law;

(d)   contracts relating to the incorporation and organisation of companies or partnerships;

(e)   terms reflecting mandatory statutory or regulatory provisions here; and

(f)   terms reflecting the provisions or principles of international conventions to which the Member States or the EU are party.

Otherwise the regulations apply to terms of all consumer contracts dealing with the sale of goods or supply of services which are not individually negotiated and they thus apply to a wide range of contracts such as:

(i)   insurance contracts (with consumers);

(ii)   credit agreements, e.g. bank loans and mortgages (the Consumer Credit Act 1995 also affects these: see **10.8** below);

(iii)   sale of goods (e.g. in shops and supermarkets);

(iv)   sale of houses to consumers by people acting in the course of a business;

(v)   supply of services to consumers (e.g. drycleaners, hairdressers, public transport);

(vi)   letting agreements;

(vii)   building contracts (for homes); and

(viii) contracts for holidays (e.g. package holidays or tours). The Package Holiday and Travel Trade Act 1995 also governs these (see **10.9** below).

Regulation 3(2) provides that for the purposes of the regulations the contractual term will be regarded as unfair if, contrary to the requirement of good faith, it causes a significant imbalance in the parties' rights and obligations under the contract to the detriment of the consumer (taking into account the nature of the goods or services for which the contract was concluded 'and all circumstances attending the conclusion of the contract and all other terms of the contract or of another contract on which it is dependent').

The definition of the main subject matter of the contract or the adequacy of the price or remuneration are not relevant in considering whether a term is unfair in so far as those terms are in plain intelligible English. The test of unfairness is applied to particular terms and not to the contract as a whole. Schedule 3 sets out an indicative and non-exhaustive list of the terms which may be regarded as unfair, as laid out in the directive. There are sixteen types of terms described. One of these is a term which has the objective or effect of 'irrevocably binding the consumer to terms with which he had no real opportunity of being acquainted before the conclusion of the contract'. This marks a change from the old theory of freedom of contract under which a person who signs a contract is usually bound by its terms even where he has not read them— agreement to the terms is presumed. It would now be advisable for a seller or supplier to allow a consumer the opportunity to read the terms of the contract beforehand.

Another term described in Schedule 3 is one having the object or effect of 'obliging the consumer to fulfil all his obligations where the seller or supplier does not perform his'. Normally where one party is in breach of a contract the other party is not necessarily entitled to breach the contract as well but may have to perform his obligations under it and sue for damages.

Three terms described in the list in Schedule 3 are disapplied in the case of suppliers of financial services.

10.7.2.3 'Good faith'

Regulation 3(3) provides that, in determining whether a term satisfies the requirement of good faith, regard will be had to the matters specified in Schedule 2. This Schedule sets out guidelines for application of the test of good faith and states that, in making an assessment of good faith, particular regard will be had to:

(a) the strength of the bargaining positions of the parties;

(b) whether the consumer had an inducement to agree to the term;

(c) whether the goods or services were sold or supplied to the special order of the consumer; and

(d) the extent to which the seller or supplier has dealt fairly and equitably with the consumer whose legitimate interests he has to take into account.

This requirement of good faith clearly involves a further move in the law away from the maxim 'caveat emptor'—let the buyer beware. It may be noted how similar the criteria in Schedule 2 (to which regard is to be had in assessing 'good faith') are to the criteria in the Schedule in the Sale of Goods and Supply of Services Act 1980 for assessing 'fair and reasonable'.

A term is always to be regarded as having not been individually negotiated where it has been drafted in advance and the consumer has therefore not been able to influence its substance, particularly in the context of a pre-formulated 'standard form' contract— in the case of the latter, the fact that a specific term or any aspect of a term has been individually negotiated will not exclude the application of the regulations to the rest of the contract if an overall assessment of the contract indicates that it is nevertheless such a contract. The terms of pre-formulated standard form contracts are therefore to be regarded as never having been individually negotiated, as are terms drafted in advance.

10.7.2.4 Definition of 'consumer'

'Consumer' is defined in the regulations as meaning a person who is acting for purposes which are outside his business (reg. 2)—a different definition from that in, e.g. the Consumer Credit Act 1995 (see **10.8** below), it will be noted. 'Seller' means a person who, acting for purposes related to his business, sells goods. 'Supplier' means a person who, acting for purposes related to his business, supplies services (reg. 2).

The regulations have no application to a term of the contract that has been individually negotiated by the parties. There is a presumption that this is not the case where a clause has been drafted in advance and the consumer has therefore not been able to influence its substance (reg. 3(4)) although the seller may rebut this by showing that it was in fact individually negotiated. The onus is on the seller or supplier to show that a term was individually negotiated if he so claims (reg. 3(6)). The basic bargain (i.e. the main subject matter and the price or remuneration) is not regulated as long as these terms are in plain, intelligible language (reg. 4). What is regulated is the 'small print' of the contract, i.e the other contractual terms.

The regulations provide that in the case of contracts where all or certain terms offered to the consumer are in writing, the seller or supplier must ensure that terms are drafted in plain, intelligible language (reg. 5(1)). Where there is a doubt about the meaning of a term, the interpretation most favourable to the consumer will prevail (reg. 5(2)). This matches the drive commenced in the 1980s to draft contracts, especially consumer contracts, in 'plain English' free of 'legalese' which mystifies the language and confuses the other party to the contract as to rights and obligations. The drafting of a mortgage deed in plain, intelligible language may not be an easy matter.

0.7.2.5 Severance

An unfair term will not be binding on the consumer (reg. 6(1)) but the contract itself will continue to bind the parties if it is capable of continuing in existence without the unfair term, i.e. if the unfair term can be severed (reg. 6(2)).

0.7.2.6 Director of Consumer Affairs

The Director of Consumer Affairs is given a role in enforcement of the regulations. He (the present Director is female but the earlier two holders of the office were both male; the legislation uses the masculine terms 'he', 'him' and 'his' and to avoid confusion this practice will be adhered to in this chapter) may apply to the High Court for an order prohibiting the use or continued use of any term in contracts adjudged by the court to be an unfair term (reg. 8(1)). This is without prejudice to the right of a consumer to rely on the provisions of the regulations in any court (reg. 8(6)). An authorised officer appointed by the Director (or the Minister for Enterprise, Trade and Employment) has powers to enter premises and inspect goods on them and any books, documents or records relating to the business (reg. 10). Anyone obstructing an authorised officer will be guilty of an offence and liable on summary conviction to a fine of up to £1,500 at the prosecution of the Director (reg. 10(7)). However, criminal liability is not imposed by the regulations on sellers or suppliers whose contracts with consumers contain unfair terms.

0.8 Consumer Credit Act 1995

0.8.1 INTRODUCTORY OVERVIEW

The Consumer Credit Act 1995 deals with all aspects of consumer credit, replacing all existing legislation on the topic and implementing two EC directives.

The Act is dealt with in detail in Chapter 4: Commercial Lending.

0.8.2 THE ACT IN DETAIL

The Consumer Credit Act 1995 gives effect to EC Council Directive 87/102/EEC of 22 December 1996, as amended by EC Council Directive 90/88/EEC of 22 February 1990, on the approximation of the laws, regulations and administrative provisions of the Member States concerning consumer credit, which required Member States to provide a minimum level of consumer protection in the area of credit. The Act, which came into operation in May 1996, introduced a body of reforms which went beyond the strict requirements of the directives, repealing all existing consumer credit law and providing one unified piece of legislation on the topic. For the purposes of the Act a 'consumer' is defined as a natural person who is acting for purposes outside his trade, business or profession. The Act repealed existing hire purchase and moneylending legislation. This was welcomed by businesses not involved in consumer transactions which had previously found that certain commercial transactions were caught, sometimes inadvertently, by that legislation. The Act substantially repeats the provisions of the Hire Purchase Acts it repealed, but confines them to transactions with consumers so that hire purchase agreements with non-consumers are now no longer regulated by specific legislation. The main features of the new Act are that it:

(a) requires credit intermediaries to obtain annual authorisation;

(b) regulates advertising of consumer credit and the form and content of credit agreements, hire purchase agreements, consumer hire agreements and housing loans;

(c) bestows a 'cooling-off' period on the consumer after signing an agreement (with some exceptions, such as housing loans);

(d) empowers the courts to reopen most credit agreements where the total cost of credit is excessive; and

(e) alters and strengthens the law in relation to money lending and requires mortgage intermediaries to have annual authorisation and pawnbrokers to have an annual licence.

The functions of the Director of Consumer Affairs were significantly increased by the Act. He has a general function to review practices in relation to obligations which were imposed on persons by the Act, to investigate such practices on his own initiative or as directed by the Minister and to request persons to discontinue or refrain from such practices under pain of enforcement proceedings initiated by him. He may publish codes of practice for businesses and advise consumers on the Act. He is responsible for authorising or licensing annually credit and mortgage intermediaries, moneylenders and pawnbrokers and for regulating customer charges set by credit institutions. He also has the responsibility for prosecuting summarily most of the offences created by the Act and must keep public registers concerning moneylenders and credit and mortgage intermediaries.

The Act gives the Director extensive powers to obtain information and documentation; he may appoint authorised officers with power to enter premises, secure records and ask questions.

10.9 Package Holiday and Travel Trade Act 1995

10.9.1 INTRODUCTORY OVERVIEW

Package holidays and tours are regulated since 1995 by the Package Holiday and Travel Trade Act, 1995 which again implemented an EU directive. The main effect of the Act is to impose considerable responsibility towards consumers on organisers of package holidays which go wrong.

The Package Holiday and Travel Trade Act 1995 ('the 1995 Act') implemented Council Directive 90/314/EEC of 13 June 1990 on package travel, package holidays and package tours. The Act also amends the Transport (Tour Operators and Travel Agents) Act, 1982.

0.9.2 THE ACT IN DETAIL

0.9.2.1 Introduction

The most significant feature of the Act is that it imposes direct liability on the organiser of a holiday for the non-performance or improper performance of the obligations under the holiday contract regardless of whether they are to be performed by the organiser or by another party involved in the provision of the holiday, i.e. the organiser is made responsible for all the elements of the package and is primarily liable for anything that goes wrong with the services, facilities or goods to be supplied as component parts of the package. It is no defence that they were supplied by other independent sub-contractors over whom it had no control e.g. airlines, hoteliers, handling agents.

0.9.2.2 Definition of a 'package'

A 'package' is defined in s. 2(1) of the Act as being:

> a combination of at least two of the following components pre-arranged by the organiser when sold or offered for sale at an inclusive price and when the service covers a period of more than twenty-four hours or includes overnight accommodation
>
> (a) transport:
> (b) accommodation;
> (c) other tourist services, not ancillary to transport or accommodation, accounting for a significant proportion of the package' (e.g. golf, fishing).

Even if the consumer has to pay separately for different components of the package it still remains a 'package holiday', although arrangements made by a tour operator or travel agent specifically for an individual carrier's requirements are not regarded as package holidays.

0.9.2.3 Definition of an 'organiser'

Section 3(1) defines an 'organiser' as being:

> a person who, otherwise than occasionally, organises packages and sells or offers them for sale to a consumer, whether directly or through a retailer.

This could conceivably include social and sporting clubs which organise educational or sports trips or pilgrimages, in appropriate circumstances, although if organised only 'occasionally' these would usually be exempted from the ambit of the Act by virtue of the Package Holidays and Travel Trade Act (Occasional Organisers) Regulations 1995 (SI 271/1995) which set out exemptions.

0.9.2.4 Definition of a 'retailer'

A 'retailer' is the person who sells or offers for sale the package put together by the organiser (s. 2(1)).

A package holiday is usually sold by a tour operator or organiser or by a retailer. The latter is almost always a travel agent and he sells the package put together by the tour operator (the organiser).

0.9.2.5 Definition of a 'consumer'

The Act's definition of a consumer is very specific and differs considerably from that in other Irish consumer legislation such as the Consumer Credit Act 1995 and the European Communities (Unfair Terms in Consumer Contracts) Regulations 1995 and from the definition of 'dealing as consumer' in the Sale of Goods and Supply of Services Act 1980.

A 'consumer' is defined as meaning:

(a) in relation to a contract, the person who takes or agrees to take the package (this person is referred to in the Act as being 'the principal contractor'), and

(b) in any other case, where the circumstances so require:

(i) the principal contractor;

(ii) any person on whose behalf the principal contractor agrees to purchase a package (referred to as 'another beneficiary'); and

(iii) any person to whom the principal contractor, or another beneficiary, transfers the package (referred to as 'the transferee').

10.9.2.6 Contents of a holiday brochure

Section 10(1) requires that an organiser must not make a brochure available to a possible consumer unless it indicates 'in a legible, comprehensible and accurate manner' the price and other essential information including:

(a) the destination and the means, characteristics and categories of transport used;

(b) the type of accommodation, its location, category or degree of comfort, its main features and, if in a Member State of the EU, its tourist classification in that State;

(c) the itinerary and meal plan;

(d) general information about relevant passport and visa requirements and any applicable health formalities required for the journey and the stay;

(e) the amount of deposit payable on booking and the timetable for payment of the balance;

(f) any tax or compulsory charge;

(g) whether a minimum number of persons is required for the package to take place and, if so, the latest time for informing the consumer in the event of cancellation; and

(h) the contingency arrangements for security for money paid over in the event of the organiser's insolvency and, where applicable, repatriation of the customer.

It is an offence for a retailer to supply a brochure knowing, or having reasonable cause to believe, that it does not comply with the requirements of s. 10(1) (s. 10(2)). The maximum penalty for a breach of s. 10(1) or (2), on summary conviction, is a fine of £1,500.

10.9.2.7 Information constitutes warranties

Where a consumer enters into a contract on the basis of information which is set out in a brochure, the particulars in the brochure (whether or not they are required by the Act to be included in it) will constitute warranties as to the matters to which they relate unless the brochure contains a clear and legible statement that changes may be made in the particulars before a contract is concluded and any such changes are clearly communicated to, and accepted by, the other party before a contract is concluded (s. 10(4) and (5)), unless the consumer and the organiser agree, when or after the contract is made, that those particulars should not form part of the contract (s. 10(6)).

10.9.2.8 Liability for misleading brochures

Section 11 supplements the contractual, tortious and statutory provisions which a consumer already had in relation to false or misleading information supplied by tour operators or travel agents.

Under the section an organiser or retailer is prohibited from supplying to a consumer a brochure or other descriptive matter concerning a package, its price, or any conditions applying to a contract in respect of it, which contains any false or misleading information (s. 11(1)).

However, it will be a good defence for a retailer to show that he did not know, and had no reason to suspect, that the brochure or other descriptive matter concerned contained information which was false or misleading (s. 11(2)).

0.9.2.9 Compensation for misleading brochures

Where an organiser provides a brochure or other descriptive matter to a consumer (whether directly or through a retailer) he will be liable to compensate the consumer for any damage caused to him as a direct consequence of and attributable to his reliance upon information which is false or misleading where that information:

(a) is contained in the brochure or other descriptive matter, or

(b) is given by the organiser in respect of the brochure or other descriptive matter (s. 11(3)).

Arguably, this could cover misleading photographs in the brochure, e.g. of a beach or swimming pool, or of the hotel. Section 11(3) would also cover advertisements, videos and leaflets supplied to the consumer.

Section 11(4) imposes a similar liability to compensate on a retailer. The term 'compensation' is a wide one and it could include consequential loss for disappointment at the quality of the holiday as well as purely financial loss.

0.9.2.10 Information to be supplied before contract concluded

A duty is imposed on the organiser before a contract is made to provide the intending consumer with information in writing 'or in some appropriate form' about essential matters such as:

(a) general information about passport and visa requirements related to the package;

(b) information about health formalities required by national administrations for the journey and the stay;

(c) where having insurance to cover the cost of cancellation by the consumer or the cost of assistance (including repatriation) in the event of accident or illness is compulsory under the contract, the minimum level of insurance cover stipulated by the organiser (the consumer cannot be forced to take out any specified insurance policy, e.g. the organiser's or retailer's insurance); and

(d) in the event of insolvency, the arrangements for security for the money paid over and (where applicable) for the repatriation of the consumer (s. 12(1)).

Contravention of s. 12(1) renders the organiser or the retailer guilty of an offence (s. 12(2)). It is a defence for an organiser to show that contravention is due to the retailer's failure to pass on to the intending consumer the information supplied to him by the organiser (s. 12(2)(a)).

0.9.2.11 Information to be provided before the start of the package

In addition to supplying the consumer with certain information before a contract is concluded between the organiser and the consumer, the organiser is required to provide the consumer with certain essential information in good time before the package is due to start including:

(a) where the package includes a transport component, the times and places of intermediate stops and transport connections and details of the place to be occupied by the traveller (including cabin or berth on ship, sleeper compartment on train);

(b) the name, address and telephone number:

    (i) of the representative of the organiser in the locality where the consumer is to stay; or

    (ii) if there is no such representative, of an agency in that locality to provide assistance to a consumer in difficulty, or, if there is no such representative or agency, a telephone number or other information which will enable the consumer to contact the organiser and/or the retailer during the course of the package (s. 13(1) and (2)).

Where an organiser fails to supply such information, he will be guilty of an offence under s. 13(3), unless the contravention is due to the failure of the retailer to pass on to the consumer, or intending consumer, the information supplied to the retailer by the organiser.

Where a retailer fails to provide the consumer, or intended consumer, with the information he will also be guilty of an offence under s. 13 (3).

10.9.2.12 The essential terms of a contract

Section 14(1) sets out the essential information which the organiser (whether dealing directly with the consumer or through a retailer) must ensure is contained in the contract if relevant to the particular package. These essential terms include:

(a) the travel destination or destinations and, where periods of stay are involved, the relevant periods, with dates;

(b) the means, characteristics and categories of transport to be used and the dates, times and points of departure and return;

(c) where the package includes accommodation, its location, its tourist category (if any) or degree of comfort and its main features;

(d) the itinerary and meal plan and any visits or excursions included in the total price agreed for the package;

(e) the name and address of the organiser, the retailer and, where appropriate, the insurer;

(f) the price of the package and method of payment and, where price revisions may be made, an indication of the possibility of such price revisions; and

(g) whether a minimum number of persons is required for the package to take place and, if so, the latest time for information of cancellation.

10.9.2.13 Form of the contract

Except in the case of a late booking, i.e. fourteen days or less before departure, the organiser is required to ensure that all the terms of the contract are set out in writing, or in such other form as is comprehensible and accessible to the intended consumer and that they are communicated to the intended consumer before the contract is made (s. 15(1)).

It is an offence for an organiser (whether dealing directly with the consumer or through a retailer) to fail to supply the consumer with a written copy of the terms of the contract, unless the contravention is due to the failure of the retailer to provide the consumer with a written copy of the terms of the contract which had been supplied to the retailer by the organiser (s. 15(3)). In the latter case the retailer is guilty of an offence (s. 15(4)).

10.9.2.14 Transfer of booking

Where the consumer is prevented from proceeding with the package, a term will be implied into the contract whereby the consumer may transfer the booking to a person who satisfies all the conditions required to be satisfied by a person who takes the package provided the consumer gives reasonable notice of his intention to transfer to the organiser or retailer (s. 16(1)).

Both the original purchaser and the transferee are jointly and severally liable to the organiser for payment for the package (or the balance of the payment, as the case may be) and for any other fair and reasonable costs incurred by him as a result of the transfer (s. 16(2)).

10.9.2.15 Contract price revision

Section 17(1) renders void a term in a contract to the effect that the prices specified in the contract may be revised, unless the contract provides for the possibility of upward or downward revision and certain conditions set out in s. 17(2) are strictly observed.

No price increase may be made later than a date specified in the contract which must be not less than twenty days before the specified departure date (s. 17(3)).

10.9.2.16 Alterations and cancellations

Where the organiser is compelled before departure to alter significantly an essential term of the contract, such as the price, a term will be implied that the consumer will be notified as soon as possible in order to enable him to take appropriate decisions and, in particular, to withdraw from the contract without penalty, or to accept a variation to the contract and that he will inform the organiser or retailer as soon as possible (s. 18(1)).

Where the consumer withdraws from the contract due to an alteration by the organiser of an essential term of the contract, or where the organiser, for any reason other than the fault of the consumer, cancels the package before the date when it is due to start, there is an implied term that the consumer is entitled to:

(a) take a replacement package of equivalent or superior quality if the organiser (whether directly or through a retailer) can in fact provide this, or

(b) take a replacement package of lower quality if the organiser is able to offer such a replacement and to recover from the organiser the difference in price between the two packages, or

(c) have a full refund (s. 18(2)(b)).

In addition, there is an implied term that the consumer is entitled, without prejudice to the above, to be compensated by the organiser for non-performance of the contract except in two situations in which the organiser may cancel a package without owing any compensation, viz where:

(i) the package is cancelled because the number of persons who agreed to take it is less than the minimum number of persons required and the consumer is informed of the cancellation, in writing, within the period prescribed in the contract, or

(ii) the package is cancelled by force majeure, i.e. by reason of unusual and unforesee-able circumstances beyond the control of the organiser, the retailer or the supplier of services, the consequences of which could not have been avoided even if all due care had been exercised (s. 18(2)). However, overbooking can never be considered as coming into this category (s. 18(3)).

10.9.2.17 Problems arising after the start of the package

Where, after departure, a significant proportion of the services contracted for is not provided, or the organiser becomes aware that a significant proportion of the services cannot be provided, there is an implied term that the organiser must make suitable alternative arrangements, at no extra cost to the consumer, for the continuation of the package and provide appropriate compensation (s. 19(1), (2)).

If such alternative arrangements cannot be made, or if they are not accepted by the consumer on reasonable grounds, there is an implied term that the organiser must, where homeward transport arrangements are a term of the contract, provide the consumer at no extra cost with equivalent transport back to the place of departure, or to another place to which the consumer has agreed. He must also compensate the consumer for the proportion of services not supplied (s. 19(3)).

10.9.2.18 Extent and financial limits of liability

Section 20(1) of the Act imposes ultimate liability to the consumer on the organiser for the proper performance of the obligations under the contract, whether or not such obligations are to be performed by the organiser, the retailer, or other suppliers of services.

This provision allows the consumer to sue the organiser for breach of contract even if the problem is with the retailer or another service provider. However, this will not affect any remedy or right of action which the organiser may have against the retailer or another supplier of services.

Section 20(2) renders the organiser liable to the consumer for any damage caused by the failure to perform the contract or the improper performance of the contract unless the failure or the improper performance is due neither to any fault of the organiser, or the retailer, nor to that of another supplier of services, because the failures in question are attributable to:

(a) the consumer;

(b) a third party unconnected with the provision of services contracted for, and are unforeseeable or unavoidable; or

(c) force majeure, i.e. due to unusual and unforeseeable circumstances beyond the control of the organiser, the retailer or other supplier of services, the consequences of which could not have been avoided even if all due care had been exercised, or due to an event which the organiser, the retailer or the supplier of services, even with all due care, could not foresee or forestall.

10.9.2.19 Exemption or limitation clauses

A contractual term which purports to exempt the organiser from liability to the consumer under s. 20(1) or (2) cannot be relied on by the organiser (s. 20(6)). However, an organiser may rely on an exemption clause or on a limitation clause in certain limited circumstances which are set out in s. 20(3), (4) and (5).

Where damage arises from the non-performance or improper performance of the services involved in the package (other than death, personal injury or damage caused by the wilful misconduct or gross negligence of the organiser), s. 20(3) permits the organiser to insert a term into the contract limiting the amount of compensation payable to the consumer. Liability may be limited to not less than twice the cost of the package holiday for an adult and not less than the cost of the holiday in the case of a minor (s. 20(4)).

The contract may provide for compensation to be limited in accordance with any international conventions in force governing such services in the place where they are performed or are due to be performed (s. 20(5)).

9.2.20 Security in the event of insolvency of operator or retailer

Section 22 requires operators and retailers to have sufficient evidence of security for the refund of money paid over and for the repatriation of the consumer in the event of insolvency. The necessary evidence of security may take the form of a bond entered into by an authorised institution (defined as a person authorised under the law of a Member State to carry on the business of entering into such bonds) either under s. 23 or a bond entered into pursuant to s. 24, depending on whether or not an approved body (as defined) of which the package provider is a member has a reserve fund or insurance cover.

9.2.21 Complaints

Holidaymakers are required to make complaints at the earliest possible opportunity and no later than twenty-eight days from completion of the holiday, both to the person responsible for their dissatisfaction and to the organiser or local representative: s. 14(1)(l).

9.2.22 Prosecutions

Summary proceedings in respect of an offence under any section of the Act may be brought and prosecuted by the Director of Consumer Affairs (s. 7(1)). The Minister for Transport, Energy and Communications is also given power to bring summary proceedings in respect of an offence under s. 21 or s. 26 (s. 6(2)). The maximum fine for most offences is £1,500. A person convicted on indictment (after prosecution by the Director of Public Prosecutions) of an offence under ss. 21, 22(3), or 26 (primarily with regard to bonding and security) will be liable on conviction on indictment to a fine of up to £50,000 or up to two years' imprisonment or to both (s. 6(2)). Where an offence under the Act is committed by a body corporate its officers may also be guilty of an offence (s. 6(3)).

9.2.23 Role of the Director of Consumer Affairs

The Director of Consumer Affairs is empowered by s. 8 to require that persons engaging in, or proposing to engage in practices or activities which are, or are likely to be, contrary to the obligations imposed on them by the Act refrain from doing so. He is also empowered to institute proceedings in the High Court for orders requiring persons engaging or proposing to engage in any such practices or activities to discontinue or refrain from doing so. His authorised officers are given wide powers of entry and inspection and power to require information, and any failure to comply with the authorised officer's request or any obstruction of his performance of his functions will be an offence (s. 21).

9.2.24 Conclusion

The intention behind the Act is to protect unfortunate consumers who enter into contracts whereby a package holiday is provided against the possibility of alterations being made to the terms of that contract to the detriment of the consumer, or against something going wrong with the holiday either prior to or after departure. The Act imposes strict liability on the organiser of the holiday subject to limited defences in which the onus of proof is on him.

A 'package holiday' may be taken at home or abroad and the Act covers holidays sold in Ireland by companies established outside Ireland as well as by domestic sellers.

9.2.25 Unfair terms

It should be noted that the European Communities (Unfair Terms in Consumer Contracts) Regulations 1995, made earlier in the same year that the Act was enacted, also apply to package holidays (as to other consumer contracts for the sale of goods or supply of services) and offer additional protection to a holidaymaker in appropriate circumstances.

10.10 European Communities (General Product Safety) Regulations 1997

10.10.1 INTRODUCTORY OVERVIEW

The European Communities (General Product Safety) Regulations 1997 (SI 197/1997) ('the 1997 Regulations') implemented directive 92/59/EEC of 29 June 1992 on General Product Safety. The main objectives of the directive are to harmonise EU product safety laws and to impose a general standard of safety in product sectors where there are no special standards already in existence, to compel producers to refrain from placing dangerous products on the market, to improve product safety monitoring and safety warnings and to permit the taking of speedy and effective action to restrict or prohibit the sale of dangerous products.

10.10.2 THE 1997 REGULATIONS IN DETAIL

10.10.2.1 Introduction

These regulations belatedly implemented EC Directive 92/59/EEC.

An obligation not to market dangerous products is imposed principally on manufacturers although it may affect others in the chain of supply. The definition of the term 'producer' is similar to the definition of that term in the Liability for Defective Products Act 1991 (see **10.6** above).

10.10.2.2 Definition of 'product'

For the purpose of the directive and the regulations made under it the term 'product' includes any product intended for consumers' use or likely to be used by consumers which is supplied, whether for consideration or not, in the course of a commercial activity and whether new, used or reconditioned (reg. 2(1)); second-hand antiques are specifically excluded from the application of the regulations (reg. 3(1)).

10.10.2.3 Definition of 'safe'

A 'safe' product is one which, under normal or reasonably foreseeable conditions of use, including duration, either presents no risk or presents only the minimum risks compatible with the product's use considered as acceptable and consistent with a high level of protection for the safety and health of persons (reg. 2(1)). Relevant factors to be taken into consideration in determining the safety of a product include:

(a) the characteristics of the product (e.g. its composition, packaging, presentation, labelling and any instructions for its assembly, maintenance, use or disposal); and

(b) its effect on other products with which it is reasonably foreseeable that it will be used and the types of consumers at serious risk when using it, in particular children (reg. 4(2)).

A product is deemed to be safe if it complies with national rules on health and safety requirements specific to that type of product (reg. 8(1)). In the absence of such rules in relation to a product certain factors will be relevant in assessing the conformity of a product to the general safety requirement. These are:

(i) voluntary national rules implementing a European standard, or

(ii) EU technical specifications,

or, in the absence of these:

(a)   national safety standards;

(b)   codes of good practice in respect of health and safety in the relevant product sector; or

(c)   the 'state of the art' and technology and the safety which consumers may reasonably expect (reg. 8(2)).

A product that is not 'safe' is a 'dangerous' product although the fact that higher safety standards could be achieved does not constitute grounds for considering products to be unsafe or dangerous; nor does the availability of other products presenting a lesser degree of risk (reg. 4(2)).

Regulation 4(1) prohibits a producer from placing or attempting to place on the market any product unless it is a 'safe' product. Contravention of this prohibition is an offence (reg. 4(3)).

0.10.2.4 Director of Consumer Affairs

The regulations give the Director quite broad powers of enforcement. He may require the withdrawal of dangerous products from the market and, if necessary, their destruction (reg. 9(1)(b)) or may direct that warnings be affixed to products (reg. 10(1)(a)). He may appoint authorised officers for the purpose of assuring compliance with the regulations (reg. 13(1)). These officers are given powers of entry, search and inspection (reg. 13(3)). Anyone who obstructs them or fails to comply with their requests commits an offence (reg. 13(11)). The Director may apply to the district court for an order for the forfeiture to him of any product on the grounds that it is a dangerous product (reg. 15(1)). A person aggrieved by the making of such an order may appeal to the circuit court (reg. 15(4)).

The Director may prosecute offences under the Act summarily (reg. 18)); penalties for an offence are a fine of up to £1,500 or imprisonment for up to three months or both (reg. 20(1)) and continued contravention after a conviction is another offence punishable by a fine of up to £250 per day (reg. 20(2)). Where the offender is a body corporate its director, manager, secretary or any other officer may also be guilty of an offence (reg. 22).

0.11 Conclusion

As can be seen, the impetus for consumer legislation in Ireland has come from the UK or Brussels rather than being exclusively home-grown. Up to and including the Sale of Goods and Supply of Services Act 1980 the main influence was from the UK but since then developments have been EU-driven and Ireland's legislation since then is generally a product of EU harmonisation measures in favour of the consumer, taking the form of directives requiring to be implemented in all Member States. In this way a certain minimum in standards is imposed and, if nothing else, it ensures that Irish traders, businesses and manufacturers are geared to EU-wide levels of consumer protection, enabling them to compete in Europe generally and even further afield.

INDEX

273

INDEX

INDEX